ARIS & PHILLIPS HISPANIC CLASSICS

ANDRÉS DE CLARAMONTE

The Valiant Black Man in Flanders

El valiente negro en Flandes

Coordinated by

Baltasar Fra-Molinero

Translated by

Nelson López

Critical Edition by

Manuel Olmedo Gobante

LIVERPOOL UNIVERSITY PRESS

First published 2023 by
Liverpool University Press
4 Cambridge Street
Liverpool
L69 7ZU

www.liverpooluniversitypress.co.uk

This paperback edition published 2025

British Library Cataloguing-in-Publication data
A British Library CIP record is available

ISBN 978-1-83764-426-1 (hardback)
ISBN 978-1-83624-547-6 (paperback)
eISBN 978-1-83764-463-6

Typeset by Tara Montane

Cover art by Astrid López.

CONTENTS

ACKNOWLEDGEMENTS

Baltasar Fra-Molinero wishes to acknowledge with gratitude the know-how and patience of his two colleagues in this endeavor, Nelson López and Manuel Olmedo Gobante. Our Saturday morning Zoom conferences took place in the midst of the COVID-19 pandemic, of which this book is not a child, but a testimony of determination. I wish to thank also Bates College Faculty Development Fund, for its help through the various stages in the process of writing this critical edition of *El valiente negro en Flandes*. To write about this play without bringing up the name of Frantz Fanon would be unforgivable. I came across *Black Skin, White Masks* when I was new to the United States, and there it was Juan de Mérida, literary archetype of the Black person in colonial subjection. Fanon was one of the readings my loving husband Professor Charles I. Nero suggested to me at the time. This was forty years ago, when a gay couple formed by a Spaniard who had lived under the Franco regime and a Black American who grew up in the segregated South sustained their love through books, films, and hope. *De manera que, continuando la posada y conversación*, we had the joy of our two children, Carlos and Bernardo. My contribution to this book has been possible only through their generosity.

Nelson López wants to thank both Baltasar Fra-Molinero and Manuel Olmedo Gobante for being invited to this *sarao*. Translating *El valiente negro en Flandes* into English has been a master class with these two amazing scholars and friends. Their help, support, reassurance, and guidance taught me a great deal. The generosity in answering my questions and questioning my choices provided clarity in rendering Claramonte's Spanish world into English. Thanks to Chloe Johnson at Liverpool Press for keeping us on course and the opportunity to bring this to fruition. Jonathan Thacker's words of encouragement, and his keen eye for details with the text. This collaborative feat could not have been possible without their support! A massive thanking to Noémi Ndiaye, John Beusterien and his students, for their correspondence and answering my every question. A shout out to my family, my colleagues, and friends, and above all, my students of Spanish and theater, whose contributions kept me honest toward the text while giving me 21st century insights on cultural nuances. Finally, a special thanks to my loving María González, life partner, friend, and confidant, who inspires me to keep fighting to make my dreams come true. I am the luckiest person in the world, with you by my side.

Manuel Olmedo Gobante is grateful to Baltasar Fra-Molinero and Nelson López for accompanying him on this journey. I thank my beloved wife Laura Tain Gutiérrez, who could not hear the end of it during the COVID-19 lockdowns, for her unlimited affection and unconditional support. I also wish to thank the University of Arkansas Humanities Center Awarding me a Grant for Humanities Research on Systemic Racism. Thanks to Juan Guilmaín Alonso and Javier García Irigoyen for their indispensable expertise and help with archival documents, and a huge thanks as well to José Luis Nogales Baena for his advice in ecdotics and his meticulous reading of the play. This book would not have been possible without the trust of Elizabeth R. Wright, who supported me from the beginning; neither without Jonathan Thacker, who fostered the project; nor without the generosity of Miguel Martínez, who gave me the intellectual tools to make it.

Finally, the three authors express their most sincere gratitude for the invaluable copy editing of Mary Susan Lederer, University of Botswana.

INTRODUCTION

Foreword

With this critical edition and English translation of *El valiente negro en Flandes* [*The Valiant Black Man in Flanders*], written by Andrés de Claramonte (c. 1580–1626), we intend to engage scholars and students of Early Modern European literature who research the formation of a discourse on Blackness and racial difference in Spain and its trans-Atlantic empire. The play offers an opportunity to address the performative elements that constitute the creation of a Black male hero through its racialized textual elements, including its use of *habla de negros*, or Black speech. *The Valiant Black Man in Flanders* has been a staple in advanced Spanish courses at several universities in the United States, as a play rich in opportunities for a post-colonial analysis (Beusterien 2006b, 177).

Frantz Fanon's *Black Skin, White Masks* addresses the figure of Juan de Mérida, the Black protagonist of *The Valiant Black Man in Flanders* as a literary example of the damage of colonialism to the Black male psyche. Fanon saw in the Black protagonist of this play the archetype of a man trying to avoid the curse of being Black in a world where anti-Blackness is a global phenomenon and the cornerstone of white supremacy. Through a partial French translation of *El valiente negro en Flandes*, Fanon discusses the contradiction of Juan de Mérida as a figure of protest and at the same time an exemplar of the anguish of the Black individual who tries to overcompensate social inferiority by excelling in things deemed white.

The popularity of the play at the time and in the following two centuries is unquestionable. Since the twentieth century, at least three stagings of *The Valiant Black Man in Flanders* have come to our attention, the first one in Havana in 1938, as part of the Negrista movement. Its English translation will allow teachers in different disciplines to study it in relation to other representations of Blackness in Europe and its different Black diasporic empires.

The textual history of the play is intimately related to its content, that is, the triumph of a Black man in the army, Juan de Mérida, later Juan de Alba. As a fictional character, he belongs in the martial tradition of the Black Diaspora, whether in the figure of the *cimarrón* – the self-liberated Black man – or the Black soldier in Spain's imperial and colonial armies. This is reflected in the play through the protagonist's violent confrontation with the white establishment, his elevation to the nobility, and his marriage to a white woman, his former owner. The play has, in fact, two endings: One edition, *P*, does not include the Black protagonist's marriage (see Textual History); the other editions contain the interracial marriage scene.[1] *The Valiant Black Man in Flanders*, therefore, is a commentary on military life, race, and sexuality, including scenes that reveal public construction of male same-sex desire and gender nonconformity in seventeenth-century Spain. It is worth noting that this aspect passed the filter of the Inquisition censors several times – the play kept being staged in different cities throughout the seventeenth century (see Performance History). Three episodes in act one and two are, on the surface, an attempt to delegitimize the public display of wealth and fashion in clothing of the upper classes. However, the play defines the Black main character as having to defend male heteronormativity in a military context that was known for its harsh treatment of male sexual deviance. The ultimate transgression is the interracial marriage at the end, when the Black male protagonist marries his white female aristocratic former enslaver.

As Moses Panford (2003) indicated in his introduction to the eighteenth-century sequel to this play, *The Valiant Black Man in Flanders* was part of an established tradition of one-act plays

---

1 The only other play ending with the marriage of a Black man and a white woman is Diego Jiménez de Enciso's *Juan Latino*, in which the protagonist, the Afro-Hispanic humanist of the same name, marries the white lady Ana de Carlobal, who was taking Latin grammar lessons from him. In Luis Vélez de Guevara's *Virtudes vencen señales*, the Black prince Filipo of Albania ends up not marrying anyone at the end of the play. In *El prodigio de Etiopia*, Princess Teodora chooses to cut her own hand off rather than marry Black bandit Filipo, who in turn retires to the wilderness to do penance.

(*entremeses*), such as Simón Aguado's *Los negros* (1602), that one can read as dramatizations of rebellion against slavery, many of them with Black women characters as protagonists (2003, 21). For Panford, Black characters in Spanish early modern theater are polysemic figures who articulate dissidence (2003, 33). *The Valiant Black Man in Flanders* is perhaps the main exponent of what Panford pointed out more than twenty years ago. This dissidence is how we understand Antón, the other Black character in the play, and a figure of comic relief who speaks in *habla de negros*, or Black Spanish. Antón uses his racialized speech, a form of linguistic blackface (in the terminology of Nicholas R. Jones), to destabilize the world that has made him a slave, in much the same way as the protagonist Juan de Mérida/Juan de Alba fights white supremacy with his words and his military prowess. *The Valiant Black Man in Flanders* is a European play that shows how the imperial armies of Spain and its adversaries started reflecting the increase in the Black population during the sixteenth century in Spain and the territories under its control over the world.

The many manipulations in the text of *The Valiant Black Man in Flanders* reveal the attempt by hands other than the playwright's to limit the transgressive aspect of seeing a Black man rising to the top of the military establishment and gaining access to the highest levels of the knighthood, including his marriage to an aristocratic (and white) woman. Juan's endeavors also echoed the desires and anxieties of white commoners who sought upward social mobility, as well as those of some women of the aristocracy at the mercy of a strict honor code that privileged white upper-class men.

Plot Summary
Act One
The play begins with a brawl involving Juan de Mérida, a Black man, who wants to enlist as a soldier in the company being formed in his hometown. Captain Don Agustín and the other soldiers reject him amidst insults, to which Juan responds with a defense of his person and his Black skin color in the first of his eloquent speeches (lines 8–32). Juan puts action to words and kills one of the soldiers, taking

refuge in the house of Doña Leonor, a local noblewoman. When Doña Leonor confronts the soldiers, she and Captain Don Agustín become smitten with each other. During their encounter that same night, the Captain promises Doña Leonor he will marry her and renounce his military career. Meanwhile Juan has come to the conclusion that he has no future in his hometown and takes leave of his former owner, Doña Juana, to fight in Flanders.

The next day, the entire company of soldiers is gone and Don Agustín with them. A distraught Doña Leonor hears a song about the fickle promises of soldiers. Outraged by Don Agustín's betrayal and the loss of her honor, she also resolves to travel to Lisbon and reach Flanders in pursuit of her wayward lover. The action moves to Flanders, where Juan is again rebuffed in his attempt to join the army. In a soliloquy he decides that daring is the only way to overcome the rejection he suffers for being Black (lines 628–653). He stands in front of the Duke of Alba, captain general of the Spanish forces, and requests permission to earn his right to be a soldier by taking the necessary weapons from the enemy by himself.

Under the cloak of night and donning a mask (lines 740–746), Juan takes Don Agustín prisoner, instead. The latter had been sent by the Duke to capture a spy and was dressed in the enemy's uniform. Juan has recognized Don Agustín in spite of his disguise and calls him effeminate and a Spaniard. Juan lets him go but not before taking his sash, the sign of his military rank as captain. Juan remains alone on stage to give his first speech praising a favorable fortune (lines 840–855). As he leaves, Doña Leonor enters dressed as a man. She is talking to Antón, her Black slave, who answers in *habla de negros*. Doña Leonor calls herself Esteban now, and promises Antón his freedom if he will help her get access to Don Agustín and make him fulfill his promise to marry her. Antón assures her he will be prudent and silent.

A commotion occurs when shots are heard coming from the enemy camp, and Juan enters with two enemy guards and the two arquebuses that he has captured from them (lines 938–965). Don Agustín sees, to his embarrassment, that Juan is the 'enemy' who during the night had taken his sash in exchange for his life. Juan asks for his appointment in the army and submits the sash to the Duke, who in a turn of dramatic irony hands it to Don Agustín, its original owner. Now Don Agustín is chafing for revenge. The Duke honors Juan with a change of name. He will be known now as Juan de Alba, in a play of words on his Blackness (*alba* means whiteness and dawn). What follows is a scene of homoerotic equivocation. Juan recognizes Antón as his friend, and Doña Leonor/Esteban reaches to embrace Juan, but he does not recognize this page, who makes him deeply uncomfortable with his words and gestures. Doña Leonor/Esteban offers to share her quarters and dinner with Juan, which he turns down. In his asides, Juan expresses his fear of physical contact with the page and calls him *maricón* (faggot, sissy), wishing for him to be burned at the stake (lines 1045–1085).

Act Two

Now promoted to sergeant, Juan de Alba reflects on his ambiguous situation. Fortune has favored his military daring, but the color of his skin makes the other Spanish soldiers threaten to resign their offices. Their leader is Captain Don Agustín. Juan hears of their plot and confronts one of the sergeants at night, forcing him to relinquish his halberd. In a new soliloquy Juan praises his fortune, which has brought him one step higher up (lines 1086–1108). However, Doña Leonor/Esteban appears again, talking to Antón about her encounter with Don Agustín. From a hiding place, Juan interprets the scene as an erotic exchange between the page and Antón. He cannot suffer the idea of Antón's possible homosexuality, but soon Doña Leonor/Esteban reveals that the object of her/his affection is Captain Don Agustín. This confirms Juan's low esteem for Don Agustín. Doña Leonor expects to marry Don Agustín after the imminent retreat of the Spanish army, now caught in a difficult situation with the winter approaching. Juan threatens to kill Antón if he does not abandon Doña Leonor/Esteban's service, to which Antón answers, "who will put food in Antón's mouth?". Antón then promises to switch masters and follow Juan (lines 1255–1345).

Surrounded by swamps and the enemy, the Duke of Alba and his army are about to accept the conditions of a humiliating defeat. Juan interrupts the council of captains and brings a banner he has captured in the Dutch camp, rallying the white officers to talk less and do the same as a Black soldier has done. An envoy from the enemy arrives full of bluster, threatening to open all the dykes of the land if the Spaniards do not retreat. He also calls for a challenge between fifteen Spanish captains and the same number of Dutch, to which Juan replies by defying and killing him. He has done what the captains have not, and he is thus promoted to that rank. Juan alone speaks up against the retreat. In a new soliloquy Juan plans to honor his new rank with an act of heroism (lines 1577–1596).

In the next scene Don Agustín and Doña Leonor/Esteban speak of their future, which Juan again interprets as a homoerotic encounter. Don Agustín, however, receives a letter from his father asking him to return to Spain and marry the very rich Doña Juana de Vera, Juan's former owner. Don Agustín is only too happy to accept the new marriage prospect.

In the next scene Juan appears with a dagger, ready to attack the enemy camp by himself. His soliloquy addresses Fortune as the giver of his Black skin, asking it not to make him an inkblot on the pages of fame. This Christmas eve he will be a different Black man, not like the ones painted in the Nativity scenes (lines 1692–1712). He immediately captures the Prince of Orange and brings him to the Spanish camp and into the presence of an astonished Duke of Alba. In an exchange of courtesies, the Prince insists on rewarding the soldier who single-handedly captured him, only to be told that the Spaniard is a Black man. After cleaning himself of the mud, Juan returns to receive the accolades of everyone, acting surprised and humble. The company breaks into song to celebrate the happy turn of the dark Christmas predicted for the Spanish army, thanks to a Black man. Fortune has changed, and now the Duke of Alba can impose the same conditions of retreat on the Dutch army in exchange for the freedom of the Prince of Orange. The Prince exchanges swords with Juan in a sign of recognition from a dignified loser (lines 1963–1974). The act ends with Doña Leonor revealing her identity to Juan and asking him to help her in recovering her honor and marrying Don Agustín. Juan accepts the request as a means of taking revenge on the double-dealing Don Agustín.

Act 3

Juan de Alba, Doña Leonor, and Antón are waiting for the Duke and the King at court, in Madrid. Some courtiers, dressed in finery, start ridiculing the two Black men. They also make jokes about the possible price Juan and Antón would fetch in a slave market. One of them farts in their presence, and Juan draws his sword and attacks all of them (lines 2099–2138). Soldiers come to arrest Juan and put him to death, as the use of a sword in the King's palace is a crime of *lèse majesté*. Only the entrance of the Duke stops Juan's imminent execution. Juan justifies himself: "This is the penalty for being this color" (line 2156). The King appears and recognizes Juan's honor in public. Juan makes his last speech, telling Fortune that it can rest now, as the King has given him honor, and through him to all Black people. The King bestows the habit of the Order of Santiago on Juan (2263–2300). He is also promoted to the rank of *maese de campo* (field marshall) and given the astronomical income of six thousand ducats. The King has bested Fortune by rewarding Juan's merit. Juan answers by comparing his glory to that of Afro-Hispanic poet Juan Latino (lines 2306–2335).

The scene moves to Mérida, where Don Agustín is preparing to marry Doña Juana. A letter arrives announcing the visit of the new *maese de campo* on his way to Lisbon to assume his new commission in Flanders. This is none other than Juan, accompanied by Doña Leonor and Antón, to the surprise of the bride Doña Juana, who recognizes Juan as her former slave. Juan speaks of the turns in the Wheel of Fortune and of how he has returned to his birthplace, where his skin color had made it impossible to be respected: Heavens give valor, while color comes from the earth (lines 2482–2519). Doña Juana proclaims that the origin of true nobility is in arms and letters. Juan wants to visit his mother, so she can see his triumph, but other characters speculate that she may have passed away (lines 2539–2563). Meanwhile, Leonor waits in hiding. In front of the entire wedding party Juan demands from Don Agustín to acknowledge his written promise to Doña Leonor and unveils her presence. Juan even threatens him with beheading, something he now has the power to do. Juan thus returns the favor to Doña Leonor, who had saved his life in act one. He then addresses Doña Juana, who feels betrayed and dishonored, and offers his money for her to choose a worthier husband. She promptly chooses him, as Juan is now her equal in nobility. Both promise to be the slave of each other, and the play ends with a double wedding (lines 2617–2644).

Claramonte and the Context of *El valiente negro en Flandes*

Andrés de Claramonte was an important figure in the theater scene of Spain during the first three decades of the seventeenth century. He was born in Murcia, in the southeast of Spain, around 1580 (Ganelin 1987, 13; Rodríguez López-Vázquez 2010, 68). Claramonte started his theater career early in his life and soon gained a reputation not only as a good actor but as a playwright as well. Agustín de Rojas Villandrando mentions him, among others, in his *Viaje entretenido* ([1603] 1995, 158). Archival documents show that he was a member of several theater companies that traveled to different places around Spain. He soon became an *autor de comedias*, that is, a theater producer in those itinerant troupes (*compañías de la legua*). He is known to have worked in Seville, Zaragoza, Valencia, Murcia, Toledo, Segovia, and finally Madrid and its surrounding area (López 2007, 8). In 1615 he obtained a license to produce *comedias* in Madrid. Later he moved to Seville, where he earned his living mostly as a playwright, and ceased to be involved in acting and directing (García Reidy 2019, 140). His Sevillian period coincides with the probable dates of composition of *El valiente negro en Flandes*. As a sought-after writer of *autos sacramentales* (religious plays that celebrated the Eucharist), he moved between Seville and Madrid, where he died in 1626 (García Reidy 2019, 136). His *Letanía moral* (Seville, 1613) provides information about other playwrights, actors, and theater producers, including a brief poem in the voice of his wife Beatriz de Castro y Virués.[2] Although she was illiterate, the poem constitutes an example of the literary involvement of women in the theatrical scene, beyond acting:[3]

> Los ratos que habéis hurtado
> del tiempo a mi compañía
> también los habéis gastado,
> que si antes celos tenía,
> ya con envidia he quedado.
>
> Pues tan santo trueco hacéis
> cantad en heroicos cantos
> los santos que engrandecéis,
> que por buscar a los santos
> es bien que a mí me dejéis.
>
> [The moments you have stolen
> From keeping company with me
> You also have spent them in things
> That if they made me jealous earlier
> Now they fill me with envy.
>
> Since you replace me for something so saintly,
> Then sing with heroic song
> To the saints thus made more praiseworthy.
> For it is fair that, going after saints,
> You leave me behind]
>
> Claramonte 1613[4]

---

2   One year after its publication, this *Letanía moral* was included by the Inquisition in its *Index of Books* to be partially censored (Montes Pérez 2019, 46). We owe this information to an online communication from Professor Alfredo Rodríguez López-Vázquez (December 15, 2021).
3   Claramonte and Castro were married before 1610. In an official document signed in Toledo that year, she is described as not knowing how to sign (Vázquez 1987, 54).
4   This and other translations are ours, unless otherwise noted.

Andrés de Claramonte's *oeuvre* has become a matter of dispute. There is a corpus of plays that most critics since the nineteenth century have attributed to him. According to the latest database research, Claramonte is the author of three *autos sacramentales* (religious plays normally staged in the streets during the Corpus Christi festival), three *loas* (dramatic poems recited as a sort of prologue to a play), and around twenty *comedias* or full three-act plays (García Reidy 2019,136).[5]

More *comedias* have been recently attributed to Claramonte, some of which were canonically considered the work of either Lope de Vega or Tirso de Molina. Rodríguez López-Vázquez created a sensation when he attributed Lope de Vega's *La Estrella de Sevilla* to Claramonte (1983), publishing it in a critical edition in 2010). Later he attributed him *El burlador de Sevilla*, the Spanish original version of the Don Juan myth. With the publication of a critical edition of this *comedia* (Claramonte 1987, 2022), Rodríguez López-Vázquez has culminated his efforts to reinstate Claramonte as one of the major *comedia* playwrights. He also has made the claim that Claramonte wrote *El condenado por desconfiado* (2016, 442). In the prologue to his 1997 edition of *El valiente negro en Flandes*, Rodríguez López-Vázquez presented a methodology of attribution based on the comparison of versification patterns and textual similarities between plays that present little or no doubt they were written by Claramonte,

---

5   In an earlier essay, García Reidy provides a slightly different list (2008, 178), including three *autos sacramentales* (*El horno de Constantinopla*, *El dote del Rosario*, and *La sinagoga*). A fourth one has been recently attributed to him, *La Araucana* (Faúndez, cited in García Reidy 2019, 1400), and even a fifth one, *El rey David* (Sentaurens 1984, 1141; cited in García Reidy 2019, 142). The two *loas* are *La Asunción de la Virgen* and *Loa sacramental en metáfora de las calles de Sevilla* (1620). The list of *comedias* that most critics seem confident in attributing to Claramonte are *El rey don Pedro en Madrid e infanzón de Illescas*; *La infelice Dorotea*; *El ataúd para el vivo y el tálamo para el muerto*; *Deste agua no beberé*; *El gran rey de los desiertos, san Onofre*; *El secreto en la mujer*; *Tan largo me lo fiais*; *El mayor rey de los reyes*; *La esclava del cielo, santa Engracia*; *El Tao de san Antón*; *Púsoseme el sol, saliome la luna*; *La católica princesa Leopolda*; *El nuevo rey Gallinato*; *El infante de Aragón*; *El valiente negro en Flandes*; *De Alcalá a Madrid*; *El honrado con su sangre*; *El inobediente o la ciudad sin Dios*; *San Carlos o las dos columnas de Carlos* and *Dineros son calidad*.

including those attributed to others. These attributions to Claramonte are not new, as in the case of *La Estrella de Sevilla*, already made by Sturgis E. Leavitt in 1931. Claramonte's case invites researchers to reconsider the concept of authorship in seventeenth-century plays, since the texts, once they were sold by the writer, became the property of theater *autores* in their dual role as producers and directors, and also the property of the owners of printing houses. All of them intervened in the texts at different times.

The last years of Claramonte's life were spent in Seville. Rodríguez López-Vázquez's thesis of Claramonte's authorship of *El burlador de Sevilla* includes the argument that this play had to be written at the time he was living in this city (1983b, 98). We also know of Claramonte's involvement in the social and religious life of Seville. His *Loa sacramental en metáfora de las calles de Sevilla* (1620) shows intimate familiarity with the geography of the city, its churches and other religious institutions.

We are persuaded that Andrés de Claramonte's sojourn in Seville during the last years of his life is related to the creation of *The Valiant Black Man in Flanders*.[6] At the time Claramonte lived in Seville, people of African descent – both free and enslaved – constituted close to ten percent of the city's total population, the largest concentration in the entire Iberian Peninsula, with the exception of Lisbon (Cires Ordóñez and García Ballesteros 1997, 493).[7] Seville, Lisbon, and Antwerp were the hubs of a financial and commercial trade system

6   Juan Barceló Jiménez (1980, 40) wrote without documented proof that *El valiente negro en Flandes* had been performed in Claramonte's hometown of Murcia either in 1610 or 1612. Although Claramonte scholar Alfredo Rodríguez López-Vázquez initially accepted an early date of composition (1983, 13), he later expressed doubts, based in the metric structure of the play, which corresponds to Claramonte's plays written between 1620–1626 (1997, 18).

7   There are no reliable records to establish the ratio of free versus enslaved Blacks in Seville. The census of the Archbishopric of Seville of 1565 stated that there were 6,327 slaves out of a population of 85,538, which amounted to 7.2 percent of the total population. Of these slaves, approximately eighty percent were Black (Santos Cabota 1997, 501–502). For the entire area surrounding Seville there were 44,670 enslaved persons out of a total of 459,362 individuals counted in the census (Pérez García and Fernández Chaves 601).

in which the presence of Blacks and the trans-Atlantic slave trade were increasing (Aguado de los Reyes 2005, 103). Even though *The Valiant Black Man in Flanders* takes place in Mérida, the relation of this city in Extremadura with Black slavery was strong. Mérida was on the road from Seville to Lisbon. Prominent Mérida families had a Sevillian origin. The names of two Sevillian families with strong ties to Mérida, the Veras and the Vargas, are present in the play (see Fra-Molinero's essay in this volume). Mérida and the region of Extremadura were also places where a large concentration of Black slaves existed at the time Claramonte conceived of Juan de Mérida as a Black military hero who travels around the Spanish European Atlantic.

The Valiant Black Man in Flanders spoke to an Afro-Hispanic community of spectators who would have found an echo of their collective aspirations represented in a Black protagonist who is constantly denouncing and overcoming the indignities of racial exclusion in a hostile environment of white enemies. The Black population of Seville was well organized and used the institutions of the time to advance their interests. Blacks were a social factor in the city, as proven by the relatively high incidence of Black and *Mulato* intra-racial marriages among both free and enslaved persons (Cires *et al.* 1989, 38). There were up to three religious confraternities (*hermandades* and *cofradías*) that had been created specifically for people of African descent. Isidoro Moreno, in his monumental study of the oldest of them, the Hermandad de los negros, uncovers a hidden history. Black confraternities were ethnically closed, meaning that they accepted only Blacks and *Mulatos*. They were also mixed, with free and enslaved members, and this created problems for their stability in the face of the authorities. Black *hermandades* and *cofradías* provided a space to create a Black collective opinion and a Black collective identity within the city in order to defend their interests and their continuity as an ethnic group (Moreno 1997, 66). By the beginning of the seventeenth century, anti-Black attitudes were increasingly violent, corresponding to a slaving city that was the main port of entry for Africans in bondage, and a city in rapid expansion. This violence took place regularly whenever Black confraternities took to the streets in processions and other public ceremonies. It had become customary for the public to use the processions of Black confraternities to yell racial insults and physically attack Black men and women. These insults included the use of *habla de negros*, or Black speech, on the part of the white public.

Noémie Ndiaye sees these incidents as a case of white people performing Blackness, a phenomenon present in European society as it developed its colonial empires and the modern trans-Atlantic slave societies. *The Valiant Black Man in Flanders* echoes some of the attitudes present among Sevillian Blacks in the 1620s. The violent scene that opens the play would be familiar to all Sevillians, but especially to Black ones: A Black man is kicked out of a public space amidst insults that are similar to the ones Black men and women suffered daily, including during said religious celebrations. Ndiaye studies these incidents by analyzing the archival testimony contained in an ecclesiastical report from 1604 (Ndiaye 2017, 184).

Reports of anti-Black incidents had reached the ears of the archbishop of Seville. White confraternities vociferously complained about having to cross paths with Black ones and even about deferring to the Hermandad de los Negros as the oldest of all confraternities in the city (Rowe 2019, 108–12). They wanted Black confraternities to be banned altogether. The anti-Black incidents were dubbed disturbances of public order, and the presence of Blacks in the streets was "the cause" that provoked the insults and unseemly scenes. The writer of the report went as far as calling the incidents a theatrical spectacle, an *entremés*, in which the assaulting white spectators used the theatrical *habla de negros* to launch insults at the members of the Black confraternities. As in the third act of *The Valiant Black Man in Flanders*, whites would sneeze and fart as the Black confraternities passed. They would stab Black women with pins and needles. Blacks were seen as a source of entertainment by whites, and an occasion for moral license:

Vio que mucha gente silbaba y hacía otros ruidos afrentosos a los dichos negros, hablándoles en guineo y afrentándoles en grande deshonor de la procesión y la representación de la Pasión de nuestro Salvador, de lo cual los negros se corrían y respondían otras palabras y juraban juramentos, diciendo palabras afrentosas a los que les silbaban; de lo cual se seguía que parecía cosa de risa y entremés más que procesión de Semana Santa.

[He saw that many people whistled and made other offensive noises directed at the said Blacks. They spoke to them in Black speech, and offended them, causing great disrespect to the procession and the representation of Our Savior's Passion. Blacks felt insulted by this and answered back with other words and curses, proffering insulting words at those who whistled at them. As a result, the whole thing looked more like the stuff for laughter and a theater skit than a Holy Week procession]

Moreno 1997, 86.

The anti-Black violence represented in Claramonte's play was not different from what happened in the streets. The performance of Blackness by whites as a form of insult (as Ndiaye understands these incidents and as described in the 1604 report) is a performance of whiteness through blackface and the use of Black speech. Ndiaye reads *The Valiant Black Man in Flanders* as a prime example of this, especially in the opening scene of act three, when three courtiers use scatological insults directed at the two Black characters, provoking a violent fight (Ndiaye 2017, 167).

The Black protagonist of Claramonte's play reacts much like the members of the Hermandad de los Negros who defended themselves physically, provoking the intervention of the authorities. These were free and enslaved people taking a stand against whites. Therefore, they were blamed for the altercations, with the added accusation that enslaved brothers and sisters stole money from their owners in order to pay for the expenses of their membership (Moreno 1997, 83). As a result, the presence in the streets of the Hermandad de los Negros and its sister Black confraternity of Triana were banned by the archbishop in 1604. This prohibition took away the main source of income for these Black organizations, because they could no longer legally ask for alms in the streets. Black confraternities were appealing this prohibition during the time Claramonte lived in Seville. They had been unsuccessful until Pope Urban VIII lifted the ban in 1625 (Moreno 1997, 90). Claramonte probably had the chance to see the Hermandad de los negros come out in procession for the first time after so many years of prohibition, now in triumph.

Performance History

The Valiant Black Man in Flanders has been the object of public attention ever since it was originally performed, possibly between 1620 and 1626. The play was staged for Philip IV on September 13, 1637, by Segundo Morales' theater company at the court theater (Shergold and Varey 1963, 231; Ferrer Valls *et al.*, n.d.). *The Valiant Black Man in Flanders* played an important political role in King Philip IV's court, as its Black protagonist was featured in at least two other dramatic spectacles in the following years.

The second time the protagonist of *The Valiant Black Man in Flanders* was featured in a theatrical performance was in 1649 in the midst of the festivities to celebrate the entrance into Madrid of Queen Mariana de Austria as the new wife of King Philip IV. The different guilds and *sesmos* (rural districts) of the city organized a series of performances and events. They included twelve dances, an acrobat show, two sword dances, a four-against-four mock fight between Moors and Christians, and a game of canes (Sánchez Cano 2005, 137). The dances could be placed into two categories. On the one hand, there were five dances of "nations" (a *danza de naciones*, several dances of "Indians", and one dance of "Moors"). On the other hand, some dances were inspired by literary and Greek mythological themes that featured Apollo, Orpheus and the Nine Muses, a group of *serranas* (female mountain dwellers), dwarves and giants. Among these literary dances was the *Baile del Valiente negro en Flandes* (Dance of the Valiant Black Man in Flanders), a show organized by the six villages that comprised the rural district of Vallecas, outside the city of Madrid (see Appendix D). The expense reports found at the Archivo General de la villa de Madrid state that this dance cost 2,400 *reales* and involved the hiring of professional dancers, a drummer, and another musician. As was customary, the dancing crew wore *libreas* (liveries) ordered for the occasion, with a cost of 1,300 *reales*, almost half of the total expenses. That the expense records identified this dance with the title of *El Valiente negro en Flandes* makes it clear that the play that inspired the dance had been quite successful. The residents of the villages outside Madrid were sufficiently familiar with the play as to have a dance included in their repertoire. This dance was performed in the Arenal Street, in downtown Madrid. Thus, we assume that the dance featured a main dancer in blackface and some sort of military attire. It probably summarized the story of the play, or some of its famous scenes, perhaps including the recitation of some text. Twenty-three years after Claramonte's death, and eleven after the publication of the play in Barcelona, the theme of this fictional Black military hero was still popular.

El valiente negro en Flandes was performed, or at least produced around December 28, 1651, in Zaragoza. This is suggested by two performing licenses signed on that date, which were included at the end of *M*, a manuscript that served as the play's prompt book (see Textual History). The acting company of Toribio de la Vega owned this manuscript, with De la Vega himself probably playing the role of Juan de Mérida/Juan de Alba, as that year he was the *primer galán* (leading male actor), according to Pérez Pastor (1913, 301). The names of other actors in Toribio de la Vega's company – Juan López, Pedro de Cifuentes, and Alonso Ortiz – are written in the margins. The last page of the manuscript suggests the possibility of a second performance in Valladolid, Spain, at an uncertain date, but more research is required to confirm this point (see witness description in Textual History).

The third presence at the royal court of the fictional valiant Black man took place between 1661 and 1663, which gives testimony of the enduring popularity of the play. He appears as a speaking character in the *Mojiganga de personajes de títulos de comedias*, a theatrical poem staged in the Buen Retiro for the birthday of Infanta Margarita Teresa of Austria, the central figure in Velázquez's painting *Las Meninas*, and daughter of the aforementioned King Philip IV and Mariana of Austria. This theatrical poem features Juan de Alba, who is referred to as *El negro* (the Black man) next to other celebrated literary characters: Miguel de Cervantes' *Licenciado Vidriera* (The Glass Graduate), Juan Pérez de Montalbán's *La doncella de labor*, *El mariscal de Birón*, and Calderón de la Barca's *La dama duende* and *El galán fantasma*. In this *mojiganga* (masquerade), *El negro* brags about having captured the Prince of Orange, a deed that is comically enhanced by a German character:

Sale El negro.

El negro	Ya no hay más Flandes que España;
	buenas noches, Caballeros.
Alemán	No es la que traéis muy mala,
	pero ¿por qué estáis aquí?
El negro	Porque con mucha arrogancia
	cogí en su tienda al de Orange.
Alemán	Pues eso a mí no me espanta,
	que es gran delito en la tienda
	andar cogiendo naranjas.

[*Enter the Black man.*

The Black Man	There is no more Flanders than Spain.
	Good evening, Gentlemen.
German	Not a bad evening indeed,
	but why are you here?
The Black Man	Because, full of arrogance,
	I grabbed the Prince of Orange in his tent.
German	It does not amaze me,
	as it is a serious crime
	to grab oranges from people's tents.]

Restori 1903, 152–53.

The valiant Black Man shows up again in the anonymous *Entremés de las naciones* (Interlude of the Nations), a one-act play published in 1691 (Micón 1691, 22–33; Ndiaye 2017, 173). In this *entremés*, a woman named Manuela convinces a man named Escamilla that she is a sorceress and tricks him into believing that he is flying across the world on a stick (*vara*), in a scene reminiscent of Don Quixote's flight on the wooden horse Clavileño (*Don Quijote* II, chapter 41). As they travel through the air, Escamilla and Manuela visit different nations: Galicians, French, Moors and Ethiopians. Two Black people, a man and a woman, share in the prank by impersonating the protagonists of four different plays in which the word *negro* appears in the title: Matos Fragoso's *El negro de Sevilla*, Claramonte's play, Lope de Vega's *El negro del mejor amo*, and Marcelo de Ayala's *El negro del cuerpo blanco*.[8]

Salen Negro y Negra, cantando y bailando.

Cante Negro	*Zucuruzú, curuzú manita,*
	zucuruzú, curuzú mandinga.
Negro	Yo zo neglo de Siviya.
Negra	Yo, negla del mejor amo.
Negro	Yo, el negro valiente en Flandes.
Negra	Yo, negla del cuelpo blanco:
	zucuruzú, curuzú manita, etc.
Escamilla	Esta es gente ruin, que todos
	se tratan como unos negros.

[*Enter Black Man and Black Woman, singing and dancing.*

Black man sings	*Zucuruzú, curuzú manita,*
	zucuruzú, curuzú mandinga.
Black man	I'm the Black man from Seville.
Black woman	I'm the Black of the Greatest Master.
Black man	I'm the Valiant Black Man in Flanders.
Black woman	I'm the Black Man of the White Body:
	zucuruzú, curuzú manita, etc.
Escamilla	These are low people, since all
	call themselves Black.]

Micón 1691, 22–33.[9]

---

8   The 'Entremés de las naciones' can be found in several manuscript copies from the eighteenth century at the Biblioteca Nacional de España (MS 14516/47 and MS 14516/60).

9   The line "quiquiribú, quiribú mandinga" appears in the chorus of Guillermo Rodríguez Fiffe's 'La negra Tomasa (Bilongo)', a famous mid-twentieth-century Cuban *son*. This suggests that the *Entremés de las naciones*'s "zucuruzú, curuzú mandinga" may be echoing a popular early modern Afro-Iberian song.

The mention of *El valiente negro en Flandes* among well-known plays by the late seventeenth century is a strong indication that the play was still performed due to its popularity. According to the DICAT and CATCOM databases, *El valiente negro en Flandes* was also performed once again at court in the Alcázar of Madrid on January 6, 1675 (significantly the feast day of the Three Wise Men, one of whom is Black) and on September 25, 1688 (Ferrer Valls *et al.*, n.d.; see also García Reidy 2019, 144).

El valiente negro en Flandes continued its presence on the stage in the eighteenth century. It was performed in Valladolid at least on three occasions, twice on December 5 and 16, 1703, and once on July 27, 1718 (Ferrer Valls, 2008). Also on February 22, 1710, at Madrid's Teatro del Príncipe. The prompt book used in rehearsals has been located (it is named *S1* in Textual History). This is a printed *suelta* (single-play booklet) with numerous manuscript marks, stage directions, and re-writings (see Critical Apparatus). The staging of *El valiente negro en Flandes* on this occasion was probably accompanied by Quiñones de Benavente's *entremés El negrito hablador y sin color anda la niña* (The Talkative Little Black and The Girl Has Lost Color). There were at least seven different editions in *suelta* in the eighteenth century, most with a high number of extant copies around the world. This is evidence that *El valiente negro en Flandes* continued to be a successful play throughout the eighteenth century, both for audiences and readers. The anonymous *Romance* or *Relación del valiente negro en Flandes* [Ballad of the Valiant Black Man in Flanders], a fictional autobiography in which Juan de Alba retells Claramonte's story, also circulated in numerous printed editions during this period (see Figure 2 and Appendix C in this volume). The play's popularity is demonstrated also by the publication of a sequel, Manuel Vicente Guerrero's *El negro valiente en Flandes* (1751). In his critical edition of this play, Panford (2003) situates the Black protagonist as an integral part of the *comedia* tradition and establishes his political and ideological significance.

The text of Claramonte's *El valiente negro en Flandes*, together with those of other plays with Black protagonists (mostly saints), appears in catalogs of the private libraries and bookstores in Mexico that were monitored by the Spanish Inquisition (Beusterien 2006a, 115; Camarena 1995, 158). Some of these catalogs were compiled as late as 1803. Readers were buying plays with Black military heroes, because the events of the Haitian Revolution (1791–1804) were inspiring the abolitionist sentiments of the war for Mexican independence.[10]

The Valiant Black Man in Flanders has been performed as an Afro-diasporic text in the twentieth century. The first was a partial staging in Havana, Cuba, in 1938, in the context of the Black cultural movement and its expression of literary Negrismo. Eduardo H. Acuña, who later became a professional movie actor, is the first Black person on record to perform in the role of Juan de Mérida (Marquina 1938, 563). Significantly, the role of Antón, the Black *gracioso*, was omitted.[11] It was not until 1997 that *The Valiant Black Man in Flanders* was performed in Alcalá de Henares, Spain; the text was reprinted as part of the celebration of the European Year against Racism (Pérez Jiménez 2000, 2). The role of Juan de Mérida was interpreted by Iranian actor Farhad Lak (Rodríguez López-Vázquez 2010, 132), and that of Antón by Victoria Buika.[12] An adaptation of the play was staged in Madrid in the summer of 2018 (Figueroa 2012, 112). [13]

---

10   Francisco Comella's abolitionist play *El negro sensible* was performed in Mexico City in 1805 and later condemned by the Inquisition in 1809 for promoting "con capciosidad la insurrección de los esclavos contra sus legítimos dueños" (Sánchez López 2019, 16–17) (promoting with mendacity the insurrection of the slaves against their legitimate masters). Comella's play inspired a second part written by Fernández de Lizardi, in the context of the political movement for the abolition of slavery in Mexico in 1825 (Young 1981, 370).

11   The play was staged as part of a larger lecture by Rafael Marquina, 'El negro en el teatro español antes de Lope de Vega'. It also included the scene from Lope de Rueda's *Comedia de los engañados* featuring Guiomar, the female Black character, interpreted by actress Felicia D. Crespo. In the lecture, Marquina echoes Juan Marinello and Fernando Ortiz's preoccupation with Black poetic expression and Black forms of Spanish as a preamble to his discussion of Lope de Rueda's creation of Black characters identified by their speech (1938, 561–62).

12   A video recording of the play is available on YouTube: https://youtu.be/ uVmerkcKHSc. Accessed 2 May 2023,

13   A workshop with the title 'Somos negros pero no tiznamos: El negro y su

The protagonist of Claramonte's *The Valiant Black Man in Flanders* was a popular Afro-Diasporic fictional character in Spanish letters for over two centuries, as shown by the number of documented instances the play was performed and printed. A variety of audiences – from royal persons to people in the street – and readers on both sides of the Atlantic Ocean have found Juan de Mérida/Juan de Alba a figure of political relevance to this day because of his Blackness. Archival research will unearth other stagings and perhaps new versions of the text, and copies with important marginalia that may shed light on the evolution of this play's performance.

Textual History

El valiente negro en Flandes is, without a doubt, Andrés de Claramonte's most successful play, at least among those attributed with certainty to him. We do not know when it was written, but Rodríguez López-Vázquez's metrical analysis safely dates it around 1625.[14] The transgressive nature of this play must have posed difficulties for its textual transmission. There are no surviving copies from before Claramonte's death in 1626. Only three witnesses of the play are dated in the seventeenth century: the oldest one from 1638 (*P*), another from 1651 (*M*), and a third one from the last decades of the century (*S1*). We can safely conjecture that *El valiente negro en Flandes* circulated widely in manuscript during the 1630s and 1640s if we consider its performance history and the circulation of other plays by Claramonte (García Reidy 2019, 144). *El valiente negro en Flandes* was the object of extraordinary interest during the entire eighteenth century. There are at least six separate editions of the play in *suelta*, some of them pirated. The collation of the

representación en el teatro del Siglo de Oro' ['We are Black, but we do not stain: Blacks and their representation in Golden Age Theater'] took place one year later in Alcalá de Henares, under the direction of Mexican theater director Brenda Escobedo. https://www.clasicosenalcala.net/2019/en/otras_actividades/1083-taller-somos-negros-pero-no-tiznamos-el-negro-y-su-representacion-en-el-teatro-del-siglo-de-oro.php.

14   See Rodríguez López Vázquez (2010, 131). Some scholars have pushed back the date of the play by at least one decade, but without much supporting evidence (Olmedo Gobante 2018, 88).

nine *sueltas* shows that all of them descend from a seventeenth-century copy – probably a manuscript – that has not survived. A precarious understanding of the textual transmission of *El valiente negro en Flandes* induced modern editors and scholars – including me (Olmedo Gobante 2018, 88) – to neglect the *sueltas* and favor the oldest witness (*P*), incorrectly considering it the closest to the author. In order to produce a critical text of *El valiente negro en Flandes*, it is necessary to study its complete textual history, for only one of the eleven surviving historical witnesses can be discarded.

Textual Witnesses[15]

P PARTE / TREYNTA / UNA, DE LAS / MEIORES COME / DIAS, QUE HASTA OY / han salido. / RECOGIDAS POR EL DOTOR FRAN. / cisco Torivio Ximenez. Y a la fin va la comedia de santa Madrona, / intitulada la viuda tirana, y conquista de Barcelona. // Año 1638 // *CON LICENCIA Y PRIVILEGIO* // En Barcelona: En la Emprenta de Iayme Romeu, de / lante de Santiago. // *A costa de Iuan Sapera Mercader de Libros*. [4], 21 h., [1] en bl., h. 22–277;

4°. There is one copy at the Austrian National Library *38.V.12. (31). I examined the digitized copy at the Biblioteca Nacional de España R/23484.

---

15 There are four copies supposedly at the Biblioteca Nacional in Madrid, that I have not been able to consult: T/14983(1), T/55273/1, T/55273/2, and T. 14974/87. Treviño Trejo describes the last one in his doctoral dissertation (1977, 28–29). Apparently, this text is quite close to *S8*. Notwithstanding its own typographic singularities. I assume that the other three are copies of this edition or any of the other ones that are described here, quite probably *S6* and *S7*. Also, I have not been able to consult the copy held at the Georg-August-Universität Göttingen 8 P DRAM II, 82:4 (10). The series number and the absence of date in this latter copy suggest that it may also be a copy of either *S6* or *S7*. The likelihood that these copies may alter the restored text of the play is slim. The same can be said of the other copies that may appear in the future, something that I am persuaded that will happen. Comparing these other witnesses with the Critical Apparatus in this volume will no doubt offer interesting data regarding the textual transmission of the play during the eighteenth century.

M Biblioteca Nacional de España MSS/15690 (Manos Teatrales 0137). Manuscript. 54 folios. With licenses to perform (*licencias de representación*) of 1551 in fol. 50v. The library acquired it from the collection of the Dukes of Osuna. Heading: "De d[on] Andrés de Claramonte / El valiente negro en / Flandes". First and last lines: "Vai ael peRo" (2r) / "j largamente las quenta" (50r).

S1 COMEDIA FAMOSA. / EL VALIENTE NEGRO / EN FLANDES / *DE DON ANDRÉS DE CLARAMONTE*. *Suelta*, Madrid: Imprenta de Francisco Sanz, calle de la Paz, no date [1672–1709]. 32 pages, 4°, no series, signatures A-D2. Text in two columns. I have found two copies: one at the Bancroft Library at the University of California, Berkeley (PQ6217.A2 C642); and one at the Biblioteca Histórica Municipal in Madrid (Tea 1-51-3,b.), which is the one I examined. The copy at the Biblioteca Histórica has a great number of manuscript marks, amendments, and annotations (see description below and Critical Apparatus).

S2 COMEDIA FAMOSA. / EL VALIENTE NEGRO / EN FLANDES / *DE DON ANDRÉS DE CLARAMONTE*. *Suelta*, no place, no date. 32 pages, 4°, series X [handwritten?], signatures A-D2. Text in two columns. Almost identical to *S1*. I have only found one copy at the Austrian National Library 38.T.12 (vol 8,10).

S3 COMEDIA FAMOSA / EL VALIENTE NEGRO / EN FLANDES / *DE DON ANDRÉS DE CLARAMONTE*. *Suelta*, Madrid: Imprenta de Antonio Sanz, calle de la Paz. 1745. 28 pages, 4° (20cm), Series 113, signatures A-C4, D2. Text in two columns. I have found ten copies of this edition. One is at the Biblioteca Municipal de Madrid C 18863; one at the University of Texas at Austin, call number 31.1; one at the Austrian National Library 600913-B.3,23; one at Wayne State University PQ 6217.A2 C6 v.3; one at the University of Pennsylvania SC75 A100 Pam v.4; one at the University of North Carolina PQ6217.T444 v. 13, no. 9 1; one at the Biblioteca Nacional de España (call number T/55273/8); and two copies at the University of Glasgow Sp Coll Scarfe 766.i.a and Sp Coll Scarfe 766.i.b. I examined the copy at the Biblioteca de la Universidad de Sevilla, call number A 250/187(19).

S4 COMEDIA FAMOSA / EL VALIENTE NEGRO / EN FLANDES. / *DE DON PEDRO CALDERÓN DE LA BARCA. Suelta*, Valladolid: Imprenta de Alonso del Riego. 1751. 28 pages, 4°, (20 cm), signatures A4-C4, D2. Text in two columns. I have found two copies of this edition: one at the Universidade de Santiago de Compostela FOLL 306-3, and another at the Biblioteca de Catalunya 83-8-C 84/18, which is the one I examined.

S5 COMEDIA FAMOSA / EL VALIENTE NEGRO / EN FLANDES / *DE DON ANDRÉS DE CLARAMONTE. Suelta*, Salamanca: Imprenta de la Santa Cruz, no date [c. 1725–1775]. 28 pages, 4° (24 cm), series Núm. 158, signatures A-C4, D2. Text in two columns. I have found twelve copies of this edition: one at Smith College, William Allan Neilson Library PQ6225.T4 42; one at Cambridge University Library (Hisp.5.76.1611), two copies at the Biblioteca Histórica Municipal de Madrid Tea 1-51-3,a1, and Tea 1-51-3,a2; three at the Biblioteca Nacional de España T/14827(6), T/55273/9, and 7/148146 v.X; two at the Biblioteca de la Real Academia Española 41-IV-50(1) and 41-V-69(2); one at the University of North Carolina at Chapel Hill: Wilson Special Collections Library PQ6217.T445 v.15, no. 21; one at the Biblioteca de Catalunya Aguiló-8-118/18; and one at the Museo Nacional del Teatro: Bueno.FA.10.COM.val, which is the one I examined.

S6 COMEDIA FAMOSA, / EL VALIENTE NEGRO EN FLANDES. / *DE D. ANDRES DE CLARAMONTE. Suelta*, no place, no date. 32 pages, 4°, series Num 23, signatures A-C4, D2. Text in two columns. I have only found one copy at the Biblioteca Nacional de España T/55273/3.

S7 COMEDIA FAMOSA, / EL VALIENTE / NEGRO EN FLANDES. / *DE DON ANDRES DE CLARAMONTE. Suelta*, no place, no date. 32 pages, 4°, series Num 23., signatures A-C4, D2. Text in two columns. I have found only one copy at Biblioteca Nacional de España T/55273/12). Folio 4 was bound before folio 3.

S8 COMEDIA FAMOSA, / EL VALIENTE / NEGRO EN FLANDES. / *DE DON ANDRES DE CLARAMONTE*. *Suelta*, Sevilla: Joseph Padrino, en calle Genova ("con licencia"), no date [c. 1741–1779 or 1748–1775, according to the BNE and comediassueltasusa.org respectively]. 24 pages, 4° (22cm), series Num. 23, signatures A-D2. Text in two columns. I have found five copies of this edition. There is one at Duke University: Rubenstein Special Collections (call number PQ6416.P756 1750z c.1), two at the Biblioteca de Castilla-La Mancha 1-906(8) and M-0297(8), and two at the Biblioteca Nacional de España: T/55273/4 and T/14798/16. I used the latter. Treviño Trejo and López Vázquez mention another copy of *S8* at the Biblioteca Nacional de España T/14789, but I could not locate it.

S9 EL NEGRO / VALIENTE / EN FLANDES. / PRIMERA PARTE. / *DE DON ANDRES DE CLARAMONTE*. *Suelta*, Valencia: Imprenta de la Viuda de Josef de Orga, calle de la Cruz Nueva. 1764. 28 pages, 4° (24 cm), series N.64, signatures A-C4, D2. Text in two columns. I have found ten copies of this edition. There are three copies at the Biblioteca Histórica Municipal de Madrid C 18764, C 18866, and Tea 1-51-3,c; one at the Austrian National Library *38.V.26.(Vol.7,9); two at the Biblioteca Nacional de España T/969 and T/19353; two at the University of North Carolina at Chapel Hill: Wilson Special Collections Library PQ6217.T445v.15,no.11, and PQ6225.T43 v.131;1; one at the University of Illinois Oak Street Library 860.82 Sp24 v.63:12; and one at the Biblioteca de la Real Academia Española 41-V-53(8). Camarena Castellanos (1993) locates a copy of *S9* in an 1803 Inquisitorial inventory in Mexico (1993, 158)16. There used to be one more copy at Smith College William Allan Neilson Library PQ6225.T4 29, but it is now lost. Treviño Trejo located two copies at the British Museum Library, but I could not confirm this.

---

16 I have not found any copies in Latin American libraries. Further research is required.

Description of the Witnesses

P (1638) is the oldest extant witness. Published twelve years after Claramonte's death, it served as the base text in modern editions until now. However, *P* contains a great number of serious errors that can be easily corrected through textual criticism. For instance, at one point, "el hado loco" (fickle fate), one of the dominant themes of the play, turns into "helado y loco" (frozen and crazy) according to *P* (line 2312). By the end of the play, a mysterious "Gobernador" (governor) enters in *P* (2586). This character was probably inserted because of an incorrect interpretation of the abbreviation *doj* (Don Juan). Many other examples come from Antón's distinctive way of speaking. This was especially challenging for *P*, which reads "aquintura" instead of *aquí*[n] *tura* (here every), and "dembera" instead of *de*[n] *Vera*, his last name. All of these errors have passed unnoticed into every modern edition.[17] One must call attention to the fact that the text was heavily censored in *P*. Some of the interventions meticulously erase references to the play's historicity. For example, they deleted most of the last names – often replacing them with extravagant substitutions –, perhaps to avoid offending the Vera, Vargas and Estrada families from Mérida (lines 171, 272, 1027, and 2383b) in the context of the performance at King Philip IV's court theatre in 1637 (Rodríguez López-Vázquez 1997, 5; see Performance History). Likewise, all allusions to the Order of Santiago are systematically suppressed, no matter how indirect they were. Most notable is the suppression of Juan de Alba's wedding engagement to Doña Juana de Vera (2629–2639), which was crossed out – although not erased – in *M*.[18] It is a mistake to say that *El valiente negro en Flandes* has two possible endings. The critical analysis of the textual history shows that these passages – the knighting of Juan and his engagement – both were in the original text, or at least in the archetype *X* restored by this edition. Some scholars

---

17 Some of the critical loci that discredit *P* are in lines 62, 136, 237, 340, 341, 427, 562, 625, 1019, 1248, 2125, 2253, 2315, 2320, 2323, 2334, 2343, 2443, 2444, and 2445. See the Critical Apparatus in this volume.

18 See lines 2280–2291, 2339, 2489, 2490, 2629–2639, 2632–2634, and 2635–2644 in the Critical Apparatus.

have dismissed these passages as improbable and ahistorical, but this conjecture has already been disproved (Olmedo Gobante 2018). As well as for reasons of censorship, *P* omits other fragments for no apparent reason,[19] but also adds some others that almost certainly were not in the original text.[20] In sum, despite being the oldest, *P* is a precarious witness not only because of its many errors, omissions, and additions but also because it stripped *El valiente negro en Flandes* of many of the transgressive elements that made it such a successful play in its time.

M (1551) is a co-penned manuscript. Treviño Trejo identified two hands (1977, 14), and at least one more could be added, as stated in our Critical Apparatus (lines 1156–1157, 1839–1927). *M* was used as a prompt book, that is, as a theater company's working copy for acting. It has many textual interventions such as added stage directions, notes in the margins, crossed out sections, highlights, re-writings, amendments, hesitations, and other kinds of marks, including the symbols = and + (see Critical Apparatus for the most conspicuous cases). In all likelihood, the manuscript was the property of Toribio de la Vega's acting company. Some names written in the margins of *M* have been identified using the online site Manos Teatrales. For example, "López" (written in folio 7v) and "Cifuentes" (written in lines 552, 865, 3141, and 1412) probably refer to Juan López de las Cuevas and Pedro Cifuentes, two actors in Toribio de la Vega's company around the year 1651 (García-Reidy 2019, 150). In addition, the name "Al[ons]o" – possibly Alonso Ortiz, actor and the company's prompter that year – also appears twice in the margins of folios 12v and 17v of the manuscript (lines 734 and 1026). I could not determine the purpose of these annotations. They could mark passages supervised by said actors or point to their interventions as characters in the play. For instance, in line 1412, instead of "Sale el sargento" (Enter the

---

19   Fragments 2345–2347 and 2404–2409 are omitted in *P* for unknown reasons.
20   The passages exclusive to *P* are 421–424, 449–450, 896–901, 1370–1377, 1621–22, 1893–1900, and 2348–2383. As explained in the Editorial Methods (see below), I included them in the present edition marking them with the + symbol in the text. These are also included in the Critical Apparatus.

sergeant) *M* seems to read "Sale Cifuentes" (Enter Cifuentes). This matter is still not clear and should be addressed in a future study. Finally, the name "Vega" has also passed unnoticed in the margin of folio 6r (line 227), something that strengthens the hypothesis that *M* belonged to De la Vega's company. This being the case, the list of eight plays featured in folio 20r, between acts one and two, would also be part of the repertoire of the company (see line 1085 in the Critical Apparatus). There, in folio 21v, we find a seemingly important note: "Ojo / [Ojo] Gregorio lo [ātagado] ni lo <\no> has de sacar / Ojo" (Careful, careful, Gregorio has crossed it out and you must not take it out?). I am unsure about the sense of this note. It may mean that the manuscript has been *atajado* (expurgated) by crossing out the passages considered inappropriate. This was advanced with a note in the margin of folio 2: <\\Ojo lo ataga ???i no> (Careful, he crosses it out and it should not...?). In any case, the name Gregorio could refer to Gregorio de Rojas, brother to playwright Francisco de Rojas. Gregorio de Rojas was a well-known actor and producer (*empresario teatral*) who worked for Toribio de la Vega's company between 1650 and 1653 (Sánchez Arjona 1898, 299–300, and 304). At the end of the manuscript, we find two licenses allowing for performing the play in Zaragoza, Spain, both from 1651 (see Critical Apparatus). The first license is signed by "El licen[cia]do Joseph Iban[ez?]", who, I believe, is wrongly identified as José Ibarra in the CLEMIT database (Urzáiz Tortajada *et al.*, n.d.). "El D[oct]or Juan Fran[cis]co Andres [de Uztarroz]" signs the second license. The same modern hand that foliated the document added the family name "de Uztárroz" in pencil, pointing to the famous poet and chronicler. Juan Francisco Andrés de Uztárroz died in Zaragoza in 1653, which makes the modern note plausible. The connection between the last folios of the manuscript and the rest of the document is not clear to me. In folio 51v there is a note signed by Andrés de Ayala: "En la ciudad de Valladolid a 2 de marzo de 16??" (In the city of Valladolid, March 2, 16??). Below, a different hand signs: "Domingo de Espinosa y Monteros, vecino de la Villa de Madrid" (Domingo de Espinosa y Monteros, from the city of Madrid).[21] In the absence of a more detailed paleographic and diplomatic study, it is reasonable to think that these last folios are unrelated to the theatrical manuscript, and were added at a later date before the manuscript was bound. As stated above, De la Vega – or whoever intervened in M – did not put on stage the lines in which Juan de Alba and Doña Juana promise each other marriage, perhaps for the same reasons that P had in censoring them (2629–2639). Someone frantically crossed the scene out, but it is still readable. The manuscript omits many other passages and contains many transcription errors that are easily identifiable and correctable by collating it with P and the *sueltas*.[22] In addition, M adapts the text of the play for a smaller cast, combining the roles of Captains Don Pedro and Don Juan in the figure of the Lieutenant, a character who does not speak in the original text beyond the first scenes of act one.

The analysis of the textual *stemma* shows that both P and M come from the same ancestor, subarchetype α.[23] The *sueltas* did not descend from α, but from subarchetype β (see the Editorial Methods section for the complete *stemma*). In other words, neither M is a copy of P (see lines 2629–2639 in the Critical Apparatus), nor do any of the *sueltas* descend from either P or M, as modern editors have suggested

---

21   To my knowledge, the full name of Espinosa has not been transcribed until now. Folio 51v contains more notes and signatures that remain to be analyzed.

22   Some of the lines omitted exclusively in M are 291–298, 381–388, 508–511, 516–519, 548–552, 556–559, 572–588, 844–847, 1308–1309, 1378–1390, 1597–1620, 1623–1630, 1699–1712, 2142–2149, and 2604–2609.

23   The *stemma* is the genealogy of the extant copies of a text, called the witnesses. It can be determined, for example, by paying attention to conjunctive errors. A conjunctive error is a mistake shared by two or more witnesses, suggesting that they copied either from the same exemplar or from sources that descend from a common ancestor, where the conjunctive error was introduced for the first time. This hypothetical ancestor is called subarchetype. The archetype (X) is the common ancestor that originated the tradition *and* is the text that I attempt to restore in this edition. Conjunctive errors that demonstrate the existence of α can be found, for instance, in lines 695 and 1952. For conjunctive errors in β, see 286, 627, 700, 779, 1357 and 2335. See the Editorial Methods section and the Critical Apparatus in this volume.

since Treviño Trejo (1977, 27).[24] In addition, it is worth noting that β provides several passages that cannot be found in α, from which P and M descended.[25] Therefore, the *sueltas* are the key to restoring the original text.

S1 is the oldest of the *sueltas*. Francisco Sanz, *impresor del reino*, printed it at a printshop in Madrid, more specifically in the square on the street of la Paz, as stated in the last page. Since Sanz had moved his printshop there from the street of los Negros by 1680 and died by 1700, he must have printed *S1* in the last twenty years of the seventeenth century (Bainton 1978, Moll 1976). *S1* introduced many errors but also many amendments, some of them of exceptional quality (e.g., lines 1412, 1575, 1765), following a tendency already started in subarchetype ε (see notes above and the Editorial Methods in this volume). The copyists of the *sueltas* descending to subarchetype ε seemed to be uncomfortable with the homoeroticism of the play, as is apparent by the many re-writings and lowering of the tone in some of the spicier passages.[26] One of the few surviving copies of *S1* served

---

24 Four critical loci problematize this textual filiation. In line 193, for example, M seems to amend an error introduced in α, agreeing with β. A possible explanation is that both P and M followed a copy that had a hypermetrical line ("soltar ... o pese"). The double reading in line 280 could possibly be a polygenetic amendment in both texts of branch α, deduced by context in both witnesses separately. Likewise, in line 537, the easier readings in M and ε could match only because of the context – seas are normally plowed through (*surcando*), not searched (*buscando*). P's *burlando* would be another solution to the strange, more difficult *buscando* of the original. Lastly, in line 763, M crosses out the more difficult reading in P, and proposes an easier one that happens to coincide with the one in β. As in previous instances, here there is no need to observe filiation or contamination between M and β, for it is more common for snowflakes (*copos*) than for mountains (*montes*), to fall from the sky. Other critical loci are more difficult to explain, as in lines 959, 971, 1002, 1138, 1164, 1276, and 1649 (see Critical Apparatus).

25 The lines that are exclusive to β are 1613–1614, 2292–2295, and 2452–2463. I include all of them in this edition, marked with the symbol +, for they could have been either added in β or suppressed in α, and thus their presence in the original cannot be determined.

26 For interventions in ε regarding homoeroticism, see 1275–1276, 1314–1318, 1328, and 1619–1620.

as a prompt book. According to the records of the Biblioteca Histórica Municipal de Madrid, *S1* was used in the rehearsal and performance of the play on February 22, 1710, at the Teatro del Príncipe in Madrid, where the text remained until its relocation to the Archivo de Villa in 1898 (Andioc and Coulon 2008, 885). As a prompt book, *S1* has a great number of manuscript marks, stage directions, and re-writings. It includes a cover page that reads: "El valiente negro en Flandes / 3° ap[un]te / El amor y la razón / y el negro hablador" (The valiant Black man in Flandes / 3° prompt / Love and reason / and the talkative Black man).[27] On the back of the cover page there is a cast of characters written by at least two hands (see Critical Apparatus). *S1* contains many amendments by at least two hands.[28]

Some of those who wrote amendments on *S1* used another edition of the play, one which I could not identify. A few of these amendments reverse the aforementioned innovations introduced in subarchetypes ε and θ. These errors would pass unnoticed by anyone who did not make a thorough comparison intending to restore a text closer to the original.[29] Some amendments, on the other hand, do not seem to be based on any other witness that we know of (line 2518). In folio 14v of *S1*, somebody glued a piece of paper on which one of the hands abridged the text, an alternative passage that can be read in Appendix A (see lines 2113–2145 in the Critical Apparatus).

S2 is almost identical to *S1*, and it shares many conjunctive errors that create the subarchetype θ (1493, 1496, 1583, and 1584). It distinguishes itself from *S1* because it does not provide any information regarding the printer and date of publication. It also has some minor typographical

---

27 'El negro hablador' could refer to the famous *entremés* (one-act interlude) by Luis Quiñones de Benavente, *El negrito hablador y sin color anda la niña*. Among Asenjo Barbieri's papers there is one reference to a play titled *El amor y la razón* around the year 1762 (Olmos 2020, 43). It could also refer to a single, long title (*El amor y la razón, y el negrito hablador*).
28   Some of the handwritten amendments to *S1* are in lines 1117, 1346,1411,1417, 1430, 1456, 1721, 1777, 1918, 1971, 2172, 2175, 2217, 2219, 2230, 2299, 2307, and 2518.
29   For examples of this kind of amendment, see 1456, 2175, 2219, 2230, 2299, and 2307.

differences (e.g., unlike *S1*, *S2*'s headers are in lower-case), and it contains a great number of exclusive although insignificant typos. All of this suggests that *S2* is a *codex descriptus* of *S1* (a copy useless for the restoration of the archetype), and for this reason, it is excluded from the index of variants in the Critical Apparatus.

S3 was published by Antonio Sanz at the same printshop where his grandfather published *S1*. And yet *S3* does not descend from the same source as *S1* but from subarchetype δ, a distant relative that does not contain all of the aforementioned innovations. The copy of *S3* at the Universidad de Sevilla also has some critically informed handwritten marks. For instance, in lines 1216–1217, somebody restored an omission in subarchetype δ by adding </hecho lo que habemos hecho>, a similar reading to the "muy bien hecho está lo hecho" that we find in γ, where *S1* comes from (see Critical Apparatus). As seen in the case of *S1*, people in the eighteenth century were not only interested in *El valiente negro en Flandes*, but were also concerned about its textual integrity, so much so that they took the trouble of comparing *sueltas* to amend errors.

S3, *S4*, and *S5* are very similar regarding their typography and textual disposition, as the three were published in the Castilian region of Madrid-Salamanca-Valladolid, and they descend from the same subarchetype δ, in opposition to γ.[30] It has been said that *S5* is identical to *S3*, but this is not the case. None of the editions of δ are identical to each other. In fact, *S3* and *S4* share errors that are not present in *S5*, thus making up subarchetype η.[31]

Subarchetype γ splits in two branches: ε, the tradition of *S1*, and ζ, represented by *S6* and *S7*.[32] *S6* and *S7* are two undated editions that at first glance are very similar. They share a notable omission at the end of

---

30   Some of the conjunctive errors that justify subarchetype δ are in lines 48, 148, 169, 200b, 349, 649, 671, 832, 893, 1217, 1241, 1971, and 2078. Conjunctive errors of subarchetype γ are in 207, 242, 338, 368, 493, 760, 771, 1138, 1216b–1217, 1256, 1319, 1326, 1774, 1980–1981, 2299, and 2393.

31   For subarchetype η, see 70, 1158, 1208, 1210, 1229, 1491 and 1756b.

32   For subarchetype ε, see 72, 134, 183, 204, 243, 307, 491, 548, 565, 573b, 694, 707, 932–933, 1137, 1346, 1431, 1606, 2393, and 2416. For subarchetype ζ, see 10, 148, 209, 210, 324, 376, 412, 444, 551, 573b, 634, 740, 784, 806, 876, 1054, 1100, 1346, 1355, 1475, 1636, 1918, 2106, 2277, and 2564.

act two (see lines 2014–2040 in the Critical Apparatus), a passage that is inserted back at the beginning of act three (2052). *S7* adds a series of alternative scenes to compensate for the omission (see lines 2007 and 2014, and Appendix A). We find more errors and additions in *S7* wherever *S6* omits (e.g., 2250), which suggests that either *S7* copied from *S6* or had a more active attitude towards amending the text.

Subarchetype ε bifurcates in two branches: θ being the two earliest *sueltas*, and ι represented by the two latest, *S8* and *S9.*[33] *S8* seems to follow *S1* closely and keeps most but not all of its errors and innovations, adding new ones (e.g., in line 889, the copyist amended a repetition).

S9 is the latest *suelta* that we know of. Apparently, it is part of the same editorial project that originated the eighteenth-century second part of the play, *El negro valiente en Flandes*, by Manuel Vicente Guerrero (Panford 2003). To keep cohesion with the second part, *S9* changed the title of the play to *El negro valiente en Flandes, primera parte* (Part One). It is worth noting that there are some minor typographic differences among the copies of *S9*, particularly in the first and last pages, although I have not found any variant reading. *S9* seems to be the first critically informed edition ever printed. The index of variants shows that, although *S9* clearly descends from γ (particularly ε), it also amends many errors by following an undetermined witness from the δ tradition (*contaminatio*).[34] In addition, *S9* offers valuable amendments and stage directions, some of which have been kept in the present edition (e.g., 96, 821, 839). For example, *S9* is the only historical edition that restores the name of captain Don Pedro (1345b *et al.*).

Modern editions
The edition that Mesonero Romanos prepared for the Biblioteca de Autores Españoles (1888) is a direct copy of *P*, with acritical

---

33   For ι, see 142, 148, 186, 243, 307, 314, 358, 368, 565, 570, 694, 707, 729, 757, 863, 1137, 1235, 1346, 2120, and 2453.

34   This is a case of *contaminatio*, that is, when a copyist combines readings from two or more different witnesses. Evidence for this contamination of *S9* with δ can be found, for instance, in lines 63, 135, 402, 477, 781, 788, 793, 812, 828, 866, 868, 887, 924, 928b, 957, 1035, 1164, 1248, 1265, 1290, 1292, 1305, 1322, 1343, 1569, 1721, 1774, 1853, 2117b, 2251, and 2345.

amendments that sometimes correct the text, and sometimes obscure it. This was noted by Treviño Trejo (1977, 26), and confirmed by Ogallas Moreno (2010). In the present edition, we eliminate Mesonero Romanos's edition as a *codex descriptus*.

Treviño Trejo (1977) was the first critical editor of *El valiente negro en Flandes*, although few credit his edition because it was published as a Ph.D. dissertation. Treviño Trejo considered six out of the eleven editions studied here. He was the first and until now last that included five of the *sueltas* in his index of variants. Treviño Trejo made two important mistakes, though. The first one was that, although he studied *M*, he did not include it in the collation with *P* and the *sueltas*. This led him to make the incorrect claim that *S8* and *S9* descend from *M*, and that *P* was the direct ancestor of *S3* and *S5*, something his own index of variants contradicts. The second error that Treviño Trejo made was to consider *P* as "la más auténtica y completa [versión] que le hace justicia verdadera a su creador, tanto en forma como en sentido poético" ("the most authentic and complete version that does his creator true justice, both in form as in poetic sense"; Treviño Trejo 1977, 23). Against his own critical apparatus, basing his interpretation only in the *aprobación* of 1638, Treviño Trejo stated that *P* "no parece haber sufrido la censura severa que se le hizo al manuscrito [*M*]" ("does not seem to have suffered the severe censorship cuts that the manuscript *M* did"; 1977, 22). It was precisely the other way round.

In his 1997 edition of *El valiente negro en Flandes*, Rodríguez López-Vázquez followed Mesonero Romanos's text, but he recovered the lines referring to the knighting and the engagement between the Black protagonist and white Doña Juana from a copy of *S4* – which he dates from 1753 (1997, 20). In addition, Rodríguez López-Vázquez's edition indicates in brackets the passages that were left out in the 1997 performance of the play in Alcalá de Henares.

Nelson López's edition (2007), based on the one he made as his 1998 Ph.D. dissertation, has the particularity of being an edition for actors. It contains a stage proposal (2007, 36–53) and offers a valuable playscript alongside with the text of the play. It did not include a critical apparatus, but López's edition is critically informed. Although López followed Mesonero Romanos closely, he takes Treviño Trejo's edition into serious consideration, and he also takes into account manuscript *M*. He restores as well several passages from the *sueltas*.

Ogallas Moreno's edition (2010) includes an important study of the play's prosody and metric scheme that supports the argument in favor of dating the play to around 1625. However, Ogallas Moreno's effort represented a step back overall, for it ignored Treviño Trejo's work, dismissed López's without much explanation, and privileged *P* as the base text, collating it exclusively with Mesonero Romanos's 1888 edition of *P*. Ogallas Moreno states that some of the *sueltas* partially or integrally descend from *M* (2010, 200), something our present study proves to be incorrect. In her 2016 re-edition, Ogallas Moreno followed the example of Rodríguez López-Vázquez and amended *P*'s suppression of the knighting and the wedding engagement – but not the many other errors and omissions.

Editorial Methods

The present edition is the first one that does not take *P* as the base text and discards Mesonero Romanos's as a *codex descriptus*. Instead, this edition restores the text closest to the original, that is, archetype *X*, critically applying the *stemma* that I justified in the Textual History section:

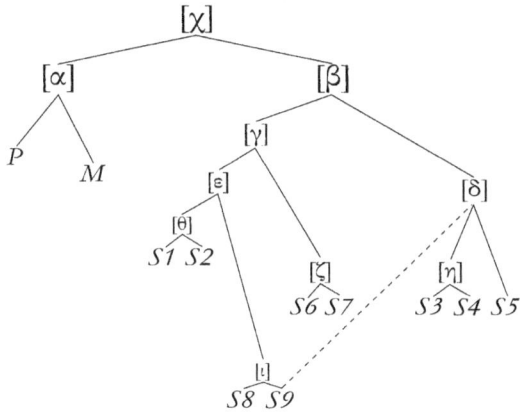

As in most stemmatic critical editions, I apply the rule of majority, and I favor more difficult readings where appropriate. I favor the α branch over the β when *P* an *M* agree, provided that they do not omit a passage or incur an obvious error, in which case I accept readings from β. I also favor *P* over *M*, and *S1* over the rest of the *sueltas* whenever the rule of majority cannot be applied and there are no obvious errors.

These criteria apply only to the parts of the text that are directly spoken by a character. The didaskalia – that is, title, headings, dramatis personae, character cues, stage directions and indications of asides – is a restoration informed by the Critical Apparatus but focused on an attempt to satisfy current theatrical conventions. Thus, I include a complete *dramatis personae* with all the characters of the play by order of appearance. I add necessary stage directions (asides in parenthesis) in order to facilitate the reading and help the possible use of this edition as a basis for performance. The original stage directions can be consulted in the Critical Apparatus. Due to the text's complex and controversial transmission, it is impossible to determine with certainty which parts were censored, and which were added later. I keep both the text passages that are exclusive to *P* and those that probably were introduced in β (see lines 2345–2347 and 2348–2383 in this section). The alternative passages that run parallel to the restored text have been edited in Appendix A.

The symbol + indicates any kind of textual intervention, amendment, and critical point. I modernize spelling, punctuation and capitalization according to current use, expanding all of the abbreviations except for *Mons.*, since it is used as a whole word in the text (see footnote to line 1426). As indicated in the Critical Apparatus, I modernize consonant groups and sounds that are subjected to dialectal variation (e.g., *dejaldo, efeto, suplicalle, estremo, traez*) as long as this does not affect rhyme (2361). I keep old forms such as *agora* and *ansí*, as well as vocalic and morphological variation common in the period (*escurecido, priesas, vistis*), but minor phonetic variations are modernized (e.g., *yelo, güele*, the conjunction *y* preceding a word that begins with the *i* sound, etc.). I also standardize and homogenize spelling inconsistencies regarding foreign names (*Lanstrac, Lastrec*, etc.) but not the variation of atonal personal pronouns (e.g., use of *le* for *la*), which is determined on a case-by-case basis by rule of majority.

As explained in the co-authored essay in this volume, Antón's text cannot be critically restored with the same certainty as the rest of the play, first because there is too much variation, and second because some of the principles of stemmatics (rule of majority, *lectio dificilior potior*, etc.) do not fully apply to Antón's textual transmission. Since *habla de negros* is a complex literary speech that preceded the creation of this Black character, it is impossible to determine when copyists were adding or deleting stereotypical traits. There were two possible critical solutions, both with serious disadvantages. On the one hand, applying the aforementioned editorial criteria would entail erasing his linguistic racialization. On the other, to amend and accommodate Antón's words to a supposed *habla de negros* – as imagined in the twenty-first century – raises many linguistic, historical, and ethical issues. I chose the former. In the present edition, Antón's text is established following general rules common in textual criticism (rules of majority and of the more difficult reading), even if this means reducing the degree to which Antón is linguistically Africanized. The index of variants may provide a useful tool for the study of the evolution of *habla de negros* through the seventeenth and eighteenth centuries (see Critical Apparatus). In any case, I keep the characteristic spelling of Antón's speech, including the use of <z> to indicate his sporadic *ceceo*, or the use of the letter <y> instead of <ll> to mark his unstable *yeísmo*, and the many ways in which Antón's nasalization is transcribed in the play, which are determined by rule of majority. Antón's exception to the modernization criteria is indicated by the use of italics – a decision also taken in the translation for similar reasons (see Lopez's Translator's Note below).

Translator's Note: Translating Blackness for the Stage in the 21st Century

This English translation has been waiting in the wings since my edition of *El valiente negro en Flandes, para actores* (López 2007). A translator's notes should explain the process and methods of translation, the mediator of the source text (ST) used for the target text (TT), in this case Castilian Spanish (ST) and modern standard English. We have come a long way in the scholarship on translating plays, moving away from the theories posited by Basnett (1991) and Pavis (1992). There has been scholarship supporting novel approaches on the degree to which theater is translatable and restoring its rightful purpose – performance (Haywood, Hervey, and Thompson 2009; Ambrosi, Bagliazi, and Kofler 2013; Hossain 2017; Brodie 2018; Johnston 2000; 2015). We agree that translating a play is not the same as translating an essay, novel, or medical treatise. There is no space here to address the latest trends and scholarship on translating plays; however, knowing that plays are to be performed, rather than read in silence at home, means rendering the play into English while serving Andrés de Claramonte, the playwright, actor, and producer. As translator, I have therefore set out a series of parameters for translating this *comedia* into a theater piece for our time.

Scholars have translated some verses of *El valiente negro en Flandes* into English (Beusterien 2007b; Ndiaye 2017; Jones 2019), but as of this writing, this is the first complete English translation of the play meant to be read out loud and performed on a stage with a live audience.

In the next section, I discuss my credentials because they color my choices for this translation. The section after that offers a brief approach, 'Translating the Performance in the Raw', a sort of homage to Antonin Artaud's idea of immediate theater, which describes the aim of theater as challenging our established notions. The final three sections are 'Translating Juan and Antón', 'Translating Dialect', and 'Self-Censorship in *The Valiant Black Man in Flanders*'.

Translating El valiente negro en Flandes: *Credentials*
Reimagining *El valiente negro en Flandes* into *The Valiant Black Man in Flanders* during the ongoing COVID-19 pandemic led me to translating the play without the help of actors to perform the lines, as opposed to what other translators have done.[35] However, I

---

35 Harley Erdman, *The Mountain Girl of La Vera* by Luis Vélez de Guevara; Kathleen Jeffs, *The Force of Habit* by Guillén de Castro; Robert

consider myself fortunate to have been trained in Spanish Golden Age theater at the University of Puerto Rico, and to have performed Spanish Golden Age *comedias* and *entremeses* in Spain and in the United States under the guidance of Dean Zayas, an international authority on staging Spanish Golden Age *comedias*. I have an MFA in theater directing, which gives me insight into visualizing the play as it unfolds in my mind's eye. A third factor in this translation is my ethnicity: I am a Hispanic person of color, a Puerto Rican, born and raised in Brooklyn, New York, with a dark-skinned father and a white mother. I have performed plays both in English and Spanish; I am classically trained, and I am bilingual and bicultural, so I have the advantages of comprehending the language, sounds, and rhythms of both languages, Spanish and English, in order to make this play performable. Canfield (1963) writes that "verse plays give the director his widest opportunities, for in them he can make use of the imagery, metaphor, meter, rhythm … any and all the other devices used in conventional poetic expression" (88). Thus, I welcome this opportunity as a person with theater knowledge, practical training, and access to the nuances of the language of Spanish Golden Age *comedias*. With this background, I set forth a series of demands. As an actor first and then as a director, I spoke these lines out loud until I did not hesitate or lose my footing, aim, or context. Rhythm and musicality are as necessary to the playscript as they are for music. One note out of place brings the whole play to collapse. But I had a bigger obstacle: the two Black characters have to struggle with slavery, but the similarity ends there.

Translating The Performance in the Raw

The first obstacle involved the translation of the title, *El valiente negro en Flandes*.[36] Although Juan is a formidable soldier, *The Brave*

Johnston's works with Spanish Golden Age plays for the Royal Shakespeare Company. He served as a translator on Tirso, Calderón, and Lope's plays.

36 James Baldwin, discussing racism with Dick Cavett in 1969, uses the term *Negro* when talking about his race: https://youtu.be/WWwOi17WHpE. In 1969 this term was used, but today it is derogatory and should not be appropriated or used by white people, because it is offensive. However, I

Black Warrior in Flanders does not convey his valor, a word that also includes characteristics such as heroism, boldness, and courage. When I think of valor, I think in terms of heroism, honesty, and humility. *The Brave Black Man in Flanders* does not represent valor either, but we kept man because

> *The Valiant Black in Flanders* [could work] too, but without '*man*', it includes or conceptualizes everyone – men, women, children, etc. It really needs 'man', I think. Man – identifies the experience and sets the stage. A black woman's experience would be completely different. Including '*man*' gives readers context and specificity, and it sets the stage for what's coming. Without 'man' – it's nebulous.
>
> Annette Powell, email to author, November 2, 2020.

The final title, *The Valiant Black Man in Flanders* results from close collaboration with two prominent scholars: Baltasar Fra-Molinero and Manuel Olmedo Gobante (as Juan de Alba says, I think Fortune has smiled upon me, because I have had their input throughout this process). Once we settled on this title, we began to address the other obstacles in translating a verse play into English. *Comedias* have complex structures and rhyme schemes, but I avoided rhyming as much as possible (due to difficulties of translating rhymes into another language), and I opted for eight-, nine-, and eleven-verse structures because of Claramonte's use of hyperbaton. In other words, I intended to get as closely as possible to the sounds of original verse structure (in Spanish) rather than to pursue 'beats', a term coined by Stanislavski and misinterpreted by the American method of acting. I do not advocate for translating beats, intentions, and/or syllables in a translation because it leads to interpretation or authorship. I attempted to recreate as much as possible the rhythm of the original and demonstrate as much as possible the language of race, the *habla de negros* (Black speech) which remains the biggest challenge for both reader and translator.

---

use the term on various occasions in act three to stress his condition among the courtiers.

Translating a play that addresses issues of race, *habla de negros*, and racial epithets from Spanish into English presents a challenge I hope I addressed with candor and justice to both Claramonte and a modern audience. This translation does not whitewash or sanitize, and (I hope) avoids offence; however, the facts of Spain's history and Claramonte's words present the harsh world of Spain's racist society.

Translating a play involves not only working painstakingly with dictionaries, thesaurus, and source texts, along with consulting others, but also taking account of a text that is meant for the stage, to be performed. Understanding theater and having theater experience helps in understanding rhythm, pace, and intonation. Play translation must communicate via speeches, actions, and other aspects of stage performance. The translator must be faithful to both the author (in this case, Claramonte), but also to the imagined actor – enabling him to speak the words effortlessly – and to the reader. Translating entails exploration of character and plot analysis, and figuring out intent, the goal of the play and its purpose, but not venturing into meaning, for "a play should provoke meanings" (Beckerman, 1979).

I approach plays by reading them backwards and then returning to the beginning, a process documented extensively in the creative process of staging plays (Ball 1983) and by other professional theater practitioners. Since plays are about cause and effect, one must trace the result back to the beginning of the play, for example to understand how the final tableau, the surprise wedding, is created in *The Valiant Black Man in Flanders*. By starting at the end and going backwards, one can recreate, like a forensic scientist, the *mise-en-scène* of the play in order to transfer the actions and culture into the TT from the ST. Still, I often found myself like the character in *An Actor Prepares* by Stanislavski (1989), at times playing the actor and then the director Tortsov in my visualization of the play. In the back of my mind, I kept Dakin Matthews's (2021) approach to translating plays, that is, reading the lines and sounding them out loud as I translated them, making them fresh to my ears, as if I were saying them for the first time.

Translating Juan and Antón: The Black Valiant and the Clever Black Man

A native Spanish speaker will recognize immediately that Juan de Mérida (Alba) and Antón speak Spanish, but Antón speaks differently. Antón's spoken Spanish differs from the 'standard' Spanish spoken by the other characters. He speaks in *habla de negros* (Jones 2019). Juan speaks the white man's Spanish, the imperial language, while Antón speaks *habla de negros*, a 'fictional' or hyperbolic Spanish spoken by Black slaves in Spain and often used in literature with the sole purpose of poking fun at them or ridiculing them. As a translator I have to think about perpetuating racial stereotypes of slow Black characters mispronouncing words. But, to posit a radical approach (using Jones' definition of *habla de negros*), we can allow the character's nuances to be subtle enough in English to distinguish his speech from Juan's. Antón may generate laughter in the way he speaks or the words he mispronounces, but he is not slow or a cowardly *gracioso*. Antón is the opposite of Juan. He has street smarts. He is keenly aware and knows how to play the system. Juan fights the system from outside, and Antón fights it from within, by using his speech patterns to navigate Claramonte's world and thus defying the *gracioso* stereotype. This approach presents two characters with different registers. Juan uses full sentences, is very articulate, and imitates white Spaniards' speech patterns, unless he is angry and rage takes over, when he might use contractions.

Antón speaks to himself in the third person and sometimes in the first-person plural. He uses contractions, and his rhythms are succinct, almost childlike. Antón appears in the secondary plot of the play, in which Doña Leonor appears dressed as a man, pursuing Don Agustín, who possessed and abandoned her in Mérida, leaving her without her honor. In the following scene, Leonor seduces Juan just to tease him, and she asks Antón to follow along with her scheme. At the beginning of the scene, Antón uses the third person and first-person plural until Leonor/Esteban asks Juan to sleep with her/him. As well as offering comic relief, the scene calls attention to both Black characters' homophobia:

Doña Leonor	Yo, no es posible que duerma
	sin compañía.
Juan de Alba	Antón puede
	dormir con vos.
Antón	Guardan fueras.
	¿Yo con brancos? ¡Osten putas!
Doña Leonor	(Bien mi venganza se ordena.
	Disimula, Antón.)
Antón	(Simulo.)

[Doña Leonor	I cannot possibly sleep
	Without company.
Juan de Alba	Antón can
	sleep with you.
Antón	Get out!
	Me with White folks! Forget that!
Doña Leonor	[*Aside*] I will get my revenge now.
	play along, Antón.
Antón	[*Aside*] I'll play along.]

From Antón's entrance, he has used "we" and the third person, but the moment Juan tells him to sleep with the white, apparently male, page, Antón switches to "I", breaking character and immediately returning to his role, radicalizing the character by stating (both in Spanish and in the English translation), "I will play along", "I will pretend, simulate": I will perform the role but I won't sleep with whites. Thus, during rehearsals, an actor or director can ask whether this line is addressed to the audience or the characters on stage.

Antón, like most *graciosos*, editorializes reality. In this case reality is being Black. The scene where he is asked to leave his mistress, Doña Leonor (disguised as Esteban) shows a typical hungry *gracioso* who trades masters for food. However, as Beusterien points out, we wonder what Antón is thinking as he picks up the halberd to serve Juan, who is now a sergeant (180). Apparently he mocks the situation of being in the service of another Black man who is a sergeant in the white Spanish army. Antón, like a character in a Brecht play, offers religious and social commentary when Juan asks what he looks like. Antón responds that he resembles one of the Magi and plays the role of servant. He finishes by saying that the whole process and pageantry seems like "a black thing" / "parecen cosas de negros" (lines 1330–1345). This scene probably resonates with the audience in Seville, and we hope Antón was portrayed by a Black actor in Claramonte's company so that a Black man's portrayal of Black speech can ring true.

Antón is in many ways Juan's cerebral counterpart. He makes clear and precise observations and editorializes throughout the play. When Antón is in the palace with Juan to meet King Philip in Act III, he says what the others in the audience may be thinking: Is he not a man [just like us]? That is, the king may be a powerful sight, a powerful man with an army and, thanks to Juan, a happy ending, but, as Antón points out: "¿Hombre no samo?" ["Aren't we men?"] (line 2205).

Antón presents a challenge for the actor and the translator because it is dangerous to attempt *habla de negros* in English and risk portraying him as a buffoon. There are obvious dangers of caricaturing him or of perpetuating the Black speech of characters that appeared in literature of the early nineteenth century and in twentieth-century English-language cinema. In order to understand the difference between these two Black characters, two distinct manners of speech must be present, both in print and in performance. The following section considers this question.

Translating Dialect: Erasing the Other
Lemuel Johnson (1971) writes that "In the discussion of the Negro in English literature a striking feature is the absence of a Negro voice. I mentioned this in relation to Othello. Othello does not speak an identifiable Negro English" (87). He continues, "The absence of such voice prevented the early exploitation of a significant element that one finds in Spanish Literature" (87). This exploitation is what readers of the Spanish *comedia* find in Black characters who do not speak the language of the Empire, but it is rather a caricaturized Black speech typical of the time, even into the late twentieth century. This "deformed Castilian" Spanish was used for satirical and burlesque

purposes in *entremeses*, *pasos*, and *comedias* in Spain and Portugal (Wynter 1977, 16).

The Valiant Black Man in Flanders presents this stereotype, this imagined, satirized, buffoon, in the character of Antón. But although Antón speaks in *habla de negros*, he is very distant from the typical *Negro* created by Claramonte's contemporaries. Claramonte clearly wants his audience to notice that Antón speaks differently from Juan de Mérida/Alba. Antón is his own person. Lemuel Johnson wonders why we do not have a similar situation in English literature. Carole Upton has an answer to his question, pointing out that "it has become commonplace for classic and contemporary plays written originally in dialect, or in a non-standard vernacular, to be translated into a standard English, so the same latitude should be extended to those who are merely applying the same approach in reverse" (2014). However, this translation considers *habla de negros* in the context of English. I use the term dialect here and define it as a playwright uses it, without political connotations or hierarchies. I use the term to refer to the speech and discourse (syntax, morphology and/or phonology) of a character.

As a theater arts practitioner, I advocate for the use of dialect in writing as long as it serves the purpose of the play, in this case the author's original character. Antón's *habla de negros*, although potentially dangerous in English, should be translated and recreated in speech to differentiate him from Juan de Alba. Not translating his speech patterns and using standard or proper English betrays both Antón and Claramonte. Claramonte purposely wrote the Black characters to show difference, the Other in the play. This brings me to my second point on the matter of dialect in translation and how it serves the play.

One has to read and see Antón as an outsider/insider; that is, if being Black in Spain in the seventeenth century is akin to being a slave, then Juan and Antón, as Black, are slaves. But Antón speaks *habla de negros*; he is the *Negro bozal* (Wynter 1977, 10), and his *habla de negros* reflects these patterns of speech. I propose that actors and producers wishing to radicalize that notion look no further than recent historical films on the Black experience, such as Colson Whitehead's *The Underground Railroad*. The same question that Beusterien's students pose about Antón and Juan surfaces with my student readers, too: "Why does the secondary character Antón speak differently from the standard spoken by Juan and the other characters in the play? If Antón is Black and speaks a form of 'Black Spanish', why does the other Black character, the protagonist, Juan, speak like the white characters in the play?" (Besteurien 2006b, 176).

Let me deflect any controversies that arise from rendering Black speech in English or creating a dialect to differentiate these two characters. I do not wish to offend, nor do I sanction any of the derogatory words (written by Claramonte) used by the characters in the play. Still, as Johnston asserts, "a translator should not forget that culture-specific items are very often parts of a linguistic code as much as they are essentially colorful motifs" (2014, 89). It is necessary – crucial – not to erase, whitewash, or colonize Antón's speech and render his words in 'proper' or standard English. Doing so erases the Other; preserving his *habla de negros*, some will argue, ridicules Antón and what he represents, summoning painful memories and stereotypes. Nicholas Jones and others have posited that this *habla de negros* was exaggerated, exploited, and distorted by white playwrights of the time; however, whitewashing this character's speech colonizes and silences the character and erases the distinction between two Black characters.

Erasing dialect and rendering it into standard English, proper grammar, perpetuates the ideals of empire, forcing people to learn the colonizer's language. I remember the experiments in Puerto Rico, when my parents and grandparents were forced to learn English, just as many Mexican migrant workers in California. We speak with an accent; we use dialects; we code-switch; we switch to Spanglish. *Habla de negros* is akin to the African American vernacular, Ebonics.[37]

---

37 Most linguists refer to the distinctive speech of African Americans as Black English or African American English (AAE), or, if they want to emphasize that this speech does not include the standard English usage of African Americans, as African American Vernacular English (AAVE). In

Writers such as Zora Neal Hurston (1937); Walter Mosley, August Wilson, Ntozake Shange, and James Baldwin have made extensive use of Ebonics. If we can no longer create dialect in characters, we cannot read the difference in characters. In *The Valiant Black Man in Flanders*, without dialect, the audience misses the nuances that separate Juan and Antón. I am troubled by these choices because of current controversies we find ourselves in regarding race, language use, appropriation, self-awareness, etc. But Claramonte, the actors, and the audience make this controversial play resonate today. Is speaking differently funny, and if so, in what way? Is a character with a stutter a laughing matter? Of course not, but the culture of that time understood them in that way. I understand that I am not translating Claramonte's play as an archaeological work of art; I am merely his translator, not his interpreter or ambassador to the English language or, as Upton points out, "This is not to suggest, of course, that the translator be reduced to a transcriber of authentic speech (see above); rather, one can exploit such language behaviors for creative effects consonant with the spirit of the play" (2014).

Self-Censorship in The Valiant Black Man in Flanders
Theater in translation has been censored and manipulated to fit the sociopolitical and religious conventions of the time and the taste of a particular few, and *comedia* has been censored for production by private companies, the Church, or resident companies, as noted in the 1651 manuscript of *El valiente negro en Flandes*, where notations such as "no se dice" or "no" abound (Figure 1). Theater has been subject to institutional censorship based on institutional and individual positions and tastes (Billiani 2007, 9). Translating into English the mindset and culture of seventeenth-century Spain for the diverse mindset and mores of a twenty-first-century general American English-speaking audience

---

theory, scholars who prefer the term Ebonics (or alternatives like African American language) wish to highlight the African roots of African American speech and its connections with languages spoken elsewhere in the Black Diaspora, e.g., Jamaica or Nigeria. In practice, AAVE and Ebonics essentially refer to the same sets of speech forms (Rickford, n.d.).

requires interpreting and translating racist language, homophobia, and antisemitism (hate speech) without risking censorship or cancellation. How does a translator serve Claramonte's world and words for the audience of our time? Do I censor Claramonte to avoid perpetuating Spain's seventeenth-century attitude towards minorities such as Blacks, homosexuals, cross-dressers, and Jews? Do I, as a person of color, use Claramonte's words to denounce his world or tame his words? Both options are dangerous, yet as a playwright, artist, actor, and director myself, my role is to render as closely as possible Claramonte's world to be performed and shared with the audience.

Translation studies is shifting to conform to the current sociopolitical arena. During the past two years language from both the left and the right has produced a rift in society. In the United States expressions such as wokeness, cancel culture, systemic racism, critical race theory, whitewashing, and white savior complex have made their way into translation studies, including texts to be performed. Translating plays for performance in these times risks being subject to censorship by editors, producers, or educational institutions. In Claramonte's play, certain words come across as objectionable today. The inherent dangers here mean the translator risks betraying the source text (ST) along with the playwright in order to render the target text (TT) appealing to the audience, producers, educational institutions, and other groups with sociopolitical agendas. Translators and playwrights face another obstacle: eliminating identity, language, and culture in the TT when rendering the dialect of ethnic characters. The translator of a ST nowadays must be careful with terms that may be perceived as triggers or as hate speech. This section addresses how as an actor, director, playwright, and translator of *El valiente negro en Flandes* I addressed these and other issues and made choices to serve the playwright of the ST.

Using racist language and attempting to render *habla de negros* into English in order to differentiate between two Black characters opens this translation to censoring or not being performed. As I listened to the congressional hearings on the events of January 6, I was shocked by the accounts of the Black police officers, who gave testimony about how white people used expletives and racist epithets against them while they protected the senators. I thought of Juan de Alba and Antón in the scene at the Royal Palace. I realized at that moment what the noblemen in the scene would call Juan and Antón at the Palace: Negroes. I originally wrote "Blacks", but when I revisited the text, I used the word *Negros* as Ndiaye does in her dissertation (2017, 166). Ndiaye believes that the word negro is "fraught with danger", and she reaffirms using *negro* in italics is best. As a Spanish Golden Age play and a historical work of art, I think it can work, but I also worry that the pronunciation of *negro* in English is not the same as in Spanish and would require constant dialect coaching, if staged in period costume to assert the racial slur.

Sanitizing the language, whitewashing it, and avoiding the language spoken by the characters would do a disservice to the playwright and his intentions. As I wrestled with this problem, I reminded myself of the role of the theater translator, not the interpreter, not the editorial commentator of a play, but the person bringing together two worlds on the stage so the reader, the audience, the performer, can have a conversation. In the words of one of my students, "You did not write or utter those words, that is the author's words and if several editions include the words, who are you to change them?" (A. Waggener, personal communication, September 22, 2021). Another student was direct and blunt: "I am ok with the words because there is a constant reference on Juan de Mérida being Black and rejected for being Black. He uses homophobic words; his antisemitism reflects not only the character but Spain's troubled past and his pain." (Dylan Long, personal email to author, August 4, 2021). A colleague phrased this situation in terms of scholarship and future historians: "Twenty-five years from now, someone will look at your play, wonder why you wrote, tawny, brown, dark-skinned, and/or omitted hate-full speech and wonder, what was your agenda, to hide the truth of the world they lived in and we are today? Where's your loyalty to the art?" (S. Roszell, personal communication, July 3, 2021). If this play creates these kinds of questions and responses, I owe it to the audience and to Claramonte to render his play as closely as possible to his intentions. What follows is a series of problematic scenes that I have not reconciled to English.

Juan begins by extolling the virtues of being Black, when he is asked what *moreno* is (a brown man, a dark-skinned or light-skinned man), because he states he is *moreno*, not *negro*.[38] According to Covarrubias, *moreno* is a person who is not "all black". I imagined the internal conflict of Juan: Is he dark-skinned, brown, tawny, or Black? Juan is conflicted about the color of his skin, so I began the passage by illustrating this conflict. In act one, scene 1, Juan's internal and external conflict comes to play in the very first lines. Italics are inserted for emphasis,

Capitán Don Agustín	¡Vaya el perro!
Juan De Mérida	No está el yerro en la sangre, ni el valor.
Sargento Barrientos	Estaralo en el color.
Juan De Mérida	Ser *moreno* no es ser perro, que ese nombre se le da a un alarbe, a un turco.
Sargento Barrientos	Bueno, pues dígame: *el que es moreno*, ¿qué vendrá a ser?
Juan De Mérida:	¿Qué? Será un borrón de la Fortuna puesto en la plana del mundo con vituperio profundo.

[Captain Don Agustín	Look at this, you dog!
Juan De Mérida	The fault is not in the blood or the courage.
Sergeant Barrientos	Maybe 'tis in the color.
Juan De Mérida	*A dark-skinned man* is not a dog; That is a name for

---

38 According to Covarrubias' *Tesoro de la lengua española* (2020), "Morena color, que no es del todo negra, como la de los moros. de donde le tomó nombre, o de mora" ["Dark colour, which is not entirely black, like that of the Moors, from which it took its name, or from mulberry"].

	An Arab or a Turk.
Sergeant Barrientos	Well,
	Then, can the one who is *dark-skinned*
	Tell me what he is?
Juan De Mérida	What is he?
	A blot dropped by Fortune
	On the page of the world
	As a profound affront]
	(lines 1–11)

I have Juan call himself dark-skinned and the sergeant call him dark-skinned also (the Spanish word in both cases is *moreno*) for dramatic purposes and to build the rhythm and pace to when he states, "so be it, I am Black". My intent is to play on the fact that Juan begins by saying he is *moreno*, but then the sergeant teases him by using the expression a white person today would use, dark-skinned. Thus, as Juan explains the fate of the Black man in a white man's world, he defines and identifies himself as Black, a darker shade than brown, dark-skinned to Black – he accepts he is Black because of the soldier's constant harassment and disparaging remarks on the color of his skin. Juan accepts he is Black to achieve his goal: to be part of the Flanders Tercios. The play does not make Juan's skin color clear, for he continues comparing himself to all shades of brown throughout the play (*moreno, nación morena, Catalina la Morena*) black, shadow, darkness, shade, and so on.

Another translation challenge occurs in the last scene of act one, when Doña Leonor dresses as a page and constantly touches and squeezes Juan's hands. Juan expresses homophobic sentiments, identifying himself with the empire (I have inserted the italics).

Toma a Juan de Alba de las manos.

Doña Leonor	…y mirad que habéis de ser
	muy mi amigo.
Juan de Alba	(*No me suena*
	a católico este paje.
	Mucho las manos me aprieta.
	No quisiera que un buen día
	nos diera…)

[Esteban takes Juan of Alba's hands.

Doña Leonor	…And know that you are to be My very best friend.
Juan de Alba	*[Aside]* This page doesn't sound like a Catholic to me. He squeezes my hands a lot. I would not like us to have good day…]

$$(1046–1051).$$

In these verses, Juan expresses a series of judgments about and accusations towards Esteban/Leonor. He becomes uncomfortable enough to call Esteban the derogatory *maricón*.

Juan de Alba	Mas, ¿qué queman a este *maricón*?[39]
[Juan de Alba	What? Why don't they burn this *faggot*?]

$$(2081–2082).$$

Act one ends revealing Juan's position, when he uses an expletive common in the Spanish of the period towards gays or queers: *maricón*. When I consulted students of color between the ages of 19 and 22 in my advanced Spanish course (which also includes white students), the consensus was that Juan, as a soldier who sides with the Spanish empire, would use the derogatory term *faggot* or *fag*. This appears to be a generational issue when translating sensitive or trigger terms that may apply to Millennials, Generation Xers, and Baby Boomers because when I asked my students if they considered the language here offensive, perpetuating stereotypes and hate speech, and not publishable, these Gen Zers and Gen Yers again said no because the world and words of Claramonte reflect the attitudes of colonizers towards minorities. In translating this scene, I initially chose "pansy" because a director does not know if Leonor/Esteban is gay or queer,

---

39   The term *maricón* is a derogatory term aimed at gay people, mostly male, referring to them as effeminate. In English it would suggest *fag* or *poof* (United States and Great Britain, respectively).

nor what it means to act gay or queer, because queer should not be conflated with effeminate. Nevertheless, I changed it to "faggot" because Juan's language in the scene reveals his attitude: The page has soft white hands; he's touching and hugging Juan and is vivacious. Initially I chose *pansy* since the *Diccionario de la Real Academia Española* defines *maricón* as 'un adjetivo despectivo y malsonante' / 'a derogatory and offensive adjective' Using *faggot* does not convey the same meaning for British readers, who would understand *poof*, but since this is an American English translation, I kept *faggot*.

These derogatory words are red flags for twenty-first-century readers, something like hate speech that perpetuates stereotypes and 'punches down' the LGTBQ community. How does a translator represent this kind of language, or should they omit this scene from the play? I suggest that directors and actors can omit these and other words from the playscript but provide explanatory notes in the program.[40]

A last issue concerns the use of Black versus Negro, which in Spain was and is not the same as for US audiences: "Simply put *'negro'* in Spanish does not mean or equal 'Negro' in English … *Negro* does not convey the same historically accrued violence that the English word 'Negro' conveys – it did not in early modernity and it does not now" (Noémi Ndiaye, email to the author, October 5, 2021). Since this is a play in which Black characters appear in seventeenth-century Spain, far removed from our culture and world, staging the play in a modern style may avoid these issues by using terms more appropriate to our times, but in prejudiced and racist Spain, this hurtful language was real.

In act three, verses 2106–2108, when Juan and Antón are in the Royal Palace to meet King Philip and the Duke of Alba, four white noblemen (courtiers) notice Juan and Antón, and one of them remarks, "¿No reparáis en los *negros*, / que son notables figuras?" ["Have you noticed those *Blacks* / Who are quite the characters?"]. In re-reading

---

40 The *Oxford English Dictionary* offers several definitions for the word *faggot*, including a kind of British sausage, a bundle of sticks or iron rods, and a derogatory term for male homosexual or (in Britain) a contemptible woman.

this scene, my theatrical instinct would have the white characters use the word *Negroes* or, as suggested by Ndiaye, the Spanish word for a Black person. Doing so shows that regardless of Juan being the hero of Spain, in Madrid, in the palace, he is still a slave: "Bien valdrán tres mil reales / el amo y paje" ["They'll be worth three thousand reales, / Both master and his page"] (lines 2113–2114). Claramonte indicates through these white characters that Juan is still a commodity to be sold.

I think theater is an immediate art that challenges our expectations or beliefs, as when Nora Helmer, of Henrik Ibsen's *A Doll's House*, does not come back for act five, or when Victor Hugo's *Hernani* revolutionized the stage in the nineteenth century for its outrageous romantic themes. Is such revolutionary art possible in our current climate, or are we to continually censor works of art and rewrite our history, even in literary translations of the classics? Mark Rylance, who used to run the Globe Theater, can offer us some insight into a cautionary tale for future translators and performers: "If a character says it, it doesn't mean the author means it but … these statements have a lot more resonance now than they did at the time" (2015).

In the end, no translation is ever final. It continues to grow on stage, for the actors make it come alive, and that is the purpose of spoken language, and of the play itself. For now, this translation allows you to discover Andrés de Claramonte. I hope you – the reader, the actor, the director, and *comedia* enthusiast – welcome this edition in English of *The Valiant Black Man in Flanders*.

THE VALIANT BLACK MAN IN FLANDERS

EL VALIENTE NEGRO EN FLANDES

EL VALIENTE NEGRO EN FLANDES

Personas que hablan en ella[+]
Capitán DON AGUSTÍN de Estrada
JUAN DE MÉRIDA (después JUAN DE ALBA)
Sargento BARRIENTOS
Un ALFÉREZ
DOÑA LEONOR
DOÑA JUANA de Vera
ELVIRA, criada
ISABEL, criada
PINEDA, criado
Capitán DON PEDRO Osorio
Capitán DON JUAN
El DUQUE DE ALBA
ANTÓN DE VERA, criado
Dos SOLDADOS FLAMENCOS
Capitán *MONS.* DE VIVANBLEC
El PRÍNCIPE DE ORANGE
General *MONS.* DE LANSTREC
General *MONS.* DE VILA
Un MÚSICO
DON GÓMEZ, caballero cortesano
DON FRANCISCO, caballero cortesano
DON MARTÍN, caballero cortesano
DON PEDRO, caballero cortesano
Dos SOLDADOS
El REY Felipe II de España
DON JUAN, padre
Dos CABALLEROS
Un CRIADO
Músicos

---

0   **Personas que hablan en ella[+]**. The symbol + next to the Spanish text indicates amendments or relevant variants. See the Index of Variants in this volume.

THE VALIANT BLACK MAN IN FLANDERS

Characters in the Play

CAPTAIN DON AGUSTÍN de Estrada
Juan de Mérida (afterwards JUAN DE ALBA)
SERGEANT BARRIENTOS
A LIEUTENANT
DOÑA LEONOR
DOÑA JUANA de Vera
ELVIRA, maid
ISABEL, maid
PINEDA, servant
Captain DON PEDRO OSORIO
Captain DON JUAN
THE DUKE OF ALBA
ANTÓN DE VERA, servant
TWO FLEMISH SOLDIERS
Captain *MONS*. DE VIVANBLEC
The PRINCE OF ORANGE
General *MONS*. DE LANSTREC
General *MONS*. DE VILA
A MUSICIAN
DON GÓMEZ, Gentleman courtier
DON FRANCISCO, Gentleman courtier
DON MARTÍN, Gentleman courtier
DON PEDRO, Gentleman courtier
TWO SOLDIERS
KING Philip II of Spain
DON JUAN, father
TWO GENTLEMEN
A SERVANT
Musicians

JORNADA PRIMERA

Salen Juan de Mérida, el capitán Don Agustín, el sargento Barrientos, un Alférez y soldados.

Capitán Don Agustín	¡Vaya el perro!
Juan de Mérida	No está el yerro
	en la sangre, ni el valor.
Sargento Barrientos	Estaralo en el color.
Juan de Mérida	Ser moreno no es ser perro,
	que ese nombre se le da
	a un alarbe, a un turco.
Sargento Barrientos	Bueno,
	pues dígame: el que es moreno,
	¿qué vendrá a ser?
Juan de Mérida	¿Qué? Será
	un borrón de la Fortuna
	puesto en la plana del mundo
	con vituperio profundo;
	aunque es cierto que ninguna
	falta recibe el color,
	siendo la naturaleza

5

10

---

1   **Vaya**. "La matraca, el trato, el vejamen que dan a uno para hacerle correr, que vulgarmente se dice *dar la vaya*. El vulgo piensa haberse dicho de 'vaya, vaya'; pero lo más cierto es ser vocablo italiano de *bayare*, que vale ladrar, porque al que siguen, dándole matraca, se puede comparar al perseguido de los perros que le van ladrando." ["The mockery, ill-treatment, humiliation they give someone to make them run, what is commonly referred to as to give someone the *vaya*. People think this comes from *vaya, vaya* – go away, go away –, but it is more probably from the Italian word *bayare*, which means to bark."] (Covarrubias 2020, 1514).

4   ***Ser moreno no es ser perro***. "Perros. Llaman a moros *y esclavos*, porque no tienen quien les salve el alma y mueren como perros" ["Dogs. They call Moors and slaves this way, because they do not have anyone to save their souls, and they die like dogs"] (Correas, refrán 18231).

6   ***Alarbe***. Arab, particularly from North Africa.

12   ***Plana***. "La escritura de una haz de la hoja del papel" ["What is written on one side of a sheet of paper"] (Covarrubias 2020, 1365).

ACT ONE

Enter Juan de Mérida, Captain Don Agustín, Sergeant Barrientos, a Lieutenant, and soldiers.

CAPTAIN DON AGUSTÍN	Look at this, you dog!
JUAN DE MÉRIDA	Neither the fault
	Nor the courage is in the blood.
SERGEANT BARRIENTOS	Maybe 'tis in the color.
JUAN DE MÉRIDA	A dark-skinned man is not a dog;
	That is a name for
	An Arab or a Turk.
SERGEANT BARRIENTOS	Well,
	Then, can the one who is dark-skinned
	Tell me what he is?
JUAN DE MÉRIDA	What is he?
	An ink blot dropped by Fortune
	placed on the world's page
	As a profound affront.
	Although, it is true that
	The color is not to blame,
	For nature being one

	una misma, y su belleza,	15
	con la variedad, mayor.	
	Blancos y negros proceden	
	de un hombre. Un ser los anima.	
	Solo la región o el clima	
	los diferencia, y si exceden	20
	los blancos en perfección	
	a los negros, es por ser	
	desdichados y tener	
	sobre ellos jurisdicción;	
	y del mismo modo, fueran	25
	abatidos e imperfectos	
	los blancos, como sujetos	
	entre los negros vivieran.	
	Y pues nos diferenciamos	
	solo en color y tenemos	30
	un ser, bien decir podemos	
	que, *aunque negros, no tiznamos*.	
SARGENTO BARRIENTOS	¡Oiga, que discursos tiene	
	filosóficos también	
	el negro envés de sartén!	35
JUAN DE MÉRIDA	Del sol nuestro origen viene,	
	que él nos abrasa.	
ALFÉREZ	Serán	
	carbón con alma.	
JUAN DE MÉRIDA	Y carbón	
	que, encendido en la ocasión,	
	rayos da por chispas. Juan	40
	de Mérida me apellido,	

16   **Con la variedad, mayor**. See Lope de Vega's *Arte nuevo de hacer comedias*: "buen ejemplo nos da naturaleza, / que por tal variedad tiene belleza" ["Nature gives us a good example, / its beauty being in its variety"] (lines 179–180).

18   **Un ser los anima**. Juan is referring to the Platonic theory of the *anima mundi*, according to which all living things in the world are part of one single being that gives them that life. It appears in *Timaeus* 34a10. Marsilio Ficino, Leone Ebreo, and other Renaissance Neo-Platonists made the idea popular among poets and philosophers.

And the same, and its beauty
Is greater in its variety.
Both Blacks and Whites come
From one man. One soul gives them life.
They differ only in climate
Or in region; and if Whites
Surpass Blacks in perfection,
It is only because of Blacks'
Misfortunes, and Whites having
Dominion over them;
And likewise, Whites would be
Downtrodden and imperfect
If they found themselves,
Subjects among Blacks.
And since we are different
Only in color, and we share
One soul, we may very well say
That, *although Black, we do not stain.*

SERGEANT BARRIENTOS   Listen to him! He comes prepared
With philosophical speeches,
This black underside of a pan!

JUAN DE MÉRIDA   Our origin comes from the sun,
He chars our skin.

LIEUTENANT   You're more
Like coal with a soul.

JUAN DE MÉRIDA   And coal,
Ignited on the spot,
Turns sparks into beams of light. Juan
De Mérida is the name,

y aunque moreno a ser vengo,
valor de Mérida tengo
porque en Mérida he nacido;
y aunque negro, mi valor   45
y mi inclinación marcial
sangre me da principal
que acredita este color,
que es capa con que se alegra
el alma de ella adornada,   50
y es siempre la más honrada
la gente de capa negra.
El azabache se aplica
a la garganta más bella.
Negra es la tinta y con ella   55
el mundo se comunica.
La pez da a los vituperios
del mar fugitivos pies.
Negra es la pólvora y es
el alma de los imperios.   60
Negro es el pórfido hermoso,
y el ébano que al sol medra.
Negra es la pentarbe piedra
contra el fuego riguroso.

52   *Capa negra*. "hombre de capa negra, ciudadano" ["a man wearing a black cloak, a citizen"] (Covarrubias 2020, 439).

57–58   *Los vituperios del mar*. Ships, because they affront the power of the sea by staying afloat. It is a metaphor in the style of Luis de Góngora's *poesía culta* (see lines 2363–2377).

62   *El ébano que al sol medra*. Ebony is a dark-colored wood that grows (*medra*) in south Asia and West Africa. In the seventeenth century, these latitudes were known as the Torrid Region because they were closer to the sun.

63   *Pentarbe piedra*. A stone with magic powers featured in the *Aithiopikai* (*Ethiopian Story*), written by Heliodorus in the 4th century CE.

and Black as I am
Mérida's valor I have.
Born and bred in Mérida
And, although Black, my valor
And martial inclination
Ennoble my blood
And accredits this color,
Which is the cloak that brings joy
And adorns my soul;
For the most honorable people
Wear black cloaks.
They place jet stone
Around the most beautiful necks;
The world expresses itself
By writing in Black ink;
Black pitch gives the ship
Speed against the affronts of the sea;
Black is gunpowder, and it is
The soul of empires;
Black is beautiful porphyry
And ebony, which thrives in sun-drenched lands;
Black is the pantarb stone,
That defends against rigorous fire;

	Negra, pule la ballena	65
	la barba que el mar honora.	
SARGENTO BARRIENTOS	Y encaje el perrazo agora:	
	"tal es la color morena".	
JUAN DE MÉRIDA	Tal es, pues.	
ALFÉREZ	Diga también	
	excelencias del hollín,	70
	que es negro.	
JUAN DE MÉRIDA	Soy negro, en fin;	
	y soy negro tan de bien,	
	que darlo a entender quisiera	
	sirviendo a su majestad	
	en Flandes.	
CAPITÁN DON AGUSTÍN	Gran novedad	75
	de aquellos países fuera.	
ALFÉREZ	Las excelencias sabemos	
	de lo negro, color vil	
	en presencia del marfil.	
	Y a él por tal le conocemos	80
	en Mérida, aunque se dice	
	que de un título de España	
	es hijo, pero es patraña,	
	que la color lo desdice.	
CAPITÁN DON AGUSTÍN	Si ser soldado desea,	85
	¿por qué a Guinea no pasa?,	
	que yo asentara su plaza	
	si fuera Flandes Guinea.	
	Y al cuerpo de guardia más	
	no llegue, que se respeta	90

66   ***Pule la barba***. "Pulido. [...] *alisar*, que es *pulir*" ["to smooth, which is the same as to comb"] (Covarrubias 2020, 1382). It may be a reference to the baleen of some whales, keratin-formed bristles. To smooth or comb one's beard with the hand may be a reference to a gesture associated to majesty in old age. In Cervantes' 'La gitanilla': "Aquí el anciano Saturno / la barba pule y remoza" ["Here Saturn, the old man, / combs his beard to look younger"] (Cervantes 1982, 80).
86   ***Guinea***. Refers to the whole sub-Saharan part of West Africa, from Senegal to Angola, identified since the fifteenth century with the slave trade.

	The whale smooths its black beard
	Which the sea honors.
SERGEANT BARRIENTOS	And let the cur end his speech:
	"This is what the Black man is."
JUAN DE MÉRIDA	So it is.
LIEUTENANT	How about
	Singing praises of soot?
	It's also black, like you.
JUAN DE MÉRIDA	I am a Black man, true;
	And an honest one.
	I want to prove it
	By serving our Majesty the King,
	In Flanders.
CAPTAIN DON AGUSTÍN	That would be something new,
	A Black man in those lands.
LIEUTENANT	We know the virtues
	Of the color black, so base
	When compared to ivory;
	And in Mérida we know
	He's Black, though some say
	He's the son of a titled nobleman,
	But that's rubbish:
	His color gives him away.
CAPTAIN DON AGUSTÍN	If you, Sir, want to be a soldier,
	Why don't you go to Africa?
	I would secure you a guard post
	If Africa were Flanders;
	And don't come near
	Our recruiting station again; or the reed

JUAN DE MÉRIDA
el junco de esta jineta
a palos.
     Palos jamás
este negro consintió
de nadie, y si el rey no fuera[+]
el que los palos me diera,   95
ansí le matara yo.

Acuchíllalos[+]

SARGENTO BARRIENTOS   ¡Oh, perro!
JUAN DE MÉRIDA   Un negro de bien
soy, y mientes si imaginas
otra cosa, que hay gallinas
con plumas blancas también.   100
Negro soy que valgo aquí
más, librando tajos francos,
que un ejército de blancos
si son los blancos ansí.
CAPITÁN DON AGUSTÍN   ¡Que el cuerpo de guardia un perro   105
de aquesta suerte alborote!
¡Prendedle, dadle un garrote!
JUAN DE MÉRIDA   En esta casa me encierro
por dejarte compañía
con que al rey puedas servir,   110
aunque, si ansí han de reñir,
mejor matarlos sería.

Éntrase JUAN DE ALBA.

---

91   *Jineta*. A short spear often used by captains to signify their rank. See Figure 9, and Olmedo Gobante's essay in this volume.

92   *A palos*. To be hit with a stick carried a very serious loss of reputation and honor that could give rise to a duel. See Olmedo Gobante's essay in this edition.

105   *Cuerpo de guardia*. This was the room where the regiment kept its banner and officers had their meetings. It was also used as a recruiting desk for new soldiers.

102   *Tajos francos*. In fencing, *franco* (free, direct) was a direct attack that hit the target.

	Of this spear will show you respect
	With a proper beating.
JUAN DE MÉRIDA	Beat me with a reed?
	This Black man has allowed no one
	To beat him; and, other than the King,
	If anyone tried to beat me with a reed,
	I would kill him.

He strikes them with his sword.

SERGEANT BARRIENTOS	Oh, you dog!
JUAN DE MÉRIDA	I am an honest Black man,
	And you lie if you imagine
	Otherwise. For there are white-feathered
	Chickens too!
	I am a Black man,
	And when I strike blow for blow,
	I'm worth more than an army of White men,
	If all Whites fight like this.
CAPTAIN DON AGUSTÍN	That a dog of this ilk
	Causes so much havoc at our Guard post?
	Seize him, and garrote him!
JUAN DE MÉRIDA	I'll seek shelter in this house,
	So you still have a regiment left
	to serve the King with;
	But if they fight like this,
	It would be best to kill them.

Exit JUAN DE ALBA

CAPITÁN DON AGUSTÍN	¡Entrad!
SARGENTO BARRIENTOS	Son casas, señor,
	de lo mejor de tu patria.
CAPITÁN DON AGUSTÍN	¡Aunque sean del rey mismo! 115

Sale DOÑA LEONOR, dama.

DOÑA LEONOR   ¿Quién la quietud de mis casas
y su decoro atropella
con descompuestas espadas,
siendo en sus puertas deidad
sus cadenas y sus armas?   120
CAPITÁN DON AGUSTÍN   Quien tras la noche venía
y halla en los brazos del alba
un sol que en su luz me ciega
y un planeta que me abrasa.
Una sombra van siguiendo   125
mis soldados, y encontrarla
ya será imposible adonde
todo es nieve y todo es nácar.
Descompuesto, ha herido un negro,
dentro del cuerpo de guardia,   130
unos soldados: injuria
y desacato a la sacra
majestad, cuya bandera
su omnipotencia declara;
y retirándose, entró   135
en vuestro cielo.
DOÑA LEONOR   Si alcanzan
mis casas plazas de cielo,
¿cómo el cielo se profana?
El cielo, con buenas obras,
y no con malas se alcanza,   140
que en él todo es gloria y paz,
si el infierno es guerra y armas.
Reportaos y haced que luego
de él vuestros soldados salgan,

113–114   ***Son casas, señor, / de lo mejor de tu patria***. The Sergeant is reminding the Captain about the privilege nobles enjoyed regarding the inviolability of their homes.

CAPTAIN DON AGUSTÍN	Go after him!
SERGEANT BARRIENTOS	Sir, this is the house
	Of the most honorable people in Spain.
CAPTAIN DON AGUSTÍN	I don't care if the King himself dwells here.

Enter DOÑA LEONOR, Lady.

DOÑA LEONOR   Who dares to disturb the peace
And dignity of these dwellings,
Trampling in with drawn swords,
Violating the sacred coat of arms
Of this noble house?

CAPTAIN DON AGUSTÍN   One who was chasing after the night
And finds in the arms of dawn
A sun whose bright light blinds me
And a planet that burns me.
My soldiers are in pursuit
Of a shadow, and finding it
Now will be impossible where
Everything is nacre and snow.
A savage Black man,
Has wounded some of my soldiers
Within the Guard post, a defiance
And a high crime against the sacred
Majesty of our King, whose flag
Declares his omnipotence;
And retreated, entering
These pearly gates of heaven.

DOÑA LEONOR   If my house
Is the pearly gates of Heaven,
Why do you profane Heaven?
With good deeds, and not evil,
Heaven is reached; for
It is all glory and peace,
Where Hell is war and arms.
Stand back and command
Your soldiers to come out at once,

	porque es su arcángel mi honor	145
	y hará que al abismo caigan.	
CAPITÁN DON AGUSTÍN	Ya a los rigores del negro	
	consagro mil alabanzas,	
	pues pudo darme su noche	
	tal día; que, aunque la fama	150
	era, en las lenguas del pueblo,	
	lisonja hermosa y gallarda	
	de ese sol que del aurora	
	por azucenas se escapa,	
	hasta llegaros a ver,	155
	no le dio crédito el alma.	
DOÑA LEONOR	¿Tan bien los soldados saben⁺	
	mentir?	
CAPITÁN DON AGUSTÍN	Verdades tan claras	
	mis palabras acreditan	
	cuando en vuestras partes hablan	160
	más espíritus que estrellas.	

Salen todos con JUAN DE MÉRIDA *sin espada.*

ALFÉREZ	¡Vaya el perro!	
JUAN DE MÉRIDA	No llegara	
	nadie, a no desguarnecerse	
	la espada, a prenderme.	
CAPITÁN DON AGUSTÍN	Basta.	
	Haced que luego le den	165
	un garrote.	
JUAN DE MÉRIDA	Aquí se acaban	
	mis honrados pensamientos.	
CAPITÁN DON AGUSTÍN	Llevadle.	
JUAN DE MÉRIDA	¡Señora!	
DOÑA LEONOR	Aguarda.	
	¿No eres tú Juanillo, el hijo	
	de Catalina, la esclava	170

---

145 ***Su arcángel mi honor***. A reference to the archangel that kept the gates of Eden closed. Doña Leonor follows the extended metaphor of her home being a new heaven, her honor keeping guard against intruders.

	For my honor is its archangel,
	And it shall make them fall into the abyss.
CAPTAIN DON AGUSTÍN	I now praise a thousand times
	The stubbornness of this Black man,
	For his night has given me such
	A Day; that, although the fame
	Of your beauty was on everyone's lips,
	As a gallant compliment
	To that sun – the sun flees
	From daybreak like lilies, –
	Until I saw you with these eyes,
	My soul could not give credit to it.
DOÑA LEONOR	Are soldiers so good
	At lying?
CAPTAIN DON AGUSTÍN	My words are obvious
	Truths. More spirits than stars,
	Speak on their behalf. Innumerable
	Stars in the sky can confirm it.

Enter the soldiers with JUAN DE MÉRIDA without his sword.

LIEUTENANT	Look at this dog!
JUAN DE MÉRIDA	If the sword
	Had not loosened,
	No one would have caught me.
CAPTAIN DON AGUSTÍN	Enough!
	Take him away and garrote
	Him.
JUAN DE MÉRIDA	Here my honorable ambition
	Comes to an end.
CAPTAIN DON AGUSTÍN	Take him away.
JUAN DE MÉRIDA	My Lady!
DOÑA LEONOR	Wait.
	Is that you, Juan, the son
	Of Catalina, the slave

	de Doña Juana de Vera	
	mi prima?	
Juan de Mérida	A mi madre llaman	
	Catalina la morena.	
Alférez	¿La negra de buena cara	
	que Extremadura celebra	175
	es su madre?	
Doña Leonor	Pues si alcanzan	
	privilegios mujeriles	
	piedades, aquí le valgan	
	los míos, pues del sagrado	
	de mi clemencia se ampara,	180
	quedando reconocida	
	al retorno de esta gracia	
	eternamente.	
Capitán Don Agustín	Si en ello	
	aquí la vuestra se gana,	
	necio sería en perderla	185
	cuando es mi intento el ganarla.	
	Por vos tenga el negro vida.	
Sargento Barrientos	Mira que de tus escuadras	
	cuatro soldados ha herido.	
Capitán Don Agustín	Aunque a los cuatro matara,	190
	se había de obedecer	
	la belleza que lo manda.	
Doña Leonor	Yo el favor estimo.	
Sargento Barrientos	¡Oh, pese…![+]	
	¡Que libre el perro se vaya,	
	vive Dios!	
Juan de Mérida	Señor sargento,	195
	bueno está.	
Sargento Barrientos	Si en la campaña,	
	perro, te cogiera…	
Juan de Mérida	En ella	
	he visto algunas espaldas	
	huir de espanto del negro.	

175. **Catalina la Negra** or *Catalina la Morena* was a historical person from Extremadura (Treviño Trejo 1977, 338). See Fra-Molinero's essay in this volume.

	Who serves my cousin,
	Doña Juana de Vera?
JUAN DE MÉRIDA	They call my mother
	Dark-skinned Catalina.
LIEUTENANT	The good-looking Black woman,
	Famous in all Extremadura
	Is his mother?
DOÑA LEONOR	Well, if female
	Privileges include
	Compassion, on his behalf
	I ask for clemency;
	For he deserves my protection.
	Knowing that I shall be forever
	Indebted to return
	This favor to you.
CAPTAIN DON AGUSTÍN	If on this occasion
	I win your favor,
	I would be foolish to lose it,
	When it is my desire to gain it.
	Because of you, may the Black man live.
SERGEANT BARRIENTOS	Look Sir, he has wounded
	Four soldiers from your squadron!
CAPTAIN DON AGUSTÍN.	Even if all four were killed,
	We should obey the beauty
	That commands it.
DOÑA LEONOR	I appreciate the favor.
SERGEANT BARRIENTOS	God Damn it! That this dog
	is set free!
JUAN DE MÉRIDA	Mister Sergeant,
	It's over.
SERGEANT BARRIENTOS	If I see your face out in the field,
	You dog…
JUAN DE MÉRIDA	I have seen there
	Some backs flee in terror
	From this Black man.

SARGENTO BARRIENTOS	Ahora, a la que te rescata	200
	de la muerte, le agradece	
	la vida.	
JUAN DE MÉRIDA	Seré en sus plantas	
	un can siempre agradecido.	
SARGENTO BARRIENTOS	Hay muchos canes que ladran	
	y después muerden al dueño.	205
JUAN DE MÉRIDA	Cuando el can muerde, es con rabia.	
DOÑA LEONOR	Juan, la vida me debéis.	
JUAN DE MÉRIDA	¿Cómo he de poder pagarla,	
	cuando un pobre negro soy?	
	Mas si gratitudes pagan	210
	buenas obras, esta vida	
	que me dais, en cualquier causa	
	vuestra, la ofreced por vuestra,	
	porque este negro en España	
	algún día piensa ser	215
	lunar de la gente blanca.	
CAPITÁN DON AGUSTÍN	Id a apaciguar la gente.	
DOÑA LEONOR	Y tú, por la puerta falsa	
	de ese jardín salir puedes.	
JUAN DE MÉRIDA	No voy porque me acobardan	220
	tropas ni escuadras por ella,	
	sino por servirte.	
SARGENTO BARRIENTOS	Extraña	
	arrogancia de moreno.	
JUAN DE MÉRIDA	Di valor, y no arrogancia.	

Vanse y quedan el capitán DON AGUSTÍN *y* DOÑA LEONOR⁺

DOÑA LEONOR	Cosas notables me cuenta	225
	de este negro Doña Juana,	
	mi prima.	
CAPITÁN DON AGUSTÍN	A pedirme vino	
	que le asentase la plaza	
	de soldado.	
DOÑA LEONOR	Es presumido.	
CAPITÁN DON AGUSTÍN	Solo la color le falta	230
	para caballero.	

SERGEANT BARRIENTOS	Now, be thankful for your life
	To the one who just rescued
	You from your death.
JUAN DE MÉRIDA	I will be at her feet
	Always a grateful hound.
SERGEANT BARRIENTOS	There are hounds that bark,
	And then bite their master.
JUAN DE MÉRIDA	When a hound bites it is with rage.
DOÑA LEONOR	Juan, you owe me your life.
JUAN DE MÉRIDA	How can I ever repay you
	When I'm just a wretched Black man?
	However, if gratitude pays
	For good deeds, this life
	You give me, I offer it for your own
	In any cause of yours,
	Because this Black man in Spain
	One day intends to be a
	Beauty mark on White people's face.
CAPTAIN DON AGUSTÍN	Go and appease the soldiers.
DOÑA LEONOR	And you, go through that door
	In the garden that leads to the street.
JUAN DE MÉRIDA	I'm not leaving because I'm intimidated
	By troops or squadrons, but
	To serve you, my Lady.
SERGEANT BARRIENTOS	Such extraordinary
	Arrogance for a Black man.
JUAN DE MÉRIDA	It's valor, not arrogance,

They exit. CAPTAIN DON AGUSTÍN and DOÑA LEONOR remain on stage.

DOÑA LEONOR	I've been told remarkable things
	About this Black man
	By my cousin Doña Juana.
CAPTAIN DON AGUSTÍN	He came to me,
	Asking me to recruit him as a soldier
	In my regiment.
DOÑA LEONOR	He's conceited.
CAPTAIN DON AGUSTÍN	He only lacks the color
	To be a nobleman.

DOÑA LEONOR   Ya
que con su vida obligada
me dejáis, segunda vez
–permitiendo que me vaya–
lo quede.

CAPITÁN DON AGUSTÍN   Con vuestra ausencia   235
en esta ocasión quedara
como sin sol queda el mundo:
metido entre sombras pardas.
Y pues quiso darme Amor
tal ocasión, malograrla   240
fuera ofender sus saetas,
fuera profanar sus alas.
Desde que le dio el abril,
coronado de esmeraldas,
al labio perfiles de oro   245
y poca aurora a la barba,
la inclinación de la guerra
me ha tenido de mi patria
ausente, siguiendo el son
de las trompas y las cajas   250
en Nápoles y en Milán.
Y agora el honor me pasa
con el Duque de Alba a Flandes,
que ya en Lisboa se embarca;
adonde mi compañía   255
con tanto cuidado marcha,
y adonde sin alma voy
porque, en tan breve distancia,
ha escurecido el amor
la gloria de mis hazañas.   260
Mas si vos le aseguráis
los premios a mi esperanza,
los rigores que he seguido
trocaré en delicias blandas
–si en la guerra de esos ojos   265
no hay más sangrientas batallas–.
Vos sola podréis torcer[+]

DOÑA LEONOR	Since
	I am indebted to you
	Because of his life,
	I'll be thankful for a second time
	If you allow me to leave.
CAPTAIN DON AGUSTÍN	With your absence
	On this occasion, I will be
	As the world is without the sun:
	Shrouded in dull grey shadows;
	And since Cupid gave me
	Such an opportunity, to misuse it
	Would be to offend his arrows,
	It would be to profane his wings.
	Ever since emerald-crowned April
	Gave my youthful lips
	Some golden strands of hair
	And a beard barely covered my face,
	My inclination towards war
	Has kept me absent
	From my homeland,
	Following the sound of trumpets and drums,
	In Naples and Milan,
	And now honor sends me
	To Flanders with the Duke of Alba,
	Where he will soon sail from Lisbon,
	Where my company,
	With worries of love goes,
	And where I go without a soul,
	For, in so short a distance,
	Love has eclipsed
	The glory of my military deeds;
	Yet, if you promise
	With rewards my hopes,
	The hardships I have endured
	Shall be turned into soft delights,
	– Though in the war of your eyes
	There are fiercer battles – .
	You alone can bend

mis intentos; vos, bizarra,
ser rémora de la vida,
y ser el fénix del alma.   270
Yo, Doña Leonor divina,
soy Don Agustín de Estrada:
con quien pretendió casaros
el señor Don Juan de Vargas⁺,
vuestro padre y mi señor   275
–que ya en el cielo descansa–,
gustando mi padre de ello;
aunque yo no di a sus cartas
la obediencia por entonces,
porque en vos imaginaba   280
más nobleza que hermosura,
que esta ha sido mi desgracia.
Mas agora que los ojos,
señora, me desengañan,
en vuestra presencia lloran   285
mi castigo y mi ignorancia.
Yo soy el que os desprecié
sin conoceros. Ya aguardan
vuestros desdenes mi injuria
y mi amor vuestras venganzas.   290
A todo rigor me ofrezco,
si puede en belleza tanta
caber rigor, aunque ha sido
siempre la hermosura ingrata.
Lo que la ausencia deshizo   295
agora el Amor lo haga.
En paz la guerra se trueque,
si Amor en la paz descansa.
Seis mil ducados de renta,
uniéndose nuestras casas,   300

---

268   **Rémora**. A tropical fish that adheres to floating vessels and other objects. It was believed to stop ships. Figuratively, an obstacle, a hindrance. It continues the series of marine metaphors initiated earlier in the act.

My efforts; you, fair and bold,
Could put my life on hold,
And be the phoenix of my soul.
I am, divine Doña Leonor,
Captain Don Agustín de Estrada:
With whom Don Juan de Vargas
Your father, and my Lord –
May God rest his soul –
Intended you to marry,
My very own father agreed to this union;
Though I paid no attention
To his letters at that time,
Because I imagined in you
More nobility than beauty,
And this has been my misfortune.
My Lady, now that my eyes
Have enlightened me,
They weep in your presence
For my punishment and ignorance.
I am the one who spurned you
Without knowing you; my wrongs
Await your disdain,
And my love your revenge;
I offer myself to all your harshness
If one can find harshness
In such beauty, though beauty
Has always been ungrateful.
What absence has undone,
Now love will do.
Let war become peace,
If peace resides in love.
I offer you an income of six thousand ducats,
If we join our houses together,

     os ofrezco, si vos sois
     de otros dos mil mayorazga.
     Ya el ser capitán renuncio,
     puesta a esos pies la bengala:
     honrad, Leonor, la jineta,   305
     siendo capitán del alma.

DOÑA LEONOR Para las flemas de Amor
     no son las priesas de Marte,
     y más cuando a Flandes parte
     lleno de sangre y rigor.   310
     Espacio pide el amor
     y más en ocasión igual.

CAPITÁN DON AGUSTÍN Ya Amor es mi general.
     Como me ilustres y mandes,
     que para mí no hay más Flandes 315
     que esa vista celestial.
     Desde hoy Mérida ha de ser
     aquel país rebelado.
     Ya soy del Amor soldado.

DOÑA LEONOR Conquistar es menester,   320
     que inexpugnable ha de ser
     el honor.

CAPITÁN DON AGUSTÍN   Solo es mi intento
     honrarme con él.

DOÑA LEONOR   Violento,
     jamás fue casto el amor.

CAPITÁN DON AGUSTÍN Hoy la violencia es honor, 325
     pues aspiro a casamiento.

---

302 ***Mayorazga****.* Woman who has inherited a *mayorazgo* (entailment), which consisted of real estate and the revenue it produced. The *mayorazgo* was inherited by the eldest male to the exclusion of the other siblings. In the absence of male heirs, it passed to the eldest female.

304–305 ***Bengala****.* A baton that denoted high military rank. See Olmedo Gobante's essay in this volume. ***Jineta****.* A ceremonial short spear. See note to line 91.

307 ***Flemas****.* Phlegm, one of the four humors (blood, yellow bile, black bile, phlegm) in ancient Greek and medieval Arab medicine that explained changes and illnesses both physical and spiritual. Phlegm was associated with women and femininity and was under the influx of the planet Venus.

	And if you are worth as sole heir,
	Another two thousand.
	I resign at once my Captain's commission,
	Laying at your feet my baton.
	Honor, Leonor, the spear
	That makes you Captain of my soul.
DOÑA LEONOR	The slow pace of Love
	Should not be hastened by Mars,
	More so when you leave for Flanders
	Full of blood and rigor.
	Love asks for more time,
	And even more so on this occasion.
CAPTAIN DON AGUSTÍN	Love is now my general.
	As you instruct and command me.
	For there's no more Flanders for me
	Than that heavenly sight.
	From this day on, Mérida will be
	That rebellious country,
	I am now Love's soldier.
DOÑA LEONOR	Conquering is necessary;
	For honor must be
	Unassailable.
CAPTAIN DON AGUSTÍN	My only intention
	Is to honor myself with it.
DOÑA LEONOR	Love
	when forced, was never chaste.
CAPTAIN DON AGUSTÍN	Today honor is forceful,
	For I aspire to marriage;

	Mi suerte impensada fue	
	y amor la ha de hacer dichosa	
	con ganaros por esposa.	
Doña Leonor	En eso, señor, vendré	330
	como asegurada esté	
	que hoy en Mérida os quedáis,	
	pero si a Flandes pasáis,	
	¿cómo queréis que lo sea?	
Capitán Don Agustín	Porque esta verdad se crea,	335
	si la palabra me dais	
	de esposa, luego un papel	
	haré aquí. Venga al momento,	
	que yo otorgaré contento	
	cuanto Amor pusiere en él.	340
Doña Leonor	¡Qué invencible, y qué cruel	
	es la ocasión!	

Don Agustín se arrodilla[+].

Capitán Don Agustín	Cobre aquí	
	lo que en la ausencia perdí,	
	que no he de dejar tus pies	
	sin que la mano me des.	345
Doña Leonor	La mano, el alma y el sí	
	os daré, como os quedéis	
	en Mérida.	
Capitán Don Agustín	Monte soy.	
Doña Leonor	(Amor, ya vencida estoy).	
	Verme esta noche podéis	350
	si en el papel concedéis	
	lo que decís.	
Capitán Don Agustín	Asegura	
	mi lealtad y tu hermosura.	
Doña Leonor	Mi gente. ¡Adiós!	
Capitán Don Agustín	Esto debo	
	a un negro.	
Doña Leonor	Suerte es que llevo	355
	semejante a mi ventura.	

Vanse. Salen Doña Juana y Juan de Mérida.

	Lady Luck has unexpectedly
	Smiled upon me, and with love
	I intend to make her happy,
	By marrying you.
Doña Leonor	That, sir, can only happen
	If you guarantee you'll stay in Mérida.
	But if you're prepared to leave for Flanders,
	How can I be sure?
Captain Don Agustín	So that you will believe me,
	If you give me your word
	To be my wife, I'll draw up
	A contract right now
	And I'll write in it everything
	That your love desires.
Doña Leonor	How unshakable and cruel
	Is the situation!

Don Agustín kneels.

CAPTAIN DON AGUSTÍN　　　　　　　Let me recover here
What I lost in my absence,
For I will not leave your feet
Without you giving me your hand.

DOÑA LEONOR　My hand, my soul and a yes,
I will grant you, as long as you
Stay in Mérida.

CAPTAIN DON AGUSTÍN　　　　　　　I'm an unmovable force.

DOÑA LEONOR　*[Aside]* Love! You've defeated me.
You can see me tonight
If you grant me in this contract
What you say.

CAPTAIN DON AGUSTÍN　　　　　My guarantee is
my loyalty and your beauty.

DOÑA LEONOR　People are coming. Farewell.

CAPTAIN DON AGUSTÍN　　　　　　　　This
I owe to a Black man.

DOÑA LEONOR　　　　　　　My luck is
as black as my fortune.

They exit. Enter Doña Juana and Juan of Mérida.

DOÑA JUANA	Ya sufrir no se pueden, negro loco,
	tanta pendencia y tanta demasía.
JUAN DE MÉRIDA	Ni en Mérida vivir puedo tampoco
	siendo quien soy.
DOÑA JUANA	Donosa perrería.	360
JUAN DE MÉRIDA	A cólera y a rabia me provoco
	cuando contemplo en la bajeza mía
	pensamientos que van a eterna fama,
	a pesar del color que así me infama.
	¡Que ser negro en el mundo infamia sea!	365
	¿Por ventura los negros no son hombres?
	¿Tienen alma más vil, más torpe y fea,
	y por ello les dan bajos renombres?
	¿Qué tiene más España que Guinea?
	o ¿por qué privilegios o renombres,	370
	si los negros valor y nombre adquieren,
	los blancos más civiles los prefieren?
DOÑA JUANA	Más bien que alborotar la compañía
	y la ciudad al perro le estuviera
	ocuparse en traer agua todo el día	375
JUAN DE MÉRIDA	¿Yo azacán?, ¿yo aguador? Antes hiciera
	la bajeza más vil.
DOÑA JUANA	¡Qué fantasía!
JUAN DE MÉRIDA	Que este valor es tuyo considera,
	pues, siendo un perro de tu casa, quiero
	ir a vencer, señora, el orbe entero.	380

372 *Civil*. Uncouth, rude, cruel.

376 *Azacán*. Water carrier, and by extension someone who worked in humble tasks. Water carrying was a typical occupation of Black people in early modern Iberia, as seen in the painting *El Chafariz d'El-Rey* (see Figure 6). Also, in Murillo's *Three Boys* (c. 1670, London, Dulwich Picture Gallery) and *The Wedding at Cana* (c. 1672, Birmingham, UK, Barber Institute of Fine Arts).

377 *Fantasía*. Fantasy, arrogance, presumption. A racial stereotype. "*Fantasía de negro*: porque los negros son amigos de andar galanes, aunque con cualquiera cosa se contentan, y siendo favorecidos, toman gran presunción" ["*A Black man's presumption*: Because Black people like to dress elegantly, although they are happy with anything, and they get very presumptuous when they are favored"] (Covarrubias 2020, 881).

DOÑA JUANA	One can no longer suffer, foolish Black man,
	So much brawling and so many excesses.
JUAN DE MÉRIDA	Nor can I live in Mérida,
	Being who I am.
DOÑA JUANA	What a fine dog.
JUAN DE MÉRIDA	I'm angered and enraged
	When I contemplate in my baseness,
	Thoughts that go to eternal fame,
	In spite of the color that shames me.
	That being Black in this world is infamy!
	By chance, are not Blacks, men?
	Have they a dreadful, fouler, wicked soul,
	And that's why they get a bad name?
	Why is Spain better than Africa?
	If Black people gain worth and fame,
	Based on what privileges or titles
	Do whites prefer Blacks uncivilized?
DOÑA JUANA	Rather than disturbing the soldiers
	And the town, the dog should busy
	Himself fetching water all day long.
JUAN DE MÉRIDA	Me? A water boy? Fetching water?
	I'd rather work in a pigsty.
DOÑA JUANA	How presumptious!
JUAN DE MÉRIDA	Consider that this valor is yours,
	For being a dog of your house,
	I want to go to conquer, my lady, the whole world.

DOÑA JUANA	Eso ha de ser, que ya a mi padre tiene
	cansado con locuras semejantes.
JUAN DE MÉRIDA	El cielo estos amagos me previene.
	Si parecen locuras, no te espantes.

Dejar luego esta tierra me conviene,   385
donde vivo comido de ignorantes[+].
Dame licencia porque trueque en brasa
este carbón, echado de tu casa.

DOÑA JUANA le da un papel[+].

Con esta carta voy contento y rico,
que es de mi libertad: con ella un clavo   390
al eje vil de la Fortuna aplico
y con la infamia del color acabo.
Ya mi valor al mundo significo,
pues, aunque negro soy, no he sido esclavo,
y miente el mismo Sol si lo imagina.   395
Señora, de mi madre Catalina
os encargo el favor que le habéis hecho,
y a vuestro padre y mi señor suplico
me perdone, pues no era de provecho
mi persona en su casa. Y cuando rico   400
vuelva y de la Fortuna satisfecho,
pagando las mercedes que hoy publico,
tendrá un esclavo en mí.

DOÑA JUANA   ¡Gentil locura!

Vase DOÑA JUANA.

JUAN DE MÉRIDA   Si no el color, mudar quiero ventura.
Pasar quiero a Lisboa y embarcarme   405
a la sombra del Duque de Alba, aurora
de quien pienso glorioso iluminarme.
Si espanto soy, si noche soy agora,
el color que hoy me afrenta ha de ilustrarme,
que la virtud triunfante y vencedora,   410
es licor celestial que no hace caso
del oro o del cristal en cualquier vaso.

DOÑA JUANA	So be it, for my father is already
	Weary of such foolish actions.
JUAN DE MÉRIDA	These actions are a sign from Heaven.
	If they seem reckless, don't be surprised.
	It's better that I leave this country soon,
	Where I live besieged by ignorant people.
	Throw this coal out of your house,
	And let me turn it into embers.

DOÑA JUANA gives him a document.

> With this paper, I feel fortunate and content,
> For it's a letter of freedom: with it, I drive a spike
> Into Fortune's evil axle,
> And end the shame of this color.
> Now I can exercise my valor in this world,
> For, although Black, I have not been a slave,
> And the sun itself lies, if it imagines otherwise.
> My Lady, on behalf of my mother Catalina,
> I thank you for the favor you have done her,
> And to your father, and my lord, I beg
> Forgiveness, for my person was of no use
> In his house. And when rich I return
> And satisfied from Fortune's wheel,
> You shall have in me a slave,
> Who will repay the favors I now declare.

DOÑA JUANA	A fool's folly!

She exits.

JUAN DE MÉRIDA	If I can't change my color, I'll change my luck.
	I shall go to Lisbon and embark
	In the shadow of the Duke of Alba,
	Whose light I intend to embrace gloriously.
	If I am the horror, if I am now the darkness,
	The color that now offends me, one day shall
	bring me fame;
	Because triumphant and victorious virtue,
	Is a celestial liquor that pays no heed
	To the gold or the glass in any cup.

Vanse y salen ELVIRA, ISABEL *y* PINEDA, *criados*[+].

ELVIRA	¿Qué dices?	
PINEDA[+]	Que yo le vi	
	salir con su compañía	
	en tropa, cuando salía	415
	el sol, fingiendo un rubí,	
	de los brazos de la aurora.	
ISABEL	Sería su alférez.	
PINEDA	Digo	
	que le vi y que habló conmigo.	
ISABEL	Reniega de hombre que llora	420
	cuando ruega, que el amor[+],	
	para atropellar antojos,	
	teniendo el alma en los ojos,	
	tiene en el pecho rigor.	
PINEDA	Mi señora sale.	
ELVIRA	Vete.	425

Vase PINEDA.

ISABEL	¿Quién las nuevas le dará?	
ELVIRA	Él, si es que en su pecho está[+].	
ISABEL	Bien cumple lo que promete	
	por su papel.	
ELVIRA	Si el papel	
	fue de este amor fundamento,	430
	llevósele, amiga, el viento,	
	que no hay más firmeza en él.	
	Mas retírate, que yo	
	con cierta industria pretendo	
	decirle el caso.	

Vanse. Sale DOÑA LEONOR.

DOÑA LEONOR	Ya entiendo	435
	que de Mérida salió	
	la compañía, aunque apenas	
	los roncos ecos he oído	
	despertar al sol, dormido	

They exit. Enter Elvira, Isabel, and Pineda, servants.

ELVIRA	What are you saying?
PINEDA	I'm saying that I saw him
	Marching with his regiment,
	When the sun was rising,
	Out of the arms of dawn
	As bright as a ruby.
ISABEL	It could've been his lieutenant.
PINEDA	I'm saying
	That I saw him, and he spoke to me.
ELVIRA	Don't trust a man who weeps
	When he begs; that love,
	In order to rush what it desires,
	Having his soul in his eyes,
	Has cruelty in his chest.
PINEDA	Here comes my Lady.
ISABEL	Leave.

PINEDA exits.

ELVIRA	Who shall give her the news?
ISABEL	The contract will, if it's kept in her bosom.
ELVIRA	He really lived up to what he promised
	In that piece of paper.
ISABEL	If that contract
	Was the foundation of his love,
	The wind, my friend, carried it away.
	It's not worth the paper it's written on.
	Now leave, for I,
	With some craftiness intend
	To tell her the news.

They exit. Enter DOÑA LEONOR.

DOÑA LEONOR	I guess
	That the company
	Left Mérida, although I barely
	Heard the hoarse echoes
	Awaken the sun, asleep

entre rosas y azucenas.   440
Ya a Don Agustín tendré
más seguro si marchó
la gente que le encargó
a su alférez; y seré
yo el capitán de rigores   445
en un soldado rendido.
Siempre gloriosos han sido
los impensados amores.
Las ternezas y favores[+]
estoy celebrando agora   450
que aquesta noche han pasado.

Canta ELVIRA *dentro*[+]   *El amor del soldado*
                              no es más de un hora.
                              En tocando la caja:
                              "adiós, señora".   455

DOÑA LEONOR   ¡Válgame Dios! Aun cantado,
                        me da el suceso temor
                        porque no es constante amor
                        nunca el amor del soldado.
                        En un hora se enamora,   460
                        en un hora es su amistad,
                        y así, la seguridad
                        de su amor no es más de un hora;
                        y aunque en amar se aventaja[+]
                        por ser el plazo menor,   465
                        el incendio de este amor
                        muere en tocando la caja.
                        Mas este discurso agora
                        es necio, porque es quimera
                        pensar que mi bien se fuera   470
                        sin decir "adiós, señora";
                        mas esta ingrata canción
                        sin propósito no viene
                        agora. Misterio tiene;
                        saber quiero la ocasión.   475

Salen ELVIRA *e* ISABEL[+].

Among roses and lilies.
Don Agustín shall be
More secure if he entrusted
The soldiers he assigned
To his lieutenant; and I shall
Become the strict captain
To a surrendered soldier.
Unexpected loves,
Have always been glorious.
I now celebrate,
The sweetness and favors
That occurred last night.

ELVIRA *[Singing off-stage]*   *A soldier's love lasts*
           No more than an hour,
           As the drums beat and slam,
           "It's Farewell, ma'am!"

DOÑA LEONOR   Good Heavens! Even though it's
Just a song, it gives me chills
Because a soldier's love
Is never constant.
In an hour he falls in love,
In an hour he's all affections,
And so, the assurance of his love
Is not more than an hour;
And, though in loving, he's more intense,
Because the time is shorter,
The fire of this love dies
With the first beating of the drums.
However, these words here now
Are nonsense, for its unthinkable
To believe that my love is gone
Without saying "Farewell ma'am";
Yet, this ungrateful song,
Is not sung now without
Purpose. There's a secret here,
I want to unravel it.

Enter ELVIRA and ISABEL.

¿Qué es esto, Elvira?

ELVIRA   Es decirte
que en la canción te prevengo.
Más que decirte no tengo.

DOÑA LEONOR   Ni yo tengo más que oírte,
porque la canción me dice[+],   480
en sus consonancias locas,
mis castigadas locuras
con tan fementidas obras.
Nuncio de desdichas eres,
y aquí cantando me informas   485
que es Don Agustín soldado
porque su engaño conozca.

ELVIRA   Ya se fue tu ingrato dueño
amparado de las sombras
del mal dibujado día   490
en los lienzos de la aurora.
Pineda sacar le vio
–calladas las cajas roncas–,
en tropas, su compañía,
que huye amor más bien en tropas.   495

DOÑA LEONOR   No me digáis más. Dejadme,
que, en desdichas tan notorias,
imaginaciones bastan
como las verdades sobran.

Vanse ELVIRA *e* ISABEL[+].

¡Loca estoy, sin seso estoy[+]!   500
Daré voces, que las oigan
las estrellas, si a ser vienen
tantas como mis congojas.
¡Oh, capitán fementido,
soldado de mis deshonras!   505
Mas no soldado, pues de él
hace el rigor que te escondas.

What's this, Elvira?

ELVIRA   Just to tell
You what the song warns you.
I have no more to say.

DOÑA LEONOR   Nor do I have anymore to hear,
Because the song tells me
In its ridiculous lyrics,
Of my follies, punished
With such deceitful actions.
Herald of misfortunes you are,
And here singing, you remind me
That Don Agustín is a soldier
So that I recognize his deceit.

ELVIRA   Your ungrateful lover is gone,
Sheltered by the shadows
Of a badly drawn day
On dawn's backdrop.
Pineda saw him
– After the hoarse snare drums fell silent –
Marching in line with his regiment,
For love flees in swarms like troops.

DOÑA LEONOR   Speak no more. Leave me alone;
For, in such well-known misfortunes,
Suspicions are enough,
As the truths are too much to bear.

Exit ELVIRA and ISABEL.

I am so mad that I would lose my mind!
I will cry out, let the stars
Hear them, if they are
As many as my pains.
Oh, you unfaithful captain,
Soldier of my dishonor!
But no, not a soldier, a soulless
Soldier that hides in the dark.

No te ha dado el *sol*, pues huyes[+]
en la noche tenebrosa,
y quien las tinieblas busca   510
los rayos del sol le asombran.
Pública sea esta afrenta
no solo en Mérida, en toda
España, para que en ella
los ingratos se conozcan.   515
Decirlo a su padre quiero[+],
y a mis deudos, porque pongan
fin con mi muerte a este agravio
y den principio a sus glorias.
¡Oh, negro vil, ocasión   520
de esta tragedia espantosa,
borrón de mi honestidad
y de mis virtudes sombra!

Saca el papel.

¡Oh fementido papel!,
¡oh, piélago de lisonjas   525
donde son más las mentiras
y las verdades son pocas!
Pues con todo he de romper,
justo será que en ti rompa
víboras en letras lirios   530
y áspides en partes rosas;
mas si mi venganza estriba
en ti y aquí me provocan
mis agravios a intentarlo,
guardarte en el alma importa.   535
Resuelta estoy en seguirlo,
buscando, desde Lisboa[+],
abismos de espuma en golfos,
montes de zafir en ondas.

---

508   *El sol*. A common Baroque play of words with the Spanish term for sun (*sol*) and the first syllable in soldier (*sol*dado). Don Agustín is not a soldier because he has fled before sunrise. The same pun is made in Ana Caro's *Valor, agravio y mujer* (1993, 135).

The sun's rays have not touched you,
And you flee through the unhappy night
Seeking the cloak of darkness as shelter,
But the sun's rays will find you.
Let this affront be well known
Not only in Mérida, but in all
Spain, so that the ungrateful
Can be singled out.
I want to tell his father,
And my relatives, so that they may
Put an end to this offence with my death
And restore their honor and glory.
Oh, despicable Black man, cause
Of this dreadful tragedy,
Blot on my honesty
And dark shadow over my virtue!

Takes out the letter.

O, deceitful letter!
O, ocean of flattery
Where there are more lies
And truths are far and few!
Since I must break and tear it all,
It will be fair to tear you too:
Vipers among your lily letters,
asps among your rosy scraps.
Yet, if my vengeance be
In you, and here I'm persuaded
By my wrongs to pursue it,
Keeping you close to my soul is vital.
I'm determined to follow him,
Overcoming from Lisbon's shore,
The ocean's depths of foam, and
Mountainous waves of sapphires.

Corra tras su honor perdido[+]   540
mi honestidad, aunque corra
vil detrimento la fama,
torpes desprecios la honra.
Sin que ninguno lo entienda,
mintiendo el hábito y forma,   545
hombre he de ser animado
de mis esperanzas locas.
Las joyas con que pensé
ser firmamento en mis bodas
vayan conmigo a servirme   550
en mis funerales pompas.
Flandes, a tus hielos voy,
que quiero que me socorran
en tanto fuego, si agravios
en los hielos se reportan.   555
¡Cielos, rayos me fiad[+]!
¡Sierpes, prestadme ponzoñas!
¡Fieras, infundid en mí
la crueldad que hay en vosotras!
Burlome un hombre, mas yo   560
más culpada que quejosa
es bien que esté, pues di el alma,
con advertencia tan poca,
a un soldado, conociendo
que, en bronces, libros e historias   565
–y en mis trágicos sucesos,
que el mundo y los tiempos lloran–,
el amor del soldado
no es más de un hora,
y en tocando la caja: 570
"adiós, señora".

Vase. Tocan cajas y salen los capitanes Don Pedro *y* Don Juan[+].

Capitán Don Pedro[+]	No se ha visto tan próspero viaje.
Capitán Don Juan	Las naos no han sido naos, sino cometas.
Capitán Don Pedro	Al Duque se le debe el buen pasaje,
	que las furias del mar tiene sujetas. 575

Let my decency run after his honor,
Though knowingly I ruin my name
And vilify my reputation.
Telling no one,
Feigning the costume and manner,
I must become a man, encouraged
By these foolish hopes.
The jewels that I wanted
To adorn me at my wedding,
Will come with me to attend me
With splendor at my funeral.
Flanders, to your cold ice I go,
I want you to help me
In so much fire, if wrongs
Can be appeased by your cold ice.
Heavens, entrust me with lightning bolts,
Serpents, lend me your venom;
Wild beasts, imbue in me
The cruelty that is in you!
A man lied to my face, but I'm
More to blame than right to complain,
for I gave my soul
With so little judgement
To a soldier, knowing
That, in bronzes, books and histories
– And in my tragic plight
That the world and times mourn – ,
A soldier's love lasts
No more than an hour,
As the drums beat and slam,
"It's Farewell, ma'am!"

She exits. Sound of drums beating offstage. Enter captains DON PEDRO *and* DON JUAN.

CAPTAIN DON PEDRO	I have never seen such a prosperous voyage.
CAPTAIN DON JUAN	The ships have not been ships, but comets.
CAPTAIN DON PEDRO	We owe this great voyage to the Duke,
	He subdued the ocean's furies.

CAPITÁN DON JUAN	Viento en popa, el felice marinaje
	tocó de Flandes los helados metas
	en ocho días.
CAPITÁN DON PEDRO	César es segundo.
CAPITÁN DON JUAN	Y fuera otro Alejandro, a hallar más mundo[+].
CAPITÁN DON PEDRO	Con gran gusto el país le ha recibido. 580
CAPITÁN DON JUAN	La plata de su barba venerable
	a unos temor y a otros respeto ha sido.
CAPITÁN DON PEDRO	Es severo.
CAPITÁN DON JUAN	Es señor.
CAPITÁN DON PEDRO	Y es todo amable.
CAPITÁN DON JUAN	El de Orange, sabiendo que ha venido,
	lamenta ya su estado miserable, 585

Dentro, tocan cajas.

	mas ¿qué es esto?
CAPITÁN DON PEDRO	La guarda al Duque meten.
CAPITÁN DON JUAN	Sus virtudes la gloria nos prometen.

Tocan cajas. Salen soldados y el sargento BARRIENTOS *echando a empujones a* JUAN DE MÉRIDA.

SARGENTO BARRIENTOS	Ya le he advertido otra vez
	que es compañía de blancos
	libres esta, y que no caben 590
	en ella negros ni esclavos.
	Váyase y no le acontezca,
	cuando venimos marchando,
	meterse entre las hileras,
	que le costará muy caro. 595

---

577   ***Meta***. End mark used in Roman circuses. In seventeenth-century Spanish it was a masculine noun.

578–579   ***César ... Alejandro***. Use of the rhetorical figure of antonomasia. He is another Julius Caesar, a new Alexander the Great, alluding to archetypes of generals and conquerors.

584   ***El de Orange.*** Refers to William of Nassau, Prince of Orange (1533–1584), the leader of the Dutch revolt against Philip II of Spain.

CAPTAIN DON JUAN	The wind at our stern, a successful voyage in Reaching Flanders' icy waters In eight days.
CAPTAIN DON PEDRO	He's a second Caesar,
CAPTAIN DON JUAN	And would be a new Alexander, if there're more worlds to Conquer.
CAPTAIN DON PEDRO	The country has welcomed him, with great pleasure.
CAPTAIN DON JUAN	The silver of his venerable beard Is feared by some and respected by others.
CAPTAIN DON PEDRO	He's an unyielding man.
CAPTAIN DON JUAN	He is Lordly.
CAPTAIN DON PEDRO	And he is all kindness.
CAPTAIN DON JUAN	The Prince of Orange, knowing that he has come, Already regrets his terrible situation…

Offstage – beating of drums.

	But what is this commotion?
CAPTAIN DON PEDRO	The guards are escorting the Duke.
CAPTAIN DON JUAN	His virtues shall grant us glory.

Sound of drums. Enter soldiers and Sergeant BARRIENTOS pushing JUAN DE MÉRIDA out.

SERGEANT BARRIENTOS	I've warned you before That this is a company of free white Men and that there is no room For black men or slaves. Get out, and don't you dare, To come among our ranks When we march, For it will cost you dearly.

JUAN DE MÉRIDA	¿Tanta bajeza es ser negro?,
	¿tanto tizna el desdichado
	color de mi rostro?
SARGENTO BARRIENTOS	Es humo.
JUAN DE MÉRIDA	Pues ya se va levantando
	a las narices, y ¡voto...

600

SARGENTO BARRIENTOS	¿He de quebrarle al perrazo
	la asta en el cuerpo?
JUAN DE MÉRIDA	Pasito,
	seor sargento.
SARGENTO BARRIENTOS	Si levanto
	la alabarda...
JUAN DE MÉRIDA	Volverá
	vuesarcé, más que de paso,

605

	a bajarla.
SARGENTO BARRIENTOS	¿Sabe el perro
	que estamos, del gran palacio
	del Duque, en la plaza de armas?
JUAN DE MÉRIDA	Pues, si como en ella estamos,
	estuviéramos agora

610

	en Mérida, ¿de dos saltos
	no estuviera en el infierno?
SARGENTO BARRIENTOS	Paso, negro.
JUAN DE MÉRIDA	Blanco, paso.
CAPITÁN DON PEDRO	¡Ah, moreno, respetad
	al que está con vos hablando,

615

	que es oficial de estos tercios!
JUAN DE MÉRIDA	Yo le respeto y le guardo
	el decoro que se debe
	a su alabarda, aunque ha dado
	en ser mi enemigo y soy,

620

	para enemigo, muy malo.
CAPITÁN DON JUAN	¡Oigan el brío del negro!

607–608   ***Palacio. Plaza de Armas***. A palace was any place where the king or his
representative was staying. The *Plaza de Armas* was the central courtyard of any
fortress or camp, often dedicated to all kinds of military maneuvers and parades.
See Olmedo Gobante's essay in this volume.

JUAN DE MÉRIDA	Is it so base to be a black man?
	Is the unlucky color of my face
	That much of a stain?
SERGEANT BARRIENTOS	It's dark smoke.
JUAN DE MÉRIDA	Well, there's no fire,
	without dark smoke, and I swear…
SERGEANT BARRIENTOS	Shall I break the dog's
	Back with this staff?
JUAN DE MÉRIDA	Careful,
	Mister sergeant.
SERGEANT BARRIENTOS	If I raise
	The halberd…
JUAN DE MÉRIDA	You will
	Lower it faster than
	You raised it.
SERGEANT BARRIENTOS	Does the dog know
	That we are in the courtyard of
	The grand duke's Palace?
JUAN DE MÉRIDA	Well, if instead of being here,
	We were in Mérida
	Wouldn't you reach
	Hell in a blink of an eye?
SERGEANT BARRIENTOS	Slow down, Black man.
JUAN DE MÉRIDA	White man, slow down.
CAPTAIN DON PEDRO	Hey, Black man, respect
	The man who's talking to you,
	He is an officer of the Spanish Army.
JUAN DE MÉRIDA	I respect him and maintain
	The proper courtesy
	To his halberd, though he chooses
	To be my enemy, and as an enemy,
	I am a very bad one.
CAPTAIN DON JUAN	Listen to this Black man's bravado!

CAPITÁN DON PEDRO	Ya de sufrirlo me enfado.
	¡Vaya el perro!
CAPITÁN DON JUAN	¡Vaya el negro!
JUAN DE MÉRIDA	¡Peor fuera ser mal blanco! 625

Suenan cajas.

CAPITÁN DON JUAN	Gentil consuelo. Venid,
	que ya va la guardia entrando.

Vanse todos, y queda JUAN DE MÉRIDA solo.

JUAN DE MÉRIDA

¿Que esto es ser negro?, ¿esto es ser
de este color? De este agravio
me quejaré a la Fortuna,   630
al cielo, al tiempo y a cuantos
me hicieron negro. ¡Oh, reniego
del color! ¡Que no hagan caso
de las almas! Loco estoy.
¿Qué he de hacer? Desesperado,   635
servirle yo solo al Rey,
siendo el capitán y el cabo
de mi compañía, y siendo
invencible y temerario.
Mas el Duque de Alba pasa   640
entre un escuadrón gallardo
de capitanes famosos
y de maeses de campo.
Retirarme quiero −¡Ah, cielos!
¡Que ser negro afrente tanto!−,   645
mas si a Flandes he venido
a servir, ¿qué me acobardo?
Hablarle quiero y decirle
mis pensamientos honrados,
que, cuando el color desprecie,   650
no dejará de estimarlos.
Leyendo una carta viene.
Quiérome poner al paso.

CAPTAIN DON PEDRO	I'm starting to lose my patience with him.
	Look at this dog!
CAPTAIN DON JUAN	Look at this Black man!
JUAN DE MÉRIDA	It would be worse to be a bad White man.

Snare drums play.

CAPTAIN DON JUAN	Those are comforting thoughts. Come,
	The guard is on its way in.

They all exit. JUAN DE MÉRIDA, alone on stage.

JUAN DE MÉRIDA	Is this to be Black? Is this to be
	This color? For this injustice,
	I'll complain to Fortune,
	To heaven, to time, and to those
	Who made me black. Oh, I reject
	This color! That they do not look
	At our souls! I am confused.
	What am I to do? In desperation,
	I'll serve the King on my own,
	Becoming both captain and corporal
	Of my regiment, and being
	Invincible and daring;
	But here comes the Duke of Alba
	Escorted by an elite squadron
	Of famous captains
	And field commanders.
	I want to withdraw, – O', Heavens!
	That being a Black man is such an affront –;
	Yet, if I have come to Flanders
	To serve, why am I so afraid?
	I want to speak to him, and tell
	Him my honest intentions,
	So that, although he may spurn this color,
	He will hold my ambitions in high esteem.
	Here he comes reading a letter,
	I must get in his way.

Sale el Duque de Alba *leyendo una carta. Salen el sargento* Barrientos,
los capitanes Don Agustín, Don Pedro *y* Don Juan *y soldados*[+].

	¡Óigame vuestra excelencia!	
Capitán Don Agustín	Apártate[+].	
Juan de Mérida	Ya me aparto.	655
Capitán Don Agustín	(Este negro me persigue).	

Se arrodilla Juan de Mérida.

Juan de Mérida	Excelentísimo amparo	
	de la milicia, gran Duque…	
Capitán Don Juan	Calla, moreno.	
Juan de Mérida	Ya callo.	
	¡Alba del Sol que en dos orbes	660
	está, glorioso, alumbrando!	
Capitán Don Pedro	Aparta.	
Juan de Mérida	Duque señor,	
	asiros tengo del brazo,	
	gran señor, porque me oigáis.	

Ase al Duque de Alba *del brazo.*

Capitán Don Agustín	¡Aparta, perro!	
Duque de Alba	Dejadlo.	665
Juan de Mérida	Perdonad mi atrevimiento.	
Duque de Alba	Atrevimientos bizarros	
	en sí la disculpa tienen.	
	¿Qué queréis?	
Juan de Mérida	Estar temblando	
	no es de miedo, es de respeto;	670
	mas no es mucho, si me hallo,	
	siendo noche, en la presencia	

---

660   **Alba del Sol.** The sun is a symbol for the king of Spain. Juan de Mérida uses
the double meaning of the name *Alba* (white, but also dawn) to address the Duke as
a champion of the Spanish king's power in Flanders. It is a dominant motif in the
play. See lines 729, 1001, and 1582.

667   **Bizarro.** Courageous, in the sense of displaying gallantry. A synonym of
valiente, this word expressed an ideal of Spanish military masculinity that could
also be applied to women in specific situations (see line 268).

Enter the DUQUE OF ALBA, reading a letter. Followed by Sergeant BARRIENTOS, captains DON AGUSTÍN, DON PEDRO, DON JUAN, and soldiers.

JUAN DE MÉRIDA	Hear me out your excellency!
CAPTAIN DON AGUSTÍN	Get out of our way.
JUAN DE MÉRIDA	I will move away soon.
CAPTAIN DON AGUSTÍN	*[Aside]* This Black man is shadowing me.

JUAN DE MÉRIDA kneels

JUAN DE MÉRIDA	Excellent protector
	Of the soldiers! Great Duke of Alba!
CAPTAIN DON JUAN	Silence, Black man.
JUAN DE MÉRIDA	I will be silent in a moment.
	Duke of Alba, dawn of the King, our Sun,
	That gloriously shines over two hemispheres.
CAPTAIN DON PEDRO	Stand aside.
JUAN DE MÉRIDA	Your Grace and my Lord;
	I will seize your arm
	To make you hear my request.

He takes the DUKE OF ALBA by his arm.

CAPTAIN DON AGUSTÍN	Out of the way, you dog!
DUKE OF ALBA	Leave him.
JUAN DE MÉRIDA	Forgive such boldness.
DUKE OF ALBA	Valiant bold actions
	Do not require forgiveness.
	What do you want?
JUAN DE MÉRIDA	I tremble,
	Not out of fear, but out of respect;
	But it is not surprising, because, I
	Am darkness in the presence

	del Alba, a quien venerando	
	están las pálidas sombras.	
DUQUE DE ALBA	Suspenso como admirado	675
	con su despejo me tiene	
	el negro.	
SARGENTO BARRIENTOS	Ya está aguardando	
	el Consejo.	
DUQUE DE ALBA	Vos despúes	
	me hablaréis con más espacio.	
JUAN DE MÉRIDA	No he de dejar vuestros pies,	680
	si aquí me hacen mil pedazos.	
CAPITÁN DON JUAN	¡Gentil desvergüenza!	
CAPITÁN DON PEDRO	¡Aparta!	
CAPITÁN DON AGUSTÍN	¡Aparta, perro!	
DUQUE DE ALBA	Dejadlo.	
JUAN DE MÉRIDA	Con intento de servir,	
	señor, en estos estados	685
	a su majestad, de España	
	he venido; y procurando	
	plaza, todos me desechan	
	por negro y por hombre bajo;	
	y así, vengo a suplicarle	690
	a vuecelencia que, en tanto	
	que este color se acredita,	
	me permita que un soldado	
	que traiga del enemigo	
	de cuerda, arcabuz y frascos⁺	695
	me provea, que yo quiero	
	por mi persona ganarlo	
	sin que me lo den a cuenta	
	del Rey, a quien le consagro	
	con obras y sin lisonjas	700
	esta negregura; y cuando	
	por negro lo desmerezca,	

---

695 ***Cuerda, arcabuz y frascos***. Arquebuses required gunpowder containers (*frascos*) as well as a match (*cuerda*) to be fired (see Figure 7). Firearms were typically provided to soldiers in the Spanish Tercios, but not always.

	Of Alba, a Dawn revered
	By faint shadows.
DUKE OF ALBA	I'm in awe and in wonder
	At the self-confidence and ease
	Of this Black man.
SERGEANT BARRIENTOS	The Council
	Is already waiting.
DUKE OF ALBA	You will have time
	To speak to me later.
JUAN DE MÉRIDA	I will not leave your feet,
	Even if I am torn to pieces.
CAPTAIN DON JUAN	What a nice insolence!
CAPTAIN DON PEDRO	Stand aside!
CAPTAIN DON AGUSTÍN	Stand aside, dog!
DUKE OF ALBA	Leave him be.
JUAN DE MÉRIDA	With the intention of serving,
	Sir, in these countries
	Our Majesty of Spain,
	I have come seeking a post
	In your regiment. But everyone rejects me
	Because I am Black and low born.
	Therefore, I come to implore
	Your Grace that, while
	This color gains credit,
	You allow me to bring a soldier
	From the enemy's camp whose,
	Gun, ammunitions, and flasks
	Will serve me well. Because I want
	To gain it by myself,
	And not have it given to me
	On account of the King, to whom I devote
	This blackness with actions,
	And not with flattery. If I am
	Unworthy because of the color of my skin,

	me sirvan los Reyes Magos	
	de abono, pues tuvo un negro	
	plaza entre dos reyes blancos.	705
Duque de Alba	El color lo da la tierra,	
	y el valor, el cielo. Honradlo,	
	que un lunar a un rostro hermoso	
	tal vez suele acreditarlo.	
	Una espía me traed	710
	del escuadrón del contrario,	
	y ved que nuestro honor pende	
	de la facción que os encargo.	
Juan de Mérida	Dadme esos pies.	
Capitán Don Juan	Gran señor,	
	aqueso ha sido afrentarnos.	715
Capitán Don Pedro	Cuando capitanes sobran,	
	¿fías de un negro los casos	
	de tanta importancia?	
Capitán Don Agustín	Mira	
	que pide mayor cuidado,	
	más valor y más persona.	720
Duque de Alba	Pues de vos quiero fiarlo.	
	Vos, Don Agustín, traed	
	la espía.	
Capitán Don Agustín	Talaré el campo	
	del enemigo si importa.	

Vase el capitán Don Agustín⁺.

703 **Reyes Magos**. The Magi or Three Wise Men. The tradition of representing one of the Magi as Black developed in Germany in the Middle Ages and soon extended throughout Europe (Kaplan 1985, 95). Juan is appealing to this example of inclusion. The Hermandad de los Negros of Seville had as its main advocation Our Lady of the Kings, represented as the Virgin Mary with the Child Jesus receiving the adoration of the Magi (Matthew 2: 1–12). Other Black confraternities in Spain and the Americas used the image of the Black Magus to gain legitimacy, as he represented royalty and sovereignty (Rowe 2019, 192).

710 **Espía o centinela**. A lone scout. See 723, 786, 851, and Olmedo Gobante's essay in this volume.

	Let the Three Wise Kings serve me
	As a precedent of a Black man
	Sharing a place between two White kings.
DUKE OF ALBA	Color is given by the land
	And heaven gives valor. Honor your blackness
	For a beauty mark on a handsome face
	Sometimes gives it credit.
	You shall bring me an enemy scout
	From the other squadron,
	And note that your honor depends
	On the mission I entrust you with.
JUAN DE MÉRIDA	Give me those feet.
CAPTAIN DON JUAN	Your Grace,
	That is an affront to us!
CAPTAIN DON PEDRO	When captains abound,
	You trust a Black man in causes
	Of such importance?
CAPTAIN DON AGUSTÍN	Consider, Sir
	That it demands greater care,
	More courage, and a more honor.
DUKE OF ALBA	Then, I want to entrust it to you.
	Don Agustín, shall bring
	The enemy scout.
CAPTAIN DON AGUSTÍN	I'll cut down
	The enemy's camp, if that's what it takes.

Exit Captain DON AGUSTÍN.

DUQUE DE ALBA	Buscad en qué señalaros	725
	vos, si es que ver pretendéis	
	el color acreditado,	
	que entonces, pues Alba soy,	
	yo os sacaré de ese ocaso.	

Vanse todos y queda JUAN DE MÉRIDA solo.

JUAN DE MÉRIDA	¡Qué desdichado que soy!	730
	Como Tántalo, no alcanzo	
	la fruta que está en la boca	
	ni el cristal que está en los labios[+].	
	¡Que haya dado en perseguirme	
	este enemigo, este ingrato	735
	de Don Agustín! Estoy,	
	¡vive el cielo!, por matarlo;	
	mas ¿qué mejor ocasión	
	para vengar mis agravios	
	puedo hallar que la presente?	740
	Tras él a la empresa salgo,	
	de donde he de hacer que vuelva	
	a coces y a espaldarazos,	
	sin espía y sin honor.	
	Pondreme, por el recato,	745
	una máscara. Yo voy.	
	Noche, pues somos hermanos	
	en el color y las sombras,	
	mi azabache te consagro	
	para que los blancos vean	750
	que, *aunque negros, no tiznamos.*	

---

729   ***Ocaso****.* A reference to sunset and night, but also to skin color and darkness in the sense of social obscurity. One of the many plays on the word *alba* (dawn, also meaning white), in contrast to Juan's blackness.

731   ***Tántalo****.* In Greek mythology, Tantalus was one of Zeus's sons. He revealed divine secrets to humankind and for this he was punished to an eternity of thirst and hunger under a tree full of hanging fruit surrounded by water. When Tantalus tried to drink or eat, water and branches withdrew.

733   ***Cristal****.* Water in the poetic language of the time.

DUKE OF ALBA   You, find something to prove
                 Yourself, if you intend
                 To see your color accredited,
                 If you do so, since Alba means Dawn,
                 I will bring you out of the shadows.

They all exit except JUAN DE MÉRIDA.

JUAN DE MÉRIDA   How wretched I am!
                 Like Tantalus, I can't reach
                 The fruit that is almost in my mouth,
                 Nor the water near my lips!
                 That I should be pursued,
                 By this enemy, this ungrateful
                 Don Agustín! I am
                 About to kill him by the heavens!
                 But what better occasion
                 To avenge my grievances
                 Can I find than the present one?
                 I'm going after his very mission,
                 From where I shall make him return,
                 With kicks and slaps,
                 Without an enemy scout and without honor.
                 I shall wear, to be discreet,
                 A mask. Here I go.
                 Night, since we are brothers
                 In color and in shadows,
                 I entrust my jet stone's color
                 With you, so that Whites may see
                 That *though Black, we do not stain.*

Vase. Sale el capitán Don Agustín *vestido de flamenco y con su banda*⁺.

Capitán Don Agustín	Del hábito contrario
	me he querido valer en esta empresa.
	Intento temerario,
	acción terrible, bárbara promesa 755
	y efecto de la envidia
	que, en el pecho, de un negro me fastidia!⁺
	La noche, tenebrosa;
	los pantanos y fosos, infinitos.
	La hazaña es rigurosa⁺; 760
	y castigando el cielo mis delitos,
	desata por los campos
	montes de nieve en cristalinos ampos⁺.
	Por este contradique,
	pues el traje es flamenco y voy seguro, 765
	mi fortuna me aplique
	espía o centinela que a lo oscuro
	–redimiendo la nieve–
	de algún álamo esté, que perlas bebe.

Sale Juan de Mérida *con máscara.*

Juan de Mérida	Aunque priesa me he dado, 770
	no he podido alcanzarle. ¡Suerte es mía!
Capitán Don Agustín	Allí suena un soldado.
	Si fuese centinela o fuese espía,
	grande ventura fuera.
Juan de Mérida	Pasos siento. ¿Qué gente?
Capitán Don Agustín	Amigos.
Juan de Mérida	Muera 775
	si no me dice el nombre.
	(Este es Don Agustín, ¡notable suerte!)
	Responda y no se asombre.
Capitán Don Agustín	¿Yo asombrarme?
Juan de Mérida	Dé el nombre, o de la muerte
	aquí no está seguro.

776 ***Nombre****. Password. See line 781.*

He exits. Enter Captain DON AGUSTÍN, *dressed as a Flemish soldier, wearing a sash.*

CAPTAIN DON AGUSTÍN   The enemy's clothes
Will serve me well in this endeavor.
These are reckless efforts,
Terrible actions, barbaric promises
And the effects of a Black man's envy
Who has become a thorn in my side!
The night is pitch black,
The marshes and moats are endless.
The task is difficult,
And the sky, punishing my crimes,
Unleashes across the fields
Mountains of snow in crystalline snowflakes.
Through this small channel
I walk confidently, for my clothes are Flemish.
May Fortune find me
Any scout spy or sentry
sheltering from snow,
Under the shade of a pearl-covered poplar tree.

Enter JUAN DE *Mérida wearing a mask.*

JUAN DE MÉRIDA   Although I have acted quickly,
I have not been able to catch up with him.
        Such is my luck!
CAPTAIN DON AGUSTÍN   There's a soldier nearby;
If he were a scout spy or a sentry,
I'd be in luck.
JUAN DE MÉRIDA   I hear footsteps. Who goes there?
CAPTAIN DON AGUSTÍN   A friend.
JUAN DE MÉRIDA   You will die
If you don't say the watchword.
[Aside] This is Don Agustín; how fortunate!
Answer me and don't be afraid.
CAPTAIN DON AGUSTÍN   Me, afraid?
JUAN DE MÉRIDA   Say the watchword, or from death
You won't escape.

Capitán Don Agustín	*San Mauricio.*	780
Juan de Mérida	No hay tal, muera el perjuro[+].	
Capitán Don Agustín	Mira que soy soldado	
	del Príncipe de Orange.	
Juan de Mérida	También mientes,	
	cobarde afeminado	
	y bárbaro español. No nos afrentes,	785
	que espía soy perdida	
	del campo del estado.	
Capitán Don Agustín	Por tu vida	
	o tu persona vengo.	
Juan de Mérida	Aquí tienes mi vida y mi persona,	
	mas advierte que tengo	790
	espíritu inmortal.	
Capitán Don Agustín	De que te abona	
	das aquí testimonio. ¿Eres hombre?	
Juan de Mérida	Hombre soy y soy demonio,	
	y más si me quitara,	
	para espantarte, la primera cara.	795

781   ***San Mauricio***. Saint Maurice. Juan asks for a watchword or password – *dé el nombre* – and Don Agustín guesses 'Saint Maurice'. This is ironic since Saint Maurice, venerated by soldiers in Germany, was from Africa and often depicted as Black (Grimm 1992, 127; Kaplan 1987). In Spain, however, most images of Saint Maurice represent him as white, as in El Greco's *Martyrdom of Saint Maurice and His Companions* (c. 1580–1582, El Escorial).

786   The words *centinela* and *espía* were synonymous in the military language of early modern Spanish. Covarrubias defines *centinela perdida* as "La que está fuera del castillo o del real en el campo, adonde en caso de necesidad no puede ser buenamente socorrida y así va a sus aventuras y a esta tal no la requieren como a las demás" [One placed outside the walls of the castle or military compound, in the open field, where he cannot receive aid in case of need. Therefore, he is on his own and does not receive orders like the rest] (2020, 502). See 710, 723, and 851.

787   ***El Estado***. The State refers here to the States General, the official name of the Dutch rebels.

791   ***Espíritu inmortal***. In war and martial arts, *inmortal* meant unbeatable, invincible, what cannot be defeated. In this context, spirit meant energy, liveliness, courage: "No tener espíritu un hombre, no tener brío" ["For a man not having spirit means not having courage"] (Covarrubias 2020, 838).

CAPTAIN DON AGUSTÍN	Saint Maurice.
JUAN DE MÉRIDA	Not even close. Die you liar!
CAPTAIN DON AGUSTÍN	Look here, that I am a soldier
	Of the Prince of Orange.
JUAN DE MÉRIDA	You lie again,
	You effeminate coward
	And Spanish barbarian; don't insult us,
	For I'm a lone scout
	From the rebel field.
CAPTAIN DON AGUSTÍN	I have come
	For you or your life.
JUAN DE MÉRIDA	Here's my life and here I am,
	But I warn you that
	I'm invincible in spirit.
CAPTAIN DON AGUSTÍN	You are proving it to be true.
	Are you a man or a demon?
JUAN DE MÉRIDA	I am a man and also a demon
	And more so if I take off
	This mask to scare you.

Riñen. Cae el capitán DON AGUSTÍN[+].

CAPITÁN DON AGUSTÍN	¡Tente!, que rendido estoy.
JUAN DE MÉRIDA	¿Quién eres?
CAPITÁN DON AGUSTÍN	Un capitán
	de España.
JUAN DE MÉRIDA	Fuerte y galán.
CAPITÁN DON AGUSTÍN	Algunas veces lo soy.
JUAN DE MÉRIDA	Mucho de verte me alegro 800
	a mis pies, vil capitán.
CAPITÁN DON AGUSTÍN	¿Quién eres?
JUAN DE MÉRIDA	Un alemán
	que ha dos horas que era negro.
	Negra ha sido esta facción,
	y esta empresa, incierta y manca; 805
	mas en la plana más blanca
	suele caer un borrón
	y en ti ha caído esta vez,
	quedando en tiempo tan breve
	yo más blanco que la nieve, 810
	tú, más negro que la pez.
	Darte puedo aquí la muerte
	y no quiero, por pensar
	que salió en negro tu azar
	y salió en blanco mi suerte. 815
CAPITÁN DON AGUSTÍN	¡Buena guerra!
JUAN DE MÉRIDA	Esa te haré
	sin que te rinda o te mate,
	mas solo por tu rescate
	una prenda llevaré.
	¿Tienes qué darme?
CAPITÁN DON AGUSTÍN	Esta banda. 820
JUAN DE MÉRIDA	Esa por rescate quiero.

Toma la banda[+].

---

816 **Buena guerra**. A just war. To engage in '*buena guerra*' was to follow the principles of 'just war', which forbade crimes and atrocities. One of those principles was to pardon the enemy who surrenders. Juan does precisely this.

They sword fight. Captain DON AGUSTÍN falls to the ground.

CAPTAIN DON AGUSTÍN	Stop! For I've been defeated.
JUAN DE MÉRIDA	Who are you?
CAPTAIN DON AGUSTÍN	A captain
	From Spain.
JUAN DE MÉRIDA	Young and refined?
CAPTAIN DON AGUSTÍN	Sometimes I am.
JUAN DE MÉRIDA	I am very glad to see you
	At my feet, you despicable captain.
CAPTAIN DON AGUSTÍN	Who are you?
JUAN DE MÉRIDA	A German
	Who was Black two hours ago.
	Black has been this action,
	And this enterprise, uncertain and bleak;
	But on the whitest plane
	A dark blot sometimes falls;
	And it has fallen on you this time,
	Allowing me in so short a time
	To be whiter than snow,
	And you, blacker than pitch.
	I can end your life right here,
	But I don't want to, since I believe
	That your venture turned out black,
	And my fortune turned out white.
CAPTAIN DON AGUSTÍN	You fight a just war!
JUAN DE MÉRIDA	And I shall fight one
	Without making you surrender, or killing you
	But as ransom
	I'll take something from you.
	Do you have anything to give me?
CAPTAIN DON AGUSTÍN	This sash.
JUAN DE MÉRIDA	I'll take it as a ransom.

He takes the sash.

	Ve en paz.	
CAPITÁN DON AGUSTÍN	Eres caballero.	
JUAN DE MÉRIDA	El valor las carnes manda.	
	Hoy, porque de mí te amparas,	
	te doy libertad aquí,	825
	mas no te fíes de mí,	
	que soy hombre de dos caras.	
CAPITÁN DON AGUSTÍN	Con esta honrarme deseas.	
JUAN DE MÉRIDA	Yo sé que en otro lugar	
	sin la tuya has de quedar	830
	cuando con otra me veas.	
CAPITÁN DON AGUSTÍN	(Corrido y sin alma voy.	
	¿Qué disculpa le daré	
	al Duque?)	
JUAN DE MÉRIDA	Soberbia fue	
	la tuya.	
CAPITÁN DON AGUSTÍN	Tu esclavo soy.	835

Vase el capitán DON AGUSTÍN.

JUAN DE MÉRIDA	Ya ha comenzado a ampararme	
	la Fortuna. Pierdo el miedo.	
	Ya soy venturoso y puedo	
	ya la máscara quitarme.	

Se quita la máscara[+].

	¡Vete, máscara!, que ya	840
	la inmortalidad me llama:	
	negro he de ser de la fama	
	que aquesta ocasión me da.	
	Ya en púrpura y rosicler	
	sale el aurora divina	845
	riéndose, que imagina	
	la acción que voy a emprender.	
	El campo del enemigo	
	agora he de alborotar,	

823 **El valor las carnes manda**. A rephrasing of the popular saying *El corazón las carnes manda* (the heart rules over the flesh). Being a valiant man, Juan substitutes *valor* for *heart*. The heart was considered the site of the noblest feelings.

	Go in peace.
CAPTAIN DON AGUSTÍN	You're a gentleman.
JUAN DE MÉRIDA	Valor commands the flesh.
	Today, since you ask for my mercy,
	I grant you here, your freedom,
	But do not trust me,
	For I am a two-faced man.
CAPTAIN DON AGUSTÍN	You want to honor me with that one.
JUAN DE MÉRIDA	I know that somewhere else
	Your expression will change
	When you see me with another face.
CAPTAIN DON AGUSTÍN	*[Aside]* Cloaked in shame and distraught.
	What excuse shall I give
	The Duke?
JUAN DE MÉRIDA	That pride has been
	Your flaw.
CAPTAIN DON AGUSTÍN	I am your slave.

Exit Captain DON AGUSTÍN.

JUAN DE MÉRIDA	Fortune's wheel has begun
	To favor me. I'm no longer afraid.
	Now I am fortunate and I can
	Take this mask off.

He takes his mask off

Begone mask! For
Immortality is calling me:
I shall be Fame's Black man,
For it grants me this opportunity.
Already in colors rose and purple,
Divine dawn appears.
It laughs because it imagines
The action I am about to take.
The enemy's camp
I shall now attack,

y al Duque le he de llevar   850
sus centinelas conmigo.
¡Haz, Fortuna, que esta acción
deje mi honor satisfecho;
y ya que negro me has hecho,
enmienda la imperfección!   855

Vase. Sale DOÑA LEONOR vestida de paje y ANTÓN⁺.

ANTÓN⁺	*Turo lo que vosancé*
	me ordenamo, Antón hacemo,
	que neglo callar sabemo.
DOÑA LEONOR	Yo libertad te daré
	si me guardas el secreto 860
	que te fío.
ANTÓN	*Preto samo*
	hombre de bien, y cayamo,
	que también sa gente preto.
DOÑA LEONOR	Notable resolución
	ha sido la mía.
ANTÓN	*Ansí* 865
	vengamo del branco aquí.
DOÑA LEONOR	Estos los palacios son
	del Duque.
ANTÓN	*Mira si sal⁺*
	aquí el falso cagayera.
DOÑA LEONOR	¡Quién esto, honor, me dijera! 870

Disparan. Salen el DUQUE DE ALBA y los capitanes DON PEDRO y DON JUAN.

CAPITÁN DON PEDRO	El campo contrario está
	alborotado…
CAPITÁN DON JUAN	Y tres piezas
	de batir ha disparado.

851 **Centinela**. Sentry. The words *centinela* and *espía* (lone scout) were synonymous in the military language of early modern Spanish. See 710, 723, and 786.

856 **Turo lo que vosancé**. Antón is a Black character who speaks in the stereotypical *habla de negros*. See the co-authored essay in this volume.

And deliver to the Duke
The sentries he requested.
Fortune, let this action
Leave my honor satisfied;
And, since you have made me Black,
Make right this wrong.

Exit. Enter DoÑA LEONOR dressed as a page and ANTÓN.

ANTÓN	*Whatever my Lady*
	orders me to do, Antón will do,
	Because we Blacks know how to hold our tongues.
DOÑA LEONOR	I will grant you your freedom
	If you keep the secret
	I entrust to you.
ANTÓN	*We are Black,*
	We're good people, we know how to keep quiet
	Because Blacks are people too.
DOÑA LEONOR	My determination
	Has been remarkable.
ANTÓN	*This is how*
	We get revenge from the White man here.
DOÑA LEONOR	These palaces here
	Belong to the Duke.
ANTÓN	*Let's see if*
	The phony craptain is here.
DOÑA LEONOR	Honor, did you foresee such fate?

Shots off stage and enter the DUKE OF ALBA and Captain DON PEDRO and DON JUAN.

CAPTAIN DON PEDRO	The enemy's field is
	In total uproar…
CAPTAIN DON JUAN	And they have fired
	Three cannon shots!

DUQUE DE ALBA	Don Agustín lo ha causado,
	que sabe cumplir proezas⁺.
DOÑA LEONOR	Este que veneran tantos
	el Duque debe de ser.
ANTÓN	*Si este sa el Duque, poner*
	podemos al mundo espantos.
DUQUE DE ALBA	La centinela o la espía
	su escuadrón alborotó.

DUQUE DE ALBA — Don Agustín lo ha causado,
que sabe cumplir proezas⁺.   875
DOÑA LEONOR — Este que veneran tantos
el Duque debe de ser.
ANTÓN — *Si este sa el Duque, poner*
podemos al mundo espantos.
DUQUE DE ALBA — La centinela o la espía   880
su escuadrón alborotó.

Sale el capitán DON AGUSTÍN.

CAPITÁN DON AGUSTÍN — (¿Quién más corrido llegó
a amanecer con el día?)
DOÑA LEONOR — Antón, el ingrato es este.
ANTÓN — *¡Ah, cagayera beyaca!*   885
Yeguemo a darle matraca.
CAPITÁN DON AGUSTÍN — (La vida la acción me cueste).
Si soy digno de esos pies,
los pies me dé vuecelencia.
DUQUE DE ALBA — Señor capitán, ¿qué es esto?   890
CAPITÁN DON AGUSTÍN — Desaciertos de la guerra.
Del campo del enemigo
con espía o centinela
prometí volver, fiado
del valor y diligencia;   895
pero, como a la Fortuna⁺
las ejecuciones dejan
los hados, los venturosos
consiguen lo que desean.
Y como la guerra es siempre   900
ardides y estratagemas,
por mayor seguridad⁺,
fingí las galas tudescas.
Camino a la ejecución
ya por pantanosas sendas,   905
ya por diques mal formados
y dibujados apenas.

906   **Diques**. Dikes. See line 764.

DUKE OF ALBA	Don Agustín has caused it,
	He knows how to accomplish heroic deeds.
DOÑA LEONOR	This one, that so many revere,
	Must be the Duke of Alba.
ANTÓN	*If this be the Duke, we can*
	Make the world tremble.
DUKE OF ALBA	An enemy sentinel or spy scout
	Must have alerted his squadron.

Enter Captain DON AGUSTÍN.

CAPTAIN DON AGUSTÍN	*[Aside]* Who has ever been more
	Humiliated before daybreak?
DOÑA LEONOR	Antón, here is the ungrateful fiend!
ANTÓN	*Oh you shitting Craptain!*
	Let's give him a hard time!
CAPTAIN DON AGUSTÍN	*[Aside]* This action will cost me my life.
	If I am worthy of those feet,
	Let me have them, your Grace.
DUKE OF ALBA	Captain, what is this?
CAPTAIN DON AGUSTÍN	Blunders of war!
	With an enemy scout or a sentry
	Relying on courage and diligence,
	I promised to return
	From the enemy's camp.
	But, since fate entrusts
	The execution
	To Fortune, the lucky ones
	Get what they wish.
	And, as war is always about
	Deceptions and stratagems,
	For greater security,
	I feigned these Flemish garments.
	Onward I went with my plan,
	Whether by marshy paths,
	Or by poorly formed dams
	And that could barely be seen.

	Discurro por varias partes	
	hasta que conmigo encuentran	
	dos capitanes que estaban	910
	de escolta con veinte o treinta	
	soldados en un casal,	
	de quien, con la resistencia	
	de caballero español,	
	por los pantanos y vegas,	915
	me escapé gloriosamente,	
	soltando el campo tres piezas	
	imaginando celada,	
	aunque algunas vidas cuesta	
	mi retirada.	
DUQUE DE ALBA	El valor	920
	se ilustra en la suerte adversa,	
	porque en las dificultades	
	está la gloria más cierta.	

Sale JUAN DE MÉRIDA *con dos* SOLDADOS FLAMENCOS *y dos arcabuces.*

SOLDADO FLAMENCO 1	*Nite.*	
SOLDADO FLAMENCO 2	*Nite.*	
JUAN DE MÉRIDA	¡Nitead,	
	y Bercebú que os entienda!	925
DUQUE DE ALBA	¿Quién es el que viene aquí?	
JUAN DE MÉRIDA	Un oso con dos colmenas.	
ANTÓN	*(Siora, también acá*	
	sa soldado gente preta).	
DOÑA LEONOR	Y es Juan de Mérida.	
ANTÓN	¿Juan?,	930
	este za la flor de Merda.	
JUAN DE MÉRIDA	Esta vez, excelentísimo	
	señor, concederme es fuerza	
	la plaza.	
CAPITÁN DON AGUSTÍN	(¡Perdido soy,	
	que este es el negro y aquella,	935
	mi banda! Bien a su cara	
	libro toda mi vergüenza).	

I wandered here and there
Until I ran into
Two captains who were
Scouting the field with twenty or thirty
Soldiers in what was a shanty house;
From which, with the endurance
Of a Spanish knight,
Through marshes and meadows,
I escaped gloriously;
The camp unleashing three battery shots,
Imagining a sudden attack;
While losing some lives
As the price of my retreat.

DUKE OF ALBA   Courage
Is exemplified in adverse fortune,
Because in hardship
Lies the most assured Glory.

Enter JUAN DE MÉRIDA with two Flemish soldiers, carrying two harquebuses

FLEMISH SOLDIER 1   *Nite.*
FLEMISH SOLDIER 2   *Nite.*
JUAN DE MÉRIDA   Nite all you want!
Not even the Devil can understand you.
DOÑA LEONOR   Who is this coming here?
JUAN DE MÉRIDA   A bear with two beehives.
ANTÓN   *Ma'am, Black people are also*
Soldiers here.
DOÑA LEONOR   And is Juan de Mérida.
ANTÓN   *Juan?*
He is Mérida's crème of the crap.
JUAN DE MÉRIDA   This time, your most excellent
Sir, you will grant me
A post.
CAPTAIN DON AGUSTÍN   *[Aside]* I'm undone,
This is the Black man and that
Is my sash! I'm shamefaced
By this Black man again.

JUAN DE MÉRIDA

Traer prometí un soldado
a que el arcabuz me diera
para serlo yo, y dos traigo⁺   940
por si el uno se revienta.
Ya os traigo dos arcabuces,
pólvora, frascos y cuerdas.
Sola la plaza me falta.
Honrad la nación morena   945
mandando asentar mi plaza,
que, como yo lo merezca,
traeré otra vez la alabarda,
la bandera y la jineta
de las tiendas del de Orange,   950
y traeré las mismas tiendas.
Ya, señores capitanes,
con la cara descubierta
puede este moreno andar,
pues, castigando soberbias,   955
quien me vio vencer con otra
me tendrá temor con esta.
A un capitán enemigo,
antes que con estos diera⁺,
le atropellé y le quité   960
esta banda. Vuecelencia
por despojos la reciba
de mis primeras empresas,
que ya a vuestros pies está
colorada de vergüenza.   965

Dale la banda al DUQUE DE ALBA.

941   ***Revienta****.* Arquebuses could blow up when fired due to improper maintenance or mechanical failure.
943   ***Pólvora, frascos y cuerdas****.* Gunpowder, flasks, and matches were essential components of the ammunition of an arquebus. See note 695 and Figure 7.
948–949   ***Bandera, alabarda, jineta****.* For the symbolic meaning and material properties of the banner, the halberd, the *jineta* spear, and the sash, see Olmedo Gobante`s essay in this volume.

JUAN DE MÉRIDA   I promised to bring a soldier
Who would give me his harquebus
So I can become one, and I brought two
In case one fails and explodes.
Here I bring you two harquebuses,
Gunpowder, flasks, and rope.
I lack only the position.
Honor the dark-skinned nation.
Make my appointment,
That I, deserving of it,
Will bring next time the halberd,
The banner, and the captain's spear
From the tents of the Prince of Orange,
And in addition the very same tents themselves.
Now, gentlemen captains,
With my face unmasked
This Black man can come and go,
By punishing arrogance because,
The one who saw me win with another face
Will be afraid of me with this one.
I came across an enemy Captain,
Before I ran into these two,
I knocked him down and took
This sash. Your Grace,
For spoils of war receive
It from my first enterprise,
Which is already at your feet
Blushed in shame.

Gives the sash to the DUKE OF ALBA

CAPITÁN DON AGUSTÍN	(¡Mataré al perro!)
DUQUE DE ALBA	La banda
	recibo por prenda vuestra,
	que es justo que se honre un duque
	con lo que un negro desecha.
JUAN DE MÉRIDA	Esta fue de un capitán
	hinchado con gran soberbia[+],
	hombre blanco y presumido.
CAPITÁN DON AGUSTÍN	(¿Quién vio mayores afrentas?)
DUQUE DE ALBA	Vos, señor Don Agustín,
	honrad esa banda.
JUAN DE MÉRIDA	Ofensa
	hacéis a tan gran soldado.
	Mirad, gran señor, que es prenda
	de un negro y lo tiznará.
CAPITÁN DON AGUSTÍN	Yo le daré a esa bajeza
	calidad.
JUAN DE MÉRIDA	Ansí lo creo.
	Guardadla bien, no se os pierda,
	que hay soldados con dos caras
	que a un capitán no respetan.
DUQUE DE ALBA	Notable negro.
CAPITÁN DON PEDRO	Admirable.
DUQUE DE ALBA	En mi compañía mesma
	quiero asentaros la plaza.
JUAN DE MÉRIDA	Ansí los príncipes premian.
DUQUE DE ALBA	¿Cómo os llamáis?
JUAN DE MÉRIDA	Juan me llamo,
	de Mérida, porque en ella
	nací libre. Y porque nadie
	jamás afrentarme pueda,
	esta es mi carta, que al cuello
	traigo como indulgencia.
DUQUE DE ALBA	Pues hoy, Juan, en la milicia
	nacéis, vuestro nombre sea
	Juan de Alba.
JUAN DE MÉRIDA	¿Queréis, señor,
	que en esta noche amanezca
	vuestra Alba?

970

975

980

985

990

995

CAPTAIN DON AGUSTÍN	*[Aside]* I will kill this dog!
DUKE OF ALBA	The sash
	I receive as a proof from you,
	That it is right for a duke to be honored
	With what a Black man discards.
JUAN DE MÉRIDA	This was from a captain
	Puffed up with great pride,
	A White man and presumptuous.
CAPTAIN DON AGUSTÍN	(Who has seen greater affronts?)
DUKE OF ALBA	You, Don Agustin,
	Honor that sash.
JUAN DE MÉRIDA	You offend
	So great a soldier.
	Beware, your Grace, it is the spoils
	Of a Black man and it will stain him.
CAPTAIN DON AGUSTÍN	I'll give that baseness
	Nobility.
JUAN DE MÉRIDA	I think you will.
	Keep it well, so you don't lose it,
	For there are soldiers with two faces
	Who do not respect captains.
DUKE OF ALBA	A remarkable Black man!
CAPTAIN DON JUAN	Admirable, indeed.
DUKE OF ALBA	In my company
	I want to place you.
JUAN DE MÉRIDA	This is how princes reward.
DUKE OF ALBA	What is your name?
JUAN DE MÉRIDA	Juan, my name is Juan
	De Mérida, for I was
	Born free there; and, so that no one
	Can ever wrong me,
	This is my letter of freedom, which I wear
	Around my neck as an indulgence.
DUKE OF ALBA	Because this day Juan, you are born
	In the military, your name shall be
	Juan de Alba.
JUAN DE MÉRIDA	Do you want, your Grace,
	That in this darkness, I become
	Dawn by naming me Alba?

DUQUE DE ALBA	Alba os llamad.
JUAN DE ALBA[+]	Basta, gran señor, que sea
	crepúsculo de vuestra Alba. 1000
DUQUE DE ALBA	El mundo en Alba tan negra
	ha de venerar el sol
	que ya a ilustraros comienza.
JUAN DE ALBA	Llamarse un negro Juan de Alba
	hoy de la misma manera 1005
	es que llamarse Juan Blanco;
	mas juro de hacer eterna
	vuestra Alba en estos países,
	que he de ser, contra estas fieras
	gentes, lebrel generoso 1010
	que los ladre y que los muerda.
DUQUE DE ALBA	Sabed de esas dos espías
	lo que imaginan o intentan
	esos rebeldes.
CAPITÁN DON AGUSTÍN	(Corrido
	voy).

Vase el capitán DON AGUSTÍN[+].

DUQUE DE ALBA	Juan de Alba, hoy comienza 1015
	vuestra vida.
JUAN DE ALBA	Pues me dais
	segunda naturaleza
	y soy negro –y Alba soy,
	ceñido de vuestras perlas–,
	el perro de Alba seré 1020
	de las escuadras flamencas.

1001   ***Alba tan negra***. In this and the following lines, the Duke of Alba and Juan play with the meanings of *alba* (white, dawn, the name of the House of Alba, the new name of Juan) in a racialization of the term.

1020   ***El perro de Alba***. A reference to the ballad *El perro de Alba*, a popular tale about a dog that harassed Jewish people in the Spanish town of Alba de Tormes in the fifteenth century. Juan had been called a dog right from the beginning (line 1). See Fra-Molinero's essay.

DUKE OF ALBA	Alba shall be your name.
JUAN DE ALBA	It suffices, your Grace, that I be
	The twilight of the name Alba.
DUKE OF ALBA	In a Dawn so black the world
	Must venerate the Sun
	That enlightens you.
JUAN DE ALBA	For a Black man to be called Juan de Alba,
	Is the same as being called Juan White;
	But I swear to make the name
	Of Alba eternal in these lands
	For I shall be against these fierce
	People, a noble hound,
	To both bark at and bite them.
DUKE OF ALBA	Find out from these two scouts
	What are the objectives or plans
	Of those rebels.
CAPTAIN DON AGUSTÍN	*[Aside]* I'm
	So ashamed!

Exit Captain DON AGUSTÍN.

DUKE DE ALBA	Juan de Alba, your life
	Begins today.
JUAN DE ALBA	Since you give me,
	A second life
	And I am Black man – and I am Alba,
	Bound to your pearls –
	I shall be Alba's hound
	To the Flemish squadrons.

| Duque de Alba | Pues tenéis dos arcabuces, |
| | dos plazas sean las vuestras. |

Vanse, y quedan solos Juan de Alba, Doña Leonor *y* Antón.

Juan de Alba	Pues ¡vive Dios!, gran señor,
	de pelear por doscientas.	1025
Doña Leonor	Lleguémosle a hablar.
Antón	¡Oh, primo,
	damo a Antoniyo de Vera
	los brazos.
Juan de Alba	Antón, amigo.
Antón	*También venimos an guerras.*
Doña Leonor	Y a mí me abrazad también,	1030
	aunque ya no se os acuerda
	de quién soy.
Juan de Alba	No caigo en vos.
Doña Leonor	Yo soy Esteban.
Juan de Alba	¿Qué Esteban?
Doña Leonor	Esteban, el que servía
	al prior Don Juan.
Juan de Alba	Las señas	1035
	conozco, mas no me acuerdo
	de vos.
Doña Leonor	Al fin, de una tierra
	somos los dos.
Juan de Alba	¿Y qué os trae
	a estos países?
Doña Leonor	La fuerza
	de mis estrellas, que son	1040
	rigurosas mis estrellas.
Juan de Alba	Pues ¿qué pretendéis?
Doña Leonor	Servir,
	amigo, hasta que edad tenga,
	a un capitán, pues soy propio
	para paje de jineta.	1045

1023 ***Dos plazas sean las vuestras.*** Receiving double pay – the pay corresponding to two soldiers – was not an unusual practice to reward merit in the Spanish military. See Olmedo Gobante's essay in this volume.

DUKE DE ALBA	Since you have two firearms,
	Let's give you twice the salary of a soldier.

They exit. JUAN DE ALBA, DOÑA LEONOR and ANTÓN, remain on stage.

JUAN DE ALBA	By God, Great Sir,
	I shall fight for two hundred more!
DOÑA LEONOR	Come, let's talk to him.
ANTÓN	*Ah brother!*
	Give little Antón de Vera
	Your arms.
JUAN DE ALBA	Antón, my friend.
ANTÓN	*We came here to fight too.*
DOÑA LEONOR	And embrace me too,
	Although you no longer remember
	Who I am.
JUAN DE ALBA	I am drawing a blank.
DOÑA LEONOR	I am Esteban.
JUAN DE ALBA	What Esteban?
DOÑA LEONOR	Esteban, the one who served
	The prior Don Juan.
JUAN DE ALBA	I remember
	Those details, but I don't remember
	You.
DOÑA LEONOR	Anyway, we are both
	From the same country.
JUAN DE ALBA	What brings you
	To these lands?
DOÑA LEONOR	The power
	Of my stars; for they are
	Very cruel.
JUAN DE ALBA	So, what do you seek?
DOÑA LEONOR	To serve,
	My friend, a captain,
	Until I'm old enough, because I'm fit
	To be a Captain's page;

Toma a JUAN DE ALBA *de las manos.*

JUAN DE ALBA	Y mirad que habéis de ser muy mi amigo.
	(No me suena a católico este paje; mucho las manos me aprieta. No quisiera que un buen día 1050 nos diera…)
DOÑA LEONOR	¿Dónde os hospedan?
JUAN DE ALBA	Donde me coge la noche. No tengo posada cierta.
DOÑA LEONOR	Pues venid y elegid una donde regalarnos puedan⁺, 1055 que yo traigo aquí dineros.
JUAN DE ALBA	(Mucho este paje me aprieta).
DOÑA LEONOR	Los dos dormiremos juntos.
JUAN DE ALBA	Yo huelo, amigo, a gragea, y por eso duermo solo. 1060
DOÑA LEONOR	Yo, no es posible que duerma sin compañía.
JUAN DE ALBA	Antón puede dormir con vos.
ANTÓN	*¡Guardan fuera!*⁺ *¿Yo con brancos? ¡Osten putas!*
DOÑA LEONOR	(Bien mi venganza se ordena. 1065 Disimula, Antón).
ANTÓN	*(Simulo).*
DOÑA LEONOR	(No me ha conocido). ¿Hay cerca de aquí hostería?
JUAN DE ALBA	No sé.

1059 *Grajea* (sweet candy). "Gragea. Una especie de confitura muy menuda." ["A kind sweet candy in the form of very small pills"] (Covarrubias 2020, 993). This may be a play on words with *grajo* (rook), and the presumed bad smell of Black people. "Heder a grajos, es de negros" ["To smell like a rook, referring to Blacks"] (Covarrubias 2020, 1033). See Fra-Molinero's essay.

She takes JUAN DE ALBA's hands.

	And know that you are to be
	My very best friend.
JUAN DE ALBA	*[Aside]* This page doesn't sound
	Like a Catholic to me.
	He squeezes my hands a lot.
	I wouldn't want one
	fine day to be f…
DOÑA LEONOR	Where are you staying?
JUAN DE ALBA	Wherever the night catches me.
	I don't have a particular place to stay.
DOÑA LEONOR	Then come and choose one
	Where I can spoil you rotten,
	For I bring here money.
JUAN DE ALBA	*[Aside]* This page squeezes me a lot.
DOÑA LEONOR	We'll both sleep together.
JUAN DE ALBA	Friend, I smell like pig farm
	And that's why I sleep alone.
DOÑA LEONOR	It is not possible for me to sleep
	Without company.
JUAN DE ALBA	Antón can
	Sleep with you.
ANTÓN	*Get out!*
	Me with White folks? Forget that!
DOÑA LEONOR	(I will get my revenge now;
	Play along, Antón.)
ANTÓN	*I'll play along.*
DOÑA LEONOR	(He hasn't recognized me).
	Is there an inn nearby?
JUAN DE ALBA	I don't know.

DOÑA LEONOR	¿Conmigo tanta extrañeza?
	Ved que de la patria somos.	1070
	Tomad mi mano.
JUAN DE ALBA	Es muy tierna
	y muy blanca, y tiznarase.
DOÑA LEONOR	Antes es la taracea
	vistosa.
JUAN DE ALBA	(¿Hay tal apretar?)
DOÑA LEONOR	Venid, y os haré en la mesa	1075
	dos brindis a la salud.
JUAN DE ALBA	Yo tengo la salud buena.
DOÑA LEONOR	¡Qué arisco sois!
JUAN DE ALBA	Soy demonio.
DOÑA LEONOR	Yo os haré, con mis ternezas
	y mis cariños y halagos,	1080
	amoroso.
JUAN DE ALBA	Mas ¿qué queman
	a este maricón?
DOÑA LEONOR	Venid,
	que me come la moneda.
JUAN DE ALBA	¡Válgate el diablo por paje
	y quien te trujo a esta tierra!	1085

1073 **Taracea**. Wood inlay. A racialized sexual reference. Leonor/Esteban indicates that the two of them together in bed would be like the darker and lighter pieces in a wood inlay.

Doña Leonor	Why are you being so timid with me?
	We're from the same country;
	Take my hand.
Juan de Alba	It is too soft
	And white, and it will tarnish.
Doña Leonor	On the contrary! Inlay is attractive
	Because it interlaces black and white.
Juan de Alba	*[Aside]* Again with the hand squeezing?
Doña Leonor	Come, and at a tavern
	I'll toast twice to your health.
Juan de Alba	I am in excellent health.
Doña Leonor	How unfriendly you are!
Juan de Alba	I am a demon.
Doña Leonor	I will make you loving with
	my tenderness, affections,
	and my adulation.
Juan de Alba	What? Why don't they burn
	this faggot?
Doña Leonor	Come,
	I want to spend some coins.
Juan de Alba	The hell with this devil for a page
	and whomever brought you here!

JORNADA SEGUNDA

Sale JUAN DE ALBA solo.

JUAN DE ALBA   Loco estoy, aunque el favor
lo debo a mi atrevimiento.
Ya el Duque me ha hecho sargento
a pesar de mi color.
Ya la Fortuna me aprueba   1090
a merecimientos grandes.
Ya hay sargento negro en Flandes:
fruta nueva, fruta nueva.
Y estoy en parte corrido
por no haber hecho facción   1095
notable en el escuadrón
contrario, y no haber traído
dos alabardas o tres,
con sus sargentos. *Grambot,*
moltuín, butir, estricot[+],   1100
cerveza, flinflán, porque es
lengua peor que la mía,
donde negro bozal soy.
Para mí, en Guinea estoy,
que por yerro blancos cría;   1105
pero aquí Barrientos viene,
y mis contrarios con él.
Retírome.

Se esconde. Sale el SARGENTO BARRIENTOS con alabarda, y los capitanes DON AGUSTÍN, DON PEDRO Y DON JUAN.

1100   ***Moltuín, butir, estricot***. These words are an imitation of the Dutch language. See the essays by Olmedo Gobante and Fra-Molinero in this volume.

1101   ***Negro Bozal***. "Boçal. El negro que no sabe otra lengua que la suya" ["*Bozal*: The Black man who does not know any language but his own"] (Covarrubias 2020, 350). It often referred to enslaved Black people whose Spanish was deemed defective. See Fra-Molinero's essay in this volume and the essay 'Antón's Linguistic Blackface'.

ACT TWO

Enter JUAN DE ALBA, Alone

JUAN DE ALBA   I cannot believe it, though I owe
                    The favor I receive to my boldness.
                    I am a sergeant now by the Duke's hand
                    In spite of my color.
                    Fortune allows me now
                    To claim greater rewards.
                    Flanders now has a black sergeant:
                    Fresh meat, fresh meat.
                    However, I am quite ashamed
                    For not making an amazing incursion
                    In the enemy's camp, and not bringing
                    Two or three halberds,
                    With some of their sergeants. *Grambutt,*
                    Molten, burr, street clod,
                    Mead, flin vlaai! This
                    Tongue is worse than mine,
                    Where I am a new Black slave.
                    I am thinking I am in Africa
                    populated by Whites,
                    But here comes Barrientos,
                    And my enemies with him.
                    I shall hide.

He hides. Enter SERGEANT BARRIENTOS with a halberd, and Captains DON AGUSTÍN, DON PEDRO AND DON JUAN.

CAPITÁN DON AGUSTÍN	¡Acción cruel!	
SARGENTO BARRIENTOS	Digo otra vez que no tiene	
	honor el que ya es sargento	1110
	donde lo es un negro vil.	
JUAN DE ALBA	(¡Oh envidia, monstruo civil	
	del más generoso intento!)	
CAPITÁN DON PEDRO	Ha dado el Duque en honrallo	
	porque es negro.	
CAPITÁN DON JUAN	Y porque ha sido	1115
	más dichoso que atrevido.	
JUAN DE ALBA	(¡Que esto sufro y que esto callo!)	
CAPITÁN DON PEDRO	Ha hecho muchas facciones	
	notables.	
CAPITÁN DON AGUSTÍN	Es temerario.	
CAPITÁN DON JUAN	Ya en el campo del contrario	1120
	temen sus resoluciones.	
CAPITÁN DON AGUSTÍN	Él es soldado, mas es	
	negro al fin.	
SARGENTO BARRIENTOS	Hoy la alabarda	
	he de dejar.	
CAPITÁN DON AGUSTÍN	Es gallarda	
	resolución, y los tres	1125
	habemos de hacer que todos⁺	
	los sargentos se amotinen.	
JUAN DE ALBA	(¡Que caballeros se inclinen	
	al mal por tan viles modos!	
	¡Vive Dios, que he de afrentallos	1130
	delante del general!	
	Pagar tengo mal con mal).	
CAPITÁN DON JUAN	Vamos, que en amotinallos	
	consiste que la jineta	
	le quite el Duque.	

Vanse los capitanes y quedan solos JUAN DE ALBA *y el* SARGENTO BARRIENTOS.

1127 *Se amotinen*. Mutinies were frequent in the Spanish army of Flanders. See Olmedo Gobante's essay in this volume.

CAPTAIN DON AGUSTÍN	Cruel affair!
SERGEANT BARRIENTOS	I'll say it again, there is no honor In being a sergeant Where a vile Black man is one!
JUAN DE ALBA	*[Aside]* Oh, envy, you vicious monster Against every noble intention.
CAPTAIN DON PEDRO	The Duke grants this honor, Because he's Black.
CAPTAIN DON JUAN	And he's been more fortunate, Than brave.
JUAN DE ALBA	*[Aside]* To endure this and hold my tongue!
CAPTAIN DON PEDRO	He has accomplished many remarkable Actions.
CAPTAIN DON AGUSTÍN	He's been reckless.
CAPTAIN DON JUAN	In the enemy's camp They dread his raids.
CAPTAIN DON AGUSTÍN	He is a soldier, yet In the end, he is Black.
SERGEANT BARRIENTOS	I shall resign from my post today And I'll turn in my halberd.
CAPTAIN DON AGUSTÍN	That is very brave of you, And the three of us Shall get the other sergeants to mutiny.
JUAN DE ALBA	*[Aside]* That these gentlemen sink So low by such vile actions! God's my witness! I will make A fool of them in front of the General; I shall pay evil, with evil.
CAPTAIN DON JUAN	Come, by staging this mutiny Our aim is to have the Duke Strip him of his command.

Exit the Captains. JUAN DE ALBA And SERGEANT BARRIENTOS remain on stage.

JUAN DE ALBA	(¡Una hormiga 1135
	tanto la envidia fatiga!
	Mas la virtud la sujeta,
	y esto es todo acrisolarme).
SARGENTO BARRIENTOS	Yo por otra parte voy,
	pues el agraviado soy, 1140
	a perseguirle y vengarme.
JUAN DE ALBA	(Esta es gallarda ocasión;
	quiero salirle al encuentro).
SARGENTO BARRIENTOS	(Este es el perro. Cogiome
	donde escaparme no puedo). 1145
	Buenos días.
JUAN DE ALBA	Buenas noches,
	dirá.
SARGENTO BARRIENTOS	¿Por qué?
JUAN DE ALBA	Porque llevo
	las noches siempre conmigo
	y, amaneciendo, anochezco.
	Los blancos son buenos días 1150
	y malas noches los prietos,
	y así, porque siempre andamos
	a escuras, vamos con tiento;
	mas, porque sé que ha de holgarse
	de mis felices sucesos, 1155
	el seor sargento sabrá
	que todos somos sargentos.
SARGENTO BARRIENTOS	Ya lo he sabido y me he holgado.
JUAN DE ALBA	De sus ausencias lo creo.
	Sargento soy, porque el Duque 1160
	ha dado, sin merecerlo,
	en honrarme; mas me falta
	la alabarda y yo no tengo
	blanca con que comprar una,
	mas ¡qué mucho, si soy negro! 1165
	Y así, atento a que soy pobre
	y atento a que lo merezco,
	me ha de honrar vuesa merced
	con la suya, que deseo

JUAN DE ALBA	*[Aside]* O, envy,
	how you torment the ant!
	But virtue restrains it,
	And what doesn't kill you, makes you strong.
SERGEANT BARRIENTOS	I'm going this way,
	For I am the one who's been disrespected,
	And I want to find him and take revenge.
JUAN DE ALBA	*[Aside]* This is my chance,
	Let me stand in his way.
SERGEANT BARRIENTOS	*[Aside]* This is the dog. I am trapped
	And I can't run away from him.
	Good morning.
JUAN DE ALBA	Good evening,
	You should say.
SERGEANT BARRIENTOS	Why is that?
JUAN DE ALBA	Because the night and I are one,
	And under the sun, I am still Black.
	Whites have pleasant days,
	Blacks have miserable nights;
	And since we always walk
	in the dark, we tread carefully;
	But I am sure you will be
	Excited by the good news,
	For as you know, mister Sergeant,
	We are all sergeants.
SERGEANT BARRIENTOS	I've heard, and I'm happy for you.
JUAN DE ALBA	By your absences, I believe it.
	I am a Sergeant, because the Duke
	Has given me,
	Despite my unworthy condition,
	This honor. But I lack a halberd,
	And have no coin to purchase one;
	What am I saying? I am just a Black man.
	So knowing that I am poor,
	And agreeing that I deserve it,
	You, Sir, will grant me this honor
	With your halberd. I hope to

| | ennoblecer mi negrura | 1170 |
| | con los honores ajenos. |

SARGENTO BARRIENTOS Quisiera, para servirle,
tener otra.

JUAN DE ALBA   Pues por eso
quiero la que tiene sola.
Trate de dármela luego   1175
o, ¡vive Dios!, que conmigo
se ha de matar, que ya el tiempo
nos hizo a los dos iguales
aunque yo no me contento
con ser su igual.

SARGENTO BARRIENTOS   Ser mi igual   1180
puede el Rey.

JUAN DE ALBA   Pues yo no quiero
–sin ser rey de Monicongo,
sino un cuitado moreno–
ser su igual.

Toma JUAN DE ALBA *la alabarda*[+].

                              Y esta le quito
por saber que está resuelto   1185
a dejarla; y porque vea
que, aunque negro, la merezco
más bien que él, a cuchilladas
aquí los dos la ganemos.

La pone en el suelo[+].

                              Aquí en el suelo la pongo: 1190
llegue y álcela del suelo,
saque la espada y rescate
su alabarda.

1181 **Ser igual al rey**. The king, as a *bellator*, or warrior, was technically a member of the same estate as a poor rank-and-file soldier. The other estates were *oratores* – those who pray – and *laboratores* – those who do manual work. This medieval ideal hierarchical system did not reflect the reality of early modern society.

	Ennoble my Blackness
	With the honors of others.
SERGEANT BARRIENTOS	I wish I had another one,
	To serve you.
JUAN DE ALBA	That is why
	I want the one you have.
	Come, give it up then,
	Or by God, we shall both
	Fight to the death; since time
	Has made us both equals in rank,
	Although I am not satisfied
	To be called your equal.
SERGEANT BARRIENTOS	Only the King is my equal.
JUAN DE ALBA	Well Sir, I would not want
	– Even if I was King Monkey Congo –
	To be your equal, when I'm just
	A pitiful Black man.

Juan takes the halberd

And I'll keep this,
Because I know you were planning
To give it up. And because I see that,
Even though I'm Black, I deserve it
more than you. Let us cross swords,
And try right here to win it.

He places it on the floor

I'll put it here on the ground.
Come, pick it up,
Draw your sword, and
Rescue your halberd.

SARGENTO BARRIENTOS   Este desprecio
no se hace a mí, al Duque se hace
y al Rey.

Saca BARRIENTOS *la espada*⁺.

JUAN DE ALBA   Pues vuelva por ellos,   1195
aunque yo, honrando su oficio,
solo a la alabarda llego
por ver que no la merece.
Y si está sentido de esto
y no se atreve por solo,   1200
junte todos los sargentos
y traigan las alabardas;
que, sin dejar este puesto
y sin desnudar la espada,
haré con todos lo mesmo.   1205
SARGENTO BARRIENTOS   Yo me voy.
JUAN DE ALBA   Vaya en buen hora
y envaine, que bien lo ha hecho.
SARGENTO BARRIENTOS   ¡Vive Dios!

Vase BARRIENTOS⁺.

JUAN DE ALBA   Y ¡vive Dios!,
que si me enojo y emperro,
que le haga al sargento blanco   1210
que obre más y que hable menos.
No lleva muy buen olor,
a buscar algún sahumerio
debe de ir con priesa tal.
Este ha de ser escarmiento   1215
de los demás.

Toma la alabarda⁺.

                               Bien me está
la alabarda, ya parezco
otro hombre; ya me ha infundido
alma y espíritu nuevo
para aspirar a ser más   1220

SERGEANT BARRIENTOS	Your insult and scorn,
	Are not aimed at me, rather at the duke,
	And our Majesty the King!

BARRIENTOS draws his sword.

JUAN DE ALBA	Well, go on and avenge them.
	Although honoring your rank,
	I only come for the halberd
	Since I see you don't deserve it.
	And if you hurt because of this,
	And you can't fight for yourself,
	Gather all the sergeants,
	And bring all the halberds;
	For without leaving this post
	And without drawing my sword,
	I will do the same to you all.
SERGEANT BARRIENTOS	I will go now.
JUAN DE ALBA	Go, in due time,
	And sheathe your sword; that's being a good boy.
SERGEANT BARRIENTOS	For God's sake!

BARRIENTOS exits.

JUAN DE ALBA	And, for God's sake!
	For if I become an angry rabid dog,
	I will force the white Sergeant
	To do more and talk less.
	He smells like crap.
	He has left in such haste,
	To cover the smell with sweet incense.
	He'll serve as an example
	To others.

He takes the halberd.

This halberd
Suits me well, I already
Feel like another man. It has given me
A new soul and spirit
To aspire to be more

con generosos trofeos.
¡Ea, Fortuna!, ya estoy
en el escalón tercero.
Si el planeta quinto es Marte,
para llegar a su cielo   1225
dos escalones me faltan.

Salen Doña Leonor vestida de paje y Antón⁺.

DOÑA LEONOR   Apenas, Antón, acierto
                   a decirte mi alegría.
JUAN DE ALBA   (A todo el campo, no temo,
                   contrario; y temo a este paje   1230
                   que me va oliendo a brasero
                   tanto como ámbar y algalia).
DOÑA LEONOR   Entre tus brazos celebro
                   mi alegría.
ANTÓN   *Turu samo*
                   contentos con sus contentos.   1235
DOÑA LEONOR   Conociome el capitán.
ANTÓN   *¿Qué decimo?*
DOÑA LEONOR   Lo que es cierto,
                   y con lágrimas y halagos
                   y con mil suspiros tiernos,
                   me ha dado tantas disculpas.   1240
ANTÓN   *¡Seso Antoniyo perdemo!*
                   Damo para que besamo
                   esa mano.
JUAN DE ALBA   (¡Malo es esto!)
ANTÓN   *Es buen cagayera.*
DOÑA LEONOR   En fin,
                   me ha dicho que nos iremos   1245
                   tras de aquesta retirada
                   que hace el Duque; y encubierto,
                   quiere que ande así hasta entonces.

1232 *Ámbar y algalía.* Juan is speculating that the perfume Esteban is using (amber and civet) is a sign of luxury, effiminacy, and sodomy. He calls for the page to be sentenced to death and burned (*brasero*), as was customary. For the discussion of the same-sex seduction, see Fra-Molinero's essay in this volume.

With noble rewards.
Look, Fortune! I am already on
The third step. If the fifth planet is
Mars, to reach its heaven,
I need two more steps.

Enter DOÑA LEONOR dressed as a pageboy and ANTÓN.

DOÑA LEONOR	Oh Antón, I can barely put into
	Words how happy I am.
JUAN DE ALBA	*[Aside]* I fear no one in the enemy camp,
	Yet I fear this page, who reeks,
	Like burned embers and arse.
DOÑA LEONOR	In your arms I celebrate
	My happiness!
ANTÓN	*We all are thrilled*
	With your thrills!
DOÑA LEONOR	The captain recognized me.
ANTÓN	*What did he say to us?*
DOÑA LEONOR	What is true;
	And with tears and compliments,
	And with a thousand tender sighs,
	Has given me so many apologies.
ANTÓN	*What? Little Antón is flabbergasted,*
	Give us your hands
	To kiss.
JUAN DE ALBA	*[Aside]* This is bad!
ANTÓN	*He's a good dung, I mean Don.*
DOÑA LEONOR	To be brief,
	He says we are going to leave
	After the Duke's planned withdrawal.
	He wants me to remain in disguise
	Until the time to leave is near.

ANTÓN	*Quieran Dioso que pasemo*	
	a España.	
DOÑA LEONOR	En ella verás	1250
	mis dichosos casamientos.	
ANTÓN	*¿Habrá notables comiras*	
	y culaciones diversos?	
	¿Grangea, culobesate	
	y cagalones?	
JUAN DE ALBA	(No tengo	1255
	enojo yo con el paje	
	–que este es vicioso en efecto–,	
	mas con Antonillo, sí.	
	¡Que haya dado en esto el perro	
	y que a afrentar pase a Flandes	1260
	el color que yo ennoblezco!	
	Antes que me descomponga,	
	importa poner remedio	
	en este fuego).	
DOÑA LEONOR	Aquí está	
	nuestro amigo.	
ANTÓN	*Sioro.*	
DOÑA LEONOR	Espero	1265
	sellar mi gusto en tus brazos.	
JUAN DE ALBA	¡Detente!	
DOÑA LEONOR	¿Al amor que muestro	
	tenerte? Es hacerme agravio⁺.	
JUAN DE ALBA	Yo, a los hombres, desde lejos	
	los abrazo.	

1253 **Culaciones diversos**. *Colaciones diversas* (various meals). For Antón's *habla de negros* and the use of scatological language, see the co-authored essay in this volume.

1255–1254 **Grangea, culobesate y cagalones**. Antón mentions three sweet desserts. *Garagea* is *grajea* (see line 1059); *culobesate* (kiss your ass) is *calabazate*, a confection made with pumpkin rind covered in honey or syrup, whereas *cagalones* (turds) refers to a type of fried dough still called by the same name in the area around Seville. A similar food catalog may be found in Simón Aguado's *Entremés de los negros* (1602; edited in Santos Morillo 2020, 414–23).

ANTÓN	*God willing we will make*
	It into Spain.
DOÑA LEONOR	Once we arrive, you will see
	The most delightful marriage!
ANTÓN	*Will there some fany meals*
	And some serious tasting?
	Crème booboole, fried fritters, and
	pahteh of far grass?
JUAN DE ALBA	*[Aside]* I'm not angry
	with the page,
	– He is quite the pervert indeed – ;
	However, with Antón, I am;
	That this dog has given into this
	Behavior and come to Flanders
	To stain the color, I ennoble!
	Before I lose my self-control,
	I must put an end
	To this wildfire.)
DOÑA LEONOR	Here comes our
	Loving friend.
ANTÓN	*Seh.*
DOÑA LEONOR	I hope to seal my happiness
	By embracing you!
JUAN DE ALBA	Stop!
DOÑA LEONOR	To disdain this
	Love? It's doing me wrong.
JUAN DE ALBA	I usually embrace men
	From a distance.

DOÑA LEONOR	Eso es ser piedra.	1270
JUAN DE ALBA	Soy piedra en el sufrimiento.	
DOÑA LEONOR	Yo, a los amigos que tienen	
	las partes de Juan, los quiero,	
	los amo, estimo y regalo;	
	y en mi mesa los asiento,	1275
	porque es la cama y la mesa⁺	
	lisonja de los deseos.	
JUAN DE ALBA	Eso, en Italia.	
DOÑA LEONOR	Dejando	
	aparte estos argumentos,	
	sabed que he hallado a mi gusto	1280
	un capitán de quien pienso	
	jamás apartarme. Es hombre	
	galán, hermoso y discreto,	
	y me regala y estima;	
	mas al fin, es caballero	1285
	de Mérida.	
JUAN DE ALBA	¿Es por ventura	
	Don Agustín?	
DOÑA LEONOR	Es él mesmo:	
	ese es mi dueño y señor.	
JUAN DE ALBA	Tenéis un gallardo dueño.	
DOÑA LEONOR	Y a vos os lo debo.	
JUAN DE ALBA	¿A mí?	1290
DOÑA LEONOR	Sí, amigo, a vos os lo debo.	
JUAN DE ALBA	¿A mí?	
DOÑA LEONOR	A vos, vos me le disteis.	
JUAN DE ALBA	¡Vive Dios, que no me acuerdo!	
	¡Válgate el diablo por paje!	
	(Los demonios le trajeron	1295
	para perseguirme. Estoy	
	por arrojarlo al infierno	
	de un puntapié).	
DOÑA LEONOR	Amigo, adiós,	
	y a la noche nos veremos,	
	que voy tras del capitán.	1300
	¿Dónde dormís?	

DOÑA LEONOR	That is being cold as stone.
JUAN DE ALBA	That's me, a stone in suffering.
DOÑA LEONOR	To me, the friends who have
	Juan's parts, I want them,
	I love, esteem, and adore them,
	And at my table I seat them,
	For the bed and the table are
	The blandishments of desire.
JUAN DE ALBA	That's in Italy.
DOÑA LEONOR	Let us,
	Leave that discussion for later,
	And know that have found to my
	Liking a captain, who I never intend
	To leave; He's a man
	Gallant, gorgeous, and discreet,
	And he showers me with such favors.
	In short, he's a nobleman
	From Mérida.
JUAN DE ALBA	Is this man by any chance
	Don Agustín?
DOÑA LEONOR	The one and only;
	He's my lord and my master.
JUAN DE ALBA	You have a very gallant master.
DOÑA LEONOR	And I owe it all to you.
JUAN DE ALBA	To me?
DOÑA LEONOR	Yes, my friend, I owe it all to you.
JUAN DE ALBA	To me?
DOÑA LEONOR	To you; you gave him to me.
JUAN DE ALBA	As God lives, I do not remember.
	The devil be damned for a page!
	[Aside] Demons brought him here to
	Hound me. I am about to
	Send him back to hell
	With the tip of my boot.
DOÑA LEONOR	Goodbye, my friend,
	And I will see you tonight;
	I go now after my Captain.
	Where do you sleep?

JUAN DE ALBA	¿Dónde duermo?
	En un pantano: hasta aquí
	el lodo.
DOÑA LEONOR	Antón y yo iremos
	allá con algún regalo
	y un *pot* de cerveza.
JUAN DE ALBA	Bebo 1305
	poco de noche.
DOÑA LEONOR	No he visto
	negro tan padre del yermo.
	A reveder. (De esta suerte
	lo confundo y lo divierto.
	Disimula, Antón).
ANTÓN	(*Simulo*). 1310
DOÑA LEONOR	(La libertad te va en ello).
ANTÓN	*¿Dónde vamo angora?*
DOÑA LEONOR	Voy
	tras mi dueño, que me pierdo
	por su talle y su donaire.
	¿No es muy lindo, no es muy bello 1315
	y no tengo muy buen gusto?
ANTÓN	*Seoro, sí.*

Vase DOÑA LEONOR.

JUAN DE ALBA	¡Qué deshonesto
	y qué lascivo demonio!
	Ya acabó de echar el sello
	Don Agustín a su infamia, 1320
	mas jamás se esperó menos
	de un hombre alindado. ¡Y tú,
	negro vil!
ANTÓN	*¿Yo sa vil negro?*
JUAN DE ALBA	¡Vive el cielo, que te mate!
ANTÓN	*¿Por qué Juan matar queremo* 1325
	a Antoniyo?

1306 *A reveder*. See you later. A common Spanish interpretation of the Italian *a rivederci*. See Olmedo Gobante's essay in this volume for this and other examples of multilingualism in the Spanish Army of Flanders.

JUAN DE ALBA	Where do I sleep?
	In a dirty, musty swamp,
	Up to here in mud.
DOÑA LEONOR	Antón and I will come
	Over with some treats
	And a pot of beer.
JUAN DE ALBA	I barely
	Drink at night.
DOÑA LEONOR	I've never seen
	A Black man be the lord of the hermits.
	Arrivederci, [Aside] In this way,
	I confuse him and play with him.
	Antón, let us pretend and play roles.
ANTÓN	*[Aside] Role play and pretend, that I know.*
DOÑA LEONOR	Your freedom depends on it.
ANTÓN	*Where are we going now?*
DOÑA LEONOR	I'm going
	After my master because I lose myself
	In his figure and his charms!
	Isn't he gorgeous? Isn't he beautiful?
	And don't I have excellent taste?
ANTÓN	*Yes Seh.*

Exit Doña Leonor.

JUAN DE ALBA	What a lewd
	And lustful demon!
	Don Agustín outdid himself
	With this one, but one cannot
	Expect less from a foppish
	Man. And you, Vile
	Black man!
ANTÓN	*I'm a Black vile man?*
JUAN DE ALBA	For heaven's sake! I will kill you.
ANTÓN	*Why does Juan want to kill*
	Little Antón?

JUAN DE ALBA	Vil, si más
	con este paje te veo
	en estos países nunca,
	en público o en secreto,
	te he de quemar.
ANTÓN	*¿Pues quién damo* 1330
	comira a Antón?
JUAN DE ALBA	Yo.
ANTÓN	*Comiendo*
	Antón, al paje olvidamo
	y a Juan por sior tendremo.
	Vamo y llevamo alabarda.
JUAN DE ALBA	¿Prometes lealtad?
ANTÓN	*Plumeto.* 1335
JUAN DE ALBA	Pues toma y sígueme.
ANTÓN	*Vamo.*
JUAN DE ALBA	Más a espacio y más severo.
ANTÓN	*Aspacio y severo andamo.*
JUAN DE ALBA	Antonillo, ¿qué parezco?
ANTÓN	*Rey Mago y yo sun lacayo.* 1340
JUAN DE ALBA	¡Antón!
ANTÓN	*¿Sioro?*
JUAN DE ALBA	Respeto,
	que soy sargento de Flandes.
ANTÓN	*Turu lu mundo sabemo.*
JUAN DE ALBA	Antón.
ANTÓN	*¿Sioro?*
JUAN DE ALBA	Camina.
ANTÓN	*Parece cosa de neglos.* 1345

Vanse. Salen el DUQUE DE ALBA *y los capitanes* DON AGUSTÍN, DON PEDRO
y DON JUAN[+].

DUQUE DE ALBA	A nuestro honor y a la opinión de España
	la retirada es vil y es afrentosa.

1345   ***Cosa de neglos*** or *cosa de morenos* (a Black people thing) may have meant
nonsense (Woodhouse 2007, 299).

JUAN DE ALBA	Villain! If I ever
	See you with this page
	In these countries,
	In public or in secret,
	I'm going to burn you.
ANTÓN	*Who will put food in*
	Antón's mouth?
JUAN DE ALBA	Me.
ANTÓN	*Well, if*
	Antón is fed the page he'll forget,
	And takes Juan as his Lord.
	Let's go and we'll carry the halberd.
JUAN DE ALBA	Do you promise loyalty?
ANTÓN	*I promise.*
JUAN DE ALBA	Then take it and walk this way.
ANTÓN	*Let's go.*
JUAN DE ALBA	Slowly and give me more space.
ANTÓN	*Slowly and we walk with more space.*
JUAN DE ALBA	Little Antón, how do I look?
ANTÓN	*Like the Wise King, and I'm his lackey.*
JUAN DE ALBA	Antón?
ANTÓN	*Seh?*
JUAN DE ALBA	Show some respect;
	For I am a sergeant of Flanders now.
ANTÓN	*Everybody knows it by now.*
JUAN DE ALBA	Antón?
ANTÓN	*Seh?*
JUAN DE ALBA	March.
ANTÓN	*This must be a Black thing.*

They exit. Enter the DUKE OF ALBA *and captain* DON AGUSTÍN, DON PEDRO, *and* DON JUAN.

DUKE OF ALBA	In the eyes of Spain and to our honor,
	The withdrawal is both contemptible and offensive.

CAPITÁN DON PEDRO[+]	Pues muramos, señor, en la campaña,
	porque vivir es imposible cosa.
	El invierno es terrible, y es extraña 1350
	la injuria de sus nieves, que en copiosa
	multitud se desata de los cielos,
	y todo es confusión y todo es hielos.
CAPITÁN DON AGUSTÍN	Los cuarteles están en los pantanos,
	y en agua y lama los soldados todos, 1355
	sobre quien nada la fajina y ramos
	resisten la Fortuna entre los lodos.
	Cada día soldados sepultamos
	que amanecen helados.
DUQUE DE ALBA	De mil modos
	nos contrasta el invierno, mas su extraña 1360
	furia no ha de poder triunfar de España.
	Resístanse las nieves y los hielos,
	las aguas y pantanos rigurosos,
	y entiendan los rebeldes que los cielos
	nos hacen contra el tiempo poderosos. 1365
	Vistamos de temor y de desvelos
	sus escuadrones locos y orgullosos,
	y conozcan, en dulce eterna salva,
	que nace el Sol aquí y que aquí está el Alba.
CAPITÁN DON PEDRO	Afrentosa es, señor, la retirada[+] 1370
	con las infamias que el de Orange pide,
	pero más afrentosa y más pesada
	será la resistencia si se mide,
	en tan fuerte ocasión, espada a espada
	cuando el rigor la ejecución impide, 1375
	quedando, entre estos lodos y pantanos,
	la importancia de España entre sus manos.
CAPITÁN DON AGUSTÍN	Los rebeldes son hijos de la nieve[+]
	y están de puesto y sitio mejorados.

1356 ***Fajina***. Brushwood used for defensive purposes. See Olmedo Gobante's essay.

1374 ***Medir las espadas***. In sword fighting, to place oneself at a short but safe distance to make the condition of the two opponents equal, what was called *medio de proporción* in the school of La Verdadera Destreza.

CAPTAIN DON PEDRO	Then let us die, your Grace, in the campaign,
	Because living here is no longer attainable;
	The winter is unbearable, and the harshness
	Of the snow is extraordinary, unleashed
	In heaving bundles from the heavens.
	And it is all confusion and ice!
CAPTAIN DON AGUSTÍN	The camps are in the swamps,
	And our soldiers, knee deep in water and slime,
	Among twigs and branches,
	Resist their fate in the mud.
	Every day, at dawn, we bury soldiers,
	Found frozen at their post.
DUKE OF ALBA	Winter opposes us
	In a thousand fronts, yet its extreme rage
	Cannot triumph over Spain.
	Let us resist the snow and ice,
	The waters and rigorous swamps,
	And let the rebels understand that the heavens
	help us overcome adverse conditions.
	Let us endow their mad and proud squadrons
	With fear and sleeplessness,
	Letting them know in sweet eternal salute
	That the sun rises here, in the Duke of Alba.
CAPTAIN DON PEDRO	Your Grace, the withdrawal is an affront
	Because of the disgraceful demands
	by the Prince of Orange;
	Yet more dreadful and a heavier still
	Will be resisting, if measured
	On such strong occasion, sword to sword,
	When the rigor prevents the execution,
	Staying in this mud and these swamps
	The reputation of Spain remains in your hands.
CAPTAIN DON AGUSTÍN	The rebels are children of the snow,
	And they are in better and more
	Advantageous positions.

	No los ofende el agua, aunque más llueve,	1380
	ni el hielo, entre quien viven conservados.	
	El sitio donde están el agua embebe,	
	defendidos de montes y collados,	
	y nosotros tenemos, importunas,	
	a la espalda, señor, cuatro lagunas.	1385
	Y ansí es acción forzosa el retirarnos	
	por la puerta que el Príncipe promete,	
	ya que el invierno así quiso encerrarnos	
	y el agua en las trincheras se nos mete.	
DUQUE DE ALBA	Negras Pascuas el cielo quiso darnos,	1390

Disparan.

mas ¿qué es esto?

Sale JUAN DE ALBA con una bandera.

JUAN DE ALBA	Señor, no se inquiete	
	vuecelencia, aunque el campo así se altera,	
	porque agora le traigo esta bandera:	
	tapete sea de esos pies en tanto	
	que voy por todas las que el campo tiene.	1395
	Y hagan los capitanes otro tanto,	
	si un negro tanta infamia les previene.	
	Negro soy que hago y digo, y pongo espanto	
	a los que hablan y no hacen, si conviene	
	el hacer y el decir en blancos pechos,	1400
	hechos de azúcar y de alcorzas hechos.	
DUQUE DE ALBA	Basta, alférez Juan de Alba.	
JUAN DE ALBA	Esos pies beso	
	por la merced.	
DUQUE DE ALBA	Alzad vuestra bandera	
	y el furor reportad.	
JUAN DE ALBA	No ha sido exceso,	
	efecto ha sido de la envidia fiera,	1405
	que ha dado en perseguirme.	
DUQUE DE ALBA	Yo os confieso	
	que, a no ser yo, Juan de Alba, os la tuviera.	

	They are not bothered by water, even
	when it rains,
	Nor by ice, where they live preserved.
	The site where they are, the soil is dry,
	Well-defended by highlands and hills,
	And to our rear, your Grace, we have
	four disadvantageous lagoons.
	And thus, it is necessary action to withdraw
	Through the passageway that the Prince promises,
	Since the winter seems to box us in,
	While the waters in our trenches rise.
DUKE OF ALBA	The heavens wanted to give us a Black Christmas.

Shots offstage

But what is this?

Enter JUAN DE ALBA carrying a flag.

JUAN DE ALBA   Your Grace, do not be alarmed
Although the enemy's camp is in uproar,
Because I have brought you this banner;
Let it be a mat for those feet while
I go for all the ones the camp has.
I encourage the captains to do the same,
If Black men make them green with envy.
I am a Black man, who does as he says,
    and I put fear
In those who are all words but no action; if
White hearts made of sugar paste
Can say and do too.

DUKE OF ALBA   Enough, Lieutenant Juan de Alba.

JUAN DE ALBA   Your feet I kiss,
For such great honor.

DUKE OF ALBA   Raise your banner,
And restrain your anger.

JUAN DE ALBA   It has not been an excess,
It has been fueled by harsh envy,
Which has been shadowing me.

DUKE OF ALBA   I must confess,
If I weren't me, Juan de Alba, I would envy you.

	De la envidia os reíd, que es desdichado	
	el que por su virtud no es envidiado.	
JUAN DE ALBA	El perro de Alba soy, vengan judíos.	1410
DUQUE DE ALBA	Bueno está, alférez.	
JUAN DE ALBA	Gran señor, soy perro,	
	y así, muero con rabia.	

Sale el sargento BARRIENTOS.

SARGENTO BARRIENTOS	¡Desafíos	
	–en un frisón más cándido que el cerro	
	que nos mira deshecho en nieve y ríos	
	tascando en el bocado plata y hierro,	1415
	que de espuma se argenta en copos fríos–	
	un capitán tudesco pide a voces!	
JUAN DE ALBA	Él viene por puñetes y por coces.	
DUQUE DE ALBA	Vendrá por la bandera.	
JUAN DE ALBA	Señor, venga,	
	que yo se la daré.	
SARGENTO BARRIENTOS	Ya está en la plaza.	1420
JUAN DE ALBA	De cólera todo hombre se prevenga,	
	mas solo a capitanes amenaza.	
DUQUE DE ALBA	Llegue a mi tienda, nadie le detenga.	
JUAN DE ALBA	Temeraria presencia. Tiene traza	
	de comernos a todos. (Yo me alegro,	1425
	porque esta vez me he de escapar por negro).	

Sale MONS. DE VIVANBLEC RAVALLAC, *tudesco.*

MONS. DE VIVANBLEC	Guárdete Dios, Duque de Alba,	
	terror de nuestros países	
	y ocasión de tantas guerras	
	por los desastrados fines	1430
	del de Hornos y el de Agamón.	

1426 **Mons**. Abbreviation of the French term *Monsieur*. The text treats the abbreviation as a full word, as noted by the text's metric.

1430 **Hornos y Agamón**. The Counts of Horns and Egmont, the two Flemish leaders who were found guilty of treason and executed on the orders of the Duke of Alba in 1568. The *desastrados fines* of the text refers to their execution.

	Laugh at envy's face; he whose virtue
	Is not envied, is an unfortunate man.
JUAN DE ALBA	I am the Alba's dog; bring on the Jews.
DUKE OF ALBA	That's enough, Lieutenant.
JUAN DE ALBA	Grand Sir, I am a dog,
	And as such, I bite with rage.

Enter Sergeant BARRIENTOS.

SERGEANT BARRIENTOS	A challenge!
	– On a Friesian, white as the snow hills,
	Who looks at us drooling snow and rivers,
	Nibbling and silvering its iron mouthpiece,
	Turning the iron into silver icy flakes –
	A Flemish captain, demands a challenge.
JUAN DE ALBA	He'll get a boot on his backside and a bloody nose.
DUKE OF ALBA	He is coming for his banner.
JUAN DE ALBA	Ah Sir! Let
	Him come. I will give it to him.
SERGEANT BARRIENTOS	He is already in the courtyard.
JUAN DE ALBA	Everyone, put on your angry faces,
	Although he only threatens captains.
DUKE OF ALBA	Let him come to my tent
	And do not stop him.
JUAN DE ALBA	What a foolish display! He looks
	as he wants to kill us all. *[Aside]* I am glad,
	because this time as a Black man I won't
	have to work.

Enter MONS. *DE VIVANBLEC RAVALLAC, Flemish captain.*

MONS. DE VIVANBLEC	God save you, Duke of Alba,
	The terror of our countries,
	The cause of so many wars
	Provoked by the unfortunate end
	Of both counts, Hornes and Egmont.

DUQUE DE ALBA	Sin que otras causas publiques,
	la ocasión de tu venida
	me di, sin pecar de libre,
	porque no hay cosa en el mundo,
	flamenco, que más castigue.
MONS. DE VIVANBLEC	A mí solo castigarme
	puede el cielo, y aun…
DUQUE DE ALBA	Prosigue.
MONS. DE VIVANBLEC	Yo soy *Mons.* de Vivanblec
	y Ravallac.
JUAN DE ALBA	(Tan terrible
	es el nombre como el talle).
MONS. DE VIVANBLEC	Yo soy capitán que sigue
	la milicia del de Orange,
	cuya disciplina envidien
	los césares soberanos,
	que no fueron tan insignes.
DUQUE DE ALBA	Tienes razón. Yo te doy
	licencia que le sublimes
	sobre el sol, que es capitán
	valeroso e invencible,
	y al fin, príncipe de Orange,
	que es cuanto puede decirse.
MONS. DE VIVANBLEC	Estas son las condiciones,

1435

1440

1445

1450

Dale un papel al Duque.

	general, de tu infelice
	retirada.
DUQUE DE ALBA	Quiere el tiempo
	y el lugar que me retire.
MONS. DE VIVANBLEC	El primer día de Pascua
	ha de ser, o no habrá dique
	que contra ti no se suelte.
DUQUE DE ALBA	Yo me veré en ello, y dime
	si con embajada vienes.
MONS. DE VIVANBLEC	No vengo sino a pedirte
	campo con tus capitanes.

1455

1460

DUKE OF ALBA	Without any other favorable words,
	State the reason for your visit
	And choose your next words with care,
	Because there is nothing in the world,
	I would punish more, Flemish Dutchman.
MONS. DE VIVANBLEC	Only heaven can punish me
	And even…
DUKE OF ALBA	Get to the point.
MONS. DE VIVANBLEC	I am *Mons.* of Vivanblec
	And Ravallac.
JUAN DE ALBA	*[Aside]* His name
	Is as dreadful as his looks.
MONS. DE VIVANBLEC	I'm a captain who follows
	The forces of Orange,
	Whose discipline is envied
	By sovereign Caesars,
	Who were not as famous as him.
DUKE OF ALBA	You are certainly right, and I
	Grant you license to praise his name
	Above the sun, for he is a captain
	Who is brave and invincible,
	And of course, Prince of Orange
	That is all that can be said.
MONS. DE VIVANBLEC	These are the conditions,

Hands a document to the Duke.

	General, of your unfortunate
	Retreat.
DUKE OF ALBA	The adverse conditions demand
	My withdrawal.
MONS. OF VIVANBLEC	It must be
	By the first day of Christmas, or there
	Will not be a levee that will not be unleashed
	on you.
DUKE OF ALBA	I will see to it myself, and tell me,
	Do you have other demands to make?
MONS. OF VIVANBLEC	I do not, but I do ask for a challenge
	With your captains.

DUQUE DE ALBA   Uno elige[+].
MONS. DE VIVANBLEC   ¿Uno me dices?
                 Campo te vengo a pedir,   1465
                 Duque, con catorce o quince.
JUAN DE ALBA   Notable cólera traes:
                 ¿son tábanos o son chinches?
MONS. DE VIVANBLEC   Son españoles.
JUAN DE ALBA   Sí son,
                 pero quiero que imagines   1470
                 que para matarte basta
                 el soldado más humilde
                 del ejército de España,
                 sin que capitán se humille
                 a tan poca hazaña; y yo,   1475
                 si el Duque me lo permite,
                 que soy un negro, un esclavo
                 que a sus capitanes sirve,
                 te haré, soberbio alemán,
                 que con el alma vomites   1480
                 la cerveza que has bebido,
                 si no es Rin el que bebiste.

Coge JUAN DE ALBA a MONS. DE VIVANBLEC en brazos, y vase[+].

DUQUE DE ALBA   ¡Alférez!
JUAN DE ALBA *(dentro)*   Señor, ya vuelvo;
                 no haré más que dividirle
                 miembro a miembro por el campo.   1485
VIVANBLEC *(dentro)*   ¡Muerto soy!

Sale JUAN DE ALBA.

JUAN DE ALBA   Tú lo dijiste.
                 Ya Vivanblec Ravallac[+],
                 sin que más nos desafíe,
                 fue a cenar con Bercebú;
                 y pues capitán deshice,   1490
                 capitán es justo que haga
                 vuecelencia.

DUKE OF ALBA	So, choose one.
MONS. OF VIVANBLEC	Only one?
	Duke of Alba, I came to request a duel
	With fourteen or fifteen men.
JUAN DE ALBA	You are a remarkably angry person,
	Is it because of the horseflies or the bedbugs?
MONS. OF VIVANBLEC	It is because of the Spaniards!
JUAN DE ALBA	Yes, the Spaniards,
	But I want you to imagine
	That to kill you, it only takes
	The humblest soldier
	Of the Spanish army, so no Spanish
	Captain will debase himself
	With such foolish action. And I,
	If the duke grants me such grace,
	Being a Black man, a slave
	Who serves his captains,
	I'll have you, arrogant Dutchman,
	Throw up not only your soul
	But all the beer you drank,
	If it is not the Rhine you've drunk.

JUAN DE ALBA grabs MONS. *DE VIVANBLEC in his arms and exits.*

DUKE OF ALBA	Lieutenant Juan de Alba!
JUAN DE ALBA	*[Off stage]* Your Grace, I will be right back.
	I just need to sever his limbs
	And scatter them across the field.
VIVANBLEC	*[Off stage]* I'm done now!

Enter JUAN DE ALBA.

JUAN DE ALBA	You said it.
	Now Vivanblec Ravallac is
	Now longer able to make challenges,
	For he went to dine with Beelzebub.
	And since I made a captain disappear
	It is only fair to make me a captain,
	Your Grace.

DUQUE DE ALBA	A voces pide
	tal hazaña tan gran premio.
JUAN DE ALBA	Todas mis hazañas tiñe
	mi negro color.
DUQUE DE ALBA	Color 1495
	es que la Fama os le envidie.
	¡Ah, señores capitanes!,
	¿vuesas mercedes qué dicen?
CAPITÁN DON PEDRO	Que le dé vuestra excelencia,
	por hazaña tan insigne, 1500
	nuestras jinetas.
DUQUE DE ALBA	El campo
	por capitán os elige.
	Dadle las gracias.
JUAN DE ALBA	Señor,
	yo prometo de servirles
	esta merced.
CAPITÁN DON JUAN	Ya es razón 1505
	que nuestros brazos le estimen.
CAPITÁN DON PEDRO	Desde hoy, señor capitán,
	por su criado me estime.
CAPITÁN DON JUAN	Y a mí por su camarada.
CAPITÁN DON AGUSTÍN	Aquí los brazos confirmen 1510
	nuestra amistad.
JUAN DE ALBA	En mí tiene,
	si a un lacayuelo despide,
	un esclavo eternamente.
CAPITÁN DON AGUSTÍN	Yo le doy de despedirle
	la palabra, aunque sé yo 1515
	que por él ha de pedirme
	que le vuelva a casa.
JUAN DE ALBA	¿Yo?
	(Este paje me persigue
	más que el color. ¿Yo, por él?
	¿Esto el capitán me dice? 1520
	Llámeme negro, cobarde

DUKE OF ALBA	Such deed cries out For a great reward.
JUAN DE ALBA	All my deeds are stained by my black color.
DUKE OF ALBA	Your color Is to be envied by Fame. Ah, My dear captains! What say you, your noble sires?
CAPTAIN DON PEDRO	Your Grace, for such grand Action, give him our captain's, Spears.
DUKE OF ALBA	The camp Has chosen you as their captain. You should thank them.
JUAN DE ALBA	Your Lordship, I promise to serve them well With this privilege.
CAPTAIN DON JUAN	It's good enough for me To welcome you with open arms.
CAPTAIN DON PEDRO	From now on, captain, Regard me as your esteemed servant.
CAPTAIN DON JUAN	And consider me as your comrade-in-arms.
CAPTAIN DON AGUSTÍN	Let us embrace To confirm our bond.
JUAN DE ALBA	You will certainly Find in me, a slave of undying loyalty, If you decide to dismiss a certain page.
CAPTAIN DON AGUSTÍN	You have my word and assurance That I will discharge this servant, Though I know that on his behalf You'll ask me to bring him back.
JUAN DE ALBA	I? *[Aside]* This pageboy shadows me More than my color; Me do what For him? What is this captain Telling me? The day that I try to persuade Someone to do such thing,

	y zurdo, para que cifre	
	en mí todos los agravios	
	el día que a persuadirle	
	vaya tal cosa).	
Duque de Alba	Del muerto	1525
	el Príncipe ha de sentirse.	
Juan de Alba	Si él, señor, vino a matarnos,	
	la defensa se permite	
	al hombre; y cuando a vengarlo	
	blancos leones envíe,	1530
	yo perro negro seré,	
	y tus capitanes, tigres[+].	
Duque de Alba	Las condiciones ver quiero	
	de la retirada.	
Capitán Don Juan	Oprime	1535
	el cielo nuestro escuadrón.	
Juan de Alba	Si los conciertos que escribe	
	no son honrosos, el campo	
	vuecelencia no retire.	
Duque de Alba	¿Pues qué se ha de hacer?	
Juan de Alba	Morir	
	con valor constante y firme.	1540
Duque de Alba	Es el sitio pantanoso,	
	y es el invierno terrible,	
	y los soldados no pueden	
	en el agua resistirse.	
	Luego el maese de campo	1545
	la retirada publique	
	para después de mañana.	
Capitán Don Agustín	Es día de Pascua.	

1522 **Zurdo**. Bias against left-handed people was pervasive in early modern Hispanic culture. Francisco de Quevedo, in his *Sueño del infierno*, portrayed left handers as "gente hecha al revés y que se duda si son gente" ["people made the wrong way, one doubts if they are even people"] (Quevedo y Villegas 2006, 25). See Fra-Molinero's essay for the meaning of *zurdo* as another term for sodomite.

1529   Juan shows knowledge of the laws concerning duels, which included self-defense as a legitimate act, based on natural law. This line of reasoning was a favorite in fencing treatises. See Olmedo Gobante's essay in this volume.

Call me Black, coward, and left-handed,
So that all misfortunes may
Fall upon me.

DUKE OF ALBA   The death of this man,
Will make the Prince quite upset.

JUAN DE ALBA   Your Grace, if he came to kill us,
A man is allowed to defend
Himself; and if or when he sends,
White lions to avenge his captain,
I will be a black dog,
And your captains will be tigers.

DUKE OF ALBA   Let me read the terms of
The withdrawal.

CAPTAIN DON JUAN   Heavens
Are bearing down on our squadron.

JUAN DE ALBA   If the arrangements of the writ
Are not honorable, do not withdraw,
Your Grace, from the field.

DUKE OF ALBA   Then what is there to be done?

JUAN DE ALBA   Die, Sir
With firm and constant valor.

DUKE OF ALBA   This place is mostly a swamp,
The winter is terribly cold,
And the soldiers cannot
Offer a strong resistance in these waters.
Have the Field Marshall at once
Relay the order of withdrawal
For the day after tomorrow.

CAPTAIN DON AGUSTÍN   Today is Christmas Eve.

JUAN DE ALBA	Tristes
	y negras Pascuas serán
	para España.
DUQUE DE ALBA	Esto consiste 1550
	en el tiempo y la ocasión,
	y cuando España averigüe
	mi retirada, verá
	que solo pudo rendirme
	el rigor del cielo, que hombres 1555
	al Duque de Alba no rinden.
JUAN DE ALBA	¡Eso sí, cuerpo de Dios!,
	fuerte y venerable cisne,
	que este cuervo a vuestros pies
	lo mismo graznando dice. 1560
DUQUE DE ALBA	Capitán, vendrá el verano.
JUAN DE ALBA	Entonces es tierra firme
	el país y se hundirá
	como vuestro pie le pise.
DUQUE DE ALBA	Honrad con una bengala 1565
	al capitán.
CAPITÁN DON AGUSTÍN	¿Cuál elige
	de todas⁺?
JUAN DE ALBA	La vuestra me honre.
CAPITÁN DON AGUSTÍN	Ella en vos honor recibe.

Entréganle la bengala, y vase DON AGUSTÍN⁺.

DUQUE DE ALBA	Bien os parece.
JUAN DE ALBA	Antes pienso
	que me mofa y que se ríe 1570
	de verse en mis manos.
DUQUE DE ALBA	Alba,
	vuestro color se acredite
	con ser Alba.

1568 *La bengala y la jineta*. The text seems to conflate the baton (*bengala*) and the spear (*jineta*), two different military insignia that marked a captain's rank (lines 1565 and 1577–1596). Sometimes the *jineta* spear was so short that it was carried as a baton. Depending on the context, the word *jineta* could also mean officer rank or captaincy. See Olmedo Gobante's essay in this volume.

JUAN DE ALBA	A sad
	And black Christmastide it will be
	For Spain.
DUKE OF ALBA	It has to do with
	Chance and the circumstances.
	When Spain learns
	Of my retreat, they will see
	That only heaven's rigor
	Could make me yield; because
	The Duke of Alba does not yield to men.
JUAN DE ALBA	By Christ's body that is true!
	Strong and venerable swan.
	Because this crow at your feet
	cawing agrees with you.
DUKE OF ALBA	Captain, summer will soon follow.
JUAN DE ALBA	Then the country's land,
	Will be firm, and sink
	Under your boot when you arrive.
DUKE OF ALBA	Honor this Captain
	With a captain's baton.
CAPTAIN DON AGUSTÍN	Which one
	Will you choose of all?
JUAN DE ALBA	Yours will honor me.
CAPTAIN DON AGUSTÍN	It gains honor by being yours.

He hands him the baton, and DON AGUSTÍN *exits.*

DUKE OF ALBA	The baton suits you well.
JUAN DE ALBA	I think instead
	That it laughs and mocks me,
	To see itself in my hands.
DUKE OF ALBA	Juan de Alba,
	Your color gains credit
	By being an Alba.

JUAN DE ALBA	Si Alba soy,
	el Alba en vos se eternice,
	y nazca en el Alba el sol 1575
	del soberano Filipe.

Vanse todos y queda JUAN DE ALBA *solo.*

Ya en el postrer escalón
de la Fortuna me siento,
y aun en él no estoy contento:
tan alta es mi inclinación. 1580
¡Quién con una heroica acción,
jineta, os engrandeciera!
¡Quién una hazaña emprendiera,
gloria del nombre español,
con que fuera el Alba el Sol, 1585
y yo rayo del sol fuera!
Jineta, cuando os recibo,
es para temblar con vos
en vil retirada, ¡ay, Dios!,
y a pesar del tiempo esquivo; 1590
mas yo os prometo, si vivo,
con mi brazo y con mi espada
dejaros acreditada
antes que el país me vea
retirar, para que sea 1595
vuestra gloria eternizada.

Salen por otro lado el capitán DON AGUSTÍN *y* DOÑA LEONOR.

CAPITÁN DON AGUSTÍN	Las horas que he estado
	sin verme en tus ojos,
	todo ha sido infierno,
	muerte ha sido todo. 1600
DOÑA LEONOR	Y en mí, ¿qué habrán sido
	los momentos solos,

1586 *Rayo del Sol*. Juan associates the name *Alba* (dawn in Spanish) to the sun, which is a symbol for the Spanish king. Being an officer in the king's army, Juan is a ray of sunlight. See lines 660, 729, and 1001.

JUAN DE ALBA	Your Grace, Duke of Alba, If I am Alba, may dawn be in you endless, And allow Alba to give life to the sun Of our Majesty, King Philip.

They all exit and JUAN DE ALBA remains onstage alone.

I can feel I am already on
The last step of my fortune,
And yet, I am not satisfied.
So lofty is my ambition.
Oh, spear, who will make you praiseworthy,
With one more heroic action?
Would I dare a legendary feat,
Worthy of the name of Spain,
Making Alba the new sun,
And making me one of his rays?
Spear, as I receive you
It is to tremble
For this shameful retreat. Oh God,
In spite of this fleeing fate,
I promise you this, spear, if I live,
With my very own arm and sword
You will get the honor you deserve
Before the country can see me
Withdraw, so that I can
Immortalize your glory.

From the other side of the stage, enter Captain DON AGUSTÍN and DOÑA LEONOR.

CAPTAIN DON AGUSTÍN	In the time I have spent Without seeing myself in your eyes, Everything has been hell, Death has been everything.
DOÑA LEONOR	And for me, what have been These lonely moments

	si soy quien te estima,	
	si soy quien te adoro?	
JUAN DE ALBA	(Digo que este paje	1605
	debe ser demonio).	
CAPITÁN DON AGUSTÍN	Dame, Leonor mía,	
	en tus amorosos	
	brazos, hermosura	
	como hiedra al olmo.	1610
DOÑA LEONOR	¡Ay, si eternos fueran!	
JUAN DE ALBA	(¡Desdichado mozo!	
	¡No sé, vive Dios,	
	cómo me reporto!	
	Decírselo quiero	1615
	a Don Pedro Osorio	
	y a sus camaradas,	
	para que ellos propios	
	escarmiento sean	
	de tales oprobios.	1620
	¡Otra vez se abrazan!	
	¿Cómo me reporto?)	

Vase JUAN DE ALBA.

CAPITÁN DON AGUSTÍN	Gente viene.	
DOÑA LEONOR	Siempre	
	los hurtados logros	
	de mis esperanzas	1625
	tienen mil estorbos.	
CAPITÁN DON AGUSTÍN	Luego volver puedes.	
DOÑA LEONOR	(¡Oh, amor, y qué cortos	
	y qué fugitivos	
	son tus gustos todos!)	1630

Vase DOÑA LEONOR, y sale el capitán DON PEDRO con una carta⁺.

CAPITÁN DON PEDRO	En los pliegos que de España	
	ha tenido su excelencia	
	–donde de la resistencia	
	del contrario en la campaña	
	le absuelve su majestad–,	1635

	If I am the one who loves you,
	If I am the one who adores you?
JUAN DE ALBA	*[Aside]* I say this page must be a demon.
CAPTAIN DON AGUSTÍN	Bedeck me, my sweet Leonor,
	With your lovely
	Arms, like ivy
	Does to an elm tree.
DOÑA LEONOR	Oh if these could be forever!
JUAN DE ALBA	*[Aside]* Oh, you wretched boy
	For God's sake! How can I keep
	Myself in check?
	I want to report this
	To Don Pedro Osorio
	And his fellow soldiers,
	So they themselves
	Serve the punishment
	For such undignified behavior.
	They are hugging again!
	How do I control myself?

JUAN DE ALBA exits.

CAPTAIN DON AGUSTÍN	Wait. People are coming.
DOÑA LEONOR	Always
	The elusive achievements
	Of my hopes meet
	A thousand obstacles.
CAPTAIN DON AGUSTÍN	You can come back later.
DOÑA LEONOR	*[Aside]* Oh, love, how brief
	And how intangible
	Are all your pleasures!

DOÑA LEONOR exits; enter Captain DON PEDRO with a letter.

CAPTAIN DON PEDRO	The letters from Spain
	His Excellency had in his possession
	– In which your Majesty absolves
	You of resisting the enemy in
	Campaign – among them,

este para vos venía,
que el secretario me dio.

Entrégale la carta.

CAPITÁN DON AGUSTÍN   Este es de mi padre. Halló
premio la esperanza mía:
Lee.

"Luego venid a casaros   1640
con Doña Juana de Vera,
que ya es única heredera
de su casa; y aunque honraros
con su nobleza pudiera,
su renta es diez mil ducados   1645
con su rostro acreditados
y con la casa de Vera.
Licencia al Duque pedid,
que amor los plazos acorta;
y pues veis lo que os importa,   1650
luego, Agustín, os partid".
¡Válgame Dios!

CAPITÁN DON PEDRO   ¿Qué tenéis?
¿Con esas nuevas lloráis?

CAPITÁN DON AGUSTÍN   ¡Ay, Don Pedro, que no amáis
ni en el punto que yo os veis!   1655
Mas pues, Don Pedro, con vos
no hay reservado secreto
y sois prudente y discreto,
sabed, para entre los dos,
que este paje de jineta   1660
es una gallarda dama
de hacienda y blasón de fama.
Es mi obligación secreta
por ser mujer de opinión.
Su honor, Don Pedro, la debo,   1665

1658   *Paje de jineta*. A page who accompanied a captain, carrying his *jineta* spear, which identified the captain's rank. See Olmedo Gobante's essay in this volume regarding early modern military insignia.

Is this letter addressed to you,
Handed to me by the secretary.

He hands him the letter.

CAPTAIN DON AGUSTÍN   This letter is from my father.
They have rewarded my hope:
[Reads.]

"Come and get married immediately
To Doña Juana de Vera,
Who is now the sole heir
Of her house, and though she could honor
You with her nobility,
Her income is of six thousand ducats,
Which accredits her beauty
And the house of Vera, of course.
Request a leave from the Duke,
For love shortens time;
And, so you see what matters to you,
You must now, Augustin, leave."
Goodness gracious!

CAPTAIN DON PEDRO   What is wrong
That this news has brought you to tears?

CAPTAIN DON AGUSTÍN   Oh, Don Pedro, you're not in love,
Nor see yourself in my predicament.
But, my dear Don Pedro, with you
There is no secret to be kept,
And you are sensible and discreet.
Between the two of us here, know
That this page, a sort of a foot-soldier
Is a noblewoman in disguise,
Famous for her wealth and noble family,
To whom I'm secretly obliged
For she is a respectable woman.
I'm, Don Pedro, indebted to her honor,

	aunque de este intento nuevo	
	es más gloriosa la acción;	
	porque Doña Juana es	
	más rica y más poderosa;	
	y aunque es rica, es tan hermosa	1670
	que oscurece el interés.	
	Y viendo que pierde y gana	
	amor los lances así,	
	en Leonor me enternecí	
	y me alegré en Doña Juana.	1675
CAPITÁN DON PEDRO	¿Vos queréis bien a Leonor?	
CAPITÁN DON AGUSTÍN	Quiérola como a gozada,	
	que en la posesión se enfada,	
	aunque se dilata, Amor.	
CAPITÁN DON PEDRO	¿Disteis la palabra⁺?	
CAPITÁN DON AGUSTÍN	Sí,	1680
	y un papel que callará	
	por su honor; que no querrá,	
	viendo esta mudanza en mí,	
	descubrirlo si ya estoy	
	con Doña Juana casado.	1685
CAPITÁN DON PEDRO	Muy bien habéis negociado.	
CAPITÁN DON AGUSTÍN	Si nos retiramos hoy,	
	pienso partirme mañana.	
CAPITÁN DON PEDRO	¿Y Leonor?	
CAPITÁN DON AGUSTÍN	¡Muera Leonor!,	
	que ha sido fénix mi amor	1690
	renaciendo en Doña Juana.	

Vanse, y sale JUAN DE ALBA con una daga desnuda⁺.

JUAN DE ALBA	Viendo al Duque afligido,	
	desesperado y loco,	
	tengo mi vida en poco	
	y, solo, tras mi muerte me he salido.	1695
	Fortuna, si has teñido	

1683   ***Casado.*** In seventeenth-century Spanish, it also meant someone who had given a promise of matrimony.

	Although, in this new endeavor,
	The end game is more glorious,
	Because Doña Juana is
	Wealthier and more powerful,
	And although she's rich, she's so beautiful,
	That it beats all the profit gained;
	And seeing that there is gain and loss to be made
	In the business of love,
	I was moved by Doña Leonor
	And I rejoiced with Doña Juana.
CAPTAIN DON PEDRO	Do you love Leonor?
CAPTAIN DON AGUSTÍN	I loved her because I had her,
	In the possession, the more love
	Lasts, the more it gets tiresome.
CAPTAIN DON PEDRO	Did you give her your word?
CAPTAIN DON AGUSTÍN	Yes,
	And a document, which she will keep secret
	For her honor's sake, seeing that
	I've moved on to another woman
	She will not unveil it, if I am by then
	Married to Doña Juana.
CAPTAIN DON PEDRO	You have negotiated well.
CAPTAIN DON AGUSTÍN	If we withdraw today,
	I am planning to leave tomorrow.
CAPTAIN DON PEDRO	What about Doña Leonor?
CAPTAIN DON AGUSTÍN	Forget Doña Leonor!;
	For my love has been a phoenix,
	Being reborn in Doña Juana.

They exit; enter JUAN DE ALBA with his dagger unsheathed.

JUAN DE ALBA	Seeing the Duke troubled,
	Overwhelmed and distressed,
	I put my life on the line,
	And I have come alone, pursuing my demise.
	Fortune, if you have stained

el rostro que me infama,
haz que borrón no sea de mi fama.
Esta es la noche día,
que al sol hace ventajas,   1700
siendo con Dios las pajas
soberana y divina jerarquía.
Parece que me guía,
resplandeciente y bella,
a ser mago de Dios su misma estrella.   1705
Negro del Nacimiento
soy esta noche santa.
La gloria el ángel canta,
y yo respondo, al son de mi instrumento
en ronco y torpe acento,   1710
canciones de Guinea,
porque la noche festejada sea.

Dentro, grita como de fiesta[+].

En el campo contrario,
sin pensar, me he metido.
¡Qué alegre y divertido   1715
está todo en su brindis ordinario!
Entre el estruendo vario
de este festín que llega
la tropa seguiré confusa y ciega;
pues tal mi suerte ha sido   1720
que, sin pensar, con máscara he venido.

Escóndese Juan de Alba, *y salen el* Príncipe de Orange, Mons. de Lanstrec *y* Mons. de Vila[+].

Mons. de Lanstrec   Diviértase vuecelencia.

1699–1707 ***La noche día … negro del nacimiento.*** Juan is referring to common motifs in Christmas carols or *villancicos*, popular songs where Black people spoke as participants in the scene of the Nativity. Christmas Eve was also called the bright night because of the conflation of Jesus with the Roman god Solis Invictus, whose birth was celebrated the same day, around the Winter solstice. See lines 703, 1340, and 1705.

This face that affronts me,
Do not let my color stain my fame.
This is the night turned into daylight,
That shines more than the sun,
Being the straw with God
In a sovereign and divine hierarchy.
The star seems to guide me
Bright and beautiful
To be God's wise man.
I am in this holy night,
A Black man from the Nativity.
The angel sings the Gloria,
And I reply with my instrument
In a hoarse, clumsy accent
Songs from Africa
To add to the Night's festivity.

Off-stage, cries of celebration and festivities

In the enemy's camp
I have entered effortlessly.
How merry and entertaining
Are all in their ordinary celebrations!
Amidst the clatter and noise
Of this party that comes near,
I will follow its drowsy and distracted troop.
Such has been my fate
That without realizing it, I've come
　　with this mask.

JUAN DE ALBA hides and enter the PRINCE OF ORANGE, MONS. DE LANSTREC, and MONS. DE VILA.

MONS. DE LANSTREC　　Savor this evening, your Excellency.

Príncipe de Orange	No sosiega el corazón
	con ver retirar mañana
	el ejército español.

    1725

Mons. de Lanstrec	¡Qué noche de Navidad
	para España!
Príncipe de Orange	Mi valor
	negras Pascuas le ha de dar.
Mons. de Vila	Pues en aquesta ocasión,
	vuecelencia se retire

    1730

	a su tienda.
Príncipe de Orange	Idos los dos,
	que solo quiero quedarme.
Juan de Alba	(Si solo queda, por Dios,
	que no tiene de perder
	el moreno la ocasión).

    1735

Príncipe de Orange	Por aqueste contradique
	un rato a solas me voy;
	y pues seguros estamos
	del escuadrón español,
	haced que el campo descanse.

    1740

Mons. de Lanstrec	Mirad, excelso señor,
	que estáis lejos de las tiendas.
Mons. de Vila	Ya la guardia se quitó.
Príncipe de Orange	Rómpase el nombre también.
Mons. de Lanstrec	Pues a publicarlo voy.

    1745

Vanse Mons. de Lanstrec *y* Mons. de Vila.

Príncipe de Orange	¡Cuál está el campo contrario!
	Contento de verle estoy.
	¡Ah, Duque de Alba! Esta vez
	tu arrogancia se postró.
Juan de Alba	No postrará mientras vive

    1750

	el del moreno color.
Príncipe de Orange	¿Qué es esto, cielos airados?
Juan de Alba	De su gente se apartó
	y a la mía he de llevarlo.
	Vamos.

PRINCE OF ORANGE	My heart will not rest Until I see the Spanish Army Withdraw tomorrow.
MONS. DE LANSTREC	What a night before Christmas For Spain!
PRINCE OF ORANGE	My valor Is going to give them a Black Christmas.
MONS. DE VILA	So for this special occasion, Your Excellency should withdraw To his tent.
PRINCE OF ORANGE	You two go ahead; I want to be by myself for a while.
JUAN DE ALBA	*[Aside]* If he is left alone, by God, There is not a moment This Black man should lose.
PRINCE OF ORANGE	I am going alone Where that second levee is, And knowing that we are safe From the Spanish army, Allow the camp to get some rest.
MONS. DE LANSTREC	Beware, most excellent Sir, That you are far from our camp.
MONS. DE VILA	And the guards have been dismissed.
PRINCE OF ORANGE	Let the men rest and change the password too.
MONS. DE LANSTREC	I shall go now and convey the orders.

MONS. *DE LANSTREC and* MONS. *DE VILA exit.*

PRINCE OF ORANGE	How is the enemy's camp doing! I am pleased to see this outcome. Ah Duke of Alba! This time Your arrogance forced you to bend a knee.
JUAN DE ALBA	He will not bend a knee while This dark-colored man lives.
PRINCE OF ORANGE	What is this, wrathful heavens?
JUAN DE ALBA	From your men you stepped away, And to mine I'll take you. Now move!

Príncipe de Orange	¡Soldados, traición!	1755
Juan de Alba	¡Traición!	
Príncipe de Orange	¡*Mons.* de Vila!, ¡amigos!	

Coge al Príncipe de Orange *en brazos, llévaselo a la tienda del* Duque
de Alba⁺.

Juan de Alba	¡Calle o, vive Dios,	
	que con esta daga	
	le haga callar yo!	
	Ya en la tienda estamos	1760
	del Duque. ¡Señor!	

Salen el Duque de Alba *y el sargento* Barrientos.

Sargento Barrientos	¿Quién llama?	
Juan de Alba	Juan de Alba.	
Duque de Alba	Conozco la voz.	
Juan de Alba	Aquí a vuecelencia	
	le entrego y le doy	1765
	al de Orange.	
Duque de Alba	¡Cielos!	
	¿Qué dice?	
Juan de Alba	Que yo	
	solo esto intentara,	
	gran señor, por vos.	
	A mudar vestido	1770
	y a limpiarme voy,	
	porque tan de lodo	
	me ha puesto esta acción.	

Vase Juan de Alba.

Duque de Alba	Deme a besar su mano vuecelencia.	
Príncipe de Orange	Si vuecelencia tales hombres tiene,	1775
	¿quién hace a su Fortuna resistencia?	
Duque de Alba	Aunque el caso Juan de Alba me previene,	
	es tal la admiración con su presencia,	
	que lo veo y lo dudo.	
Príncipe de Orange	Ya es solemne	
	noche de Navidad esta conmigo.	1780

PRINCE OF ORANGE	Soldiers, this is treachery!
JUAN DE ALBA	Treachery it is!
PRINCE OF ORANGE	*Mons.* de Vila! Friends!

He takes the PRINCE OF ORANGE in his arms and carries him to the DUKE OF ALBA's tent.

JUAN DE ALBA	Silence, or as God lives
	With this dagger
	I will silence you myself.
	We are back at the tent
	Of the duke. Your Grace, sir!

Enter Sergeant BARRIENTOS.

SERGEANT BARRIENTOS	Who goes there?
JUAN DE ALBA	It is I, Juan de Alba.

Enter the DUKE OF ALBA.

DUKE OF ALBA	I recognize the voice.
JUAN DE ALBA	Your Excellency here
	I give you
	The one called the Prince of Orange.
DUKE OF ALBA	Oh, good heavens!
	What are you saying?
JUAN DE ALBA	Only I could attempt,
	My great dear lord, this for you.
	Forgive me, I am going to change
	These clothes and clean myself up,
	For I am covered with mud
	From this mission.

Exit JUAN DE ALBA.

DUKE OF ALBA	Your Grace, let me kiss your hand.
PRINCE OF ORANGE	If Your Grace has such men,
	Who shall dare to oppose your fortune?
DUKE OF ALBA	Although Juan de Alba has informed me of this,
	Such is the admiration by your presence,
	That I see it and I don't believe it.
PRINCE OF ORANGE	It is already
	a solemn Christmas eve.

DUQUE DE ALBA	Gloria eterna es vencer tal enemigo.
	¿Dónde halló a vuecelencia?
PRÍNCIPE DE ORANGE	Imaginallo

es perder el juicio. De mi tienda
me sacó el español. El modo callo,
porque el cielo de oírlo no se ofenda.   1785
Soldado insigne, debe el Rey premiallo,
y yo, aunque agora su valor me ofenda,
le he de premiar también, que estoy pagado
de que me haya vencido tal soldado.
¿Quién es? ¿Es capitán?

DUQUE DE ALBA	No oso decille 1790

–puesto que es capitán– quién es.

PRÍNCIPE DE ORANGE	¿No es hombre?
DUQUE DE ALBA	Quiso su suerte este valor teñille

porque con su color el mundo asombre.

PRÍNCIPE DE ORANGE	¿Pues es negro?
DUQUE DE ALBA	Negro es.
PRÍNCIPE DE ORANGE	Cuando me humille

a un negro, la Fortuna, de tal nombre,   1795
estoy glorioso, y en mi mal, me alegro.
¡Quién no fuera quien soy, y fuera el negro!

Salen los capitanes DON AGUSTÍN, DON PEDRO y DON JUAN.

CAPITÁN DON AGUSTÍN	El campo del de Orange, alborotado,

se apercibe a batalla, y ya en el nuestro
en arma puesto está el menor soldado.   1800
¿Qué será la ocasión?

DUQUE DE ALBA	La que aquí os muestro.
PRÍNCIPE DE ORANGE	Yo la ocasión del alboroto he dado,

aunque de él nacerá el sosiego vuestro.
Esta sortija un capitán le entregue
a Lanstrec porque el campo se sosiegue,   1805
y diga cómo estoy con su excelencia
y que él y *mons.* de Vila vengan luego,
asegurando el campo con su ausencia.

DUQUE DE ALBA	Vaya Don Pedro Osorio.

DUKE OF ALBA	Eternal glory is to defeat such enemy.
	Where did he find your Grace?
PRINCE OF ORANGE	To relive it
	Is to lose one's mind. From my tent
	The Spaniard took me away. The how, I won't say,
	For I don't want the heavens to be outraged:
	A remarkable soldier! The King must reward him;
	And I, even though his valor amazes me,
	I will reward him, too, for I am satisfied
	That such a soldier has defeated me.
	Who is he? Is he a captain?
DUKE OF ALBA	I dare not tell you
	Who he is, yet he is a captain.
PRINCE OF ORANGE	Is he not a man?
DUKE OF ALBA	Fortune wanted to blacken his valor,
	So that his color would surprise the entire world.
PRINCE OF ORANGE	Well, is he Black?
DUKE OF ALBA	Black he is.
PRINCE OF ORANGE	Since fortune forces me
	To bend the knee to a Black man of such renown,
	I am glorious and in my grief I am glad.
	If only I was not who I am, and I was
	the Black man!

Enter captains DON AGUSTÍN, DON PEDRO, and DON JUAN.

CAPTAIN DON AGUSTÍN	The camp of Orange is in up in arms
	Preparing for battle, and already in ours
	We armed every soldier at his post.
	What can the cause be of such commotion?
DUKE OF ALBA	The one that I show you here.
PRINCE OF ORANGE	I have caused this commotion,
	But from it, you shall have some peace of mind.
	Have this ring delivered by a captain
	To Lanstrec, so that the battlefield calms down,
	And tell them that I am with your Grace,
	And let him and *Mons.* de Vila come at once,
	Securing the camp in their absence.
DUKE OF ALBA	Go ahead, Pedro Osorio.

Príncipe de Orange	Ya me entrego
	prisionero a esos pies y a esa clemencia, 1810
	con los partidos que ordenare luego,
	pues ha querido, loca e importuna,
	darme tan negras Pascuas la Fortuna.

Vase Don Pedro.

Soldado (*dentro*)	¿Prisionero el de Orange?
Capitán Don Juan	El campo todo alborotado llega.
Duque de Alba	Sosegallo 1815
	puede el maese de campo.
Capitán Don Agustín	¿De qué modo
	ha sido la prisión?
Capitán Don Juan	Yo no lo hallo.
Duque de Alba	Hagamos colación.
Príncipe de Orange	Ya me acomodo
	a obedecer. ¿Y el negro?
Duque de Alba	Id a llamallo.
Capitán Don Juan	No conocemos rancho donde acuda. 1820
Capitán Don Agustín	En el pesebre le han de hallar, sin duda,
	que esta noche los negros y pastores
	le están diciendo a Dios sus villancicos.

Sacan la mesa.

Duque de Alba	¡Cuán ajenos están de sus honores!
Príncipe de Orange	¡Ricos aparadores, vasos ricos! 1825
Duque de Alba	Es hacerme lisonjas y favores,
	cuando son de esos pies despojos chicos.
	Aqueste es su lugar.
Príncipe de Orange	Señor.
Duque de Alba	Paciencia,
	pues es mi prisionero vuecelencia.

Siéntase a la mesa y sale Juan de Alba⁺.

Juan de Alba	(Más de tres cargas de leña 1830
	he gastado en enjugarme.

PRINCE OF ORANGE	Now I submit myself to you
	As a prisoner at your feet and mercy
	With accords you will immediately demand
	Because Fortune, unstable and tiresome,
	Has given me such a black Christmas.

DON PEDRO exits.

SOLDIER	*[Off stage]* The Prince of Orange a prisoner?
CAPTAIN DON JUAN	The enemy camp
	Has shown up ready for battle.
DUKE OF ALBA	Let the Field Marshall
	Quiet down their uproar.
CAPTAIN DON AGUSTÍN	How
	Was he captured?
CAPTAIN DON JUAN	I cannot figure it out.
DUKE OF ALBA	Let us break bread, your Grace.
PRINCE OF ORANGE	I am now taking
	Orders from you; and the Black man?
DUKE OF ALBA	You two find him.
CAPTAIN DON JUAN	We do not know where he spends his time.
CAPTAIN DON AGUSTÍN	No doubt they will find him in the manger,
	Because tonight Blacks and shepherds
	Are singing a thousand carols to God.

They bring out a makeshift dining table.

DUKE OF ALBA	How oblivious they are of their honors!
PRINCE OF ORANGE	Rich sideboards, exquisite glasses!
DUKE OF ALBA	You flatter me with these favors,
	When these are just small scraps for your Grace.
	This here is your spot.
PRINCE OF ORANGE	Your Grace!
DUKE OF ALBA	Patience,
	Your Grace, you are my prisoner.

The Prince of Orange sits at the table and enter JUAN DE ALBA

JUAN DE ALBA	*[Aside]* Over three loads of firewood
	I have used cleaning myself.

	Ya vengo limpio y caliente,	
	mas no he podido limpiarme	
	el rostro; pero ¿qué mucho,	
	si la mancha está en la carne?)	1835
Duque de Alba	Este es Juan de Alba.	

Se levanta el Príncipe de Orange⁺.

Príncipe de Orange	Decid	
	el soldado más notable	
	que monarca ha conocido.	
Juan de Alba	Gran señor, no se levante	
	vuecelencia a honrar un negro.	1840
Príncipe de Orange	Vuesa merced levantarme	
	pudo en sus hombros y fue	
	para que yo me humillase;	
	y así, que me humille a quien	
	me levantó no se espante.	1845
Duque de Alba	Siéntese vuestra excelencia.	
Príncipe de Orange	Gran señor, no he de sentarme	
	si el capitán no se sienta.	
Juan de Alba	¿Yo, señor?	
Príncipe de Orange	Quien triunfar sabe	
	del de Orange también puede	1850
	sentarse con el de Orange.	
Duque de Alba	Juan de Alba es de casa.	
Juan de Alba	El can	
	soy del Duque, y contentarme	
	con los huesos de su mesa	
	suelo.	
Príncipe de Orange	Soldado tan grande	1855
	con grandes sentarse puede.	
Duque de Alba	No aguarde que se lo mande,	
	capitán, segunda vez	
	el Príncipe.	
Juan de Alba	¿Que sentarme	
	tengo de veras, señores?	1860
	De rodillas…	
Príncipe de Orange	Es cansarse.	

	I come back clean and warm,
	But I couldn't wipe my
	Face clean; yet why would it be any different,
	Since the stain is in the flesh?
DUKE OF ALBA	This is Juan de Alba.

The Prince of Orange rises.

PRINCE OF ORANGE	Rather say the most remarkable soldier
	That a monarch has ever known.
JUAN DE ALBA	Great Lord, please do not rise
	Your Grace, to honor a Black man.
PRINCE OF ORANGE	Sir, you were able to lift me up
	On your shoulders and it was
	That I might humble myself;
	And thus, if I humble myself before
	The one who lifted me up, don't be surprised.
DUKE OF ALBA	Be seated, Your Grace.
PRINCE OF ORANGE	Your Grace, I shall not take a seat
	If the captain does not sit.
JUAN DE ALBA	Me, Sir?
PRINCE OF ORANGE	Whoever can be victorious
	Over the Prince of Orange, can also
	Be seated with the Prince of Orange.
DUKE OF ALBA	Juan de Alba is from the house of Alba.
JUAN DE ALBA	I am the Duke's
	Dog. And I tend to be pleased
	With the bones from his
	Table.
PRINCE OF ORANGE	Juan, a soldier so great
	Can sit down at table with the greatest.
DUKE OF ALBA	Captain, do not wait
	For his Grace, the Prince,
	To give you the order twice.
JUAN DE ALBA	Must I truly
	Sit, excellent sirs?
	On my knees...
PRINCE OF ORANGE	This is useless.

DUQUE DE ALBA	Excuse que tanto tiempo
	el Príncipe en pie le aguarde.
JUAN DE ALBA	Por obediencia me siento
	y seré, entre dos cristales, 1865
	negro azabache.
PRÍNCIPE DE ORANGE	Quisiera
	más, capitán, su azabache
	que el marfil que me engrandece.

Siéntase JUAN DE ALBA.

CAPITÁN DON AGUSTÍN	(¡Que esto la virtud alcance!
	Corrido estoy)
DUQUE DE ALBA	Esta noche 1870
	quiero que los capitanes
	sirvan al Príncipe.
JUAN DE ALBA	Un negro
	les da negras Navidades
	a todos.
DUQUE DE ALBA	Pascuas tan negras
	jamás, capitán, me falten. 1875

Salen MÚSICOS, y los capitanes DON AGUSTÍN y DON JUAN sirven a la mesa⁺.

Cantan MÚSICOS	*Haciendo está colación*
	con el Príncipe de Orange
	y con el gran Duque de Alba
	el negro terror de Flandes⁺.
JUAN DE ALBA	¿Tan presto hay coplas?
MÚSICO	Tan presto 1880
	que soy, en hacer romances,
	ira de Dios. De repente,
	hago ciento en una tarde
	sin que me falte concepto
	ni se me pierda asonante. 1885
JUAN DE ALBA	Sin duda debéis de ser
	poeta flujo de sangre.
	Tomad este plato, digo,
	lo que tiene, y perdonadme,
	que la cáscara no es mía. 1890

DUKE OF ALBA	Excuse yourself for keeping the Prince
	On his feet for such a long time.
JUAN DE ALBA	In obedience I shall sit,
	And I will be amongst two crystals,
	A piece of black jet.
PRINCE OF ORANGE	I rather prefer,
	Dear Captain, the jet of your blackness
	Than the ivory that makes me great.

JUAN DE ALBA sits

CAPTAIN DON AGUSTÍN	*[Aside]* To see virtue, reach so high!
	I am shamed again!
DUKE OF ALBA	Tonight
	I want the captains
	To serve the Prince.
JUAN DE ALBA	A Black man
	Gives a black Christmas
	For everyone.
DUKE OF ALBA	Such a black Christmas,
	Captain, may I never be without.

Enter MUSICIANS and captains DON AGUSTÍN and DON JUAN, serving at the table.

MUSICIANS *sing*	*Partaking a meal as homage*
	Was his Grace, the Prince of Orange
	The Grand Duke of Alba and his commanders
	and the Black terror of Flanders.
JUAN DE ALBA	So soon there are songs about me?
MUSICIAN	So quick;
	That I am with my rhymes,
	God's wrath. I can suddenly
	In one afternoon, write a hundred
	Or two, without missing a beat
	Nor losing sight of the feet.
JUAN DE ALBA	With no doubt your
	Poetry must be like bloodletting.
	Here, take this plate, I mean,
	What is in it, and forgive me,
	For the dark meat is not mine.

DUQUE DE ALBA	Los desperdicios que salen
	de mi mesa no se vuelven.
MÚSICO	Mil años el cielo os guarde[+].
Cantan MÚSICOS	*Sirviendo estaban las mesas*
	soldados y capitanes:
	unos traen la bebida 1895
	y otros la vianda traen.

Salen DOÑA LEONOR *y* ANTÓN.

ANTÓN	¿*Sioro*?
JUAN DE ALBA	¿Qué hay, Antonillo?
	A muy buen tiempo llegaste.
	Toma esta presa también
	para ti y para ese paje. 1900

Sale el capitán DON PEDRO.

CAPITÁN DON PEDRO	Aquí los dos generales
	mons. de Lanstrec y de Vila
	están.
DUQUE DE ALBA	Las mesas levanten,
	porque del Príncipe luego
	las libertades se traten.

Quitan la mesa, y salen los generales MONS. DE LANSTREC *y* DE VILA[+].

MONS. DE LANSTREC	Las manos de vuecelencia 1905
	nos dé.
DUQUE DE ALBA	A los brazos alcen
	vueseñorías.
MONS. DE VILA	Señor,
	¿qué es esto?
PRÍNCIPE DE ORANGE	Son disparates
	de la Fortuna.
MONS. DE LANSTREC	Al revés
	la retirada nos sale. 1910
PRÍNCIPE DE ORANGE	Con cualquier partido acepto
	de su excelencia las paces.
DUQUE DE ALBA	Con las mismas condiciones
	serán que se hacían antes
	conmigo.

DUKE OF ALBA	The scraps that leave my table
	Shall not return.
MUSICIAN	May the heavens keep you for a thousand years.
MUSICIANS *sing*	*Waiting tables with wine and booze*
	Soldiers bringing all kind of brews
	Captains came with plenty of food
	All were merry and in good mood.

Enter DOÑA LEONOR and ANTÓN.

ANTÓN	*Seh?*
JUAN DE ALBA	What's going on Little Antón?
	You have come at a good time;
	Take this piece of meat,
	For you and for that page, too.

Enter Captain DON PEDRO.

CAPTAIN DON PEDRO	The two Generals,
	Mons. de Lanstrec and de Vila,
	Are here.
DUKE OF ALBA	Clear the tables,
	So that we can begin talks
	Regarding the Prince's release.

They remove the table, and enter the generals MONS. OF LANSTREC and MONS. OF VILA.

MONS. DE LANSTREC	Grant me your hands, your Grace.
DUKE OF ALBA	Your lordships come
	To my arms.
MONS. DE VILA	Your Highness,
	What is this?
PRINCE OF ORANGE	It is Fortune's
	Tricks on us.
MONS. DE LANSTREC	The withdrawal has
	Backfired for us all.
PRINCE OF ORANGE	I will accept whatever agreements
	Of peace from your Grace.
DUKE OF ALBA	With the same terms and conditions
	That were made with me earlier.

Mons. de Lanstrec	Es vuecelencia,	1915
	por las acciones, notable.	
	Mucho a su Fortuna debe.	
Duque de Alba	Y más le debo a mis partes.	
Mons. de Vila	¿Quién es quien imaginó,	
	señor, acción tan notable?	1920
Juan de Alba	Yo, que solo un negro pudo,	
	por ser nada, aventurarse.	
Mons. de Vila	No fue acción de negro, fue	
	acción de príncipe.	
Juan de Alba	Baste	
	que esté servido mi rey	1925
	en tan riguroso trance.	
Duque de Alba	Son, al fin, las condiciones	
	que de los países saque	
	el de Orange sus banderas,	
	y que por seis años guarde	1930
	lealtad y obediencia al Rey;	
	y que sus soldados marchen	
	con los arcabuces vueltos.	
	Ítem, que también arrastren	
	las picas, y las banderas	1935
	vayan cogidas.	
Príncipe de Orange	Infames	
	condiciones son.	
Duque de Alba	Quejaos	
	de vos, que las ordenasteis.	
Príncipe de Orange	Esto a un negro el Rey le debe.	
Duque de Alba	Los rehenes han de darse	1940
	antes que dejéis mis tiendas.	
Mons. de Lanstrec	Los rehenes y el rescate	
	está prevenido.	
Mons. de Vila	Aquí	
	en oro y piedras se trae.	
Príncipe de Orange	Abrid esos cofres. Tome	1945
	de ellos lo que más le agrade.	

Juan de Alba reparte el tesoro.

Mons. de Lanstrec	Your Grace's Decision is magnificent. You owe a lot to your fortune.
Duke of Alba	And I owe much more to my skills.
Mons. de Vila	Who could have imagined, Sir, such formidable action?
Juan de Alba	I, because only a Black man could, Being nothing, risk his own life.
Mons. de Vila	It was not a Black man's action. What you did was a princely deed.
Juan de Alba	I am satisfied enough if By this my king is served In this difficult situation.
Duke of Alba	In sum, our conditions are That the Prince of Orange shall withdraw His banners from the country, And that for six years he shall Be loyal and obedient to the King, And that your soldiers march With their harquebuses pointing down; Equally, that while marching, drag Their pikes and that the banners Shall be folded and secured.
Prince of Orange	These are Shameful conditions!
Duke of Alba	They are your conditions, You have only yourself to blame.
Prince of Orange	The King owes all this to a Black man.
Duke of Alba.	You must hand the bonds Before you leave.
Mons. de Lanstrec	Both the bonds and the ransom Are already prepared.
Mons. de Vila	In these coffers We bring gold and precious stones.
Prince of Orange	Open them and take From them whatever you like best.

Juan de Alba distributes the treasure.

JUAN DE ALBA	Para el Duque, mi señor,	
	este collar de diamantes	
	y este tusón.	
DUQUE DE ALBA	Yo lo acepto.	
JUAN DE ALBA	Esta cadena de esmaltes	1950
	del señor Don Pedro sea;	
	y estos trencellines guarden[+]	
	Don Juan y Don Agustín;	
	y estos, por iguales partes,	
	si son escudos, se den	1955
	a los soldados.	
PRÍNCIPE DE ORANGE	¡Notable	
	negro! Excederme procura	
	en todo.	
DUQUE DE ALBA	A la tierra espante	
	tal valor.	
ANTÓN	*¿Y a Antón qué damo?*	
JUAN DE ALBA	Yo, negro, sabré pagarte;	1960
	y pues me sirves a mí,	
	no pidas el premio a nadie.	
PRÍNCIPE DE ORANGE	Ya que ha repartido a todos,	
	¿para sí qué elige?	
JUAN DE ALBA	Honrarme	
	solo con su espada quiero,	1965
	que es la joya que más vale	
	porque acreditada está	
	de la cinta del de Orange.	
PRÍNCIPE DE ORANGE	Yo se la doy, pero advierta	
	que es condición que ha de darme	1970
	la suya.	
JUAN DE ALBA	Es una perrera	
	que me costó nueve reales.	

1949 **Tusón**. The Golden Fleece, the decoration of the Catholic Order of the Golden Fleece (*Toisón de Oro*), associated with the Hapsburg dynasty. The Duke of Alba was a knight of this order, and he was portrayed wearing it in official paintings.
1952 **Trencellines**. Gold or silver bands sometimes adorned with gems used as decoration in hats.
1971 **Perrera**. A cheap sword. Literally, a dog's sword. See Olmedo Gobante's essay in this volume.

JUAN DE ALBA	For the Duke, my Lord,
	This diamond necklace
	And this Golden Fleece pendant.
DUKE OF ALBA	I accept it.
JUAN DE ALBA	This colorful chain
	Is for Don Pedro,
	These precious stones belong
	To Don Juan and Don Agustin.
	And these, if they are coins,
	Give them to the soldiers,
	In equal parts.
PRINCE OF ORANGE	What a remarkable
	Black man! He really tries to
	Best me in everything.
DUKE OF ALBA	May the land
	Be in awe by such valor.
ANTÓN	*And Antón, What do we give him?*
JUAN DE ALBA	I, Black, will know how to pay you,
	And since you are in my service,
	Do not ask for a reward from anybody.
PRINCE OF ALBA	Since you have given to everyone,
	What do you choose for yourself?
JUAN DE ALBA	I want to honor myself,
	Your Grace, only with your sword,
	Which is the most valuable jewel
	Because it is accredited by the
	Crest of the house of Orange.
PRINCE OF ORANGE	I will give it to you, but be aware
	That as a condition you have
	To give me yours.
JUAN DE ALBA	It is a cheap dog's sword
	That cost me a few coins.

PRÍNCIPE DE ORANGE	Más la estimo por ser suya
	que a todo mi estado.
DUQUE DE ALBA	Tarde
	es ya. Vamos, porque un poco 1975
	vuestra excelencia descanse,
	que Estos son de la Fortuna
	sucesos.
PRÍNCIPE DE ORANGE	Mañana sale
	de los países mi gente.
MONS. DE LANSTREC	¡Qué vuelta tan miserable 1980
	dio en un hora la Fortuna!

Vanse todos, y quedan JUAN DE ALBA, el DUQUE DE ALBA, ANTÓN y DOÑA LEONOR.

DUQUE DE ALBA	Capitán, yo he de embarcarme
	y he de llevarle conmigo
	a que su valor ensalce
	su majestad, de quien soy 1985
	ya mayordomo.
JUAN DE ALBA	Tan grande
	príncipe ser mayordomo
	puede de Dios, no de nadie.
DUQUE DE ALBA	Advierta que es nuestro rey
	majestad de majestades. 1990
JUAN DE ALBA	¿Pues qué me hará a mí, si al Alba
	su mayordomo le hace?
	Mozo de cocina es mucho.
DUQUE DE ALBA	Del Rey un gran premio aguarde,
	que es justo que premie a quien 1995
	tales Pascuas pudo darle.

Vase el DUQUE DE ALBA.

DOÑA LEONOR	Señor capitán
JUAN DE ALBA	¿Quién llama?
DOÑA LEONOR	Yo soy.
JUAN DE ALBA	¿Qué me quieres, paje
	de Bercebú? ¡Vete luego
	o, vive Dios, que te mate! 2000

PRINCE OF ORANGE	I value her more for being yours
	Than all my lands.
DUKE OF ALBA	It is now
	Late. Let us go, Your Excellency,
	So you can get at least some rest
	For these our Fortune's
	Effects.
PRINCE OF ORANGE	By tomorrow my people
	Will leave the countries.
MONS. DE LANSTREC	What a miserable reversal of Fortune
	Has occurred in a blink of an eye!

They exit, and JUAN DE ALBA, the DUKE OF ALBA, ANTÓN and DOÑA LEONOR remain on stage.

DUKE OF ALBA	Captain, I am going to embark
	And you are coming with me
	So that his Majesty, of whom
	I am already his Majordomo,
	Rewards your valor.
JUAN DE ALBA	Such a great
	Prince can be God's Majordomo
	Only, and no one else's.
DUKE OF ALBA	You should know that our King
	Is the Majesty of Majesties.
JUAN DE ALBA	Well, what will he give me,
	If he makes Alba his majordomo?
	Kitchen boy would suffice.
DUKE OF ALBA	A substantial reward from the King awaits you,
	For it is fair to reward those who
	Could give him such Christmastide.

The DUKE OF ALBA exits.

DOÑA LEONOR	Captain?
JUAN DE ALBA	Who is calling me?
DOÑA LEONOR	I am.
JUAN DE ALBA	What do you want from me, page
	Of Beelzebub? Get out of my sight at once,
	Or, for God's sake, I will kill you.

DOÑA LEONOR	¿Matarme por qué?
JUAN DE ALBA	¿Por qué?
	Tú mejor que yo lo sabes.
DOÑA LEONOR	Oye una palabra a solas.
JUAN DE ALBA	Un tigre a solas te aguarde.
DOÑA LEONOR	Yo sé que me aguardarás,
	capitán, cuando repares
	en que soy Doña Leonor+.
JUAN DE ALBA	¿Tú, Leonor? ¿Qué dices?
DOÑA LEONOR	Hablen
	mis ojos.
JUAN DE ALBA	¡Cuerpo de Dios!
	¿No lo hubieras dicho antes?
	Dame esa mano.
DOÑA LEONOR	La vida
	me debes, y a que me pagues
	desde Mérida he venido.
JUAN DE ALBA	Mira en qué puedo pagarte+.
DOÑA LEONOR	En que el vil Don Agustín,
	tras burlarme, no se case.
JUAN DE ALBA	¿Débete honor?
DOÑA LEONOR	Tras él vengo.
JUAN DE ALBA	¿Y de quién, señora, sabes
	que no se casa contigo?
DOÑA LEONOR	De esta carta que al cobarde
	de un bolsillo le saqué.
JUAN DE ALBA	Bueno está. Vendrá a casarse
	de rodillas a tus pies.
	Deja que el Duque se embarque,
	que la vida que te debo
	quiere el cielo que te pague
	en el mismo lugar.
ANTÓN	*Sioro,*
	venganza de branco infame,
	que con siola venimo
	de Merda a vengamo.

Line numbers in right margin: 2005, 2010, 2015, 2020, 2025

DOÑA LEONOR	Kill me? Why?
JUAN DE ALBA	Why?
	You know better than I do.
DOÑA LEONOR	A word. A word with you alone.
JUAN DE ALBA	A tiger can meet with you alone.
DOÑA LEONOR	I know you will refrain,
	Captain, when you learn
	That I am Doña Leonor.
JUAN DE ALBA	You, Leonor? What are you saying?
DOÑA LEONOR	Let my
	Eyes speak for me.
JUAN DE ALBA	Jesus Christ!
	Couldn't you have said this before?
	Give me that hand.
DOÑA LEONOR	You owe me
	Your life, and I have come here
	From Mérida to collect the debt.
JUAN DE ALBA	Just tell me how I can repay you.
DOÑA LEONOR	Stopping that vile Don Agustín
	From marrying after he deceived me.
JUAN DE ALBA	Does he owe you honor?
DOÑA LEONOR	That brought me here.
JUAN DE ALBA	And how, my Lady, do you know
	He will not marry you?
DOÑA LEONOR	From this, a letter that I took
	From the coward's pocket.
JUAN DE ALBA	Well, that settles it. He will come to marry
	You on his knees and be at your feet.
	Let the Duke embark
	The heavens want me to pay you
	The life I owe you
	In the same place.
ANTÓN	*Seh,*
	I come with the Lady from Merida
	To get revenge on the infamous
	White man.

JUAN DE ALBA	¿Y sabes	2030
	que era mujer?	
ANTÓN	*Sí, sioro.*	
JUAN DE ALBA	(¡Que este perro me engañase!	
	Corrido quedo).	
ANTÓN	(*Mamolas,*	
	que Antón simulas).	
JUAN DE ALBA	¡Que a un ángel	
	se atreva a burlar un hombre!	2035
	En ocasión semejante,	
	quisiera que un césar fuera	
	Don Agustín, por casarte	
	con un césar, porque fuera	
	mi venganza más notable.	2040

2030   ***Merda***. Shit in Portuguese, for Mérida. This is another case of the scatological use of words in Antón's *habla de negros*. See Fra-Molinero`s essay in this volume.
2033   ***Mamolas***. *Hacer la mamola.* To put one's finger or hand under someone else's chin as an insult or a joke.

JUAN DE ALBA	You knew she was dressed as a man?
ANTÓN	*Yes, seh.*
JUAN DE ALBA	*[Aside]* That this dog could deceive me!
	Well, that is embarrassing.
ANTÓN	*[Aside]* *Har I gotcha,*
	Take that; Antón can role play).
JUAN DE ALBA	That a man dares to deceive
	the sweetest angel!
	On such an occasion,
	I would like Don Agustin to be
	A Caesar, in order to marry you
	To a Caesar, because that would
	Make my revenge more remarkable.

JORNADA TERCERA

Salen JUAN DE ALBA muy galán, DOÑA LEONOR de lacayuelo, y ANTÓN de paje.

JUAN DE ALBA	¡Vive Dios!, que ya me enfada	
	la corte, donde estoy viendo	
	a ejércitos los hermosos,	
	cansando y haciendo gestos.	
ANTÓN	*Aquí tura gente brancas*	2045
	sa fisgonera y hacemo	
	den preto burla y, peor,	
	que estornudamo y peemo.	
DOÑA LEONOR	Si estos una noche, Antón,	
	se vieran entre los hielos	2050
	de los países supieran	
	obrar más y fisgar menos[+].	
JUAN DE ALBA	Ya ha tres días que estos patios	
	de palacio estoy midiendo	
	losa a losa; y ¡vive Dios!,	2055
	que quisiera estar primero	
	en un pantano, hasta aquí	
	el agua, que estar sufriendo	
	la dilación que he tenido	
	del Duque; y vengo resuelto[+]	2060
	a salirme de Madrid	
	sin ver al Rey.	
DOÑA LEONOR	Yo deseo	
	partirme también.	
JUAN DE ALBA	Pues, alto:	
	no hay sino partirse luego,	
	que esta es la carta del Duque	2065
	para que no tenga efecto	
	su maldad hasta que yo	
	llegue a hacer que los conciertos	
	de esa cédula se cumplan.	
DOÑA LEONOR	En ti estriba mi remedio.	2070

ACT THREE

Enter JUAN DE ALBA, dressed as a nobleman (courtier), DOÑA LEONOR dressed as footman, and ANTÓN as a pageboy.

JUAN DE ALBA   For God's sake! I am getting tired
       Of the court, where I am seeing
       Armies of pretty men,
       Looking down on us as they mock us.

ANTÓN   *Here all White people*
       Laugh at us and make
       Fun of us Blacks, and worse
       They sneeze and fart at us.

DOÑA LEONOR   If they, Antón, found themselves
       One night among those frozen
       Lands, they would know
       How to do more and have less fun.

JUAN DE ALBA   For three days now, I've been counting
       The stone slabs of this courtyard,
       Stone by stone; and by God!,
       I'd rather be in a swamp
       Up to my neck
       In water, than suffer
       Waiting all this time
       For the Duke; I'm ready
       To leave Madrid
       Without seeing the King.

DOÑA LEONOR   That is my
       Wish as well.

JUAN DE ALBA   That settles it.
       We must leave at once.
       Here is the duke's letter,
       So that the captain's treachery
       May have no effect until I
       Come to make sure the accords
       Of this contract are enforced.

DOÑA LEONOR   The remedy of my predicament is on you.

JUAN DE ALBA	Con ella se ha de partir,
	y con prudencia y secreto,
	después de habérsela dado,
	encerrarse en el convento
	de Santa Olalla, de donde 2075
	a castigar los desprecios
	de caballero tan vil
	saldrá.
DOÑA LEONOR	Mi venganza dejo
	en tus manos.
JUAN DE ALBA	Suyo soy,
	suya es la vida que tengo, 2080
	que de él me la ha reservado
	para vengarla de él mesmo.
	Hasta llegar yo, esta carta
	suspenderá el casamiento
	de Doña Juana; que allá, 2085
	si los dos juntos nos vemos,
	a cuchilladas y a coces,
	haré que se acabe el pleito.

Vase DOÑA LEONOR.

ANTÓN	*Lleguemo a buscamo al Duque.*
JUAN DE ALBA	Por Dios, Antonillo que entro 2090
	con más miedo en estas salas,
	palestras de lisonjeros,
	que en el campo del contrario.
	Ponte bien el ferreruelo
	y no me dejes jamás. 2095
ANTÓN	*Santiguamo antes que entremo.*
JUAN DE ALBA	Entra sin dar ocasión
	que nos pierdan el respeto.

2075 **Santa Olalla**. Saint Eulalia in Mérida was a convent of nuns (Freylas de Santa Olalla) founded in 1530 under the sponsorship of the Vargas family, two of whose members appear in this comedy: Doña Juana and Don Juan. See Fra-Molinero's essay in this volume.

2095 **Ferreruelo**. A small cape, fashionable at the time, and a sign of wealth.

JUAN DE ALBA	You shall leave with this writ,
	And with prudence and secrecy,
	After he receives it,
	Go to the Convent
	Of Santa Olalla, from where
	You will come out
	To punish the scorn made by
	Such a wretched gentleman.
DOÑA LEONOR	I leave my vengeance
	In your hands.
JUAN DE ALBA	I am yours,
	The life I have is yours;
	One that you saved from him,
	so you can take revenge against him;
	Until I arrive, this letter
	Will suspend Doña Juana's
	Marriage; and there,
	If the captain and I meet,
	With my fist and my sword
	I will put an end to this business.

Exit DOÑA LEONOR.

ANTÓN	*Let's find the Duke.*
JUAN DE ALBA	By God, Little Antón, I enter
	These halls with more fear,
	Where sycophants compete,
	Than I do in an enemy's camp;
	Adjust your short cape well,
	And never leave me.
ANTÓN	*Let's cross ourselves before entering.*
JUAN DE ALBA	Come, and give them no reason
	To disrespect us.

Salen Don Francisco *y* Don Gómez *por una parte, y* Don Martín *y* Don Pedro *por otra⁺.*

Don Gómez *[a* Don Pedro*]* Pues sale su majestad,		
aquí aguardarle podemos.		2100

Don Francisco *[a* Don Martín*]*   El Rey pasa a la capilla;
                                    darle un memorial deseo
                                    mil días ha.
Don Martín   Al Duque de Alba
                                    he hablado dos veces.
Don Francisco   Eso
                                    es la vida perdurable.   2105
Don Pedro *[a Don Gómez]*   ¿No reparáis en los negros,
                                    que son notables figuras?
Don Francisco *[a Don Martín]*   Dos días ha que los veo
                                    en la antecámara ansí.
Don Martín   Con qué gravedad el perro   2110
                                    se pasea.
Don Francisco   Y las pisadas
                                    el paje le va midiendo.
Don Pedro *[a Don Gómez]*   Bien valdrán tres mil reales
                                    el amo y paje.

Estornudan⁺.

Juan de Alba   ¿Qué es esto?
Antón   *Estornudar gente branca*   2115
                                    haciendo burla de preto.
Don Francisco   ¡Uchúa!

2107   **Figura**. Someone at court who lacks favor of the powerful and is the object of jokes. It was a theatrical term.

2113   **Tres mil reales**. Three thousand reales would be the average price for two healthy enslaved men between twenty and thirty years of age in Extremadura (Periáñez Gómez 2008ab, 202).

2115   **Estornudar**. To sneeze and to fart in the presence of Black people were forms of insult. By sneezing, the offender was pretending to be reacting to the presence of black pepper.

Enter Don Francisco *and* Don Gómez *on one side of the stage, and* Don
Martín *and* Don Pedro *on the other side.*

Don Gómez *[To Don Pedro.]* His Majesty is coming out,
                                  We can wait for him here.
Don Francisco *[To Don Martín.]* The King is off to the chapel;
                                  For a thousand days I have been
                                  Longing to give him this report.
Don Martín   I have spoken
                                  Twice with the Duke of Alba.
Don Francisco   That's
                                  Like waiting for life everlasting.
Don Pedro *[To Don Gómez.]* Have you noticed those *Negroes*
                                  Who are quite the characters?
Don Francisco *[To Don Martín.]* I have seen them for two days
                                  In the corridors as well.
Don Martín   How solemn is the dog's
                                  Swagger.
Don Francisco   And the page
                                  Follows his every step.
Don Pedro *[To Don Gómez.]* They'll be worth three thousand *reales*,
                                  Both master and his page.

They sneeze.

Juan de Alba   What's this?
Antón   *White people sneezing*
                                  Making fun of us Blacks.
Don Francisco   Achoo!

Don Pedro	¡Mandinga!
Don Martín	¡Aché!
Juan de Alba	Calla, y no hagas caso de ellos.
Antón	*¿No hagan caso? ¡Jur' an Dioso,*
	si espadan saco...!
Don Pedro *[a Don Gómez]*	¡Qué tieso
	y qué grave va el perrazo!

Don Pedro *[a Don Gómez]* ¡Qué tieso   2120
y qué grave va el perrazo!
Don Francisco *[a Don Martín]* Las plumillas del sombrero
son muy donosas.
Don Martín   Serán,
a mi parecer, del cuervo
de San Antón.
Don Gómez   ¡Pu, pu, puy!   2125
Don Pedro *[a Don Gómez]*   ¡Con qué majestad ha vuelto
el rostro!
Juan de Alba   ¿Peyeron?
Antón   *Sí.*
Juan de Alba   ¿A quién de los dos peyeron?
Antón   *A vosancé.*
Juan de Alba   Negro, a ti.
Antón   *¿A Antón?*
Juan de Alba   Sí.

Vuelven a peer.

Antón   *¿Y a quién peemo*   2130
angora?
Juan de Alba   Ya huele mal;
que a mí me han peído pienso.
Mas yo haré que los cobardes
tengan más comedimiento:

2117   **Mandinga**. A person of West African ethnic identity. A Black person, as a form of insult. Lope de Vega, *El santo negro Rosambuco*: "¡Buen socorro / Me viene el perrazo a dar! ¿Quién le mete en predicar, / Padre Mandinga, modorro?" ["What help is this dog going to give me! Who are you to be a preacher, you dozing Father Mandinga?"] (1894, 381). Quevedo, *Poema heroico de las necedades y locuras de Orlando el Enamorado*, Canto II: "El mundo está mandinga anochecido" ["The world is mandinga as the night"] (Quevedo 1971).

DON PEDRO   Mandinka.
DON GÓMEZ   Achoo!
JUAN DE ALBA   Shut up and ignore them.
ANTÓN   *Ignore them? I swear to God,*
                      If I draw my sword!
DON PEDRO *[To Don Gómez.]*   How stately
                      And grave the mongrel carries himself.
DON FRANCISCO *[To Don Martín.]* The feathers of the hat
                      Are very dashing.
DON MARTÍN   It seems to me, they come from the raven
                      Of Saint Anthony Abbot.
DON GÓMEZ   *Phbbbbt! Prarrp!*
DON PEDRO, *to Don Gómez*   He has turned around with such
                      Majesty.
JUAN DE ALBA   Did they fart?
ANTÓN   *Yes.*
JUAN DE ALBA   Which one of us did they fart at?
ANTÓN   *At you, sir.*
JUAN DE ALBA   No, at you, *Negro*!
ANTÓN   *At Antón?*
JUAN DE ALBA   Yes.

They fart again.

ANTÓN   *And who of us did*
                      They fart at now?
JUAN DE ALBA   It smells bad already.
                      I think it's me they're farting at;
                      But I'll make these cowards
                      Be more respectful.

así desvergüenzas tales   2135
a calabazadas suelo
castigar.

Acuchíllalos[+].

DON FRANCISCO	¡Muero!
DON PEDRO	¡Ay de mí!
JUAN DE ALBA	¡Peedme agora!

Salen SOLDADOS *1 y 2*[+].

SOLDADO 1	¿Qué es esto?
JUAN DE ALBA	Un negro que hace a los blancos
	comedidos y compuestos. 2140
SOLDADO 2	¡Oh, negro!
DON MARTÍN	¡Oh, vil!
DON FRANCISCO	¿Tú, a nosotros?
DON GÓMEZ	¡Matadlo o llevadlo preso!
JUAN DE ALBA	¿Preso, a mí?
DON PEDRO	¡Asidlo!
JUAN DE ALBA	¡Cobardes!
	¡De esta suerte asir me dejo!
DON FRANCISCO	Llegad por aquí.
JUAN DE ALBA	¡Ah, villanos, 2145
	por detrás!
DON PEDRO	Muera este perro.
ANTÓN	*También, pobre Antón, morimo.*
DON GÓMEZ	El Duque sale.
SOLDADO 1	Ha de hacerlo
	colgar de una reja.

Sale el DUQUE DE ALBA *con bastón de mayordomo.*

DUQUE DE ALBA	¡Hola,
	soldados! Ahorquen luego 2150
	al villano que ha tenido
	tan bárbaro atrevimiento.
SOLDADO 2	Este perro es.

2149 **Reja**. Possible reference to grilled windows in the Royal Palace at El
Escorial.

I usually punish such
Shamelessness with
A good head bashing.

He strikes them with his sword.

DON FRANCISCO	I am a dead man now.
DON PEDRO	Ah I'm done!
JUAN DE ALBA	Fart at me now.

Enter SOLDIERS 1 and 2.

SOLDIER 1	What's going on?
JUAN DE ALBA	A Black man teaching whites
	How to behave properly.
SOLDIER 2	You worthless *Negro*!
DON MARTÍN	O' you scum!
DON FRANCISCO	You dare to challenge us?
DON GÓMEZ	Kill him or seize him!
JUAN DE ALBA	Imprison me?
DON PEDRO	Get him.
JUAN DE ALBA	Cowards,
	I will not make this easy for you.
DON FRANCISCO	All of you, come this way.
JUAN DE ALBA	O' you bastards!
	You got me from behind!
DON PEDRO	Kill this dog.
ANTÓN	*Poor Antón, he will die, too.*
DON GÓMEZ	Here comes the Duke.
SOLDIER 1	He shall hang him high
	From a balcony's railing.

Enter the DUKE OF ALBA with a majordomo's staff.

DUKE OF ALBA	Hallo,
	Soldiers! Hang now
	The scoundrel who has had
	Such barbaric nerve.
SOLDIER 2	It is this dog.

DUQUE DE ALBA	¡Aguardad!	
	¡Tened, soldados! ¿Qué es esto,	
	señor capitán Juan de Alba?	2155
JUAN DE ALBA	Vuecelencia puede verlo:	
	pensiones de mi color.	
	Ocasionados, me han hecho	
	salir de mí unos hidalgos;	
	y si castigo merezco	2160
	o prisión, aquí me tiene	
	vuecelencia.	
DUQUE DE ALBA	En lazo estrecho,	
	la prisión sea en mis brazos.	
DON MARTÍN	(Corrido estoy).	
DON FRANCISCO	(Muerto quedo).	
DON GÓMEZ	(Este es el negro de Flandes).	2165
DON FRANCISCO	(Dile el negro del infierno,	
	pues pega como demonio	
	calabazadas).	
JUAN DE ALBA	Defectos	
	son de mi color.	
DON GÓMEZ	(Con él	
	se pasea).	
DUQUE DE ALBA	Caballeros:	2170
	el que veis es el señor	
	capitán Juan de Alba, opuesto	
	con su color a la fama,	
	donde hará su nombre eterno.	
	Yo, por su noche, Alba soy;	2175
	y sol del polo flamenco,	
	su majestad: tanta gloria	
	a este color le debemos.	
ANTÓN	*Y yo so Antonillo…*	
JUAN DE ALBA	Calla.	
ANTÓN	*Callamo, mas ya habraremo.*	2180
JUAN DE ALBA	Yo soy el que a vuecelencia	
	debo todo el ser que tengo,	
	pues siendo noche tan vil,	
	Alba de su luz parezco.	

DUKE OF ALBA	Stop,
	Hold on soldiers. What is
	Going on Captain Juan de Alba?
JUAN DE ALBA	As your Grace can see,
	This is the penalty for being
	This color; some irritating gentlemen
	Have made me lose my temper
	And if I deserve punishment,
	Or prison, here I am,
	Your Grace.
DUKE OF ALBA	Let my arms,
	In a tight embrace, be your prison.
DON MARTÍN	*[Aside]* I am embarrassed.
DON FRANCISCO	*[Aside]* I am surely dead.
DON GÓMEZ	*[Aside]* This is the Black Man of Flanders.
DON FRANCISCO	*[Aside]* Call him the Black Man from hell
	Because he bashes heads
	Like a demon.
JUAN DE ALBA	These are the flaws
	Of my color.
DON FRANCISCO	*[Aside]* He walks
	with him by his side.
DUKE OF ALBA	Gentlemen:
	This man you see here
	Is Captain Juan de Alba, who challenged
	Fame with the color of his skin,
	Where his name shall be eternal;
	Because of his darkness, I am the Dawn,
	And his Majesty, our King, is the Sun
	Of the region of Flanders; so much glory
	We owe to this color.
ANTÓN	*And I am Little Antón...*
JUAN DE ALBA	Be quiet!
ANTÓN	*We'll be quiet, but we'll talk later.*
JUAN DE ALBA	It is I, your Grace,
	Who owes you everything,
	For I being such a vile night
	Your name has enlightened me;

	Mas, por Dios, que vuecelencia	2185
	me excuse de estos aprietos
	en que me pone en palacio
	mi color.
Duque de Alba	Ya de su premio
	su majestad ha tratado.
Juan de Alba	¡Vive Dios, que estoy temiendo	2190
	mi condición en la corte!
Duque de Alba	Pues de ella saldrá tan presto
	vuesa merced qué será
	mañana o esotro.
Juan de Alba	Beso
	a vuecelencia sus manos.	2195
Duque de Alba	Deseo tiene de verlo
	su majestad; y así, agora
	famosa ocasión tenemos
	porque a la capilla pasa.
	Póngase aquí,

Ruido dentro[+].

	mas ya siento	2200
	el ruido de las astas,
	que es señal que va saliendo.
	Quiero llegar a advertirle
	que está aquí.

Vase el Duque de Alba.

Juan de Alba	Antonillo, temo
	ver al Rey.
Antón	*¿Hombre no samo?*	2205
Juan de Alba	Hombre es, mas dice que ha puesto,
	cuidadoso, el cielo en él
	tal majestad y respeto
	que cuantos lo ven se turban,
	y como me considero	2210
	cuervo vil en la presencia
	del águila a quien dan feudos
	trópicos tan dilatados
	y tan remotos imperios,

But for God's sake, your Lordship,
Release me from the predicaments
In which my color puts me
In this palace.

DUKE OF ALBA　　　　　　His Majesty has
Already addressed your reward.

JUAN DE ALBA　　As God lives, I am afraid
Of seeing myself in this court.

DUKE OF ALBA　　Your mercy, you shall leave here promptly
By tomorrow or the next day.

JUAN DE ALBA　　　　　　　　　　　I kiss
Your hands, your Grace.

DUKE OF ALBA　　His Majesty wishes
To see you; and look, now
Is an opportune moment
For he is going towards the chapel.
Stand here;

Noise Off-Stage.

　　　　　　　　　for I hear
The sounds made by the guards' halberds,
Which means he's coming this way.
I will let him know
Of your presence.

The Duke of Alba exits.

JUAN DE ALBA　　Little Antón, I am afraid
To meet the King.

ANTÓN　　　　　　　　　*Aren't we men?*

JUAN DE ALBA　　He is a man, and yet they say heaven
Has thoughtfully vested him
With such majesty and respect,
That those who meet him are perplexed;
And, since I consider myself
A vile raven in the presence
Of the eagle respected in
Such vast remote regions
And such vast empires

no es mucho que me acobarde,   2215
aunque en mi vida lo he hecho.

Sale el DUQUE DE ALBA, *y el* REY, *tomando memoriales.*

DUQUE DE ALBA   Aquel, sacra majestad,…
JUAN DE ALBA   (Antón).
ANTÓN   *(¿Sioro?)*
JUAN DE ALBA   (Ya tiemblo).
DUQUE DE ALBA   … es el capitán Juan de Alba.
REY   Hacedle llegar, que quiero   2220
                       admirarme, Duque, un rato
                       con tan prodigioso negro.
DUQUE DE ALBA   Capitán: llegad, llegad.
JUAN DE ALBA   ¿Tan invencible un rey es
                       que me hace temblar?
DUQUE DE ALBA   Los pies   2225
                       pedid a su majestad.
JUAN DE ALBA   Señor, yo…
DUQUE DE ALBA   Llegad.
REY   ¡Notable
                       negro! Admirándole estoy.
JUAN DE ALBA   …soy un negro, un negro soy…
DUQUE DE ALBA   Sosegaos.
JUAN DE ALBA   …tan miserable   2230
                       que en Flandes con mi color
                       vuestra sacra majestad
                       afrento.
DUQUE DE ALBA   La Navidad
                       pasada, gloria y honor
                       fue de España, pues se alegra   2235
                       por el negro que está aquí.
JUAN DE ALBA   Yo a España, señor, le di
                       negro día y Pascua negra.
                       El Duque en su luz me baña,
                       que fuera, sin luz tan pura,   2240
                       negra como mi ventura,
                       señor, la Pascua en España:
                       sombra de sus rayos fui.

It is not remarkable if I cower,
Though I have never done so in my life.

Enter the DUKE OF ALBA and the KING, taking legal briefs.

DUKE OF ALBA	That one, your Sacred Majesty…
JUAN DE ALBA	*[Aside]* Antón.
ANTÓN	*Seh?*
JUAN DE ALBA	*[Aside]* I'm trembling.
DUKE OF ALBA	…Is Captain Juan de Alba.
KING	Let him come, Duke, I want
	To be amazed for a while
	With such a wondrous Black.
DUKE OF ALBA	Captain: come, come.
JUAN DE ALBA	So invincible a king is
	That he makes me tremble?
DUKE OF ALBA	Ask
	For his Majesty's feet to kiss.
JUAN DE ALBA	Sir, I…
DUKE OF ALBA	Come forth.
KING	Remarkable
	Black man! I am admiring him.
JUAN DE ALBA	…I am a Black man, a Black man I am…
DUKE OF ALBA	At ease.
JUAN DE ALBA	…so miserable
	That in Flanders, with my color,
	I affront your sacred
	Majesty.
DUKE OF ALBA	This past Christmas,
	The honor and glory belonged
	To Spain, as it rejoices
	For this Black man here.
JUAN DE ALBA	I, sir, gave Spain
	A black day and a black Christmas.
	The Duke shines his light upon me,
	Which would have been
	Without light so pure,
	A Black Christmas in Spain,
	As my fortune would be:
	I was a shadow of his rays.

REY	Capitán Alba, por vos,	
	mis reinos ensalza Dios	2245
	y el premio os da a vos por mí.	

Vanse todos, y quedan solos JUAN DE ALBA y ANTÓN.

ANTÓN	*¿Esta sa el Rey? ¡Jur' an Dioso,*	
	que branco tornamo al preto	
	den temor y den respeto!	
	Cagayera sa espantosa.	2250
	Sioro, sioro, estamo	
	belesados.	
JUAN DE ALBA	Sin mí estoy.	
ANTÓN	*Ya podemo decir hoy*	
	que, "aunque negro, gente samo".	
JUAN DE ALBA	¡Que la majestad a quien	2255
	tiemblan dos mundos así	
	me hablase y me honrase a mí!	
	Gracias los negros me den,	
	pues a su color he dado	
	nuevo aumento y calidad.	2260
ANTÓN	*Ya habramo a su majestad,*	
	¡ah, preto za ya entonado!	
JUAN DE ALBA	Ya en mí descansar podrás,	
	Fortuna, pues para honrarme,	
	ni tú tienes más que darme	2265
	ni yo, que pedirte más.	
	Ya el Rey me honró, ya al Rey vi:	
	no quiero suerte mayor.	
	Ya, Fortuna, a mi color	
	más que imaginé le di.	2270

Sale el DUQUE DE ALBA.

DUQUE DE ALBA	Ya tiene vueseñoría	
	su despacho aquí.	
JUAN DE ALBA	¿Se... qué?	
DUQUE DE ALBA	Señoría.	
JUAN DE ALBA	A decir fue	
	vuecelencia "perrería",	

KING   Captain Alba, because of you,
        God increases my kingdoms
        And rewards you on my behalf.

They all exit. JUAN DE ALBA and ANTÓN remain on stage.

ANTÓN   *Was that the king? I swear to God,*
        That Black men turn White
        Out of fear and respect.
        He's the Knight of Knights.
        My Seh, my Seh, we
        Are dumberstruck.
JUAN DE ALBA   I am at a loss for words.
ANTÓN   *We can now say today,*
        That "although Black, we are people."
JUAN DE ALBA   That the majesty that makes
        Two worlds tremble should
        Honor and speak to me like this!
        Black brothers, you should be grateful to me,
        For I have given your color
        A new status and prestige.
ANTÓN   *His Majesty has spoken to Black folks,*
        We Blacks can boast about it now.
JUAN DE ALBA   Now you may rest in me
        Fortune, you have nothing
        Left to give me nor I
        to ask of you. The King
        Honored me; I saw the King:
        I require no greater favor.
        Fortune, now, I have given my color
        More than I ever imagined.

Enter the DUKE OF ALBA

DUKE OF ALBA   My Lord, here is your
                Dispatch.
JUAN DE ALBA   My? What?
DUKE OF ALBA   My Lord.
JUAN DE ALBA   You are mistaken
                Your Grace. No doubt you intended

	sin duda, y se equivocó.	2275
	¿Yo señoría? ¿Yo, yo?	
DUQUE DE ALBA	Quien sabe ser, dando honores,	
	señor de grandes señores	
	señoría mereció.	
	De un hábito de Santiago	2280
	le ha hecho su majestad	
	merced.	
JUAN DE ALBA	Con dificultad,	
	las mercedes satisfago	
	si en Guinea se han de hacer	
	las pruebas.	
DUQUE DE ALBA	Hechas están	2285
	ya en Flandes, y un capitán	
	tan grande no ha menester	
	más pruebas que su valor.	
	Hijo de sus obras es,	
	y la Fortuna, a sus pies,	2290
	acredita su color.	
	La cruz su valor publica⁺	
	sin que su color la ultraje,	
	porque comienza un linaje	
	en el que le califica.	2295
	Y por agora, le da	
	seis mil ducados de renta.	
JUAN DE ALBA	¿Qué dice?	
DUQUE DE ALBA	Que ansí le aumenta	
	la virtud.	

2285 *Pruebas*. Candidates for membership in a military order needed to undergo an investigation with written proof of *limpieza de sangre,* or purity of blood, ascertaining that none of their ancestors were of Jewish, Muslim, or heretical descent. This investigation would be conducted in the place where the candidate's forebears allegedly lived, normally small rural enclaves in northern Spain, maintaining the fiction that these places were inhabited mostly by old Christians in previous generations. The place of origin in Juan's case would have to be in West Africa, in Guinea, which is meant as a joke. See Fra-Molinero's essay in this volume.

	To say "My dog."
	A Lord? Me? Me?
DUKE OF ALBA	Who bestows honor, and knows how to be
	A Lords among Lords,
	Deserves to be called a Lord.
	His Majesty the King has
	Awarded you with
	The order of Saint James.
JUAN DE ALBA	With adversity,
	I will satisfy the award
	If proof of my noble ancestry
	Has to be searched in Africa.
DUKE OF ALBA	Your nobility has already been asserted
	In Flanders, and so great a captain
	Requires no more proof
	Than his valor.
	You are the son of your deeds,
	And Fortune, being at your feet,
	Credits your color.
	The cross of Saint James displays your valor,
	And the Black color does not disgrace it,
	Since it begins a new lineage
	that makes your color a proof of nobility.
	And, for now, he provides you
	with an income of six thousand ducats.
JUAN DE ALBA	What do you say?
DUKE OF ALBA	That virtue makes you
	Greater.

JUAN DE ALBA	Los negros ya	
	truequen en honra su ultraje.	2300
	¡Seis mil ducados!	
DUQUE DE ALBA	¿Qué espanto?	
JUAN DE ALBA	¿Cuándo pensó valer tanto	
	el perro de mi linaje?	
DUQUE DE ALBA	Maese de campo, en esta,	
	general también le ha hecho	2305
	su majestad.	
JUAN DE ALBA	Yo sospecho	
	que esta es, gran señor, apuesta	
	entre el Rey y la Fortuna,	
	mostrando cuál puede más.	
	¿Quién imaginó jamás	2310
	tal extremo? Mas, si alguna	
	vez ha andado el hado loco,	
	agora lo anda conmigo.	
	¿Por vuecelencia consigo,	
	siendo el mérito tan poco,	2315
	tanta merced y favor?	
DUQUE DE ALBA	De la Fortuna el osado	
	es dueño, y tan gran soldado	
	no aspira a premio menor.	
	Maese de campo es ya,	2320
	general, vueseñoría;	
	que esto alcanza la osadía	
	y esto la osadía da⁺.	
JUAN DE ALBA	En mí España ha procurado,	
	señor, a lo que imagino,	2325

2300   *Ultraje*. Reference to slavery, which is the insult made to Blacks through history. See Fra-Molinero's essay in this volume about the role of Fortune in the fate of Black people.
2297   *Seis mil ducados*. An annual income of six thousand ducats was an outrageous amount. These exaggerated figures were customary in early modern Spanish theatre.

JUAN DE ALBA	Black people will now
	Turn their disgrace into honor.
	Six thousand ducats!
DUKE OF ALBA	Is it surprising?
JUAN DE ALBA	Since when did the dog of my lineage
	Think it was worth so much?
DUKE OF ALBA	His majesty has made you
	A Field Commander of the Army
	Under the rank of General.
JUAN DE ALBA	I suspect
	This is, your Grace, a wager
	Between the King and Fortune,
	Showing who can outdo the other.
	Who has ever imagined
	Such extremes? Yet, if fate
	Has ever been fickle,
	It favors me now.
	Why do I receive so much reward and favor
	through your Grace,
	since my merit is so little?
DUKE OF ALBA	A bold man masters
	Fortune; and so great a soldier
	Does not aspire to a lesser prize.
	You are now a Field Commander,
	A General, and a Lord;
	This is what being bold achieves
	And this is what being bold grants.
JUAN DE ALBA	Your Grace, to what I imagine,
	Spain has achieved with me,

	como tiene un Juan Latino,	
	tener otro Juan Soldado;	
	mostrando, en tales disfraces	
	–dando al color opinión–,	
	que en letras y en armas son	2330
	de honor los negros capaces;	
	pero si de esa Alba bella	
	soy rayo, el color me salva:	
	blanco soy, hijo del Alba,	
	que es del Sol de España estrella.	2335
DUQUE DE ALBA	Vuestra luz en el aurora	
	eterna y blanca será.	
ANTÓN	*Primo, estimamo que ya*	
	ay neglo comendadora.	
DUQUE DE ALBA	Vamos, porque el Rey me envía	2340
	a que el hábito le den.	

Vase el DUQUE DE ALBA.

JUAN DE ALBA	Antonillo.	
ANTÓN	*¿Sior?*	
JUAN DE ALBA	Prevén	
	postas, porque antes del día	
	habemos de caminar	
	a Mérida.	
ANTÓN	*Vamos.*	
JUAN DE ALBA	Vamos⁺,	2345
	y a Don Agustín hagamos	
	a mojicones casar.	

Vanse. Salen MÚSICOS, el capitán DON AGUSTÍN y DOÑA JUANA⁺.

2326   *Juan Latino* (c. 1516–c. 1594). A university professor in Granada, and the first known early modern Afro-European writer. He authored *Austrias Carmen* (Latinus 1573), a Neo-Latin epic poem celebrating the triumph of Don John of Austria, half-brother of Philip II of Spain, at the battle of Lepanto in 1571. See Fra-Molinero's essay in this volume.
2338   *Primo.* Cousin, friend, fellow Black person. It was used also among non-Blacks to address persons of shared class, ethnicity, or race.

Since it already has a Juan Latino,
To have a Juan Soldier.
Showing in such masquerades –
Giving color a good name – ,
That in arms and letters,
Blacks are capable of honor;
But, if I am a beam of light from
That fair Alba, the color saves me:
For Alba means white, so do I,
Who is a star of the sun of Spain.

DUKE OF ALBA   Your light shall be white
And eternal at daybreak.

ANTÓN   *Brother, me thinks that we*
Have now a Black Commander.

DUKE OF ALBA   Come, for the King sends me
To give you the Order of Saint James.

The DUKE OF ALBA exits.

JUAN DE ALBA   Little Antón.
ANTÓN.   *Sir?*
JUAN DE ALBA   Ready
The horses, because before morning ends,
We'll have to travel
To Mérida.

ANTÓN   *Let's go.*
JUAN DE ALBA   Let's go,
And let's slap Don Agustin
Into marriage.

They Exit. Enter MUSICIANS, Captain DON AGUSTÍN and DOÑA JUANA.

Cantan Músicos	Toque alarma la gloria[+],
	aunque agravien,
	en la paz de Cupido, 2350
	guerras de Marte.
	Venturoso el soldado
	que alcanza suave,
	entre guerras sangrientas,
	tan dulces paces. 2355
Doña Juana	Amor, el nombre yerras,
	pues las paces en él todas son guerras.
Capitán Don Agustín	De los hielos de Flandes
	me trujo amor a méritos tan grandes.
Doña Juana	Dichosa yo, pues de ellos 2360
	en Mérida he venido a merecellos.
Capitán Don Agustín	Todo el tiempo lo alcanza.
Doña Juana	Y todo lo consigue la esperanza,
	pues ver –pálido y frío,
	llorando soles– que burló el estío 2365
	el erizado invierno
	–preso en las sombras del rigor eterno
	y anegado en la nieve
	que copo a copo en horizontes bebe–
	sin ver cándido rayo 2370
	del sol –vida de abril, alma de Mayo–
	y –cuando transparentes
	culebras de cristal enlazan fuentes–,
	de tan fieros rigores,
	salir pisando márgenes de flores 2375
	en verde primavera,
	símbolo generoso del que espera.
Capitán Don Agustín	Dichoso el que ha esperado.
Doña Juana	Y dichoso mil veces mi cuidado.
Capitán Don Agustín	Al fin será mañana 2380
	nuestro vínculo eterno en soberana
	y sacra unión de estrellas.
Doña Juana	Cuando espira el amor, ¿no influyen ellas[+]?

2363–2377   An example of *poesía culta*, a poetic style popularized by Luis de Góngora in the early seventeenth century. See Fra-Molinero's essay in this volume.

MUSICIANS *sing*	*Glory sound the alarm*
	Even if they harm
	Mars wars
	In Cupid's peaceful times.
	How lucky is the soldier
	Who gently achieves,
	Amidst bloody wars,
	Such a sweet, lovely peace.
DOÑA JUANA	Love, your name is misleading
	Because there is no peace,
	It is but a constant battle.
CAPTAIN DON AGUSTÍN	From the frozen land of Flanders
	Love brought me to such glorious rewards.
DOÑA JUANA	I am blessed, because in Mérida,
	I've come to deserve them.
CAPTAIN DON AGUSTÍN	Everything happens in good time.
DOÑA JUANA	And hope achieves everything.
	For to see that summer has outwitted
	The bristling winter – where the latter
	Being pale and cold, cries for the sun,
	While the former imprisoned
	In the shadows of timeless rigor, drowned
	In the snow that swallows the horizon,
	Snowflake by snowflake unable to see
	The sun's candid rays,
	Being the life of April and the soul of May.
	And when the fountains snake their way
	Linking themselves with transparent crystals,
	The summer steps out into flowerbeds,
	In the green of spring,
	As a noble symbol of the one who waits.
CAPTAIN DON AGUSTÍN	Happy is the one who has waited.
DOÑA JUANA	And blissful a thousand times, my love.
CAPTAIN DON AGUSTÍN	At last, our eternal bond
	Will be tomorrow in a sovereign
	Sacred union of stars.
DOÑA JUANA	And when love exhales, don't they influence it?

Sale Don Juan, padre.

Don Juan⁺	Un mozo de camino
	este pliego me ha dado.
Capitán Don Agustín	Yo imagino 2385
	que es orden que me llama,
	y más quiero la paz que no la fama.
	(Mas si de Leonor fuera,
	mi máquina el amor descompusiera;
	pero, temor, ¿qué quieres, 2390
	si con Don Pedro la dejé en Amberes?)
Don Juan	¿Quién firma?
Capitán Don Agustín	El Duque firma.
Don Juan	Provocando a respeto está la firma.

Lee Capitán Don Agustín   Los rigores de aquellos rebeldes países quiere su majestad que, por agora, resista en su real palacio, donde le sirvo de mayordomo mayor. Y así, ha sido fuerza nombrar un maese de campo general para mis ausencias. Este ha de pasar por Mérida, porque va a Lisboa a embarcarse y quiero que asista a sus bodas del señor capitán, a quien pido no las celebre antes que llegue, que quiero que conozca el amor que le tengo obligándole con esta demostración, que vea que soy muy suyo y guárdele Dios.

Madrid y mayo,
El Duque de Alba.

2384   *Sale **don Juan**, padre*. The text is unclear whether this is Don Juan de Vera, Doña Juana's father, or Don Juan de Estrada, Captain Don Agustín's father, who is mentioned in the two previous acts (lines 275 and 1638). Both Doña Juana and Don Agustín call him *padre* and *señor* (2399 and 2423). In line 2438 he is referred to as Doña Juana's father. But if he were Don Juan de Vera, Doña Juana's father, it is odd that he does not seem to recognize Juan de Alba as his daughter's servant, the one who made him so tired with his acts of insubordination in the first act (line 381). If he were Don Agustín's father, it would be unseemly for Doña Juana to be seen alone in the company of her betrothed and her future father- in-law. In any case, this Don Juan should never be confused with Don Juan de Vargas, who is Doña Leonor's father (274), nor with Captain Don Juan (1953), or even Prior Don Juan (1035).

Enter Don Juan, her father.

Don Juan	A traveling porter Has given me this letter.
Captain Don Agustín	I imagine That it is command summoning me; Yet I want peace more than fame; *[Aside]* But, if it were Leonor's, Love would break down my plan; But, fear, what do you want from me, Since I left her with Don Pedro in Antwerp?
Don Juan	Who signs it?
Captain Don Agustín	The Duke himself.
Don Juan	That signature demands respect.
Captain Don Agustín	(*Reading the letter*) Because of the hardships of those rebellious countries, his Majesty wants me to remain in the palace, for the time being, where I serve him as his Chief Majordomo; and so, I have seen myself forced to appoint a General Field Commander during my absence. Since he must pass through Merida, because he is on his way to Lisbon to take ship. And I want him to attend your wedding, my dear sir and Captain, I ask of you not to celebrate it before he arrives. I want you to know the love I have for you, and compel you with this demonstration, so you may see that I am very much yours; and may God keep you safe. Madrid and May. The Duke Of Alba.

DON JUAN	Gran favor.
CAPITÁN DON AGUSTÍN	Más quisiera
	que en tan fuerte ocasión no me le hiciera, 2395
	que es infierno el deseo
	cuando en los ojos la esperanza veo;
	y glorias dilatadas
	muchas veces, señor, son desdichadas.
DON JUAN	Cuando el plazo es tan breve 2400
	–y hace por vos el Duque lo que debe–,
	la dilación es justa.
CAPITÁN DON AGUSTÍN	Amor en las tardanzas se disgusta,
	y en el más breve instante⁺,
	hace quejoso al más pagado amante. 2405
DON JUAN	Aquí es finezas todo.
CAPITÁN DON AGUSTÍN	¡Pues dilátese el bien si es de este modo!
DON JUAN	No es dilación dos días.
CAPITÁN DON AGUSTÍN	Volved a celebrar las glorias mías⁺.
	No pienso más dilatar, 2410
	padre y señor, mis empleos,
	que amor muere en los deseos
	y es infierno el desear.
	No es casarse el asaltar
	muros, ni vencer trincheras 2415
	ni fajinas, que deseas
	de tu general la vista.
	Amor sus glorias alista,
	y en la paz los pies estampo;
	y así, el maese de campo 2420
	sobra en tan dulce conquista.
DOÑA JUANA	Ya está, señor, convocada
	de Mérida la nobleza,
	prevenida la belleza
	y la casa alborotada. 2425
DON JUAN	Siendo así, ya es escusada
	la dilación.
CAPITÁN DON AGUSTÍN	Hoy, señor,
	los logros de tanto amor
	he de conseguir.

DON JUAN	What a great honor.
CAPTAIN DON AGUSTÍN	I would prefer
	Not to be so honored on such untimely occasion,
	For desire is hell when I see
	My hopes within reach; and delayed glories,
	Sir, are often unhappy.
DON JUAN	When the wait is so short
	– And the Duke does for you what he must –
	The delay is just.
CAPTAIN DON AGUSTÍN	Love dislikes delays
	And, the briefest of moments,
	Makes the best rewarded lover complain.
DON JUAN	He's regaling you properly.
CAPTAIN DON AGUSTÍN	If that's so, let the joy be delayed.
DON JUAN	Two days' delay is not so bad at all.
CAPTAIN AGUSTÍN	*[To the musicians]* Come and sing my glories.
	[To Don Juan] I will no longer delay
	Father and my lord, my task at hand,
	That love dies in desire
	And to desire is hell.
	They do not make marriage to assault
	Walls, nor to conquer trenches
	Or do soldierly tasks that requires
	Your general's command.
	Love prepares its glories
	And, in peace, I set my feet;
	And so, in such sweet conquest
	There's no need for Field Commander.
DOÑA JUANA	Sir, the nobility of Mérida
	Has already been called to attend,
	The decorations are all set,
	And the household is in frenzy.
DON JUAN	That being the case,
	There's no point in putting it off.
CAPTAIN DON AGUSTÍN	Sir, today,
	I shall harvest the fruits
	Of so much love.

DON JUAN	No quiero	
	impedirlo, antes espero[+]	2430
	hacer el plazo menor	
	haciendo que luego sea	
	el desposorio.	

Salen dos CABALLEROS.

CABALLERO 1	¿Qué hacéis,	
	si en vuestra casa tenéis,	
	sin que ninguno lo crea,	2435
	el padrino que desea	
	vuestro padre y mi señor	
	en Mérida?	
DOÑA JUANA	Amor y honor	
	hoy me eternizan.	
CABALLERO 2	Galanes,	
	soldados y capitanes,	2440
	con sombreros de color,	
	bandas y plumas, le dieron	
	a la ciudad primaveras,	
	cuyas luces lisonjeras	
	firmamentos parecieron.	2445
DON JUAN	¿Quién los vio?	
CABALLERO 1	Muchos los vieron	
	y yo los vi.	
DON JUAN	Sí es así,	
	hijo, ¿qué hacemos aquí?	
CAPITÁN DON AGUSTÍN	Mientras yo el cuarto prevengo	
	y en mil cosas me detengo	2450
	id a disculparme a mí.	
DON JUAN	Del tálamo de flores[+]	
	dilatéis, dando vida, eternidades,	
	gloriosos sucesores,	
	y generosos en las cuatro edades.	2455

2455 *Las cuatro edades*. The four ages were childhood, youth, maturity, and old age. They were the subject of allegorical paintings in the Renaissance. The Three Wise Men have been interpreted as representations of three of the four ages: youth, maturity, and old age, with the Black King being depicted as a young man (Rowe 2019, 23).

DON JUAN	I won't
	Get in the way,
	I rather hope to shorten
	The wait and let the marriage
	Take place at once.

Enter two noblemen.

NOBLEMAN 1	What are you still doing
	Here when you have in your house,
	And no one can believe it,
	The Godfather, that your father, My Lord
	Desires in all Merida?
DOÑA JUANA	Love and honor
	Intend to make me eternal today.
NOBLEMAN 2	Gallant Knights,
	Soldiers and captains
	With colored hats, sashes,
	And feathers
	Brought spring to the city,
	Whose brilliance is so
	Pleasing, it seemed like the starry sky.
DOÑA JUANA	Who saw them?
NOBLEMAN 1	Lots of people
	And I saw them too.
DON JUAN	If that's the case, my son,
	What are we doing here?
CAPTAIN DON AGUSTÍN	Go ahead, while I attend
	To the room and other things
	And please apologize on my behalf.
DON JUAN	From the flowery bed of marriage
	May you grow, giving eternal life,
	To glorious and noble successors;
	In the four ages of man,

	Excedan todos almas	
	a los cogollos de las verdes palmas.	
	El vínculo amoroso	
	eterna paz y eterno gusto sea;	
	y en tan gallardo esposo	2460
	Mérida el Fénix de las galas vea,	
	que, en su esposa divina,	
	el gozo y la grandeza se imagina.	
DOÑA JUANA	Más ventura no quiero+	
	que el dueño que me ha dado mi ventura.	2465
CAPITÁN DON AGUSTÍN	Ni yo más bien espero	
	que el que Amor en tus ojos me asegura.	
DOÑA JUANA	¿Quién tan dichosa ha sido?	
CAPITÁN DON AGUSTÍN	¿Ni quién tanta ventura ha merecido?	

Sale un CRIADO.

CRIADO+	Ya el señor maese de campo	2470
	está aquí.	
DON JUAN	¿Qué dices? Llego	
	a sus pies.	
CAPITÁN DON AGUSTÍN	(Amor permita	
	que Doña Leonor no venga	
	con él).	

Sale JUAN DE ALBA *con el capitán* DON PEDRO *y toda la compañía.*

JUAN DE ALBA	(Aquí es el espanto).	
CAPITÁN DON AGUSTÍN	Vueseñoría me tenga	2475
	por su criado, mas ¿quién	
	es a quien mis labios besan	
	las manos?	
JUAN DE ALBA	A mí.	
CAPITÁN DON AGUSTÍN	Mil años	
	vueseñoría lo sea.	
DOÑA JUANA	¡Válgame Dios! ¿No es Juanillo,	2480
	mi negro?	
JUAN DE ALBA	(Todos se alteran).	
CAPITÁN DON AGUSTÍN	Mas, ¿cómo?	

	May all souls outperform
	The blossoming of the green palms.
	May the bond of love be
	Of eternal peace and everlasting joy;
	And, Mérida may see the Phoenix
	Of all dashing husbands,
	That in his divine wife
	The joy and greatness is unimaginable.
DOÑA JUANA	I seek no more fortune
	Than the man my good fortune has given me.
CAPTAIN DON AGUSTÍN	Nor do I hope for anything more,
	Than what love in your eyes assures me of.
DOÑA JUANA	Who has been so blessed?
CAPTAIN DON AGUSTÍN	Who has deserved so much happiness?

Enter a servant

SERVANT	The Field Commander
	Is already here.
DON JUAN	What do you say? I will
	Kneel at his feet.
CAPTAIN DON AGUSTÍN	*[Aside]* Love, let
	Doña Leonor not be with him.

Enter JUAN DE ALBA with Captain DON PEDRO and the entire regiment.

JUAN DE ALBA	*[Aside]* This is going to be good.
CAPTAIN DON AGUSTÍN	Your Lordship shall regard me
	As your servant; but, to whom
	Do these hands belong that my
	Lips kiss?
JUAN DE ALBA	To me.
CAPTAIN DON AGUSTÍN	May you
	Live a thousand years, my Lordship.
DOÑA JUANA	God help me! Isn't this Little Juan,
	My Black boy?
JUAN DE ALBA	*[Aside]* Everyone's confused.
CAPTAIN DON AGUSTÍN	But, how?

JUAN DE ALBA   De la Fortuna,
                    señor capitán, son estas
                    las mudanzas prodigiosas.
                    Así su inconstante rueda   2485
                    los imposibles allana,
                    y así la virtud se premia.
                    Su majestad mi color
                    ha honrado con la venera
                    de Santiago, a quien añade   2490
                    seis mil ducados de renta;
                    y de maese de campo
                    general, quiere que tenga
                    la honrosa plaza, gustando
                    que esto todo lo merezca   2495
                    un negro a quien dio su espada,
                    su valor y fortaleza
                    merecimientos de blanco,
                    porque los blancos adviertan
                    que el valor lo dan los cielos   2500
                    y el color lo da la tierra.
                    En este mismo lugar,
                    si vuesa merced se acuerda,
                    no quiso asentar mi plaza
                    movido de mi bajeza;   2505
                    y en él me ha venido a ver
                    –¿quién tal suceso creyera?–
                    su general. Mas el tiempo
                    ansí las fortunas trueca,
                    y cuando de estos agravios   2510
                    aquí vengarme pudiera,
                    como negro, quiero, honrando
                    su persona, que en mí vea
                    un negro blanco en las obras
                    y que a los blancos afrenta.   2515
                    Y así, en mi tercio, le elijo
                    coronel de seis banderas,

2517   **Bandera**. Each of the companies in which the Spanish Tercios were divided.
See Olmedo Gobante's essay in this volume.

JUAN DE ALBA   Captain,
                    These are the extraordinary
                    Turns of Fortune.
                    This is how its fickle wheel
                    Makes the impossible possible,
                    And how virtue is rewarded.
                    His Majesty the King has honored
                    My color with the insignia
                    Of Saint James, to whom he adds
                    Six thousand ducats of income;
                    And, as a Field Commander
                    General, he wants me to have
                    Such an honorable post, content
                    That all this a Black man
                    Should deserve because his sword,
                    His valor, and strength
                    Made him equal to White men in merit.
                    Because White people should know
                    That valor is given by the heavens
                    And color is given by the land.
                    In this same place,
                    If my dear captain remembers,
                    You did not want to give me a post,
                    Based on my inferior status;
                    And here you are before me
                    As your general – Who would
                    Believe such an event? – ; but time,
                    Brings about a change in fortunes,
                    And when I could avenge
                    These wrongs right here,
                    As a Black man, I want to honor
                    Your person, so you see in me
                    A Black man, white in his deeds
                    Shaming white folks;
                    So, I pick you to be in my company
                    As a colonel of six regiments,

aunque en tan grande soldado,
es poca correspondencia[+].

CAPITÁN DON AGUSTÍN   Vueseñoría me dé   2520
sus manos.

JUAN DE ALBA   Los brazos sean
el vínculo más glorioso.
Y agora, con su licencia,
besar quiero a mi señora
los pies.

DOÑA JUANA   Confusa y suspensa   2525
estoy.

JUAN DE ALBA   Yo, señora, soy
quien siempre se estima y precia
de ser vuestro negro, que es
vil el que el principio niega
a su Fortuna e, ingrato,   2530
de lo que ha sido se afrenta.
Mejorado prometí
volver a vuestra presencia:
favorecedme y honradme.

DOÑA JUANA   Antes nuestra casa queda   2535
desde hoy, con vueseñoría,
honrada.

JUAN DE ALBA   Que me dijera
vuesamerced *señoría*,
¿quién lo imaginara?

DOÑA JUANA   Aumenta[+]
los méritos la virtud,   2540
y las armas y las letras
han sido siempre en el mundo
los polos de la nobleza.
En ellos comienzan todos
los linajes.

JUAN DE ALBA   Y comienzan   2545
los negros en mí a ser nobles;
y así, permitid que vea
a la negra Catalina,
mi madre.

	Even though it is too little a reward
	For such a noble soldier.
CAPTAIN DON AGUSTÍN	Your Lordship, give me
	Your hands.
JUAN DE ALBA	Let my arms be
	The most glorious bond;
	And, now, forgive me,
	I want to kiss my Lady's
	Feet.
DOÑA JUANA	I am confused and
	In suspense.
JUAN DE ALBA	My Lady, I am
	The one who always esteems and cherishes
	Being your Black man, for he who denies
	His humble beginnings, is vile
	Of his Fortune and ashamed of what he has
	Been in the past, is ungrateful.
	I promised to return to your presence
	In better standing:
	You may favor me and honor me now.
DOÑA JUANA	On the contrary, our house from this day
	Forward is honored with
	Your Lordship.
JUAN DE ALBA	Who would have ever imagined,
	That your Grace would call me
	'Your Lordship?'
DOÑA JUANA	Virtue
	Increases merits;
	And arms and letters
	Have always been in the world
	The poles of nobility.
	In them, all lineages
	Begin.
JUAN DE ALBA	And Blacks begin
	To be noble with me;
	And, therefore, allow me to see
	Catalina, the Black woman,
	My mother.

Capitán Don Agustín	Dichosa negra,
	con hijo que es señoría. 2550
Doña Juana	Catalina está en la aldea,
	pero luego iremos todos
	a darle la norabuena.
Juan de Alba	Pues yo ofrezco las albricias.
	Haced, señora, que venga 2555
	a hablarme con *señoría*
	y a verme con tanta renta.
Capitán Don Agustín	(¿En fin, que más no la vistis?)
Capitán Don Pedro	(No la vi más, aunque enferma
	oí que estaba, después, 2560
	Doña Leonor en Bruselas;
	y pues nada se ha sabido,
	sin duda alguna que es muerta).
Capitán Don Agustín	(Buenas nuevas os dé Dios).
Juan de Alba	No pensó bodas tan negras 2565
	el señor Don Agustín
	tener.

Sale Antón.

Antón	(*Leonor sa a la puerta*
	de la cámara esperando).
Juan de Alba	(Dile que entre).
Capitán Don Agustín	Antes tenerlas
	tan alegres no entendí 2570
	jamás; y pues la presencia
	de vueseñoría basta
	a ilustrar las bodas nuestras,
	con su licencia, la mano
	le daré a mi esposa.
Juan de Alba	Tenga, 2575
	que si a su esposa ha de darla,
	su esposa, señor, es esta.

Antón *saca a* Doña Leonor.

Antón	*En la trampa hemos caído,*
	¡par Dios!, como en ratonera.

CAPTAIN DON AGUSTÍN	A fortunate Black woman,
	With a son who is a Lord.
DOÑA JUANA	Catalina is in the village.
	But we can all go afterwards
	To congratulate her.
JUAN DE ALBA	I will reward the first one to give her the news.
	My Lady, make her come
	To speak to me as her Lordship
	And to see me with so much revenue.
CAPTAIN DON AGUSTÍN	*[Aside]* So, you didn't see her anymore?
CAPTAIN DON PEDRO	*[Aside]* I never saw her again, although,
	I heard later, Doña Leonor was in Brussels,
	And sick. And since we have heard nothing,
	There's no doubt that she must be dead.
CAPTAIN DON AGUSTÍN	*[Aside]* Splendid news!
JUAN DE ALBA	My dear Don Agustín, you did not think
	Of a wedding as black as this one.

Enter ANTÓN

ANTÓN	*[Aside] Leonor is at the door*
	And waiting.
JUAN DE ALBA	*[Aside]* Tell her to come in.
CAPTAIN DON AGUSTÍN	On the contrary,
	I could never picture them happier;
	And since the presence
	Of your Lordship is enough
	To exalt this our wedding,
	With your permission, I will
	Give my hand to my wife.
JUAN DE ALBA	So here it is,
	if you must give your wife your hand,
	Your wife, Sir, is this one.

ANTÓN brings forth DOÑA LEONOR.

ANTÓN	*In the trap we've fallen,*
	By God, like a mousetrap.

CAPITÁN DON AGUSTÍN	¿Mi esposa?, ¿cómo ha de ser? 2580
JUAN DE ALBA	Como quiere que lo sea
	la palabra y la justicia.
CAPITÁN DON AGUSTÍN	Señor…
JUAN DE ALBA	¡Cásese con ella
	luego o, por vida del Rey,
	que le corte la cabeza! 2585
DON JUAN	Señor maese de campo,
	esto no ha de ser por fuerza.
JUAN DE ALBA	La obligación fuerza le hace.
DOÑA JUANA	(Salió mi esperanza incierta).
DON JUAN	¿Qué obligación?
JUAN DE ALBA	Esta diga 2590
	su obligación y su deuda.

Dale un papel.

DON JUAN	¿Es esto así?
CAPITÁN DON AGUSTÍN	Señor…
DON JUAN	Basta.
	Quién se obliga pagar piensa,
	y así, pues tú te obligaste,
	debes pagar.
JUAN DE ALBA	La belleza, 2595
	honestidad y virtud
	de Doña Leonor pudieran
	haberte obligado a ser
	reconocido. Y pues de ella
	recibí en este lugar 2600
	–contra tu enojo y fiereza–
	la vida, es razón que aquí
	la vida y el honor le vuelva.
	Por ella me diste vida
	y, pues yo llego a tenerla 2605
	por ti por ella, los dos
	por mí que tengáis es fuerza

CAPTAIN DON AGUSTÍN	My wife? How could she be?
JUAN DE ALBA	Just as the word is your bond
	So is its justice.
CAPTAIN DON AGUSTÍN	Sir ... I...
JUAN DE ALBA	Marry her
	Now or, by the King's life,
	I'll chop your head off.
DON JUAN	My Lord field commander,
	This shall not be by force.
JUAN DE ALBA	His word compels him to do so.
DOÑA JUANA *[Aside]*	My hope became uncertain.
DON JUAN	What obligation?
JUAN DE ALBA	This here
	States his debt and obligation.

Hands him the document.

DON JUAN	Is this true?
CAPTAIN DON AGUSTÍN	Sir...
DON JUAN	Enough.
	An obligation made is a debt to pay.
	And so, you made an obligation,
	You have a payment to make.
JUAN DE ALBA	Doña Leonor's
	Beauty, honesty, and virtue
	Could have obliged you to be
	Grateful; and, since I received
	Life from her in this very place
	– In spite of your anger and cruelty –
	It is reasonable that I here
	Restore her life and honor.
	For her sake, you allowed me to live;
	And since I have my life
	thanks to you both,
	Both of you should share, thanks to me,

	una vida, un ser, un alma,	
	en nueva naturaleza.	
Capitán Don Agustín	Sea ansí, pues tú lo mandas.	2610
Juan de Alba	Yo lo suplico, y lo ordenan	
	amor y la obligación	
	que en este papel confiesas.	
Capitán Don Agustín	Suya es mi mano y mi vida.	
Doña Juana	(Corrida estoy).	
Doña Leonor	Señor, deja	2615
	que a tus pies te rinda el alma.	
Doña Juana	¿Tú, contra mí? ¿Tú, en mi ofensa?	
Juan de Alba	Esto es, señora, volver	
	por tu honor; que si te diera	
	Don Agustín con engaño	2620
	la mano, quedaras necia	
	y burlada. Y si aquí yo,	
	aunque sin razón te quejas,	
	te he quitado esposo, elige	
	en Mérida el que en tu idea	2625
	fabricares; que ese, al punto,	
	con mi aumento y con mis rentas,	
	te ofrezco.	
Doña Juana	Pues, si ha de ser	
	ya el casarme por tu cuenta	
	–y el cielo te ha dado honor	2630
	que ha igualado a mi nobleza–,	
	de negro quiero que subas	
	a dueño.	
Juan de Alba	¿Qué dices?	
Doña Juana	Que esta	
	es ya mi resolución.	

2609 **En nueva naturaleza**. Juan gives a new life to Doña Leonor and Don Agustín through their marriage, an idea that echoes Juan's new life as an Alba (see line 1017).

	A life, a being, and a soul
	In a new beginning.
CAPTAIN DON AGUSTÍN	So be it, for you command it.
JUAN DE ALBA	I beseech you, as I charge it
	By the love and obligation
	You have confessed in this writ.
CAPTAIN DON AGUSTÍN	My hand and my life are hers.
DOÑA JUANA	*[Aside]* This is embarrassing.
DOÑA LEONOR	My lord, allow
	Me to surrender my soul at your feet.
DOÑA JUANA	You against me? You, my enemy?
JUAN DE ALBA	This is, my lady, defending
	Your honor; because if
	Don Agustín gives
	His hand with deceit,
	You would have remained
	Foolish and tricked; and, if here I –
	Against your baseless complaint –
	Have taken away your husband,
	Pick in Mérida whomever
	You have in mind; and that one,
	At once, with my current status
	And revenue, I offer to you.
DOÑA JUANA	Well, if I am going to be
	Married out of your bounty
	– And Heaven has given you honor,
	making you my equal in nobility –
	From a Black man, I want you to rise
	As my Master.
JUAN DE ALBA	What are you saying?
DOÑA JUANA	That I have made my
	Choice.

JUAN DE ALBA	(¿Quién tal suceso creyera? 2635
	Vueltas son de la Fortuna[+]).
	Vueseñoría me tenga
	por su esclavo.
DOÑA JUANA	Yo, desde hoy,
	he de ser esclava vuestra.
JUAN DE ALBA	Pues tal suceso han tenido 2640
	tan varias fortunas, sean
	las bodas aquesta noche.
DON JUAN	Y el regocijo y las fiestas
	comiencen desde mañana.
JUAN DE ALBA	Reservando a otra comedia 2645
	de este negro las hazañas,
	cuya historia verdadera
	largamente las aclara
	y largamente las cuenta.

Fin.

JUAN DE ALBA	*[Aside]* Who would believe such an event?
	These are turns of the wheel of Fortune.
	Your ladyship shall
	Regard me as your slave.
DOÑA JUANA	From this day on,
	I shall be your slave.
JUAN DE ALBA	Since such an event has had
	So many twists and turns of Fortune,
	Let the weddings be tonight.
DON JUAN	And the joy and celebrations
	Will begin tomorrow!
JUAN DE ALBA	Saving for another play
	Of this Black Man's exploits
	Whose true story
	Will greatly unfold
	And at length will be told.

The End.

CRITICAL ESSAY

Black Pride, Honor, and Sex: Dramatis Personae in *El valiente negro en Flandes*

Baltasar Fra-Molinero
Bates College

El valiente negro en Flandes [*The Valiant Black Man in Flanders*] is a text in conflict with itself. The protagonist is a Black man who is not a saint.[1] The play was transgressive enough to merit excisions in some key episodes, including that of the protagonist's final interracial marriage. The action in the comedy rests on three main breaches. The first is the prospect of a Black man attacking white men on his way to build a military career. The second occurs in the protagonist's relation to sexual ambiguity on the part of the play's principal female character, who dresses as a man for most of the comedy. The last transgression is built on the final interracial marriage between the Black male protagonist and his former white female owner.

Juan de Mérida is a proud Black man. His first words are a defense of his Blackness against the soldiers who oppose his wish to enlist in the imperial army that is about to sail for Flanders. His speech is direct, and when his words move the others to insult him, he thrashes them:

---

1 Lope de Vega wrote *El negro de mejor amo* and *El santo negro Rosambuco de la ciudad de Palermo*. Another such play attributed to Lope de Vega is *El prodigio de Etiopia*, or *Saint Moses of Ethiopia*, the same subject of Juan Bautista Diamante's *El negro más prodigioso*. Mira de Amescua's *El negro del mejor amo* is a different play from that of Lope de Vega with the same title. Its protagonist is Saint Benedict of Palermo, the same saintly protagonist of Luis Vélez de Guevara's *El negro del Serafín*. Calderón de la Barca is the only playwright who created a religious Black female character in the *comedia La sibila de Oriente* and the *auto sacramental El árbol del mejor fruto*, both with the Queen of Sheba as protagonist. However, this play did not present characters who are ostensibly racialized as Black in the modern sense used in Spain at the time. Andrés de Claramonte's *El gran rey de los desiertos, san Onofre* also presents a non-racialized African.

CAPITÁN DON AGUSTÍN	¡Vaya el perro!
JUAN DE MÉRIDA	No está el yerro
	en la sangre, ni el valor.
SARGENTO BARRIENTOS	Estaralo en el color.
JUAN DE MÉRIDA	Ser moreno no es ser perro,
	que ese nombre se le da
	a un alarbe, a un turco

[CAPTAIN DON AGUSTÍN	Look at this, you dog!
JUAN DE MÉRIDA	The fault is not
	In the blood, nor the courage.
SERGEANT BARRIENTOS	Maybe 'tis in the color.
JUAN DE MÉRIDA	A dark-skinned man is not a dog;
	That is a name for
	An Arab or a Turk]

(lines 1–6)

There are other times when Juan is called a dog, and at times he calls himself a dog. The opening insult is interpreted by Juan in its racial context. He knows he is being called a dog because he is Black. There is nothing wrong (*yerro*) with being Black. In fact, he is playing with words, as the word *yerro* (error, wrong) is a homophone of *hierro* (iron), the mark with which slaves were sometimes branded on the face.[2] Juan states that military virtue (*valor*) is the source of nobility, and military virtue is not present in one's blood. It is neither inherited nor inheritable.

Juan de Mérida is a Spanish-born Black man. He is an Afro-diasporic character, the product of modernity, understood as the age ushered in by the Atlantic slave trade. He is not a *bozal*, an African brought to Spain into slavery who does not speak Spanish well. His eloquence, marked by his use of standard Spanish, stands in contrast and as a reminder to himself and others that he comes from a line of

---

2   In Mira de Amescua's *El esclavo del demonio*, Lisarda, dressed as an enslaved man, has branded her own face as penance for her past mistakes: "No quiero ser conocido. / Estando así, se repara / un yerro que he cometido / con los hierros de mi cara" ["I do not want to be known. / In this way I turn right / a wrong I committed / through the iron brand on my face"] (150–53).

Black people. As an Afro-diasporic character, his slave genealogy is present in the play. His mother Catalina is mentioned three times, the first as an act of filiation, when he is identified as the son of "Catalina the slave" (I: 173); the second before he takes his leave (I: 395), when he asks his former owner Doña Juana to look after his mother; the third at the end, when he returns in triumph to Mérida (III: 2548). Juan's mother, who never appears on stage, may have been created based on the historical Catalina la Morena, an enslaved Black woman who lived in Philip II's time and was renowned for her beauty.[3] Other soldiers comment on this fact, which makes Juan and his family well known. Juan is not a *Mulatto* either, for both his parents appear to be Black. His skin color leaves no doubt that he is not the son of a white man. His Blackness is turned into a form of purity of blood, for he is not a bastard:

ALFÉREZ	Las excelencias sabemos
	de lo negro, color vil
	en presencia del marfil.
	Y a él por tal le conocemos
	en Mérida, aunque se dice
	que de un título de España
	es hijo, pero es patraña,
	que la color lo desdice.
CAPITÁN DON AGUSTÍN	Si ser soldado desea,
	¿por qué a Guinea no pasa?,
	que yo asentara su plaza
	si fuera Flandes Guinea.
[LIEUTENANT	We know the virtues
	Of the color black, so base
	When compared to ivory;
	And in Mérida we know
	He's Black, though some say

---

3   She was from Extremadura. She was known as *Catalina la Morena de buena cara* (Catalina, the Black woman with a pretty face). There was a Catalina among the slaves Philip II manumitted, according to his famous secretary Antonio Pérez (Treviño Trejo 1977, 338).

He's the son of a titled nobleman,
But that's rubbish:
His color gives him away.
CAPTAIN DON AGUSTÍN   If you, Sir, want to be a soldier,
Why don't you go to Africa?
I would secure you a guard post
If Africa were Flanders.]

(lines 77–88)

Captain Don Agustín, however, insists on characterizing this Black man as a permanent foreigner by mentioning Guinea in Africa as the appropriate place for Juan de Mérida to be a soldier. Guinea is not only a place of origin for Blacks but a place that designates the geography of slavery, as Sancho Panza knew so well (*Don Quijote* I, chapter 29). Captain Don Agustín articulates an anti-Black discourse in opposing Flanders and Guinea, Flanders being a place for white soldiers only. Juan makes this equation a false one as the play moves on.

Juan de Mérida is a man of words and action. The eloquence of this Black man is a sign of his power and dignity. In the Renaissance, the exercise of power was associated with mastery over language (Todorov 1987, 87). Eloquence preceding righteous violence was the sign of the choleric Black man, according to swordman Luis Pacheco de Narváez in his *Grandezas de la espada* (1600), a choleric Black man:

Es de pocas palabras y comedido... Si es nacido en España, se precia de hablar bien. Tiene buena expresiva o pronunciación; y, conforme a su capacidad, es abundante de términos; y, si lo traen de su tierra, en breve tiempo sabe hablar nuestra lengua.

[He is a man of few, measured words… If born in Spain, he is proud of speaking well. He expresses himself and has good pronunciation. And depending on his ability, his vocabulary is abundant. If he was brought from his native land, in a short time he can speak our language.]

Pacheco de Narváez 1600, 259v; see Olmedo Gobante 2018, 81.

The construction of Blackness in *The Valiant Black Man in Flanders* is a manifestation that Spain was a slave society.[4] The contradiction of

---

4   The study of Spain as a slave society has produced a rich bibliography regarding

being Black and free is the cornerstone of the play up to the last scene. The color of freedom is white, and in order to be free, Juan de Mérida needs to adopt a mask of whiteness. He has to wear a mask, literally, in act one, during his first military action, in which Don Agustín, his white nemesis, will be the enemy:

> Pondreme, por el recato,
> una máscara. Yo voy.
> Noche, pues somos hermanos
> en el color y las sombras,
> mi azabache te consagro
> para que los blancos vean
> que, *aunque negros, no tiznamos.*
>
> [I shall wear, to be discreet,
> A mask. Here I go.
> Night, since we are brothers
> In color and in shadows,
> I entrust my jet stone's color
> With you, so that whites may see
> That *though Black, we do not stain.*]
>
> (lines 745–751)

Juan appears with the face of a white man he is not. His whitening is an act of equalization with whites: I am as good as any white.

---

different cities and regions, but not an organic study of its evolution as a whole that includes the lives and the institutions of the enslaved and the society they helped shape. The seminal studies by Antonio Domínguez Ortiz from 1952 (2003), Cortés López (1989), and William Phillips (1990) are still a referent. Historians have tended to focus on the data obtained from different archives, and they tend to be circumscribed to cities and regions (Seville, Málaga, Granada, and Cádiz in Andalusia, Canary Islands, Extremadura, Madrid, Valladolid, Valencia). The historiography of Seville is abundant in this respect (Franco Silva, Isidoro Moreno, Fernández Chaves, Pérez García). Cultural critics (Alessandro Stella, Aurelia Martín Casares, Isidoro Moreno, Méndez Rodríguez) have combined archival documents with literary and visual sources. In a 2008 essay that guides students to the study of early modern slavery in Spain, Rocío Periáñez Gómez advocates for a more interdisciplinary methodology that diversifies the sources of information and focuses more on the lives and work of the enslaved (2008b, 280).

Whiteness, after all, is nothing more than a mask. After he is elevated to the position of captain, most references he makes, or others make, to his Blackness are positive. Blackness is good.

John Beusterien (2006a, 115) reads Juan de Mérida as an example of textual whitening, referring to Frantz Fanon's analysis of the mask scene. However, the whitening of Juan is different from the whitening of Black saints in Spanish *comedias*. The latter have their souls and bodies whitened after death, a trope that became a standard in Black saints' hagiographies (Rowe 2016, 749).[5] Juan dons the mask of whiteness of his own accord, not by metaphysical imposition. Juan never changes color, and he asserts that his Black skin is a social, not a theological, category. He makes the association of Black skin color with the devil (*demonio*) an advantage on two occasions: line 793 ("hombre soy y soy demonio") and line 1078 ("soy demonio"), in response to Doña Leonor/Esteban's erotic advances, and on one occasion his prowess in fighting is compared to the devil's: "Dile el negro del infierno / pues pega como demonio / calabazadas" ["call him the Black Man from hell, because he bashes heads like a demon"] (lines 2166–2167).

Only after Juan de Mérida's first action does valor add value to his Black face, which, by itself, was deemed unworthy for a soldier. In act two, as his military star is rising, Juan again passes for a white man donning a Black face, as if he were attending a celebratory masque on Christmas Eve, on his way to capture the Prince of Orange:

> Entre el estruendo vario
> de este festín que llega
> la tropa seguiré confusa y ciega;
> pues tal mi suerte ha sido
> que, sin pensar, con máscara he venido.

---

5   The protagonists of Lope de Vega's *El santo negro Rosambuco* and *El negro del mejor amo* show the whiteness of their souls ascending to heaven at the moment of their death (Fra Molinero 1995, 56; 121–22). This miraculous whitening could happen to Black religious persons, as in the Afro-Mexican nun Sor Esperanza de San Alberto, whose fasting practices made her look Mulatto to the other nuns, or Sor Teresa Chicaba in Spain, whose body whitened after death (Benoist 2014, 30ff).

[Amidst the clatter and noise
Of this party that comes near,
I will follow its drowsy and distracted troop.
Such has been my fate
That without realizing it, I've come
 with this mask.]
(lines 1717–1721)

As mentioned earlier, Juan de Mérida caught the attention of Frantz Fanon. In chapter seven of *Black Skin, White Mask*s (1967), Fanon uses Juan de Mérida as the epitome of the colonial condition of the Black man. The Black man stands for comparison, since he is always comparing himself to other Black people, self-evaluating in order to gain a sense of worth, which makes Fanon pronounce that "The Antilleans have no inherent values of their own, they are always contingent on the presence of The Other" (211). Fanon presents Juan de Mérida as an early example of overcompensation, the psychological result of experiencing and rejecting racial inferiority yet being trapped in the governing fiction of whiteness (215). In some ways, Juan represents the colonizer's fantasy of imagining the colonized as someone desiring to become the colonizer (Irigoyen-García 2005, 151). Juan de Mérida represents a desire for inclusion of the dispossessed in the global imperial idea of the Hispanic monarchy, which is a contradiction in itself. In the soliloquy commented on by Fanon, Juan de Mérida protests his right to have a place where he was born:

	¡Que ser negro en el mundo infamia sea!	365
	¿Por ventura los negros no son hombres?	
	¿Tienen alma más vil, más torpe y fea,	
	y por ello les dan bajos renombres?	
	¿Qué tiene más España que Guinea?	
	o ¿por qué privilegios o renombres,	370
	si los negros valor y nombre adquieren,	
	los blancos más civiles los prefieren?	
Doña Juana	Más bien que alborotar la compañía	
	y la ciudad al perro le estuviera	
	ocuparse en traer agua todo el día	375

JUAN DE MÉRIDA	¿Yo azacán?, ¿yo aguador? Antes hiciera la bajeza más vil.

[That being Black in this world is infamy!
By chance, are not Blacks, men?
Have they a dreadful, fouler, wicked soul,
And that's why they get a bad name?
What has Spain more than Africa,
Or what privileges or reputation,
If Black people gain worth and name,
More uncivilized White people prefer them?

DOÑA JUANA   Rather than disturbing the soldiers
And the town, the dog should busy
Himself fetching water all day long.

JUAN DE MÉRIDA   Me? A water boy? Fetching water?
I'd rather work in a pigsty.]

                          (lines 365–377)

Juan accuses white people of choosing to consider Black people uncouth (*civiles*), a word akin to barbarian, unfit for social intercourse, in spite of the evidence to the contrary. He refuses his assigned role of debasement as a Black man: "¿Yo azacán?, ¿yo aguador?" He will not accept being a water seller, claiming his right to occupy a position of dignity.[6]

Juan de Mérida's discourse on Black value is steeped in the modern idea of the common man, which Olmedo Gobante addresses in its military context in his essay in this volume. The discourse of the common man, in the mouth and actions of a Black man, shows the cracks and anxieties of the beneficiaries of the ideological construct we call whiteness. Juan de Mérida racializes his position as the common man through a lamentation that will elicit the sympathy of the audience:

                y procurando
                plaza, todos me desechan

---

6   Black water carriers appear in the Portuguese painting *El Chafariz d'El-Rey* (Figure 6) and also in Bartolomé Esteban Murillo's *Three Boys* (c. 1670, Dulwich Picture Gallery, London, UK) and in the religious painting *Wedding at Caná* (1670–1675, Barber Institute of Fine Arts, Birmingham, UK). For an analysis of *Three Boys*, see Carmen Fracchia (2019, 95–97)

por negro y por hombre bajo

...

         que yo quiero
por mi persona ganarlo
sin que me lo den a cuenta
del Rey, a quien le consagro
con obras y sin lisonjas
esta negregura...

[I have come seeking a post
In your regiment. But everyone rejects me
Because I am Black and low born.

...

         Because I want
To gain it by myself,
And not have it given to me
On account of the King, whom I devote
This blackness with actions,
And not with flattery]
         (lines 688–690 and 696–701)

Juan is everyman. This is emphasized in the abundance of characters in the play called Juan or Juana: Juan de Mérida, Don Juan de Vera, Don Juan de Vargas, Captain Don Juan, Doña Juana, the mention of a priest also called Don Juan – Juan is every John. The idea of the nobility of the common man based on his worthy actions flattens the conception of honor rooted in genealogy and inheritance. Juan de Mérida embodies a new conception of honor based on personal merit. His is the story of social ascent through valor, notwithstanding one's humble social origins. Claramonte spoke of himself in similar terms.[7]

Juan's Blackness puts him at the bottom of the social scale. He chooses the military as the best way to move up in society. His main adversary, Captain Don Agustín, represents the opposite idea

---

7   "Otros dirán que el autor es humilde, y que por él desmerece. A quien respondo que la ciencia y el trabajo muchas veces hace a los hombres señores de sus mayores" ["Others will say that the author is of lowly origins and thus the piece is worth less. To these I answer that knowledge and work very often gives men lordship over their ancestors] (*Letanía moral*, quoted in Barceló Jiménez 1978, 57).

of honor, the one defended by the ruling classes. He is an aristocrat whose ancestry is the source of his honor. In a society so preoccupied with *limpieza de sangre* (blood purity), Blackness had become the mark of absolute lack of honor.

At the lower levels of society, economic competition in urban settings generated racial barriers that extended the exclusionary practices of *limpieza de sangre* to more and more groups of people. The play shows how religion – being of Jewish or Muslim descent – was becoming less a factor for social exclusion than skin color and association to slavery.

Associating with Blacks brought dishonor, and practices of exclusion targeted Blacks in guilds, liberal professions, the army, and the Church, both in Spain and Spanish America (Méndez Rodríguez 2001, 249).[8] Exclusion of Blacks was a social practice that rarely resorted to religious narratives for justification. As discussed in Olmedo Gobante's essay in this edition, the military was an exception, however conflicted. Juan has to fight his fellow soldiers, who are planning a rebellion as a response to having to share military rank with him. In this context, Captain Don Agustín, although a nobleman, collaborates with the mutineers in order to maintain his own status against someone who is rising in the ranks but who does not possess the required ancestry:

CAPITÁN DON AGUSTÍN	¡Acción cruel!
SARGENTO BARRIENTOS	Digo otra vez que no tiene
	honor el que ya es sargento
	donde lo es un negro vil.
JUAN DE ALBA	(¡Oh envidia, monstruo civil
	del más generoso intento!)

---

8   Eighteenth-century Spanish convents rejected the presence of Black nuns as a blemish on their houses, as exemplified in the hagiography of the African nun Sor Teresa Chicaba (c. 1676–1748). An aristocratic nun in Alba de Tormes balked at the Black postulant with these words: "¡Una negra, decía, en mi convento! No en mis días; no está fundada esta casa para negras. Y así señoras, pongan fin a la plática, pues para que no tenga efecto, pondré todas las diligencias posibles" ["A negress," she said, "in my convent! Not for as long as I live. This house was not founded for negresses. So, ladies, stop the talking because I will make every effort possible to stop this from happening"] (Pan y Agua, Houchins, and Fra-Molinero 2018, 187).

| CAPITÁN DON PEDRO | Ha dado el Duque en honrallo |
| | porque es negro. |

[CAPTAIN DON AGUSTÍN	Cruel affair!
SERGEANT BARRIENTOS	I'll say it again, there is no honor
	In being a sergeant
	Where a vile Black man is one!
JUAN DE ALBA	(Aside) Oh, envy, you vicious monster
	Against every noble intention.
CAPTAIN DON PEDRO	The Duke grants this honor,
	Because he's Black.]

(lines 1108–1115)

The opposition of the sergeants to the action of the Duke in honoring (*honrar*) this Black man corresponds to the anti-aristocratic impulse of the concept of *limpieza de sangre*, which could be claimed by the lower classes, following the fiction that most people in rural Spain – the majority – descended from Old Christians. Juan confronts this opposition to his quest of honor with verbal and physical violence (Irigoyen-García 2005, 154).

To claim honor was a common practice for a soldier, as honor was achieved through the practice of righteous, legitimate violence (Harden 2020, 46). Juan's quest for honor is in itself aristocratic. His merit is only recognized by the Duke of Alba, and ultimately the King. This dependence on hierarchy is symbolized in his change of name. The Duke of Alba changes Juan's name to Juan de Alba as a reward after Juan shows up with two enemy soldiers as his prisoners. Juan de Mérida is the old name associated with slavery and Blackness. The new name is associated with the noble house of Alba, but also with symbolic whiteness. It is also reminiscent of the change of name enslaved persons received upon arrival in the land of their 'un-freedom'. This is the point at which the discourse of honor, *limpieza de sangre*, and defense of Blackness clash.

The name Juan de Alba increases the tension in the text because in the end the protagonist, a Black man, marries the white lady who had been his legal owner. The fiction of Spain as a white country is challenged in this play, as much as other texts of the time engage issues of gender, nation, and empire (Fuchs 2003, 18). The *Valiant Black Man in Flanders* does not cast doubt on the Christianity of Spain, or its Catholicity, but on its whiteness.

A significant change in social mores regarding *limpieza de sangre* was taking place in Spain and its overseas empire. Genealogy, one of the legs of *limpieza de sangre*, fostered an 'anxiety of sameness' among old Christians. They had to create a discursive difference between themselves and those who were of Jewish and Muslim descent (Lee 2016, 103). Skin color added a new layer to the genealogical proof of purity. Phenotype was now a visual marker of the religion of one's ancestors.

Religious orthodoxy was the other leg in the construction of *limpieza de sangre* (Martínez 2008, 80). For Juan, being Black – the visible mark that he is not of Old Christian stock – is a social problem that he wants to resolve. Juan's discourse assails the two-forked tenet of *limpieza de sangre*: ancestry and religion, religion that has become biology. He proclaims the biblical Adam as his ancestor, thus negating the theological validity of any notion of exclusion based on lineage or national origin. Thus, he proclaims that he is not a dog, because that insult should be reserved for Muslims (the enemies of Spain), Turks, and Muslim Arabs of his time.[9] Juan de Mérida is no Othello, whose phenotype and geographic origin make him suspect as possibly being a member of the enemy religion, Islam (Hall 2005, 359).

By re-directing the dog insult to the religious enemies, the anti-Black insult loses theological justification. In a twist of words later in the play, after the Duke of Alba recognizes his valor, Juan calls himself "Alba's dog" and threatens to attack his enemies as if they were Jews, in a reference to an anti-Semitic *romance* that the audience would have known: "El perro de Alba soy, vengan judíos" (Martin 2014, 300).[10]

---

9   "Ya pues si con esto les tratassen bien de palabra, todo lo demás perdonarían, porque esto suelen sentir más que todo, su nombre apenas es otro, que perro, vozal, cavallo y otros innumerables baldones, con los cuales el amo infierna su alma..." ["If at least they were treated with kind words, they would forgive everything else. Because they usually take offense of this more than anything else, as they are called nothing if not dog, muzzle-mouth, horse, and numberless insults with which the master fills their souls with hell..."] (Sandoval 1987, 236).

10   The worthiness of Blacks as paragons of anti-Jewishness occurs in different

The dog in the ballad of *El perro de Alba* could smell Jews, making them visible (Beusterien 2006a, 119). Juan makes his Blackness – what equates him to a dog – into visible proof of his contradictory *limpieza de sangre*: Because he is not white, he cannot be Jewish. Juan cancels the dog insult by calling all of his enemies, all white, Jews. All the Jews are white, so all the whites may be Jews for this Black man who turns whiteness on its head.[11]

The Valiant Black Man in Flanders decouples religion from race. The religious conflict that originated in the rebellion of the Low Countries against Philip II receives no attention in this comedy, throughout which the words heretic (*hereje*) or Lutheran (*luterano*) are not uttered one single time. Instead, the Dutch enemies are dubbed rebels (*rebeldes*). The political legitimacy of the Prince of Orange is not questioned. Unlike other Black protagonists, Juan de Mérida rejects association with Islam or the wars Spain fought in the Mediterranean against the Ottoman Empire.[12] The presence of this Black military hero in Flanders corresponds to a different imperial narrative that avoids the quagmire of the religious confrontation between Catholics and Protestants.

---

plays, but it is best exemplified in Diego Jiménez de Enciso's *Juan Latino*, in which the Afro-Hispanic humanist of the same name has to compete for a professorship chair against an anti-Black opponent. Juan Latino counters by attacking his opponent as someone of Jewish descent (Fra Molinero 1995, 152; Panford 1999, 4).

11   Black people insulted whites by calling them Jews. A witness testifying about the altercations that led to the 1604 banning of Black confraternities in Seville said that whites attacked Blacks during their processions: "picándoles con alfileres, de los cual se enojan y llaman a los blancos judíos" ["stabbing them with pins, which angers them, and they answer by calling whites Jews"] (Moreno 85). For more on these repeated incidents, see the section 'Claramonte and the context of *The Valiant Black Man in Flanders*'.

12   The Black protagonists of most plays were related to Islam and the conflict between Spain and the Ottoman Empire. These include Lope de Vega's *El negro del mejor amo*, *El santo negro Rosambuco*; Enríquez Gómez's *El negro más alevoso*, *Las misas de san Vicente Ferrer*; Vélez de Guevara's *El negro del mejor amo*; or Diamante's *El negro más prodigioso*. The relation to Islam is also present in Jiménez de Enciso's *Juan Latino*, in which the Islamic rebellion in Granada is initiated by the Black character Cañerí.

Religion was made to justify Black slavery, since the Pope allowed the Portuguese to raid the coasts of West Africa and capture its 'Pagan' population.[13] Christian salvation was linked to the institution of Black slavery as its main justification.[14] Juan de Mérida defends his Blackness and attacks anti-Blackness through a clear rejection of the notion of Black inferiority of any sort, or the religious justification of the enslavement of Blacks as ransom for their salvation.[15] Religion is not discussed in part because the military model Juan de Mérida contemplates is not that of the *Reconquista*, with its Apocalyptic goal in the conquest of Jerusalem. The chivalric military hero responded to a hierarchical model of society that the modern military structure of permanent standing armies was struggling with. Juan de Mérida exemplifies the professional soldier of the present, not the medieval crusader. Juan de Mérida is a soldier of fortune.

Fortune and Being Black

In his *De instauranda aethiopum salute* (1627, 1647), the Sevillian Jesuit Alonso de Sandoval asks himself about the circumstance of Blacks in his time. He was writing in Cartagena de Indias, where he was charged with the evangelization of the newly arrived enslaved

---

13   Nicolas V's papal bull *Dum diversas* (1452) allowed the Portuguese to conquer the Islamic enemies (Saracens) and other non-Christians (pagans) and subject them to perpetual slavery. The same pope, in *Romanus Pontifex* (1455), affirms that the conquest and enslavement of Blacks (Guineans) is legitimate. These bulls were confirmed by Pope Calixtus III in his *Inter caetera* (1456), in which he proclaims the right of the Crown of Portugal to conquer the western and eastern coasts of Africa all the way to India (*usque ad indos*) (Adiele 2017, 309–64).

14   Jesuit Alonso de Sandoval, in his *De instauranda aethiopum salute* (Seville 1627 and 1647), talks about the need to baptize and evangelize newly arrived enslaved people to the Americas, denounces their abject situation and mistreatment, but refrains from condemning slavery itself (Olsen 2004, 105).

15   The natural inferiority of Blacks was a reformulation of Aristotle's notion of natural slavery expressed in his *Politics* (Frank 2004, 91–92). Jesuit Father Antonio de Vieira, who attacked slave owners in Brazil for their cruelties, nevertheless asked enslaved Blacks to accept their travails as similar to Christ's suffering on the cross: "a natureza gerou os pretos da mesma cor da sua fortuna" ["nature dressed Blacks in the same color as their fortune"] (Sermon XL: 311, quoted in Martínez-López 1998, 96 n. 135).

Africans. At one point in his treatise, Sandoval cites Aristotle's opinion that some people were born to be servants. However, he immediately says that it is Fortune, that is, lack of fortune, that brings Blacks to the wretched state caused by their owners. He does not mention Providence, or any divine design, but human agency.

> Mas dexando aparte estos males, no por menores, sino por sabidos, y comunes a todos, trataremos de los que les ocasiona su fortuna, que tan escaza fe mostró con ellos, haziéndolos, o por mejor dezir, permitiendo que fuesen esclavos de hombres que con ellos son más fieras que hombres.

> [But setting aside these calamities, not of a lesser kind just because they are common knowledge, we will address the evils caused by their fortune, which has been so mean with them. It has made them slaves to men who are more beasts than men to them.]

Sandoval 1987, 215.

Fortune is the preferred trope in the racial discourse of *The Valiant Black Man in Flanders*. Juan de Mérida's first speech is a defense of his Blackness and of all Blacks through an original take on the Renaissance notion of Fortune applied to racial difference. That Blacks are in a situation of disadvantage is purely a stroke of fortune:

SARGENTO BARRIENTOS Bueno,
pues dígame: el que es moreno,
¿qué vendrá a ser?
JUAN DE MÉRIDA: ¿Qué? Será
un borrón de la Fortuna
puesto en la plana del mundo
con vituperio profundo

[SERGEANT BARRIENTOS Well,
Then, can the one who is dark-skinned
Tell me what he is?
JUAN DE MÉRIDA What is he?
A blot dropped by Fortune
On the page of the world
As a profound affront]

(lines 5–10)

The present situation of Blacks is a product of world history – in a reference to the global character of the Atlantic slave trade – and their skin color is no fault but rather a consequence of the beauty and variety of nature:

> Aunque es cierto que ninguna
> falta recibe el color,
> siendo la naturaleza
> una misma, y su belleza,
> con la variedad, mayor.
> Blancos y negros proceden
> de un hombre. Un ser los anima.
> Solo la región o el clima
> los diferencia, y si exceden
> los blancos en perfección
> a los negros, es por ser
> desdichados y tener
> sobre ellos jurisdicción;

> [Yet, the truth is that
> The color is not to blame,
> For nature is one
> And the same, and its beauty
> Is greater in its variety.
> Both Blacks and whites come
> From one man. One soul gives them life.
> Only in climate or in region
> They differ; and if whites
> Surpass Blacks in perfection,
> It is only because of Blacks'
> Misfortunes, and whites having
> Dominion over them]
> (lines 12–14)

All humans descend from Adam (*un hombre*), a theological argument that could not be challenged. In many ways, this pronouncement of one single human nature for Blacks and whites turns the

Requerimiento formula of the Spanish conquistadors upside down.[16] The *Requerimiento* had a white Spaniard proclaiming the unity of mankind as a preamble to the threat of destruction and enslavement of an addressee who could not understand the message. Now it is a Black man who tells an audience of white soldiers that they all come from the same origin. And since they do not accept this religious truth, he will act against them in the fashion of the conquistadors, with violence. All, therefore, share the same nature. Skin color difference is the product of region and climate, according to the discourse of the time. Once again, if whites have achieved more perfection than Blacks, that is, if they have been more successful, it is a matter of Fortune. Blacks have had bad luck (*ser desdichados*), and whites have taken advantage to rule over them:

> y del mismo modo, fueran
> abatidos e imperfectos
> los blancos, como sujetos
> entre los negros vivieran.
> Y pues nos diferenciamos
> solo en color y tenemos
> un ser, bien decir podemos
> que, *aunque negros, no tiznamos.*

> [And likewise, whites would be
> Downtrodden and imperfect
> If they found themselves,
> Subjects among Blacks.
> And since we are different
> Only in color, and we share
> One soul, we may very well say
> That, *although Black, we do not stain*]
>   (lines 25–32)

---

16 Quoted from Legnani (2020, 52): "un hombre y una mujer, de quien nosotros y vosotros y todos los hombres del mundo fueron y son descendientes y procreados" ["one man and one woman from whom we and you and all the men of the world were and are descendants"], followed by an explanation of the dispersal and variety of existing humans.

Juan de Mérida ends his speech of racial political analysis with a call for equality as a logical conclusion with a phrase often repeated in songs: *aunque negros no tiznamos.*

Although Black, we don't stain. Sylvia Wynter has stated that Blacks constitute the only race whose humanity has been put into question (1972, 69). Being Black is not a defect. Juan de Mérida implicitly rejects the categorization of Blackness as an ontological defect that political thinkers have been using since the Renaissance to justify Black slavery as natural (Sorentino 2019, 632). For Juan de Mérida, Black slavery is contingent; it is only a historical phenomenon, therefore changeable. The book of history is not finished yet. Juan sees himself as a soldier with a mission to erase the blot of Fortune against Blacks. He will re-write history.

Blacks at present suffer the power of whites. This is due to contingency, not merit on the part of white people. There is no divine order in this hierarchy, and in fact, it could be quite the other way around, should circumstances obtain differently, with whites suffering under the power of Blacks. Juan's discourse echoes words said by Black humanist Juan Latino a few decades earlier, addressing King Philip II:

> Quod si nostra tuis facies Rex nigra ministris
> displicet, Aethiopum non placet alba viris.
> Illic Auroram sordet qui viserit albus.
> Suntque duces nigri Rex quoque fuscus adest.

> [Because if our Black face displeases your ministers, oh king, a white one is not pleasant either among the Ethiopians. Anyone visiting the parts of the East will not be held in esteem if they look white. Leaders there are all Black, as so is their king.][17]

---

17 "Ad catholicum ... elegia" (Latinus 1573, 10). For Juan Latino's defense of his Blackness, see Fra-Molinero (2005). Juan Latino was the author of the neo-Latin epic poem *Austrias carmen*, dedicated to the naval victory of Don John of Austria at Lepanto over the Ottoman Empire in 1571. Elizabeth Wright published a modern edition with an English translation. For an updated and documented biography of Juan Latino, see Aurelia Martín Casares (2016).

Juan's frequent use of the term Fortune rang in the ears of those who were attuned to political philosophers of the time. *Fortuna* appeared in visual representations and in literary works and political essays to express the sensation of the chaos that modernity brought, as compared to the perceived order of the past (González García 2017, 108).[18] Fortune was a complex political metaphor both negative and positive, the latter associated with the sense of opportunity and favorable occasion a ruler needs to seize (González García 2006, 47–48). In the defense of his Blackness and his right to have a place in society, Juan de Mérida's discourse employs the two competing notions of the old Roman goddess Fortuna. First was the image of the Wheel of Fortune, the notion of change and unpredictability, tied to the idea of Fate (*hado*) and Time. But a new notion of Fortune was coming into being, one in which change was seen as something positive, even desirable, a factor that could even be mastered.

But Fortuna seemed to be at odds with the Christian concept of God as ruler of history and human actions. In the late sixteenth century Justus Lipsius had run into trouble with the Catholic Church for alluding to Fortune as predestination when explaining the sudden turn of events in war and the destiny of rulers.[19] He was alluding to the

---

18 González García (2017) provides a useful catalog of Spanish authors and works – Juan de Mena, Jorge Manrique, Fernando de Rojas, Cervantes, Lope de Vega, Calderón de la Barca, Francisco de Quevedo – in which Fortune is prominently featured (2017, 107–108).

19 According to Miguel Martínez (2020a), Cristóbal Rodríguez Alva, the author of *La inquieta Flandes* (1594), saw how the censors scratched the following lines of his heroic poem that equate the concept of Fortune with that of predestination:

> Contra el factal destino es devaneo
> querer torcer el hombre cosa alguna,
> pues no puede eximirse del trofeo
> que va predestinado su fortuna.

> [Against fateful destiny it is folly
> for a man to try and twist anything at all,
> as he cannot avoid the trophy
> that Fortune predestined for him.]

wars of religion in the Netherlands. As a Catholic, Lipsius defended the position of Spain. How then could one explain military setbacks if Spain defended the Catholic faith and was on the side of God? Lipsius and other fellow neo-Stoics had been forced to accommodate their ideas under the cloak of religion to announce that Fortune was nothing if not divine providence in action, the expression of divine order (Mout 2017, 66–67). Lipsius came to defend the idea that one's virtue in action can call in good fortune, and this is the duty of a military leader or a prince: to practice virtue and defeat Fortune, as in some depictions of Emperor Charles V's controlling the Wheel of Fortune (González García 2017, 111).

Juan de Mérida's defense of his actions reads like Lipsius's explanation in his *De Politica* (1589) regarding the role of Fortune in the life of a prince or a military ruler. His actions will turn Fortune in his favor.[20] Juan's speech attributes the debasement of Blackness in his time to the vagaries of Fortune, not to divine providence. Any religious justification for Black slavery and Black exclusion is not even contemplated. To be Black is to be a blot Fortune made on the pages of humanity. The inferiority of Blacks is due to the actions of whites, who have been fortunate in subjugating Blacks to their present condition, and therefore not to any innate inferiority, or as part of a divine order. Juan sees whites' overlordship as an insult (*vituperio*). Fortune, not divine providence, is blamed for the situation of Blacks:

JUAN DE MÉRIDA   ¿Que esto es ser negro?, ¿esto es ser
de este color? De este agravio
me quejaré a la Fortuna,
al cielo, al tiempo y a cuantos
me hicieron negro. ¡Oh, reniego
del color!

As Martínez points out, "Predestination was undoubtedly one of the most divisive theological issues in post-Reformation Europe. However, simplified in this stanza, Rodríguez Alva's usage of loaded terms ('factal destino', 'predestinado', 'decreto') must have triggered all the alarms for some readers..." (2020a, 99).

20   "It is the soldier's and his commander's task not to fail Fortune when she offers herself, and when she happens to do so, to bend her towards their strategy" (Lipsius 2004, 623).

[JUAN DE MÉRIDA	Is this to be Black? Is this to be
	This color? For this injustice,
	I'll complain to Fortune,
	To heaven, to time, and to those
	Who made me black. Oh, I reject
	This color!] (lines 628–633)

One is not born Black, one is made Black, Juan says. In his time, to be Black is an insult. Juan de Mérida is bent on demanding satisfaction from those responsible for his situation, especially "those who made me Black". Fortune, heaven, the times, and people have made his skin color signify an insult (*agravio*). Being Black is a matter of natural contingency, an accident in Aristotelian categorization. Being Black is a historical category, Juan says. Black is an accident with negative meaning. Nature is the signifier; its meaning is given by people. Therefore, he rejects that meaning.[21]

The debasement of all Blacks is just a matter of contingency, which was one of the meanings of Fortune. Juan's discourse in defense of Blackness is the result of the modern idea of Blacks as enslavable in a global context.[22] Therefore a Black man like Juan de Mérida does not have to accept his lot and is justified in confronting what he sees as a grievance (*agravio*). He will change the insult of being Black into praise. Juan de Mérida wants a change in his own Fortune and that of the other Blacks in the world through his feats. Like other modern military heroes, he expresses his desire through the *topos* of stopping the Wheel of Fortune:

---

21   The medieval legal code of *Las Siete Partidas* defined slavery as unnatural (quoted in Lucena Salmoral 1995, 35). In its distinction between substance and accident, Aristotelian philosophy elaborates on the concept of accident. Blackness is an 'inseparable accident', and Aristotle gives the example of the crow and the Ethiopian (García Norro 2002, 176–77).

22   In his *De instauranda Aethiopum salute* (1627 and 1647), Seville-born Jesuit priest Alonso de Sandoval dedicates a large portion of his religious treatise to an ethnographic and historical account of Blacks (Ethiopians, in his terminology) as a global human category of people of dark complexion that included most of the African continent, parts of the Arabian Peninsula, the Indian subcontinent and South Asia, the Philippines and islands of what Spanish geography called Maluco, but also the area of New Granada and Peru on the American continent (Olsen 2004, 81).

Con esta carta voy contento y rico,
que es de mi libertad: con ella un clavo
al eje vil de la Fortuna aplico
y con la infamia del color acabo.
Ya mi valor al mundo significo,
pues, aunque negro soy, no he sido esclavo,
y miente el mismo Sol si lo imagina.

[With this paper, I feel fortunate and content,
For it's a letter of freedom: with it, I drive a spike
Into Fortune's evil axle,
And end the shame of this color.
Now I can exercise my valor in this world,
For, although Black, I have not been a slave,
And the sun itself lies, if it imagines otherwise.]

(lines 389–395)

Juan alludes to visual images of the time showing military leaders like Hernán Cortés putting the brakes on the Wheel of Fortune, represented in his case by a water wheel, through the use of a hammer and a nail (González García 2017, 117–18).[23] Claramonte was probably familiar with the trope of controlling the Wheel of Fortune with a nail.[24] But

---

23   Cortés chose the Wheel of Fortune as his device after the fall of Mexico-Tenochtitlan with the motto: "Clavaré cuando me vea do no haya más que posea" ["I shall hammer in the nail when I see that there is nothing more to possess"] (Elliott 1989, 34).

24   It appears in Machiavelli's *History of Florence*, signifying that virtue can stop the Wheel of Fortune from turning (González García 2006, 286), and in emblem 65 of Sebastián de Covarrubias' *Emblemas morales* (1610) as a sign of the power of military and political virtue over Fortune (González García 2017, 219). Lope de Vega, in *El perro del hortelano*, repeats the commonplace: "Ludovico: Detenga / la fortuna, en tanto bien, / con clavo de oro la rueda" ["May Fortune stop its wheel with a golden spoke in the midst of all this goodness"] (lines 3349–3351), meaning stopping the Wheel of Fortune when good events take place. It is associated with prudence in Covarrubias' *Tesoro de la lengua castellana*: "Echar un clavo a la rueda de la Fortuna es asegurar que no vuelva atrás. Esto hace el hombre cuerdo, cuando reconociendo su volubilidad, asegura lo mejor que puede el estado en que se ve colocado, conservando amigos, ganando voluntades, y no se desvaneciendo, que los vagidos de la cabeza son peligrosos para los que andan por lugares altos y de

the meaning of the Wheel of Fortune for Juan de Mérida, a Black man, is markedly different from that of Hernán Cortés. Juan is to become a military leader too, but his goal is collective and liberatory. He will stop the running of the Wheel of Fortune for all people of his skin color, all Black people. The *conceptista* use of the word *clavo* (nail) acquires significance in the opposition of freedom and slavery. The S and I (spoke, nail, *clavo*) became a sign branded on the face of slaves, associated with their legal status.[25] Juan will use his freedom, contained in his *carta de ahorro* – letter of freedom, a piece of paper – to stop the Wheel of Fortune that has made him Black and his Blackness an insult. The spoke, the nail, written/branded on the bodies of Blacks, becomes a symbolic tool to write his liberation. He will stop the infamy for all Blacks. Military valor will be the means.

Now a soldier in his own right, Juan dares anyone to say he has ever been a slave. Being a soldier is a mark of his freedom, for slaves are

poco campo y margen" ["To put a nail in the Wheel of Fortune is to make sure it does not turn backwards. Acknowledging its fickleness, a judicious man does this and ensures the best way he can the estate in which he is placed by keeping friends, earning good will, and avoiding false self-esteem, because dizziness is dangerous for those who tread on high and narrow places"] (2020, 556).

25   The S and the I (*ese y clavo*, S and nail) were iron marks branded on the faces of some fugitive slaves, although this was not always the case (Stella 1998, 24). In some cases, the brand contained the entire name of the owner (Fernández Martín 34–36), and even the owner's address (N'Damba Kabongo 1975, 76). Covarrubias: "Esclavo: El siervo, el cautivo. Algunos quieren se haya dicho del hierro que les ponen a los fugitivos y díscolos en ambos carrillos de la S y del clavo; pero yo entiendo ser dos letras S y I que parece clavo y cada una es iniciativa de dicción, y vale tanto como *sine iure* porque el esclavo no es suyo sino de su señor y así le es prohibido cualquier acto libre y de aquí resultó el nombre de esclavo" ["Slave: Serf, captive. Some believe it comes from the iron used to brand those who are fugitive and disobedient in each cheek with the S and the nail. However, I think they are the two letters S and I, the latter looking like a nail, but each being the initials for *sine iure*, because the slave does not belong to himself, but to his master, and any free act is forbidden to him, and from this resulted the name slave"] (2020, 811). The popularity of the S and nail topos is present in Baltasar del Alcázar's poem on the theme of the slave of love: "Púsome en el alma el clavo / su dulce nombre y la S / porque ninguno pudiese / saber de quién soy esclavo" ["Her sweet name put in my soul the nail and the S / so no one could know whose slave I am"] (Buchanan 2016, 52).

by definition not soldiers. No slave owner would be foolish enough to allow the enslaved to bear arms. Juan de Mérida, however, still needs the letter of freedom to move around and travel. As other Black people before and after him, Juan de Mérida knows that in a slave society he will be presumed a slave until he demonstrates otherwise. He knows that his skin color requires an official written document stating that he is free. This is not just a personal quest, because he wants to end the infamy his skin color is held in. In his determination to join the military, he wants to decouple the twin notions of Blackness and slavery. He will render obsolete the need to carry a *carta de ahorro* for himself and for other Black people.

Juan de Mérida is a man of the Renaissance, and Fortune helps those who are in possession of the *virtù* Machiavelli spoke about, which consists of valor, prudence, and daring.[26] Juan's military virtue will defeat the Fortune of being Black. Fortune will be dominated by this Black man, for even though Fortune is blind to justice, it is movable. His actions will sway it to his side. Acquiring Fortune – honor, money, success – had become a new concept in the Renaissance. Juan rejects the idea of accepting his assigned social position when he tells his former owner, Doña Juana, that he will not be a water carrier (*azacán*) in his hometown.

Juan conflates Fortune and skin color again in the scene when he captures Captain Don Agustín. The night scene allows Juan to tell the Captain, as he did in the first scene of the play, that skin color is not related to blood, in the sense of moral virtue or military valor. When the surprised Captain asks for his captor's identity, Juan answers in a *conceptista* tone that puts racial and national identities upside down:

JUAN DE MÉRIDA   Un alemán
                        que ha dos horas que era negro.
                        Negra ha sido esta facción,
                        y esta empresa, incierta y manca;
                        mas en la plana más blanca
                        suele caer un borrón;

---

26   For the role of Fortune in a military career, see the essay by Olmedo Gobante in this edition.

y en ti ha caído esta vez,
quedando en tiempo tan breve
yo más blanco que la nieve,
tú, más negro que la pez.
Darte puedo aquí la muerte
y no quiero, por pensar
que salió en negro tu azar
y salió en blanco mi suerte.

[JUAN DE MÉRIDA   A German
Who was Black two hours ago.
Black has been this action,
And this enterprise, uncertain and bleak;
But on the whitest plane
A dark blot sometimes falls;
And it has befallen on you this time,
Allowing me on such short notice
To be whiter than snow,
And you , blacker than pitch.
I can end your life right here,
But I don't want to, since I believe
That your venture turned out black,
And my fortune turned out white.]
(lines 802–815)

Juan could be a German for all that matters, and the Captain a Black man. By passing as a German – white – and then revealing his racial identity as a Black man, he puts his aristocratic adversary in a contradictory position. If Juan is a German, he will have to be a natural enemy of Spain, but if he now reveals himself as Black, he cannot be mistaken for a German. To be Black means to be a Spaniard. He cannot be Don Agustín's enemy, but Don Agustín has declared Juan his enemy on account of his Black skin. Through his valor in the defense of the Spanish cause, Juan has equated being a Spaniard with being Black. In capturing Don Agustín, Juan has captured "a German". Whiteness becomes an unstable sign, shared by Germans and white Spaniards like Don Agustín. Juan changes the terms of the racial discourse in a second reference to writing. He is the blot on the white paper of white supremacy. Juan's actions are the ink with which he writes history. In this continued metonym, Don Agustín has the unenviable role of being the white paper on which Juan writes a new account. There is an added sexual subtext here, in which Don Agustín is placed in a subjugated female position. Juan also refers to Fortune in terms of gambling, an activity that was common among soldiers and frequently criticized. Luck has inverted their roles. But it is Don Agustín's luck, not Juan's Fortune, that is, his prudence and daring.

Captain Don Agustín is an unworthy aristocrat, and a poor example of the good soldier Juan represents. Don Agustín is dishonorable in matters of love, and a coward in military affairs. As seen above, he voices the pervasive anti-Black discourse of the other white soldiers. He represents one of the meanings of Fortune, that of those who were born with means, Fortune as inherited (and unmerited) wealth.[27]

Juan's pursuit of Fortune is in stark contrast to that of Don Agustín, his nemesis. The latter shows lack of prudence and decorum. The audience sees and hears that Don Agustín has no virtue. Don Agustín only means luck when he applies the term Fortune to his chances to do something advantageous to his military career. The contrast is visible in the scene when he disguises himself in the enemy camp, ironically using the night as a darkening aid in the same way Juan does:

> Por este contradique,
> pues el traje es flamenco y voy seguro,
> mi Fortuna me aplique
> espía o centinela que a lo oscuro
> −redimiendo la nieve−
> de algún álamo esté que perlas bebe.

---

27   In the Prologue of *Lazarillo de Tormes*, the protagonist compares his own life of effort to that of those who were born wealthy: "consideren los que heredaron nobles estados cuán poco se les debe, pues Fortuna fue con ellos parcial, y cuánto más hicieron los que, siéndoles contraria, con fuerza y maña remando salieron a buen puerto" ["those who inherit noble estates may consider how little they deserve them, Fortune having been so very partial to them in its gifts; and how much more those have done who, not being so favoured, have, by force and management, arrived at a good estate"] (Anonymous 1908, 3; 1982, 89).

[Through this smaller channel
I walk safely, for my clothes are Flemish.
May Fortune find me
any scout spy or sentry
– sheltering from snow –
under the shadow of a pearl-covered
      poplar tree.]
(lines 764–769)

Don Agustín's disguise has a negative effect, as he becomes equal to Juan. By dressing as other than himself he becomes visually identified as the enemy. Out on a hunt for a spy, he will be Juan's prey in a reversal of roles. Juan's Blackness thus becomes identified with Spanishness, as said before.

Juan's military virtue is chiefly opposed to the lack thereof in Don Agustín, who proves to be daring but cowardly, imprudent, and, most of all, devoid of a sense of justice, a virtue most necessary in a military commander. Juan's actions, presided over by virtue, are also in contrast with those of the Prince of Orange, who is captured by Juan as a consequence of his lack of prudence, even though as a prince he shows himself to be a man of honor in defeat:

PRÍNCIPE DE ORANGE   Si vuecelencia tales hombres tiene,
        ¿quién hace a su Fortuna resistencia?
        …

DUQUE DE ALBA   Gloria eterna es vencer tal enemigo.
        ¿Dónde halló a vuecelencia?

PRÍNCIPE DE ORANGE   Imaginallo
        es perder el juicio. De mi tienda
        me sacó el español. (El modo callo,
        porque el cielo de oírlo no se ofenda).
        Soldado insigne. Debe el Rey premiallo;
        y yo, aunque agora su valor me ofende
        le he de premiar también, que estoy pagado
        de que me haya vencido tal soldado.

[PRINCE OF ORANGE   If Your Grace has such men,
        Who shall dare to oppose your fortune?
        …

DUKE OF ALBA	Eternal glory is to defeat such an enemy.
	Where did he find your Grace?
PRINCE OF ORANGE	To relive it
	Is to lose one's mind. From my tent
	The Spaniard took me away. The how, I won't say,
	Because I don't want the heavens to be outraged:
	A remarkable soldier! The King must reward him;
	And I, even if his valor amazes me,
	will reward him, too, for I am satisfied
	That such a soldier has defeated me.]

(lines 1775–1776 and 1781–1789)

The incorporation of Fortune in Juan's racial discourse also changes his relation to the Duke of Alba. Fortune was a factor the Renaissance military leader had to acknowledge and dominate. As war's events turn against the Spanish armies of Flanders, the Duke of Alba displays temperance as he faces defeat and the need to withdraw on less than honorable terms (lines 1550–1556). At this point Juan's actions to turn Fortune in his favor coalesce with the Fortune of the Duke of Alba and his armies. The message would not be lost on the audience. A Black soldier saves the day, and his new name, Juan de Alba, is a change of symbolic color.

Like Hernán Cortés, Juan's military actions will turn Fortune to his favor, but as in the case of the conquistador, this can only happen with royal favor (González García 2017, 117). Kingly magnanimity is the ultimate Fortune, for the King is the origin of all legitimate power and prosperity:

JUAN DE ALBA	Yo sospecho
	que esta es, gran señor, apuesta
	entre el Rey y la Fortuna,
	mostrando cuál puede más.

JUAN DE ALBA	[I suspect
	that this is, your Grace, a wager
	between the King and Fortune,
	showing which can outdo the other.]

(lines 2307–2310)

But Juan's discourse on Fortune is different from others. Hernán Cortés mentioned royal fortune (*real ventura*) as a necessary element in political and military success (Elliott 1989, 35). Cortés also mentioned the help of God, adding the vagaries of royal fortune in a political argument to request the favor of the King. It was almost a demand and a criticism of the King's fickleness towards those he should reward. Juan does not mention divine providence, but rather the King himself in competition with good fortune. The King will always best Fortune in the drive to reward those who deserve it. This unflinching praise of the King in his practice of rewarding military virtue is not coupled with any mention of divine providence. The absence of God's will at this juncture is consistent with Juan's argument that blames Fortune, and not God, for his condition as a Black man. It is Fortune – historical contingency – that has to be dominated. The Duke of Alba confirms it by spelling out a variation on the adage *Audaces fortuna iuvat*:[28]

> De la Fortuna el osado
> es dueño; y tan gran soldado
> no aspira a premio menor.
> Maese de campo es ya,
> general, vueseñoría;
> que esto alcanza la osadía
> y esto la osadía da.
>
> [A bold man masters
> Fortune; and so great a soldier
> does not aspire to a minor prize.
> You are now Field Commander,
> a General, and a Lord;
> this being bold achieves
> and this is being bold grants.]
>
> (lines 2318–2324)[29]

---

28   'Fortune helps those who dare'. It is a variation of the original 'audentis fortuna iuvat' (*Aeneid* X: 284).

29   A variant of this concept is present in Alciati's emblem 118: "Virtuti fortuna comes" ["Fortune is virtue's companion"]. The text of the emblem states that Fortune is abundant with those who use eloquence with equity and good counsel (Alciato 1549).

The Duke of Alba uses the word "dueño" (master, owner) to concretize the relation between Fortune and Juan. He, like the King, sees only the results of military virtue. The audience knows better, for the audacious Juan had to dominate the very reason that makes him Black in seventeenth-century Spanish society. Juan enslaved Fortune, became its master; that is, he physically defeated those who held him in lesser esteem (see Olmedo Gobante's essay in this volume). His anti-Black enemies were fellow Spaniards. They embodied Fortune, the historical reality of modern slavery.

In the notes on performance in this volume we propose that Claramonte had Black spectators in mind when he wrote *The Valiant Black Man in Flanders*. In all plays there is a pact between the playwright, director, actors, and those who engage with the dramatic proposal in front of them, the spectators. The audience of spectators, however, is not uniform. While white spectators of the lower classes would see *The Valiant Black Man in Flanders* as a comedy of upward mobility, military valor, and thrashing of unmerited privilege, Black spectators might see *The Valiant Black Man in Flanders* differently. The play lends itself to being read as an argument for freedom and against slavery. If we take into account that it was written and possibly staged in Seville, as Claramonte's biography suggests, Black spectators would have had a say in its future popularity. Black spectators were poised to see in Juan de Mérida someone who claimed Spain as his birthplace. They would see his Afro-diasporic condition in the fact that he is a Black man with ties to family and place. The second mention of his mother Catalina makes him a returning son who lets white audiences know that his roots are in Spanish soil. He calls for his mother Catalina as soon as he shows up back in Mérida, now in military triumph and with the new name Juan de Alba. A Black woman, Catalina, is now the origin of a new genealogical tree. Mérida had made Juan a Black person by connecting him to slavery. Now ennobled, he will make Mérida the site of freedom for himself, his progeny, and all Blacks. Slavery can be defeated through fighting.

Juan de Mérida's Afro-diasporic condition is celebrated with his elevation to a position of honor at the end of the play, when the King bestows on him the habit of the Order of Santiago.[30] A Black man's induction to this elite institution was extraordinary yet not unique.[31] But someone decided to remove this passage and that of Juan de Alba's marriage from the 1638 Barcelona edition. The scene (lines 2277–2291) makes fun of the *probanzas* (proof of purity of blood), the investigation into the candidate's ancestry prior to the concession of the honor. These proofs also served to show the candidate's *hidalguía*, that is, that he descended from warriors and not peasants. This vetting system was notorious, for money made it easy to obtain favorable reports.[32] In the case of Juan, he says, the request should be sent to Africa (*Guinea*), where his ancestors came from. To all spectators this is an impossible proposition. The choice of the word *Guinea* immediately conjured the geography of slavery, and the contradiction was served. Proof of purity of blood was meant to root out men of Jewish and Muslim descent. By having *Guinea* as their ancestral land, Blacks could prove they did not descend from Jews and Muslims. This point was something any white person in Spain would have a hard time contradicting. The scene would serve as a send-up to the aristocracy: Blacks could be considered to be just as pure in blood as lower-class Old Christians.[33]

---

30   The military order of Santiago (Saint James) was created in the twelfth century to protect pilgrims to Santiago de Compostela from Muslim attacks. It was incorporated to the Crown by the Catholic monarchs in 1493. By the seventeenth century, the King conferred the Cross of Santiago and its habit to distinguish military merit.

31   A Black knight of Santiago on horseback is featured in the Portuguese painting *El chafariz d'El-Rey* by an anonymous Flemish artist at the end of the sixteenth century (Olmedo Gobante 2018, 70–71, figure 6). The painting is remarkable because it also depicts numerous other Black individuals, some of whom are water carriers. The painting thus represents opposite social positions among Blacks. Juan is now a knight of Santiago after refusing to accept his lot as a humble *azacán*, a water carrier, in act one, as discussed earlier in this essay.

32   Its elitist membership excluded people of Jewish and Muslim descent, in addition to those who descended from people condemned for heresy. People whose ancestors had practiced mechanical arts (agriculture, artisans) or who had engaged in mercantile activities were also barred.

33   Juan de Alba could claim, from Spain, that he did not know who his pagan ancestors in Africa were. This doctrine, however, was not followed in Spanish

Doña Leonor, Don Agustín, and the Queerness of Whites

Doña Leonor and Don Agustín are the protagonists of the love story without which a Spanish seventeenth-century *comedia* would be almost unthinkable. Because this is a play in which the protagonist is neither aristocratic nor white, the love story serves the purpose of setting the honorable behavior of Juan de Mérida in contrast with the less-than-honorable acts of his adversary, Captain Don Agustín.

Doña Leonor and Don Agustín are two flawed characters. Doña Leonor has entrusted her sexual honor to a man's written word, Don Agustín's. From the start of the play, he is depicted as cruel and an unworthy *galán* (male lover). Don Agustín does not embody the knightly virtues of the early modern European armies (see Olmedo Gobante's essay in this edition). Captain Don Agustín is a calculating schemer who puts his economic interest ahead of his written promises: He will ditch Doña Leonor for the wealthier Doña Juana. In the military field, Don Agustín cannot be trusted either, as he proves himself to be a lying coward. He lacks manliness in both love and war. His inconstancy in love is a at a par with his effeminacy. He is called a *lindo*.[34] Furthermore, his betrayal of Doña Leonor changes the gender dynamics of the play.

A woman dressed as a man in Spanish *comedia* forms a question

America. Martínez (2008) mentions, as one of the elements of *limpieza de sangre*, the doctrine that explained being an old Christian as someone whose non-Christian ancestors could not be traced back in memory (2008, 203).

34   Cervantes in 'El amante liberal' presents Cornelio as a *lindo*, both rich and effeminate and the opposite of military spirit: "¿piensas, quiero decir, que este mozo, altivo por su riqueza, arrogante por su gallardía, inexperto por su edad poca, confiado por su linaje, ha de querer, ni poder, ni saber guardar firmeza en sus amores…? …Vete, vete, y recréate entre las doncellas de tu madre, y allí ten cuidado de tus cabellos y de tus manos, más despiertas a devanar blando sirgo que a empuñar la dura espada" ["Do you think, in other words, that this boy, haughty because of his wealth, arrogant because of his handsome bearing, lacking in experience because of his youth and presumptuous because of his lineage, will wish or be able or know how to keep constancy in his love…? …Go, go and amuse yourself among your mother's maidservants and there tend to your hair and to your hands, which are better suited to winding soft silk around a reel than to taking up the harsh sword"] (Cervantes 1982, 160–61; 2013, 107–109).

mark. The question is one of honor: how did she lose it? The answer almost always lies in an act of injustice, the broken word of a man. Doña Leonor, after being abandoned by Don Agustín, has to reclaim her most valuable social possession, her sexual honor. The letter Don Agustín wrote indicating his promise of marriage is a parallel document to the letter of freedom Juan must carry with him. Doña Leonor's letter is proof of her social worth, what makes her marriageable and not someone destined to social death.

White women and Blacks depend on papers to establish their worth and to have freedom of movement. Olmedo Gobante discusses the role of written culture in this play, and how letters actually make action move forward. The relation between Juan's letter of freedom and Doña Leonor's written promise of marriage is one of wealth. Without his letter, Juan is a slave, subject to be sold for a monetary price. No other episode makes it more evident than the one at the Royal Palace, where two white men speculate over the possible monetary worth of Juan and Antón (line 2113). The letter Doña Leonor carries with her to Flanders, like Juan's, denotes her social worth, something that translates into money. Don Agustín, after all, is ready to leave Doña Leonor for the wealthier Doña Juana. Doña Leonor's letter of promise is indeed a commercial document worth money, like Juan's letter of freedom.

The transfer of the play's location from Mérida, in Spain, to Flanders allows the love story to develop as one of loss and recovery of honor. Doña Leonor's quest to regain her honor joins Juan's attempt to build his own through military valor. Her sexual honor will be tied to his success as a soldier. The mismatch is evident. Dressed as a page and calling herself Esteban, Doña Leonor joins the hundreds of *comedia* ladies who dress as men for reasons of love and honor (although not always).[35] But Doña Leonor does not travel alone, bringing her Black

---

35 One out of four *comedias* written by Lope de Vega and Tirso de Molina have a woman cross-dressed as a man as protagonist, according to Anita K. Stall (2000, 86). *La mujer vestida de hombre en el teatro español (siglos XVI–XVII)*, the pioneering work of Carmen Bravo-Villasante, defined some of the categories: *doncella guerrera* (war-like maid), *mujer hombruna* (man-acting woman), *mujer varonil* (manly woman), which initially were met with strong criticism (Ashcom

male slave Antón with her. Antón's presence is a reminder of her position of power as a white woman in Spain, which includes being a slave owner.[36]

In *The Valiant Black Man in Flanders*, Flanders becomes a stage where whiteness is performed in a series of situations that belong in the category of dishonor. The first two situations of dishonor are, respectively, a broken promise of marriage and gender crossing through a change in dress. Upon encountering Juan in Flanders, Doña Leonor/ Esteban decides to make her male attire an instrument for further sexual transgression. Her male dress and her equivocal offers of friendship make Juan believe that he is being wooed by another man. He is deeply alarmed (lines 1042–1085). It is important to note that in the construction of this episode, Juan does not recognize Doña Leonor as the lady who saved his life earlier in the first act, but he recognizes Antón as a friend and neighbor from Mérida. When Doña Leonor, a white woman, dresses as a man, her identity becomes unreadable to Juan.

Doña Leonor/Esteban's homoerotic actions are predicated on a contrast between her/his whiteness and Juan's masculine Blackness. The entire episode is a power game in which whiteness appears as menacing to the honor and physical integrity of a Black man. Doña Leonor's disguise hides her gender but not her whiteness. Her whiteness is performed as queer, and this is the message Juan de Mérida reads in the sexual advances of which he is the object.

1960, 44). Melveena McKendrick established the field of female cross-dressing studies in 1974. A critical assessment of scholarship on cross-dressing women, gender as performance, and same-sex attraction in Spanish *comedia* is to be found in Jonathan Thacker's study of three plays by Tirso de Molina.

36   The Morisco population of Granada, for instance, had been forbidden to own Black slaves through a royal order from Philip II in 1566 that also restricted most of their acts and signs of cultural difference (dress, language, food). There was fear that Morisco owners would convert their Black slaves to Islam or allow them to continue practicing it. Don Francisco Núñez Muley, speaking for the Moriscos, wrote a famous *memorial* excoriating these measures in what is one of the first documents that expresses the right to be ethnically different. Núñez Muley's arguments appear in Calderón de la Barca's *Amar después de la muerte, o el Tuzaní de la Alpularra* and in Jiménez de Enciso's *Juan Latino* (Fra-Molinero 2005, 335, n. 19 and 20).

Juan de Mérida's Blackness is gendered in a form of masculinity that resolves conflict with violence, but in his encounter with Doña Leonor/Esteban, direct violence appears not to be an option. For one, the setting is the Spanish military camp, a public space, where Juan's violent reaction would be judged harshly. Instead, Juan has to perform his Blackness as separate from his masculinity. He will have to use the rhetorical device of Black self-deprecation.

Juan has to play into the idea of Blackness as negativity. He rejects the sexual advances of this young white man by asserting the undesirability of his black body, objecting that he will stain the page's white hands with "the soot" of his skin: "es muy tierna / y muy blanca y tiznaráse" (lines 1071–1072). This phrase is in direct contrast to what he had stated earlier to the other soldiers in Mérida: "aunque negros no tiznamos" (line 32). He further rejects the offer to sleep with Esteban, going to the point of self-insult: Like all Blacks in literature, he says he smells bad ("huelo a grajea").[37] The only problem is that he is supposed to say "a grajos" ["like a crow"], and he says *grajea*, a piece of confectionery.

In his anxious defense of a heteronormative masculine sexuality Juan claims his Blackness. His resort to some of the negative stereotypes used against the Black body on the stage and in poetry – presumed bad smell and skin color as something that smears like soot – is a strategy of survival against the menace of a queer white individual. Juan presents his Black body's perceived undesirability – it smells, its color stains – as a shield against a white person's unlawful desire. Leonor/Esteban sexualizes Juan's Black body and her/his white one when she compares their two bodies in bed to *taracea* (inlay in marquetry), two pieces of different wood intertwined, with its phallic element included.

---

37 Covarrubias in *Tesoro de la lengua castellana* (2020, 1033): "heder a grajos, es de negros" ["to smell like a rook, referring to Blacks"]. The popularity of this phrase associated to non-whites is attested in Lorenzo Franciosini's *Vocabulario italiano e spagnuolo*: "heder a grajos: puzzare di sudore, o di certa materia cattiva, come talvolta si sente ne' Mori, quando uno s'accosta loro" ["to stink of sweat, or of something bad, like sometimes it feels among the Moors when one gets close to them"] (1638, 2nd volume, 434).

The homoerotic advances of Leonor/Esteban are a threat to Juan's honor, defined as fear of penetration. In Spanish *comedias* the male protagonist defends himself from real or symbolic penetration: his body, his home, his womenfolk (Stroud 2007, 114). Doña Leonor/ Esteban's homoerotic proposition turns Juan's Black male body into an object of desire. Doña Leonor/Esteban puts him in the same position as a white woman or an enslaved Black person. The white woman, the Black person, fears to be touched, to be desired and ultimately penetrated. Both have to counter the desire their bodies provoke: submit to it or face violence.

The honor Juan de Mérida is trying to gain through his military valor is challenged by someone white. Doña Leonor/Esteban destabilizes Juan's body as a marker of masculinity by simply letting him know of her/his desire. Doña Leonor/Esteban uses the *camarada*, a homosocial space among soldiers, to present herself/himself as a fellow soldier and friend from Mérida to which Juan responds with fear and rage. After all, Juan is a lonely hero, with no friends in the military. The offer of friendship and material comfort is seductive, but Juan sees it as a trap.

The performance of homoeroticism hinges on the creation of Doña Leonor/Esteban as a dual character in terms of gender, but not in terms of race and social class. As observed earlier, Doña Leonor becomes unknowable to Juan. The white female body performs typically female gestures and words that change meaning through the signifier of her male attire, including the mention of perfume (line 1232), associated with effeminacy in a soldier. Whiteness is further marked as upper class in the offer of money that Doña Leonor/Esteban makes to Juan so they can become friends. Doña Leonor/Esteban's conspicuous wealth constitutes a serious risk for Juan.

The presence of money complicates the situation for Juan even further: He sees himself as a male prostitute. The encounter is being dictated by the white other who could bring catastrophe to his life. At the time, there were well-known cases of men of African descent burned at the stake for sodomy.[38] Sodomy and Blackness become equally damning social attributes:

> (Este paje me persigue
> más que el color ¿Yo, por él?
> ¿Esto el capitán me dice?
> Llámeme negro cobarde
> y zurdo, para que cifre
> en mí todos los agravios
> el día que a persuadirle
> vaya tal cosa)

[[Aside]]

> This pageboy shadows me
> More than my color; I wonder, What?
> What is this captain telling me?
> The day that I lead you to believe that you
> Can call me Black, coward, and left-handed,
> So that all misfortunes fall upon me]
> (lines 1518–1525)

Zurdo (left-handed) was a popular term for a sodomite. The play's public was familiar with the puns and jokes regarding the punishment of sodomy by burning at the stake, as the victims were referred to as *quemados*, *morenos*, and *mulato*s.[39] Not only is Juan's male honor at stake; his own life is in danger. For Juan, Leonor/Esteban is the white phantom of homosexuality that haunts him as an attribute associated to Black men in Spanish cities. This ghost follows him to Flanders.

---

38 In a letter dated November 30, 1611, to the Duke of Sessa, Lope de Vega comments on the burning at the stake of a Mulatto hermit accused of sodomy in Madrid (Lope de Vega 1985, 106). The poem 'A un ermitaño mulato' by Francisco de Quevedo may be addressing the same person (Fra Molinero 2000, 129). Another famous case is that of Machuco, a freed Black man sentenced to death in Seville in 1585 for procuring same-sex encounters among upper-class men (Martin 2008, 113–114). Statistics from criminal records also indicate that 55 percent of Black and Muslim men accused of sodomy were sentenced to death or to the galleys (Berco 2007, 114).

39 See Francisco de Quevedo's *jácara*: "Montúfar se ha entrado a puto / con un mulato rapaz / que por lucir más que todos / se deja el pobre quemar" ["Montufar is now a punk whore with a mulatto lad as his pal. To show off more than anyone he'll go through fire"] (Quevedo y Villegas 2007, 15).

Leonor/Esteban's homosocial invitation implies a change of physical space for Juan. Throughout the play, Juan occupies public spaces, and rarely domestic ones: the square in Mérida, the tent of the Duke of Alba, the fields of Flanders, the waiting halls of the Royal Palace in Madrid. The domestic space of the dinner table and the bed at the inn, a space indoors, is the space of domestic enslavement or servitude he rejected by leaving Mérida. Domestic space meant servitude and dependence for Juan, as signified in act one when he takes refuge in Doña Leonor's house, or in his exchange with Doña Juana in her house (line 356), in which he rejects servitude. As a Black servant he had been part of a world of luxury, in which he had been one more commodity. Consequently, Juan's sense of masculinity is rooted in heterosexual normativity, one of whose performative markers is opposition to ideas of comfort and luxury.

Luxury, sodomy, and foreignness go hand in hand in Spanish seventeenth-century literature. Italians and Italy as a site of male homosexual practices were a commonplace (Martin 2008, 212). Juan says that homoeroticism belongs in Italy (line 1278). Leonor/Esteban uses *a reverder* (line 1308) to say good-bye to Juan, in a display of linguistic foreignness that points to modern fashion and queerness. The other site of sodomy was the Muslim Mediterranean world.[40] While the connection between Algiers and the nefarious sin was a topos to describe the religious abyss Islam represented – so close geographically and so distant in the imaginary – the display of Italian words by Leonor/Esteban provokes a more profound destabilization. The scene takes place in Flanders, where an Italian, Alessandro Farnese, succeeded the Duke of Alba as commander of the Spanish armies.

Doña Leonor, as a female character, is tied to sexual and linguistic deviance. Her passionate exchanges with Captain Don Agustín are perfect examples of *poesía culta*, the poetic style made fashionable

---

40 Algiers and the Ottoman Empire were also frequently associated with sodomy. Cervantes refers to Algiers in this sense in the episode of Ana Félix, whose boyfriend has to dress as a woman to avoid being the object of same-sex desire in Algiers (*Don Quijote* II, chapter 65).

by Luis de Góngora (1561–1627) that many, including Francisco de Quevedo, dubbed a form of heresy. Góngora's style was dubbed *culteranismo*, a word that alliterates with *luteranismo* (Lutheranism), that is, a heretical poetic religion, according to opponents of *Gongorismo*. Doña Leonor's seduction by Don Agustín materializes through this form of poetic deviance that at the same time can be read as a form of female sexual affirmation. *Gongorismo* expressed luxury and the love of expensive foreign things as related to sexual deviation from heteronormativity. This new style became the poetic norm for the following century on both sides of the Atlantic, emphasizing a display of new words and old ones of Latin origin with difficult meanings, a sort of linguistic luxury (Valencia 2021, 201).

As a sign of luxury, sexual deviance expressed in the *Gongorista* style ends up being associated with whiteness in the play. Every love scene in the play adopts the new poetic fashion. Doña Leonor and Don Agustín stop their frenetic pursuit of a fleeing Juan de Mérida to fall for each other in a parody of verbal luxury:

> y, pues quiso darme Amor
> tal ocasión, malograrla
> fuera ofender sus saetas,
> fuera profanar sus alas.
> Desde que le dio el abril,
> coronado de esmeraldas,
> al labio perfiles de oro
> y poca aurora a la barba,
> la inclinación de la guerra
> me ha tenido de mi patria
> ausente, siguiendo el son
> de las trompas y las cajas.

> [And since Cupid's love gave me
> Such an opportunity, to misuse it
> Would be to offend its arrows,
> It would be to profane its wings.
> Ever since emerald-crowned April
> Gave my youthful lips

> Some golden strands of hair
> And a beard barely covered my face,
> My inclination towards war
> Has kept me absent
> From my homeland,
> Following the sound of trumpets and drums.]
>
> (lines 239–250)

Emeralds or the golden facial hair of Don Agustín (*al labio perfiles de oro*) are signs of the cant in Don Agustín's words and actions, and they are expressed in his letter promising marriage. Doña Leonor vents her anger at having given in to her sexual desire with the freedom this new poetic style affords her:

> ¡Oh fementido papel!,
> ¡oh, piélago de lisonjas
> donde son más las mentiras
> y las verdades son pocas!
> Pues con todo he de romper,
> justo será que en ti rompa
> víboras en letras lirios
> y áspides en partes rosas.

> [Oh, deceitful letter!
> Oh, ocean of flattery
> Where there are more lies
> And truths are far and few!
> Since I have to break with everything,
> It will be fair that I tear
> Vipers among lettered lilies,
> asps in scraps of roses.]
>
> (lines 524–531)

Leonor and Don Agustín are not the only ones indulging in *Gongorismo*. Doña Juana also expresses her love for her briefly betrothed Don Agustín in act three (lines 2365–2378). In act two Sergeant Barrientos uses a language that parodies the style associated with already famous poems like the Fábula de Polifemo:

SARGENTO BARRIENTOS ¡Desafíos
—en un frisón más cándido que el cerro
que nos mira deshecho en nieve y ríos
tascando en el bocado plata y hierro,
que de espuma se argenta en copos fríos—
un capitán tudesco pide a voces!
JUAN DE ALBA Él viene por puñetes y por coces.

[SERGEANT BARRIENTOS A challenge!
In a Friesian, white as the snow hills,
Who looks at us undone in snow and rivers,
Nibbling and silvering its iron mouthpiece,
Turning the iron into silver icy flakes,
A German captain demands a challenge.
JUAN DE ALBA He'll get a boot on his backside
and a bloody nose.]
(lines 1412–1418)[41]

Juan de Alba's comment "Él viene por puñetes y por coces" ["He'll get a boot on his backside and a bloody nose"] translates the showy display of words from the sergeant into the common language of violence against the enemy.

Gongorismo is the new poetic commodity of the ruling classes, the ones Juan has to confront to defend his Blackness as a form of humanity and not as another commodity. In his demonstration of eloquence, Juan also uses *Gongorismo* in defense of the Black color (lines 38–66). Juan de Mérida's adoption of the luxurious and foreign *Gongorista* style goes beyond using a rhetorical mask of whiteness by appropriating it. His defense of Blackness in this style becomes an ironic exercise in historical references to the horrors of slavery represented in the sailing ships of modernity. Black tar is what keeps ships afloat on the waters: "la pez da a los vituperios / del mar fugitivos pies" ["Black pitch provides the ship / With speed against the affronts of the sea"] (lines 57–58). He sees himself as the Black man of the

---

41 The second stanza of Góngora's *Fábula de Polifemo y Galatea*: "tascando haga el freno de oro, cano, / del caballo andaluz la ociosa espuma" ["biting the golden bridle the Andalusian horse makes it white and idle foam"] (Góngora III: 13).

Renaissance who changes the fortune of an entire race by excelling in military virtue and the eloquence that goes with it. His visible triumph comes in his marriage at the end of the play.

The 'Two Endings' of *El valiente negro en Flandes*

The Barcelona edition of 1638, *P*, is the only one that omits Juan de Alba's marriage to his former owner Doña Juana at the end of the third act (as well as Juan's induction into the Order of Santiago, see Textual History in this volume). This omission, or rather erasure, is retained in the 1857 edition of the Biblioteca de Autores Españoles (under the care of Ramón de Mesonero Romanos) and its subsequent reprints; this was the standard edition throughout the Spanish-speaking world for most of the twentieth century. As explained in the Textual History section, the manuscript of 1651 and all the eighteenth-century printed versions of it include these two scenes.[42]

It is quite possible that the 1638 edition came from a version of the play that might have been staged at court (see Performance History), rather than in one of the popular *corrales* (theater houses). The excision of these two scenes would have suited the political and social interests of a more aristocratic and conservative audience (Rodríguez López-Vázquez 1997, 5). Possible proof of the discomfort that Juan's marriage could produce appears in the 1651 manuscript, where the text of the final marriage proposal is crossed out and marked with "no" in the margin (see Figure 1).

In *comedias* that ended with weddings, it was customary for the young, single protagonist to be rewarded with one. Juan de Mérida has no love interest throughout the play, and all love scenes are limited to Don Agustín, Doña Leonor, and the third-act addition of Doña Juana de Vera to the triangle. At the apogee of his glory and power, the newly appointed *maestre de campo general* Juan de Alba becomes the referee who restores the honor of the two ladies. He forces Don Agustín to fulfill his written promise to Doña Leonor, and seeing that Doña Juana is left without a husband, he accepts her offer of marriage.

---

42   See Editorial Methods in this volume for the stemma with all the extant texts prior the nineteenth century.

In a play where characters disguise their identity in different fashions day and night, the controversial marriage between Juan de Alba and Doña Juana is preceded by an act of misrecognition. Don Agustín does not recognize Juan de Alba back in Mérida, now promoted to the office of field marshal general. This is the final instance in which the aristocratic Don Agustín misreads Juan's body. Juan's new status, signalled by clothes and language tone, mystify Don Agustín. But the play has come full circle back to Mérida, the site where Juan's Blackness was associated with slavery. Doña Juana immediatly recognizes Juan as "mi negro", "my Black boy", in a verbal act of (re)possession, all of Juan's protestations of freedom from birth notwithstanding: "¡Válgame Dios! ¿No es Juanillo, / mi negro? ["God help me! Isn't this Little Juan, my Black boy?"] (lines 2481–2482).

In a baroque tour de force, the institutions of slavery and aristocracy end up embodied in Juan de Mérida/Juan de Alba. The descendant of slaves is now in a commanding position over the local aristocracy of Mérida. The inclusion in the play of the name Vera, the last name of Doña Juana and also of Antón, is not fortuitous. Many *comedias* insert names of members of the aristocracy as a form of literary homage, sometimes seeking patronage. At other times it could be a form of veiled political attack. The Vera family were members of the nobility in Mérida and originally from Seville, the city where Andrés de Claramonte most likely lived while writing *The Valiant Black Man in Flanders*. The first and third acts of *The Valiant Black Man in Flanders* take place in Mérida, and two characters, Doña Juana and her father Don Juan de Vera, are fictitious members of this noble house. In a possible nod to members of the Vera family, the place where Juan de Alba sends Doña Leonor to await the final denouement of her honor's restoration is the convent of Santa Olalla, founded by the Vera family.[43] All this indicates that Claramonte had

---

43 The convent of Santa Olalla was founded in 1530, and its building still exists today (Lozano Bartolozzi 1997, 129). Claramonte might have obtained information from Juan Antonio Vera y Figueroa (1583–1658), count of Roca and a member of the Vera family of Mérida. He studied in Seville, where he published *El embajador*

an interest in connecting Mérida and the Vera family to this Black protagonist.

Juan de Alba, now a powerful man, has come back to Mérida to impose a new, legitimate order. His word is authorized by the King. From being rejected by the army in act one, he now comes to raise an army, occupying a position even higher than the one Captain Don Augustín had at the beginning. His first act of power is to make Don Agustín marry Doña Leonor. For a second time, but this one in public, he threatens Don Agustín's life if he doesn't take Doña Leonor's hand in marriage:

JUAN DE ALBA   Cásese con ella
                         luego o, ¡por vida del Rey!,
                         que le corte la cabeza.

[JUAN DE ALBA   Marry her
                         now or, by the King's life,
                         I'll chop your head off.]
                                         (lines 2584–86)

From being a Black man who attacked soldiers in the first act, Juan is at the end of the play the Black man who threatens violence in the King's name and with his legal power. If Don Agustín defies him, he is defying the King and his punishment will be decapitation, as corresponds to someone of his rank who publicly disobeyed a military superior. The visual aspect of a Black man rhetorically overpowering a white and aristocratic one must have been pleasurable to some and unsettling to others. This violent reversal of racial dynamics could only be contemplated in a few churches, where statues of Saint Elesbaan, a Black military Christian king of Ethiopia, theatrically present him in the act of slaying a white king, a pagan (Rowe 2019, 148).

Acts of power are represented in increases. From restoring the honor of Doña Leonor, Juan moves to restore Doña Juana's honor. This is a complicated moment that conflates slavery and freedom.

(1620), an influential book on diplomacy that caught the attention of the Count-Duke of Olivares. Vera y Figueroa was active in the literary circles of Seville. All this activity took place at the time Andrés de Claramonte lived there.

The play maintains the ambiguity of Juan de Alba's legal status as a free man when he left Mérida. Doña Juana, betrothed to Don Agustín, now finds herself without a husband. Powerful and rich with a huge revenue, Juan offers to pay for Doña Juana's dowry to whomever she chooses as a husband. It was common at the end of *comedias*, for upper-class characters to pay the dowry of their female servants upon marrying male servants.[44] It was unheard of that a Black man born of a slave woman would endow his former mistress. But marriage, like slavery, was part of the economic structure.

The play makes clear that, among upper-class people, marriage was in essence a financial transaction. Don Agustín wanted to marry Doña Juana because of her money. Money and honor go together. Juan de Alba knows this when he offers to pay Doña Juana's dowry, even though she is wealthy already. Is this dowry a symbolic payment of Juan's manumission? Ostensibly, by offering to endow the rich Doña Juana, Juan is making her an irresistible marriage option to all men of her social status. But this is odd.

It is odd too, and significant, that Doña Juana takes the initiative to choose Juan de Alba as her husband instead of any of the men who would find her wealth quite attractive. Doña Juana's choice brings back the issue of Juan's freedom. Why is Juan free in the first place? Was he given freedom? Was he born free? Is his mother Catalina also free? One is reluctant to think that Claramonte disregarded clarifying these issues out of carelessness. Ambiguity plays a role in this play of social ascent.

As a Black man in Doña Juana's household, Juan had been a problem at the beginning of the play. He brought dishonor to her father due to his rebellious outbursts. He was a free Black, a walking contradiction. We must remember that *negro* was a synonym of slave that needed the adjective free (*horro, libre*) to negate the equivalence of blackness and slavery. Consequently, Doña Juana's surprising

---

44 In Lope de Vega's *El perro del hortelano*, newly ennobled and enriched Teodoro gives a dowry to Dorotea, a servant, so she can marry his male servant Tristán, "moreno de color quebrado" ["a dark man of broken color"] (lines 2434 and 3370–3377), that is, of mixed race with Black.

decision to propose marriage to Juan de Alba exposes the inherent negativity of Blackness:

DOÑA JUANA	Pues, si ha de ser ya el casarme por tu cuenta –y el cielo te ha dado honor y te ha igualado a mi nobleza–, de negro quiero que subas a dueño.
JUAN DE ALBA	¿Qué dices?
DOÑA JUANA	Que esta es ya mi resolución.

[DOÑA JUANA	Well, if I am going to be married out of your bounty – and Heaven has given you honor and has made you my equal in nobility – from a Black man, I want you to rise as my Master.
JUAN DE ALBA	What are you saying?
DOÑA JUANA	That I have already decided.]
	(lines 2629–2635)

Juan is stunned. He has reached the highest rung on the ladder of Fortune: *de negro a dueño*, from Black to master/owner. Although free, Juan's Blackness cannot deny the attached meaning of slavery. The answer Juan gives makes the play a rhetorical closed circle by repeating the words in act one in which he declared himself her slave, which legally he was no longer:

JUAN DE ALBA	(¿Quién tal suceso creyera? Vueltas son de la Fortuna). Vueseñoría me tenga por su esclavo.
DOÑA JUANA	Yo, desde hoy, he de ser esclava vuestra.

[JUAN DE ALBA	*[Aside]* Who would believe such an event? These are turns of the Wheel of Fortune. Your ladyship shall

DOÑA JUANA   regard me as your slave.
     From this day on,
     I shall be your slave.]
         (lines 2636–2640)

By declaring himself Doña Juana's slave, Juan re-signifies the meaning of the word through the metaphor of love enslavement that circulated in poems, novels, and plays through the early modern period.[45] This metaphorical enslavement to each other bridges the chasm of Doña Juana and Juan's social difference. Juan de Alba's mention, in an aside, of Fortune and its turns brings home the fact that he is in a position to change the meaning of being Black in Mérida and the rest of the world.

Weddings restored the broken order in the *comedia* (López 2007, 239). Thus, the two weddings at the end result in the recognition that Juan de Alba is the new source of honor. Honor is life in the value system of the *comedia*, or rather loss of honor is death. If Doña Leonor had saved Juan from being killed by the soldiers in act one, now Juan pays her back by restoring her honor and rescuing her from social death. For a popular audience that would include Black people, seeing a Black man bestowing honor would be a comforting proposition. A Black man has honor and gives honor to others, who accept it gladly. Thus, honor is a transferable entity: Since Juan has received his honor from the King – the origin of all honor – he can legitimately give honor to his new white wife, who appears not to be ashamed of marrying a Black man.

This multiracial social order is honorable and legitimate. The marriage of a Black man to an aristocratic white woman would usher in a nation where purity of blood is canceled. The play ends with the

---

45   The slavery metaphor of love had been made famous in many poetic compositions: "esclavo soy pero cúyo / esto no negaré yo, / que cúyo soy me compró / y estoy herrado por suyo" ["I am a slave but to whom / I shall not refuse to say / that whose I am bought me / and I have been branded as their belonging"]. There were many versions of these verses, repeated since the fifteenth century. Lope de Vega used variations in at least seven *comedias* (Fra Molinero 2014, 23). The metaphor of enslavement was made popular also in religious language, as many Catholic lay confraternities adopted the name slave in their names, in reference, among other things, to Christ's suffering on earth (Rowe 2019, 117).

enshrinement of blood mixture, but blood mixture that is endowed with social honor and wealth. This proposal for blood mixture with Blackness fed the anxiety around the image of Spain in Northern Europe as a country of mixed-race people, a country of Blacks (Fuchs 2009, 123ff). Perhaps this is why the episodes of the Order of Santiago's knighthood, and the multiracial wedding were absent in the 1638 Barcelona edition. Censorship would reflect this anxiety.

With Juan's marriage to Doña Juana, *The Valiant Black Man in Flanders* imagines a future in which a Black man, the son of a Black enslaved woman, is the genesis of a new society that descends from the lowest stratum imaginable. The irony is that in the end, Juan de Alba's plan to end slavery for all Blacks by uniting the enslaved with the enslaver is done on his own terms, not in the terms dictated by a male enslaver. To make this future imaginable, the proposed multiracial family will have a Black male patriarch, but also a woman who makes a choice against the racial norms.

CRITICAL ESSAY

A Black Soldier's Trophies:
Military Culture in *El valiente negro en Flandes*

Manuel Olmedo Gobante
Cornell University

As its title suggests, *Un cuerpo de guardia* (*A Guard Post*; Figure 5) is not meant to be an exceptional painting. Abraham Teniers produced this oil on copperplate along with a great number of extremely similar artworks (Israel 1995, 559). Painted in the mid-seventeenth century, right after the end of the Eighty Years' War, it depicts a scene of everyday military life. Every garrison or military camp had at least one of these guard posts, a space where watchmen took turns to protect the regiment's banner and other valuables such as weapons or the treasure. Teniers's strategic use of light dissuades us from focusing on the guards themselves, whom we can barely see smoking and drinking in the background. Instead, our attention is drawn to a series of objects that are laid at the forefront, framing the scene, as if they could better convey the essence of the guard post and the living experiences and serving conditions of the common soldier. Among these objects, a young Black man stands as the protagonist of the tableau. There is nothing exceptional about him. We can confidently assume he is a *paje de jineta* (an officer's assistant) because of his young age, his expensive outfit, and the fact that he is allowed to enter a highly restricted military zone. This Black page is portrayed with an individualized subjectivity, since he seems to have noticed something that his fellow soldiers have not. The adjacent watchdog that replicates the young man's posture hints at an undefined acoustic element. Although we ignore the cause of their alertness, both the page and the dog redirect our view towards the regiment's banner, a trophy whose strong symbolic power we will discuss later.

Much like Teniers's military genre paintings, Andrés de Claramonte's

El valiente negro en Flandes is a mise-en-scène of everyday soldierly life that places a Black man at the center.[46] Both the painting and the play were produced at a time when war fashioned every aspect of early modern culture, particularly in the Low Countries during the revolt against the Spanish monarchy.[47] They are, in a broad sense of the term, war narratives, for they allow the spectator to experience life at the front from the safety of either their home or the playhouse. Painting and play use the same technique: the accumulation of military objects of culture.[48]

In this essay, we examine how military culture permeates *El valiente negro en Flandes*, focusing on the study of materiality. In section one, we explore what being a Black man in Flanders was like. By comparing the story of the play's main character with similar accounts of the experiences of Black soldiers in the Spanish army, we posit that Claramonte critically engaged with contemporary military history. In section two, we inquire into the everyday life of a soldier. By surveying the material culture recreated in the play, we argue that *El valiente negro en Flandes* is a thorough and relatively accurate depiction of the living conditions of the common soldier serving in Flanders. Last, in section three, we identify the objects that characterize a valiant man, that is, the ideal image of the extraordinary early modern soldier. The critical analysis of the cultural objects – the trophies – that are prominently displayed in the play helps us to understand *El valiente negro en Flandes* in its theatrical context.

I. Black Men in Flanders
The Eighty Years' War (1568–1648), also known as the Dutch Revolt – or the Flemish Wars, as the conflict was framed in mainstream

---

46   The living conditions of early modern Spanish soldiers have received significant attention in the last few decades. See Hale (1985), Parker (2000), Thompson (2013), Calvo (2019), Harden (2020) and Martínez (2016 and 2020a and b).

47   For the centrality of warfare in early modern Spanish culture, see Espino López (2001), García Hernán (2006), Rupp (2014) and the volume edited by Vélez Sainz and Sánchez Jiménez (2016).

48   See the collective volume edited by Barnard and De Armas (2013).

Spanish discourse – was told through a wide array of forms and media, from personal letters, printed pamphlets, and war chronicles, to many visual and literary representations. Theater was a privileged medium to narrate the Revolt in the Low Countries.[49] At least thirty-five *comedias* were set in Flanders (Rodríguez Pérez 2008, 24), the most studied being Lope de Vega's *Los españoles en Flandes*, *El asalto de Mastrique por el príncipe de Parma*, and *Pobreza no es vileza*; Calderón de la Barca's *El sitio de Bredá*; and *Los amotinados de Flandes* by Luis Vélez de Guevara.[50] *El valiente negro en Flandes* takes place during the tenure of Fernando Álvarez de Toledo, third Duke of Alba, as governor of the Spanish Low Countries (1567–1573) and his military campaign against the Protestant uprising led by William of Nassau, Prince of Orange. The play was written much later, in the first half of the 1620s. By then, the Habsburg monarchy had abandoned the grand strategy of the *Pax Hispanica* signaled by the Twelve-Year Truce (1609–1621) and its brief cessation of military action in the Low Countries (Israel 1995, 404; Allen 2000, 234–44).

El valiente negro en Flandes engages with military history in its own way. There are some precise references to historical events, such as the execution of the Counts of Egmont and Horn by the Duke of Alba's Council of Troubles (lines 1430–1431; Israel 1995, 156–69). Other historical events are heavily redacted to fit a specific narrative, but still demonstrate a distinct interest in historical accuracy. For example, in order to emphasize the economy of honor that drives the entire play (Harden 2020), the Duke of Alba is rewarded with the position of *mayordomo mayor* of Philip II at the end of Act II (lines 1985–1988), even though he had occupied the position since the reign

---

49   For the variety of contemporary accounts of the Eighty Years' War, see Parker (2000, 284–85), García García (2006), and the volume edited by Raymond Fagel, Leonor Álvarez Francés, and Santiago Belmonte (2020).
50   For plays set against the background of the revolt in the Low Countries, see Loftis (1987), Gómez-Centurión Jiménez (1999), Shannon (1995), Sanz Camañes (2004), Kirschner (2002), Whicker (2002), Barsacq and García García (2005), Crowe Morey (2010), Torrico (2008), Peale (2007), Pérez Fernández (2007), Rodríguez Pérez (2008), Pedraza Jiménez (2012), Roncero López (2014), Usandizaga (2015), Samson (2016) and Fagel (2017).

of Charles V (Parker 2014, 68). The play also includes non-historical events that, in the context of the war, could be interpreted as wishful thinking, for they portray William of Nassau and the rebels as an enemy that could be defeated again. Examples of this are the capture of the Prince of Orange, or the six-year truce that followed the Duke's withdrawal (lines 1927–1931 of the play).

The historicity of Juan de Alba, the protagonist of the play, has been the subject of significant attention. For instance, scholars such as Panford (2003, 55–58) and Beusterien (2006a, 114) link him to Juan Valiente, an enslaved Black conquistador of the sixteenth century who bought his freedom by participating in the colonization of modern-day Guatemala and Chile in the first half of the sixteenth century (Restall 2000). However, as I argued elsewhere (2018, 70–71; 2022), the story of a successful Black soldier in the early modern period should not be considered categorically exceptional, nor necessarily traced back to a single individual. To give just one example, the Black knight of the Order of Santiago prominently featured in the painting *Chafariz d'el Rey* (see Figure 4), whether real or imagined, most probably also achieved his status through military exploits, as did many Afro-descendants in the period.[51] Fagel (2020) provides yet another reason not to consider Juan de Alba an oddity by comparing him to Alonso Venegas, a historic Spanish soldier in Flanders who was often racialized either as *negro* or as *mulato* (2020, 204). The many similarities between Venegas and De Alba suggest to Fagel "an undefined sense of recognition" that we will examine in greater detail (2020, 293).

The story of Captain Alonso de Venegas can be found in Captain Alonso Vázquez's account of the Flemish Wars, titled *Los sucesos de Flandes y Francia del tiempo de Alexandro Farnese* (Appendix B).[52] As stated in this account, Venegas was born in Andújar, Andalucía,

---

51   There are not many studies of early modern Black soldiers, other than of their role in the colonization of the Americas. See Restall (2000), Mattos (2008) and Fagel (2020).

52   Alonso Vázquez's *Relación...* is kept in manuscript at Spain's National Library (BNE Mss/2767. *olim* I.132, vi). It was first published in the nineteenth century (Vázquez 1897; Rodríguez Pérez 2005). See Appendix B for a transcription and a translation of the account.

a region Vázquez knew well. Venegas had occupied a prominent position at the French court before serving on the Flemish front under the command of the Duke of Alba. There he enjoyed the personal protection of Fadrique de Toledo, the Duke's son. Like the protagonist of *El valiente negro en Flandes*, Venegas was a member of 'the School of Alba', a select circle of military appointees who gained celebrity in their time (González de León 2009, 62–88). Venegas distinguished himself from the beginning. Because he had more and better arms than his peers, he was placed at the front row of his squadron, a more dangerous albeit lucrative position. As Claramonte's play exemplifies, outstanding soldiers commonly received double pay (*dos plazas*) by the same rationale: Juan de Alba was paid twice because he procured two arquebuses for himself (lines 1022–1023).[53] Venegas's promotion, Vázquez explains, provoked the envy of his fellow soldiers ("envidiosos desto" ["Envious of this"]).[54] One officer in particular, a historic version of Don Agustín, abused his power upon Venegas ("atropellarlo") despite the protection of his mentor. Like Captain Don Agustín de Estrada in *El valiente negro en Flandes*, this officer encouraged other soldiers to spite him for being Black ("despreciasen como a negro"). Venegas was called a dog, a racial slur commonly used against Black people, as shown from the very first line and at many other points in the play (Fagel 2020, 293).[55]

---

53 The common practice of the double pay, or *duplicarius*, can be traced back to the Ancient Roman army (Speidel 1992, 100; Londoño 1593, 11v).

54 Envy is also a recurrent theme in *El valiente negro en Flandes* (see lines 756, 1112, 1136, 1405, 1408–1409, and 1496). It is depicted in the play as a necessary 'effect' of Juan's valor, or military virtue (see Fra-Molinero's essay in this volume). As the Duke of Alba sums up, a man's valor could be determined by the number of people who envy him: "De la envidia os reíd, que es desdichado / el que por su virtud no es envidiado" ["Laugh at envy's face; he whose virtue is not envied is an unfortunate man"] (1408–1409).

55 According to Correas's *Vocabulario de refranes y frases proverbiales* (1627), "Perros: Llaman a moros y esclavos, porque no tienen quien les salve el alma y mueren como perros" ["Dogs: They call Moors and slaves this way, because they do not have anyone to save their souls, and they die like dogs"] (Correas, *refrán* 18231). Juan de Alba is called a dog (*perro, can*) sixteen times by others (1, 96, 105, 162, 194, 197, 374, 606, 624, 664, 683, 966, 1144,

Venegas did not take this lightly and challenged the officer to a duel. The officer rejected Venegas's challenge, arguing that fighting with a Black man was beneath his status. According to Vázquez, this is not the only instance in which Venegas proved to be an active duelist. Sometime earlier, he had moved from Flanders to France "to seek an enemy he had" (Appendix B). As we will discuss later, taking part in the culture of dueling was an essential part of performing valor, and *El valiente negro en Flandes* illustrates this to a considerable extent.

The officer's anti-blackness was partially contested by some of Venegas's fellow soldiers, who claimed that he was "an honest man" (*hombre de bien*) and therefore the challenge should be accepted. This echoes Juan de Mérida/Alba's assertion that he is "an honest Black man" (*negro de bien*) on two separate occasions (lines 72 and 97). Antón, the Black *gracioso* of the play, also claims to be an "hombre de bien" (line 862), suggesting that this was a common discursive strategy to fight racism in that period.

Venegas's and Alba's stories diverge at a crucial point. Not being able to withstand the racial harassment, Venegas decided to switch sides and become a confidant of William of Orange in an episode that evokes Juan de Alba's cordial dinner with the selfsame Prince in *El valiente negro en Flandes* (Fagel 2020, 293). Unlike the Spanish soldiers, the Prince of Orange rewarded Venegas's military prowess by promoting him to the rank of captain and arranging his marriage with a noble Flemish lady. From then on, Venegas continued to serve the rebels to the detriment of the Spanish army. According to Vázquez, he was singly responsible for the Spanish loss of Diest, as he climbed the city's wall during open combat ("a escala vista"), one of the most dangerous actions described in military treatises (Appendix B).[56]

2110, 2146, 2153), and ten times by himself (203, 206, 379, 1020, 1209, 1410, 1411, 1531, 1852, 2304). He also calls Antón a dog in two instances (1259, 2032). For more on this racial slur, see Fra-Molinero's essay in this volume.
56   Probably following another source, Fagel (2020) states that Venegas and his soldiers "silently climbed the city walls" (289), contradicting the famous engraving by Hogenberg (see Figure 6), who shows the walls being climbed in plain sight during the battle. If this was the case, Venegas would share yet one more point with Juan de Mérida/Alba, who also distinguished

As we will see later, Juan de Alba engages military actions single-handedly, which is framed as heroic.

The positive light in which Captain Vázquez portrays Venegas and other Spaniards who changed sides in the conflict may seem striking at first glance. According to Fagel, Vázquez "was praising a defector's qualities in order to promote the sending of more Spanish soldiers to Flanders" (289). However, the captain's many digressions point to a different interpretation, for they all criticize practices he considered harmful to the army. According to Vázquez, Alonso Venegas and others did not betray the Spanish army of Flanders willingly, but rather were "driven out" of it ("echado de Flandes"). In other words, defection is not a personal flaw, but a systemic problem with disastrous consequences. By stating the legitimate reasons that some soldiers had to change sides, Vázquez suggests that military authorities should institute reforms to prevent defection. Simply put, Vázquez argues that Spanish soldiers should be treated with more respect, or else they will keep joining the enemy: "se ve claro que, por haber en nuestros ejércitos tenido en poco algunos soldados, [puede] sucedernos lo que con Alonso de Venegas" ["since it is clear that, because we have thought little of some soldiers in our armies, the same thing will happen to us as happened to Alonso de Venegas"] (Appendix B). In light of *El valiente negro en Flandes*, Vázquez's message comes across even louder. Racial discrimination – any sort of in-fighting, for that matter – is harmful, not only for honest individual soldiers, but also for the greater cause.[57] This rationale explains why both Vázquez

---

himself in four stealth missions in acts one and two of the play: the subduing of Don Agustín (line 769), the capture of the two Dutch arquebusiers, the seizure of the enemy banner (1391), and the apprehension of the Prince of Orange (1712).

57 The Habsburg Monarchy was aware of this, at least in theory. The statutes of *limpieza de sangre* did not apply to the Spanish army, and there were no legal restrictions regarding the enrollment of any racial or ethnic group (Martínez 2016, 13). On the other hand, armed Black civilians were usually perceived as a threat in early modern Spain, and were frequently discriminated against and harassed despite the absence of specific legislation (Olmedo Gobante 2022).

and Claramonte portray the Dutch rebels as not anti-Black. Venegas "jamás se vio menospreciado, antes favorecido y estimado de todos los enemigos de S. M." ["all his Majesty's enemies did not despise him, but all favored and esteemed him"]. Juan de Alba's Flemish enemies do not seem to discriminate based on race either. The Prince of Orange, for example, reaches the extreme of wishing to be Black at two points of the play: "Quién no fuera quien soy, y fuera el negro!" ["If only I was not who I am, and I was the Black man!"] (line 1797, see 1866–1868). One may understand the perhaps exaggerated racial inclusiveness of the rebels as a narrative scare tactic, a spur for change.

The story of Alonso Venegas shows that *El valiente negro en Flandes* could have had an alternative ending. This possibility invites us to reconsider the common interpretation of the play as a triumphant celebration of the allegedly meritocratic structure of the Habsburg military empire (Tobar y Morabito 2017, 116). Ndiaye sums up this line of interpretation perfectly: "That system came with built-in pressure outlets, that is, with poster boys and success stories for allegedly exceptional black subjects that made a slaving society look like a fair system of racial meritocracy" (2022, 82). The eventual yet contingent success of Juan de Alba has obscured the critical, reformist, and anti-racist elements of the play, which are unmistakable in Vázquez's account.

El valiente negro en Flandes does not glorify the deeds of a living patron, unlike other commissioned historical plays of the time (Pedraza 2012), but describes the valor of a common soldier, a Black man. The play neither celebrates nor even justifies the war in Flanders. The greatest achievement of the Empire from a military point is a temporary truce agreement that was never respected. Furthermore, as we have already seen, rebels are portrayed in a sympathetic manner.[58] For example, the Duke of Alba's dreadful Council of Troubles is mentioned in the play from the perspective of Monsieur de Vivanblec. The daring rebel captain confronts the Duke at one point and blames him for starting the war, an accusation that goes undisputed (lines 1427–

---

58   There is one comical albeit veiled reference to Protestantism in the play (line 1438).

1432). As Rodríguez Pérez (2008) explains, Spanish theater since the beginning of the Twelve-Year Truce lost interest in demonizing the Flemish rebels and focused its attention more on pursuing an image of Spain (135). Claramonte's exploration of Spanish identity explains why the play does not detail macro-historical military events. As a war narrative, it engages with history by re-telling the stories of the many Black soldiers who were forgotten or deemed exceptions by historians.

That said, *El valiente negro en Flandes* is not exclusively about racial relations. After all, discrimination was only one among the many hardships that Black soldiers experienced in their everyday lives on the Flemish front.

A Soldier's Everyday Life

Winter is the real enemy in *El valiente negro en Flandes*. This is illustrated by the scene in which Captains Don Agustín and Don Pedro convince the Duke of Alba to withdraw (lines 1345–1390). Far from being an exaggeration, the two captain's complaints – "Cada día soldados sepultamos / que amanecen helados" ["Every day, at dawn, we bury soldiers, found frozen at their post"] (1358–1359) – accurately describe actual conditions of service. The real-life Duke of Alba faced a mutiny in which the soldiers protested "the great sufferings caused by frosts and the cold which have caused many soldiers to die, frozen to death on the open road or keeping watch in the trenches."[59] Indeed, during the Little Ice Age, temperatures in Europe were significantly lower (Le Roy Ladurie 1971, Degroot 2018). Among the most common causes of death on the Spanish side, the "ices of Flanders", mentioned many times throughout the play, were also prominently featured in literary narratives of the Flemish Wars, especially at the earlier stages (Martínez 2016, 169–71).

Water was another fierce enemy. The high precipitation rates and the fact that the Low Countries are so named for being below sea level were significant causes of distress for the Spanish in Flanders.

---

59 Archivo General de Simancas. Estado 558, 51, Article 18, quoted in Martínez (2016, 169). See Parker 2004, 169.

Flooded trenches, wet grounds, and muddy waters are also recurrent themes in the play.[60] Captain Don Agustín's comment, "y el agua en las trincheras se nos mete" ["While the waters in our trenches rise"] (1389), clearly echoes Captain Vázquez's historical account of the siege of Torney, where

> Llovió tanto y las aguas eran tan recias, que se anegaban en las trincheras; y en dos meses que duró el sitio pasó el ejército católico muchos y excesivos trabajos, tanto de la inclemencia del tiempo como de necesidad de bastimentos y otras cosas no menos necesarias.

> [It rained so much and so hard, that water flooded the trenches; and in the two months that the siege lasted, the Catholic army suffered many and excessive hardships due to the inclement weather and the lack of supplies.]

Vázquez 1879, 309.

One can understand the ubiquitous presence of winter in the play as an excuse for the Habsburg's inability to end the revolt, or as the Duke of Alba puts it, "que solo pudo rendirme / el rigor del cielo, que hombres / al Duque de Alba no rinden" ["that only heaven's rigor could make me yield, because / the Duke of Alba does not yield to men"] (lines 1554–1556). This may be an echo of the well-known quote wrongly attributed to king Philip II: "I did not send my fleet to fight the elements". However, by narrating with such emphasis the hardships of many who departed to the front and echoing the testimonies of the few who returned home, the play appeals to the common men present among the standing audience of the playhouse, who not by chance were called *mosqueteros* (musketeers) in Spain and were a deciding factor in the economic success or failure of a play. *El valiente negro en Flandes* is not a simple piece of military propaganda.

The play also provides a vivid description of common military tactics of the period. It does not feature any siege or battle, which were relatively infrequent events. Instead, the play focuses on *acciones* and *empresas*, that is, common small-scale actions. Juan's incursions into

---

60   Mentioned in lines 759, 905, 915, 1303, 1357, 1376, 1541, 1772, and 2057.

the enemy's field, although hardly achievable single-handedly, must not be interpreted as a mere flight of fancy on Claramonte's part. Official chronicles and other accredited accounts of the war are peppered with anecdotes in which common men individually accomplish far more spectacular martial deeds.[61] Juan's missions are not only within the realm of possibility but also credible in their military context. His first mission is to capture a spy (*espía*, line 710), that is to say, a type of scout who was routinely deployed alone to gather intelligence in the surroundings of the enemy camp (Quatrefagges 1983, 183). As shown in the play and in military treatises, capturing a lone sentinel was commonly rewarded with a pay raise.[62]

El valiente negro en Flandes furthers its depiction of military tactics by detailing its material elements. There are several mentions of the use of brushwood (*fajina*), which was also a prominent element of military material culture in the Eighty Years' War. These bundles of thin branches had a variety of purposes. *Fajina* was used as construction material for housing, as shown in a sonnet by Captain Rey de Artieda.[63] It could also be used to cover and neutralize enemy

---

61   For example, Captain Vázquez's account of the Flemish Wars tells the anecdote of "Un pastelero que salió en camisa, con una pica mató tantos franceses, que estando cansado de hacerlo a pie, cerró con uno de a caballo y lo mató, y subiendo en él siguó el alcance, haciendo cosas muy señaladas" ["A pastry maker who went out in shirtsleeves killed so many French men with a pike that, being tired of doing it on foot, engaged with a horseman and killed him; and mounting on his horse, began the chase doing truly remarkable things"] (Vázquez 1879, 406).

62   "El soldado ha de ser aventajado cuando con orden mata o toma una centinela de los enemigos" ["A soldier must be given a raise when he kills or captures a spy from the enemy by command"] (Isaba 1594, 95r). Covarrubias defines *centinela perdida* as: "La que está fuera del castillo o del real en el campo, adonde en caso de necesidad no puede ser buenamente socorrida y así va a sus aventuras y a esta tal no la requieren como a las demás" ["One placed outside the walls of the castle or military compound, in the open field, where he cannot receive aid in case of need. Therefore, he is on his own and does not receive orders like the rest"] (2020, 502).

63   "Quién hace casa de fajina y paja" ["One builds a shelter out of brushwood and straw"]. See Martínez (2020b, 34).

pits (*fosos*). Lope de Vega's *El asalto de Mastrique* features this deployment of brushwood ordered by Alejandro Farnesio, Duke of Parma, during the siege of Maastricht (Vega y Carpio, lines 1795–1800).[64] Not by coincidence, Captain Alonso Vázquez 's account of the same event describes an almost identical tactic (Vázquez 1879, 206).

Nonetheless, the main use of brushwood both in the Flemish Wars and in the play was to build dams and dikes, on top of which one could walk or transport supplies, as explained by Captain Vázquez in his description of the province of Friesland:

> Su tierra es fuerte por estar ceñida de diversos diques, que son unos caminos hechos a mano con mucha tierra, estacas y fajina para detener las aguas que no se junten, y caminan sobre ellos de unas partes a otras en carros y como les parece. Los suelen romper o cortar para inundar la tierra cuando se les ofrece en ocasiones de guerra, con que se defienden y están muy fuertes por los grandes pantanos que se extienden por toda la tierra, y para hacer guerra se aguarda al rigor del invierno cuando están helados.

> [Their land is strong because they enclose it with various dikes, which are roads made by hand with a lot of soil, stakes and brushwood to stop the waters from pooling, and they walk over them from one part to another in wagons and as they see fit. They usually break or cut them down to flood the land when it is presented to them in times of war, with which they defend themselves, and are very strong because of the great marshes that are spread all over the land, and to wage war, they wait for the rigor of winter when they are frozen.]

Vázquez 1879, 18.

The maze-like topography of Flanders's wetlands plays a major role in the play. Captain Don Agustín's encounter with Juan takes place

---

64   "Y será ardid belicoso / ir siempre cegando el foso / con tierra, leña y fajina. / Tome cualquiera soldado, de guarda o no de guarda, entre / la leña y ramas que encuentre, / un manojo grande atado" ["As a warlike trick, we will constantly cover the pit up with soil, firewood and brushwood. Every soldier, watchman or otherwise, should make a big and tight bundle with all the wood and branches he finds"] (lines 1795–1800).

in this setting, after wandering "ya por pantanosas sendas, / ya por diques mal formados / y dibujados apenas" ["whether by marshy paths, or by poorly formed dams, that could barely be seen"] (lines 905–907). More specifically, the Captain gets caught by Juan while walking over a *contradique* or minor road dam (764),[65] in the precise manner the Prince of Orange is captured in act two (1736). As Mons. de Vivanblec threatens – "o no habrá dique / que contra ti no se suelte" ["or there will not be a levee that will not be unleashed on you"] (1458–1459) – breaking dikes was a common tactic of the Flemish rebels. Indeed, battles could be won, or sieges could be lifted just by breaking a dam or opening a floodgate.[66]

The repeated use of the now common words *dique* and *contradique* – instead of the Spanish-vernacular *presa* – is highly significant in the linguistic construction of Flanders as a locus of action. The Habsburgs' many military campaigns had the unintended effect of expanding the Spanish lexicon by borrowing from other languages such as Italian, French, and Dutch, as well as American languages (Lapesa 1981, 408–13). This was specially the case during the Duke of Alba's government, the time of the play and a period described as the beginning of a stage of multilingualism in the Low Countries (Verdonk 2017, 113). *El valiente negro en Flandes* reflects this linguistic diversity by featuring innumerable loanwords, all of them related to everyday soldierly life. Words of French origin such as "trinchea" (*trench*, 2416) and "pot" (*jar*, 1305), German expressions like "brindis" (*toast* or *party*, from the German *Ich bring dir's*; 1076, 1716), Italian borrowings such as "foso" (*pit*, 759) and derivatives of "marcha" (*march*, 256, 1932), were all relatively new to the Spanish language and still perceived as exotic during that period (Lapesa 1981, 410; Coromines 2008). The play goes further by featuring a few bilingual exchanges. On the one hand, the two Flemish soldiers captured by Juan repeatedly use the

---

65 "Diques y contradiques son todos caminos, unos más grandes y cosarios que otros." ["*Diques* and *contradiques* are both roads, the former being larger and more travelled than the latter"] (Vázquez 1879, 515).
66 This tactic is pervasive in the accounts of the war. See Vázquez (1879, 425, 505, 509, 524–25).

word "nite" (924) as an expression of the negative.[67] Esteban/Leonor, on the other, performs his/her sophisticated queerness by saying goodbye to Juan with the common Spanish-Italian phrase "a reveder" (*a rivederci*, 1308).[68]

Learning the front-line jargon was one of the first things a recruit had to do, as illustrated by many literary products (Verdonk 1986; Canonica-de Rochemonteix 1991, 417–56). In *Mentir y mudarse a un tiempo* – a mid-seventeenth century play by Diego and José Figueroa y Córdoba that was also in the repertory of the theatre company that produced *El valiente negro en Flandes* in 1651[69] – a soldier sums up his experience in Flanders as a linguistic challenge:

> No huvo más lugar en Flandes, / que de aprender el lenguaje / del pais, y el que la guerra / en sus términos encierra, / llamando al hurtar pillaje; / a la presa, contradique; / a la manteca, buturo; […] / que son menester diez años / para entrar en la cabeza. / Nos ofuscamos de modo / que en aquesto consumimos / el tiempo que allí estuvimos,/ y aun no lo aprendimos todo.

> [I didn't have time in Flanders, but to learn the language of the country, and that which War contains in its terms; where stealing is *pillaje*, and the dam is *contradique*, and lard is *buturo* … And you need ten years to get it into your head. We got so confused that in this we spent all the time we were there, and yet we did not learn it all.]
> Figueroa y Córdoba 2014; also quoted in Verdonk 2017, 114.

As discussed in Fra-Molinero's essay in this volume, Juan de Alba also struggles to adapt to the multilingual context. At one point, he

---

67 *Nite* as *no* may be related to a popular expression of the negative, the pseudo-Dutch word *nitefistón*. Derived from the Flemish pronunciation of *niet te verstaan* (meaning *I don't understand*), the word meant 'not at all' and was utilized in several plays as a comic marker of Flemishness (Canonica-de Rochemonteix 1991, 449, 478).

68 *A reveder* appears in one play by Lope de Vega (Canonica-de Rochemonteix 1991, 150) and in two short plays by Quiñones de Benavente (2019, 207). For the Italianization of Esteban/Leonor, see Fra-Molinero's essay in this volume.

69 See the Textual History and Critical Apparatus (line 1085b) sections in this volume.

reflects on his linguistic abilities by enumerating a series of words foreign to him: "*Grambot, / moltuín, butir, estricot, / cerveza, flinflán*" (lines 1099–1101). With the exception of "cerveza" (*beer* in Spanish), Juan's polyglot litany is pure gibberish for the modern audience, but perhaps not for a soldier of that period. We have already seen the Dutch word "butir" (*lard* or *butter*), whose variants *buturo* and *butiro* have been extensively documented as 'Spanish of Flanders' (Cano Aguilar 2009, 99). "Grambot" has been interpreted as a boat (*boot* in Dutch, Beusterien 2006a, 121), but it may be also a distortion of *grand pot* (*big jar*), a Gallicism mentioned in the play as well. "Estricot" could be an approximation of *tricot* (knit, derived from *estrique*), and "moltuin" sounds like *moestuin* (kitchen garden) or literally, *garden of moles* in Dutch.

The frontier lexicon teaches us that combat was only a minor portion of military service. As depicted in Teniers's genre paintings (Figure 5), soldiers typically spent most of their time idling at a guard post (*cuerpo de guardia*, mentioned in lines 89, 105, 130), which was located next to the camp courtyard (*plaza de armas*, 608, 1420) or at a town square, where it also served as a recruiting station, as shown in the first scenes of the play (Rodríguez Hernández y Díaz Paredes 2020, 17). At the guard post, soldiers also performed ordinary tasks such as maintaining the arsenal, reading posted news (lines 1546 and 1745), or learning the watchword (*nombre*, 776, 779, 1744), a sort of password, usually a Saint's name, that was reset every day to deter spies and other intruders (Quatrefages 2015, 231). Soldiers slept in multiple locations, depending on their status and particular situation. Some slept in tents (*tiendas*)[70] at the camp; some were billeted in housing provided by local civilians. Juan de Alba, however, lived outdoors and alone (1051–1055). This fact dramatizes his marginalization, for soldiers typically slept and had their dining gatherings (*ranchos*, 1820) always with a closer group of comrades (*camarada*, 1509, 1617). Defined as informal bands of friends or roommates, the *camarada* was the core of a soldier's social life (Martínez 2016, 18–21; Harden 2020, 31–32). The intimate affections fostered in such homosocial

---

70 See lines 950–951, 1423, 1731, and 1756.

spaces often led to something more. As Fra-Molinero's critical essay in this volume shows, homosexual relationships were frequent and brutally punished in early modern armies (Prickett-Barnes 1999; Muravyeva 2014; Martínez 2020a, 37–38). As Martínez explains, the strong social bonds of the *camarada* also allowed soldiers to unite and protest their often-precarious conditions. As illustrated in the scene where Sergeant Barrientos and the three captains discuss their plan to demote Juan de Alba (1108–1135), mutinies were extremely frequent in the Spanish Army of Flanders.[71]

Indeed, conflict and violence permeated everyday life in the military, even in times of peace. As seen previously in the case of Black soldier Alonso de Venegas, dueling, for example, was also common among soldiers (Taylor, 2008, 22–23). In 1596, the practice was strictly prohibited by an edict signed by Cardinal Albert, Archduke of Austria and captain general of the Spanish Army of Flanders. The decree explained in great detail how dueling had become "mala costumbre y uso frecuentado entre la gente militar" ["a bad habit and frequent practice among the military"] (Austria 1597, s.p.). Apparently, soldiers experienced great social pressure, and many of them felt compelled to fight, fearing "que si los llamados no salen, incurren en caso de menos valer" ["that if the challenged do not accept, they fall into a case of being worth less"]. Cardinal Albert's edict set out severe punishment for soldiers "of any rank and status" who engaged in duels or even participated as intermediaries or bystanders. Among the possible sentences, the edict stated twice that perpetrators – and not people who rejected challenges – would be the ones who "incurran por ello en pena y nota de perpetua infamia, alevosía, caso de menos valer" ["because of that, will fall in perpetual infamy, malice, and into a case of being worth less"] (Austria 1597, s.p.). Cardinal Albert's edict was printed and re-published a year later, showing that the dueling culture was far from being eradicated.

Duels are theatrical commonplaces, especially in historical

---

71   For the high frequency of mutinies during the Eighty Years' War, see Parker (1975, 185–206), González de León (2009, 107–19), Rodríguez Pérez (2009), and Martínez (2016, 209; 2019; 2020a; 2020b).

dramas.[72] However, in its soldierly context, dueling was about proving a man's worth or value. Being *valiente* (valiant, literally worthy), Juan de Alba is a duelist. He demonstrates it at many points in the play. In the first scene, for example, he expresses great concern about the prospect of being hit with a stick, one of the worst offenses in dueling culture (lines 92–96, Chauchadis 1996, 116–17); at another point, he eloquently comments on the right to self-defense (1526–1528), another commonplace in dueling culture. In fact, Juan takes part in two duels during the play – not including Juan's showdown with Don Agustín (795), for it is part of a military action. Juan re-enacts the story of the Afro-Andalusian captain Alonso Venegas, following even more closely the steps of Diego García Paredes, a most celebrated Spanish soldier born like Juan in Extremadura and the subject of many literary works (Sánchez Jiménez 2006). When Juan challenges Sergeant Barrientos following the codified protocol of placing the disputed halberd on the ground to be rescued, he echoes the episode in which Paredes literally throws down the gauntlet to defend his general's honor (2006, 27). In addition, the merciless dismemberment of Captain Vivamblec evokes the decapitation of Captain Cesare Romano by Paredes at the end of their fight (2006, 17). In sum, dueling was a way for a common soldier to perform the role of the extraordinary, valiant man, a script that we will examine next.

To recapitulate, *El valiente negro en Flandes* captures a soldier's everyday life through a meticulous portrait of its material culture. In the play, the elements we have seen so far serve mainly as a backdrop to the action. However, Claramonte places a specific set of objects at the forefront. To understand the material making of a valiant man, we need to pay close attention to his trophies.

A Valiant Man's Trophies

Julián Romero, a play dubiously attributed to Lope de Vega, re-imagines the life of a historic soldier who, like the valiant Black man,

---

72 Miguel de Cervantes famously questions the verisimilitude of duels between champions from opposite sides in plays such as *El gallardo español* and *Tragedia de Numancia* (2015). However, these situations are described in some military treatises (Isaba 1594, 95r).

served with distinction in Flanders as a *maestro de campo* general under the Duke of Alba. At the end of that play, Romero sums up his outstanding career ascent from a poor sacristan and a drummer's servant to – again, like Juan de Alba – a knight of Santiago.

> Luego fui vuestro soldado,
> cabo de escuadra, y allí
> pasé a ser sargento, y fui,
> subiendo de grado en grado
> por mis servicios, a ser
> alférez y capitán.

> [Then I was your soldier,
> then corporal of the squadron, and there
> I became a sergeant, and went,
> rising step by step
> because of my service, to become
> lieutenant and captain]
> Vega y Carpio, lines 2450–2458.

Like other early modern plays, *Julián Romero* and *El valiente negro en Flandes* have much in common. Essentially, they both tell the same story: that of a poor man who dares to challenge Fortune and enroll in the Spanish army.[73] There, each protagonist is harassed by his peers because of his low status, and yet their martial prowess and the support of a powerful mentor allow them to prosper and become knights and generals at the end of their respective plays.[74]

As in *Julián Romero*, the plot of *El valiente negro en Flandes* is paced through a scripted sequence of five ascending steps (*escalones*) on a ladder to breach the Wheel of Fortune, as if it were a fortress.

---

73   For the theme of Fortune regarding Juan de Alba's discourse on race, see Fra-Molinero's essay in this volume.

74   Other plays that have the same synopsis, with minor changes, are *El valiente Céspedes* by Lope de Vega, and Vélez de Guevara's *El valiente Toledano* and *El Hércules de Ocaña*. To the best of my knowledge, the specific genre of *comedias* about military valiant men has never been studied as such. See Olmedo Gobante's forthcoming paper, 'Soldados de Fortuna: Hacia el género de la comedia de valientes militares'.

Force – not Fortune, Time, or Fate – decides a valiant man's position in society.[75] His ascending steps correspond to those of military ranks: common soldier, corporal, sergeant, lieutenant, and captain. At the beginning of act two, we find Juan is already at step three, for he has become a sergeant:

> ¡Ea, Fortuna!, ya estoy
> en el escalón tercero.
> Si el planeta quinto es Marte,
> para llegar a su cielo
> dos escalones me faltan.
>
> [Holla, Fortune! I am already on
> The third step. If the fifth planet is
> Mars, to reach its heaven,
> I need two more steps.] (lines 1222–1226)

As we will discuss later, when he reaches the rank of captain, he feels at the top of his career: "Ya en el postrer escalón / de la Fortuna me siento" ["I can feel I am already on the last step of my fortune"] (1577–1578).

Eight objects mark Juan's ascension, here called trophies: the sword, the arquebus, the halberd, the banner, the sash, the baton, the *jineta* spear, and paper. All of them, without exception, either were worn historically as military insignia or played a crucial role in everyday soldierly life.

The SWORD is the only trophy Juan owns at the beginning of the play. Although it is rather cheap – it only cost nine *reales* and breaks apart easily (lines 163–164, 1972)[76] – it is still a precious possession for him. He proudly alludes to it throughout the play (1592, 1965,

---

75 Of course, these dreams of social up-ward mobility were mostly just dreams. However, they had some grounding in reality. The record shows that, for a lowborn common soldier, ending his career as a captain, or even higher, was definitely not unthinkable. Certainly, there were ongoing profound social and demographic transformations in the period, at least partially due to the European military revolution. See Martínez (2016, 3–5).

76 At the time the play was written, nine *reales* was the fixed price of a Genoan blade. Swords made in Genoa were notorious for their poor quality and tendency to bend or break (Girón 2016, 164).

2497). However, when forced to choose among the numerous treasures from the Prince of Orange's lavish ransom, Juan picks a new sword to replace his old one: "Honrarme / solo con su espada quiero, / que es la joya que más vale" ["I want to honor myself, Your Grace, only with your sword, which is the most valuable jewel"] (1964–1966). Swords were commonly featured in early modern theater to symbolize unequivocal power and masculinity (Quintero 2013). However, for Juan, the sword is not only a symbol, but an actual instrument to accomplish things (1592),[77] to actively improve his social status and his living conditions. This also is the case for Antón, who will have more confidence in his sword as the play progresses (2120). In the last scene of act three, Juan de Alba will define himself as a Black swordsman, made chiefly by his weapon:

> ...un negro a quien dio su espada
> su valor y fortaleza
> merecimientos de blanco

> [...a Black man ... because his sword,
> his valor, and strength
> made him equal to white men in merit]
> (lines 2497–2499)

The question of who could have a sword. and who could not, was a serious matter in early modern society. Owning and carrying swords was strictly regulated by many laws that specifically legislated against Black people and other racial minorities (Olmedo Gobante 2022). Despite this, Juan, like many others, overtly engaged with the martial arts culture of the time. Through his behavior, Juan seems to diligently follow a fencing manual, Pacheco de Narváez's *Grandezas de la Espada* [Greatness of the Sword] (1600). In this treatise on swordplay, Narváez states that there are "a great number" of Black fencers who show courage, gravity, pride and social intelligence, neatness, and articulateness, traits that perfectly define Juan de Alba's personality (Olmedo Gobante 2018, 77–82). Juan's attachment to

---

77   For the semantic and instrumental versatility of the sword in early modern Europe, see Neuschel (2020, 129–59).

his sword proves, in his words, his "inclinación marcial" ["martial inclination"] (line 46), a claim often made in the context of fencing and other martial arts of the time (2018, 79–80). An innate martial predisposition is also the key marker of a valiant military man. Julián Romero states that he is "a las armas inclinado" ["inclined towards arms"] (Vega y Carpio, line 66). The protagonist of *La monja alférez*, a play likely by Juan Ruiz de Alarcón, would be even more explicit: "mi natural / inclinación es marcial" ["my natural / inclination is martial"] (Pérez de Montalbán 1998).[78] Even Don Agustín in *El Valiente negro en Flandes* claims to feel "la inclinación de la guerra" ["the inclination towards war"] (line 247).

The ARQUEBUS is the first trophy that Juan de Mérida wins in the play.[79] When he presents the two arquebuses he has captured from the enemy to the Duke, he takes the first step in his siege of Fortune, having a "second birth" as Juan de Alba and becoming a rank-and-file soldier (lines 924–1025). The symbolic power of this scene cannot be overstated. At that time, the arquebus had already become the embodiment of a social revolution. As the nobility gradually lost their military role, some of their knightly privileges increasingly became available to more people. Consequently, the traditional literary ways of narrating war had to adapt to the strident presence of gunpowder, or "the soul of empires", as Juan de Alba calls it (60).[80] From the point of view of performance, the mere presence of a gun is already intrinsically unsettling. In its social context, it conveyed still stronger

---

78 For the debated authorship of *La monja alférez*, see Vega García-Luengos (2021).

79 Arquebuses are depicted in virtually all military genre paintings. Figure 5 depicts an arquebusier entering the guard post. Gunpowder flasks, mentioned twice in the play (lines 695, 943), are also scattered throughout Figure 5, and they are conspicuously displayed in Figure 7.

80 See Murrin (1994) and Martínez (2016, 54–85). Although swords kept their same essential role in war as secondary weapons until the early twentieth century, the commonly named 'death of courage' was a frequently disputed question in early modern European thought. It was famously discussed by authors such as Cervantes, Quevedo, and Gracián. For more on this, see Olmedo Gobante (2019, 103).

emotions. At one point in the play, the Duke of Alba orders that the defeated rebels shamefully "marchen / con los arcabuces vueltos" ["march with their harquebuses pointing down"] (1932–1933). The standing *musketeers* at a playhouse – that is, the bulk of the male audience – could understand this gesture as the death of the common soldier's dreams of moving to a higher position in society, regardless of his humble origins. When questioned about his linage, the valiant Julián Romero proudly responds: "El arcabuz es mi padre" ["my father is this arquebus"] (Vega y Carpio, line 2462). Powerful both as a symbol and as a weapon, the arquebus also allows Juan to cancel his enslaved ancestry, to be born again as an Alba. In short, the arquebus enables him to change not only his own destiny but also his past.

As soon as Juan officially joins the army, he reveals both his plans and the script of the play:

> Honrad la nación morena
> mandando asentar mi plaza,
> que, como yo lo merezca,
> traeré otra vez la alabarda,
> la bandera y la jineta
> de las tiendas del de Orange.
>
> [Honor the dark-skinned nation.
> Make my appointment,
> That I, deserving of it,
> Will bring next time the halberd,
> The banner, and the captain's spear
> From the tents of the Prince of Orange.]
>   (lines 945–950)

Juan enumerates steps three, four, and five on the ladder in his siege of Fortune, represented by the respective insignia of the ranks he intends to reach: the sergeant's halberd, the lieutenant's banner, and the captain's *jineta* spear (Quatrefages 2015, 124). These trophies were an essential part of military culture. They were often carried by officers themselves or by their assistants to make their ranks visible.

When Barrientos considers turning in his HALBERD – "hoy la alabarda / he de dejar" ["I shall ... turn in my halberd"] (1123–1124) – he means resigning from his position as a sergeant. The audience of the time could certainly recognize this common metonymy, showing how deeply military culture permeated early modern society (Figure 8).[81] According to Captain Barroso's treatise titled *Teórica, práctica, y ejemplos* [Theory, Practice, and Examples], a halberd is designed to intimidate, for it was an "arma … más fanfarrona que provechosa" ["a more showy than advantageous weapon"] (1628, 33). Hence, it was often employed to physically discipline the troops.[82] When Barrientos threatens Juan with his halberd (lines 603–604), he performs his expected role as a figure of authority. Although Juan is appointed sergeant in the lapse between acts one and two, he does not take the position *de facto* until he picks up the halberd he took away from Barrientos. As soon as Juan holds the weapon in his hands, he feels transformed:

> Bien me está
> la alabarda, ya parezco
> otro hombre; ya me ha infundido
> alma y espíritu nuevo
> para aspirar a ser más
> con generosos trofeos.
>
> [This halberd
> Suits me well, I already
> Feel like another man. It has given me
> A new soul and spirit
> To aspire to be more
> With noble rewards.]
> (lines 1216–1221)

---

81   In Lope de Vega's *El galán Castrucho*, a sergeant alludes to his rank in a similar manner: "Aunque pierda *el alabarda*" ["Even if I lose my rank"] (line 1205).

82   As Sancho Londoño explains in his well-known military treatise: "Si conveniere castigar in fraganti, hágalo el sargento con la alabarda o jineta" ["If it is necessary to punish in the act, the sergeant must do it with his halberd or *jineta*"] (Londoño 1593, 5v). Note that the word *jineta*, in this context, refers to the halberd as a weapon of rank or insignia, as illustrated in line 1134 of *El valiente negro en Flandes*, as well as in military treatises of the period (Barroso 1628, 33).

From now onward, Juan will walk differently. His seemingly magical transformation is grounded not only in the symbolic but also in the material dimensions of his new trophy. Lifting a weapon for the first time means feeling a new texture, experiencing a particular weight, and adjusting your body to counterbalance it. Indeed, war changed people.[83]

The BANNER marks Juan's fourth step on his way up. Protected in the guard post at all times, as illustrated in Figure 5, the banner was the symbol of the regiment (Barroso 1628, 34). The banner was also the insignia of the lieutenant, his duty being to raise and defend it with his person, although at times it could be carried by a subordinate standard bearer or *abanderado* (Londoño 1593, 5r; Quatrefages 2015, 65). After Juan captures an enemy banner,[84] the Duke of Alba confirms his promotion to lieutenant (*alférez*) immediately and without much ceremony: "Basta, alférez Juan de Alba" ["That's enough, Lieutenant Juan de Alba"] (1402). More than a reward, it was an acknowledgment. In line with the logic of trophies, Juan had already become a lieutenant the very moment he seized the flag. As implausible as it may sound, this was a common scenario, not only in literature but in war narratives. The historic Catalina or Antonio de Erauso, also known as the Lieutenant Nun, was promoted to that rank for re-capturing the regiment's banner (Erauso 2021, 142). Following the same script, Sergeant Julián Romero requested a promotion to the fourth rank right after seizing an enemy flag. In that precise scene, the word *bandera* is used with the meanings of both the banner and the

---

83 Fagel (2020) mentions the interesting testimony of the Spanish commander Francisco Valdés, who claimed that "the moment a man picked up a pike, he stopped being a Christian" (2020, 45). As Fagel suggests, this partially contradicts Harari's thesis on "war as the ultimate experience" as a distinction between early modern and modern war narratives (2008).

84 Capturing the enemy flag was a common practice on the early modern battlefield because the banner was an essential visual marker for coordinating the squadron (Barroso 1628, 36). Losing it or capturing a new one often had a great effect on a soldier's morale. Unsurprisingly, the lieutenant and the banner play the leading roles in innumerable war stories, literary or otherwise (Sánchez Jiménez 2006, 244).

rank of lieutenant (Vega y Carpio, lines 976–1093). Like the arquebus, this trophy was meant to convey powerful emotions, as shown in *El valiente negro en Flandes*, namely, in the scene in which the Duke of Alba orders the rebel soldiers to march with their banners folded (lines 1935–1936).

Juan is finally at the fifth and last step of his siege of Fortune, when he is made captain. Although not the highest rank, a captain was considered the core of the army.[85] For Juan, becoming one leads to a radical improvement of his position in society. In the context of the European military revolution, the image of the modern captain had replaced the medieval knight as the embodiment of the aristocratic ideals of the warrior class.[86] For this reason, while common people did not face specific legal restrictions to become captains, this rank was typically reserved for noblemen.

Captains and other officers wore a SASH (*banda*, see Figure 9) to signify their status. At a time when military uniforms were not yet in use, a captain's identity was closely attached to items like this. Captains strongly identified themselves with their sash in Lope de Vega's *La contienda de García de Paredes y el capitán Juan de Urbina*, where Captain Urbina talks directly to his sash as if talking to himself – a trope also present in *El valiente negro en Flandes* (Sánchez Jiménez 2006, 256). Only by taking into consideration the dramatic and symbolic value of this trophy can we appreciate the scenes in which Captain Don Agustín loses his sash. Being the only ransom demanded by Juan after the captain's defeat, the sash signified both Don Agustín's lost honor and Juan's career aspirations, for he wants to be a captain (line 820). However, unlike the halberd or the banner, the sash Juan took did not allow him to get promoted immediately. At the moment he seized it from Don Agustín, he was a rank-and-file

---

85 Most officers above this rank were captains as well.

86 The image of the 'perfect captain' – that is to say, the aristocratic military leader suitable for modern warfare – was widely popularized in the early modern period through visual and literary representations. Many treatises were published to divulge the the skills, virtues, and knowledge required to be a perfect captain (Faini and Severini 2016, Londoño 1593, Barroso 1628).

soldier, and only lieutenants could become captains. Fortune's ladder is to be climbed step by step, or rank by rank, as regulations specified (Londoño 1593). For this reason, the sash is returned to Captain Don Agustín, who had visibly lost his (974). Before he recovers it, the sash has been transferred from hand to hand, a symbol of his contested military dignity.

The BATON (*bengala*) is the second trophy that Juan takes away from Don Agustín, this time permanently, as he becomes a captain himself (lines 1565–1570). When asked whose baton he wants, Juan furthers his revenge by choosing Don Agustín's. Much earlier in the play, Don Agustín had explicitly linked his baton with his rank.

> Ya el ser capitán renuncio,
> puesta a esos pies la bengala:
> honrad, Leonor, la jineta,
> siendo capitán del alma.
>
> [I resign at once my Captain's commission,
> Laying at your feet my baton.
> Honor, Leonor my spear
> That makes you Captain of my soul.]
> (lines 303–306)

As we see here, the *JINETA* SPEAR is also a mark of the captain.[87] The specific length and form of this weapon varied, but generally fitted Covarrubias' description: "lanza corta con una borla por guarnición junto al hierro dorado, insignia de los capitanes de infantería" ["a short spear whose gilded head is garnished with a tassel, the insignia of infantry captains"] (Covarrubias 2020, 1126).[88] Typically short, the

---

87 We see a captain carrying a *jineta* spear in Figure 9. The *jineta* spear signifies captaincy also in the last scene of Lope de Vega's *El galán Castrucho*, in which the leading *valiente* receives a captaincy as a dowry (lines 2985–2986).

88 The word *jineta*, which etymologically means *horseman's* had very different meanings in early modern Spanish. It most commonly referred to a well-known Spanish horse-riding style. According to Covarrubias, the *jineta* spears have nothing to do with the lances typically used by horsemen, but may owe them the name because they are short, like the stirrups of

purpose of a *jineta* spear was not to kill enemies but to assert the captain's authority both symbolically and materially. Like the halberd, it was usually employed to physically punish disobedient soldiers.[89] Being hit with the staff of a *jineta* spear, as Juan is threatened with at the beginning of the play (lines 90–92), was commonplace in early modern theater. In Lope de Vega's *El vaquero de Moraña*, a captain also uses his *jineta* spear to threaten two peasants who do not seem to understand the point of a tasseled, miniature weapon.[90] Like Juan de Mérida, the hero of Lope de Vega's *Julián Romero* is also threatened with the *jineta* spear in his first interaction with a captain at the beginning of the play.[91]

The *jineta* spear was rarely carried by the captain himself, but by his *jineta* page ("paje de jineta", lines 1045 and 1660), a young boy who served and accompanied him, as illustrated by the main figure in Teniers's painting (Figure 5) or by Esteban/Leonor and Antón in *El valiente negro en Flandes*. The page's duties were to carry the

the *jineta* mount: "púdose decir así por ser corta y recogida, y no porque sea arma de los jinetes, cuyas lanzas son muy largas" ["it could have been named like that for being short and cut down, and not because it is wielded by horsemen, whose lances are very long"] (Covarrubias 2020, 1126). The word *jineta* also alluded to a specific type of one-handed sword from fifteenth-century Al-Andalus. However, in a soldierly context, *jineta* had the meaning of *rank*, usually that of captain but also the sergeant, as we have seen before (Barroso 1628, 33).

89   "A los inobedientes en las órdenes y escuadrones, guardias y centinelas, deben castigar con las ginetas o bastones" ["Those who are disobedient when receiving orders, or forming squadrons, watchguards or sentries, should be punished with *jineta* spears or quarterstaffs"] (Londoño 1593, 13v).

90   "CAPITÁN: Si le alzo, haré respetar / al Conde y a la jineta. / ANTÓN: Pedro, jineta la llama, / luego a la jineta viene. / DON JUAN: Sí, Antón, ¿no ves cómo tiene / borlas, flecos, como cama?" ["CAPTAIN: If I raise it, I'll make you respect the Count and the *jineta*. ANTÓN: Pedro, he called it *jineta*, thus he came riding that way. DON JUAN: Yes, Antón. Don't you see it has tassels and fringes like a bed?"] (Lope de Vega's *El vaquero de Moraña*, lines 2380–2386).

91   "¿Mas que os tengo de romper / la jineta en la cabeza?" ["Do you want me to break this *jineta* on your head?"] (Lope de Vega's *Julián Romero*, lines 127–128).

captain's panoply, chiefly his round shield (*rodela*),[92] his helmet, and his *jineta* spear. Typically, but not always, the captain's page came from a noble family. Thus, Esteban/Leonor is presenting himself as an upper-class young man when he says that he intends to "servir, / amigo, hasta que edad tenga, / a un capitán, pues soy propio / para paje de jineta" ["To serve, my friend, a captain, until I'm old enough, because I'm fit to be a Captain's page"] (1042–1045).

For all these reasons, Juan's intimate connection to his *jineta* cannot be overstated. At one point, he even treats it as a sentient being.[93] Indeed, as soon as he becomes captain, he addresses a long monologue to it, saying that being on Fortune's "last step" is not enough for him (1577–1596). As we are about to see, Juan de Alba's final ascent comes with the ultimate trophy.

PAPER, with its innumerable applications, was an essential component of early modern warfare (Martínez 2016, 21–22). Written documents were a valiant man's most valuable possession, for his career ultimately depended on his ability to capitalize on his merits and service by following a wide array of writing strategies, which included petitions, reports, accounts, recommendations, and requests (Quafrages 2015, 122; Harden 2020, 13–14). As we have seen with Juan de Alba, promotions were highly performative, both on stage and in real life, but still depended on their respective formalizations on paper. The play is full of documents that constantly circulate from hand to hand, and dictate the course of the plot, so much so that one could say there are eight parallel paper characters in *El valiente negro en Flandes*. These are as follows.

Paper 1:   Juan de Mérida's Letter of Freedom (mentioned in lines 389–391, and 990–993).

Paper 2:   Don Agustin's letter of promise to Leonor (337, 350, 429, 523–535, 1681, 2069, 2591, and 2614).

Paper 3:   Letter to the Duke of Alba from an unknown person (652).

---

92   For an illustration of a captain's *rodela*, or round shield, see the upper-left corner in Figure 5.

93   There is the possibility that Juan is talking to his baton (*bengala*) or even to his new rank. See note to line 1568.

Paper 4: The paper with the Prince of Orange's conditions for the truce (1453).

Paper 5: Letter from the King to the Duke of Alba, making him *mayordomo real* (1631).

Paper 6: Letter from Don Agustín's father to his son (1631, also mentioned in 2020).

Paper 7: Letter from the Duke to Don Agustín (2065, mentioned in 2083 and 2386, read aloud in 2394).

Paper 8: Dispatch signed by the King (2273, mentioned again in 2305).

The LETTER OF FREEDOM (Paper 1) that Doña Juana hands to Juan at the beginning of the play officially sets him free from slavery (lines 389–391). As a valiant man's trophy, the letter of freedom is perceived by Juan as his only chance to defeat Fortune: "Con esta carta voy contento y rico, / que es de mi libertad: con ella un clavo / al eje vil de la Fortuna aplico" ["With this paper, I feel fortunate and content, for it's a letter of freedom: with it, I drive a spike into Fortune's evil axle"] (389–391). Unsurprisingly, Juan wears this document around his neck as an amulet at all times, feeling its liberating power in his chest throughout the play (992–993).

Doña Leonor also wears a document. The LETTER OF PROMISE (Paper 2) that Don Agustín writes at the beginning of the play is so important to her that she even speaks to it at one point (lines 523–535). It is arguably the most consequential piece of paper for the development of the plot, and also the one that circulates the most, traveling from Mérida to Flanders and back, and being passed from Don Agustín to Doña Leonor, to Juan, and back to Don Agustín. At the end of the play, this paper puts an end to the conflict when Juan uses it to 'restore' Doña Leonor's honor and to cement his final triumph over Don Agustín.

Other documents are used in the play to evoke the famously bureaucratic government of Philip II, who was known as the Paper King (Parker 2014, 61–77). The Duke of Alba is shown reading a LETTER (Paper 3) at his first entrance on stage. Similarly, the Spanish king is also shown in his first entrance receiving written petitions others put in his hands ("Tomando memoriales" ["Taking legal briefs"], line 2216). As the play shows, war veterans inundated the palace's corridors with paper looking for a reward for their services (Martínez 2016, 183). Juan de Alba was one of them, and although he feels uncomfortable at the court, he perfectly understands its bureaucratic mechanisms.[94] Juan is ready to use force to re-arrange Don Agustín's marriage (line 2348), yet he eventually uses paper instead. First, he asks the Duke for a LETTER (Paper 7) to delay the Captain's wedding with Doña Juana. Then he turns Don Agustín's own letter of promise against him (Paper 2). Finally, Juan's ascent culminates with his final trophy, the royal DISPATCH (Paper 8), his commission as a *maestro de campo general* (the second highest rank in the army). Signed by the King and handed by the Duke (2273), this document also confirms Juan's nobility, makes him a knight of the Order of Santiago, and grants him an astronomical income.

To conclude, the valiant man's trophies comprised the common soldier's dreams of defeating Fate and Fortune and achieving upward social mobility. They are extremely meaningful, but not just as symbols. Their material properties enable human agency. In short, a valiant man is made by his trophies.[95]

* * *

On November 15, 1649, not long before Teniers produced his genre paintings and nearly a year after the end of the war in Flanders, the rural district of Vallecas, now a district in the city of Madrid, organized a public dance entitled *El valiente negro en Flandes* to celebrate the entrance of Queen Mariana of Austria into the city. The venue chosen

---

94   Juan's and Antón's violent experience in the corridors of El Escorial illustrates the clash between the courtier and the soldier (Olmedo Gobante 2016). It would be closely echoed in an episode of Alonso de Contreras's account of his own life, in which the soldier also visits El Escorial in search of a reward and ends up killing an official (Contreras 1988, 214–19). A similar scene is echoed at the beginning of act three of *Julián Romero*.

95   For an introduction to material culture studies and 'how things people make make people', see Hicks and Beaudry (2010) and Miller (2005, 2017).

for this dance, "in the street, in front of the steps of San Felipe,"[96] was highly significant. The surroundings of the convent of San Felipe in Madrid were a notorious gossip locale (*mentidero*) in which all sorts of people exchanged news, rumors, opinions, and even literary texts about foreign policy and military matters. They gathered there, attracted by the many war veterans who, like Juan de Alba, went to the Court in hopes of improving their precarious living conditions. As Castro Ibaseta explains (2010), both the soldiers at the *mentidero* and the *mosqueteros* of the playhouses fostered a particular social space for public opinion and political criticism. This soldierly context may give us a key for interpreting *El valiente negro en Flandes*, not just as historical drama, but as a way to discuss the Flemish war in the present. As with the stories told at the steps of San Felipe, the play minimizes allusions to imperial pride, the deeds of Spanish military leaders, or the justification of war. Instead, it focuses on the hardships faced by rank-and-file soldiers. Indeed, war veterans in the social space of the San Felipe *mentidero* did not focus on ideals but on material conditions. Accordingly, the play emphasizes soldierly material culture and strategically places trophies to further the plot. Juan de Alba was a juicy subject for the *mentidero* – "Tan presto hay coplas?" ["Are there ballads about me so soon?"], he once said (line 1880). So was Alonso de Venegas, the Black man in Flanders, used by Captain Vázquez to criticize the Spanish army's inability to keep some of its best soldiers on its side. Claramonte knew this and put Blackness at the forefront of a vivid tableau of everyday military life.

Juan's pursuit of equality is not free from moral contradictions. He fights racism by following the script of the valiant man, the epitome of a toxic masculinity based on ableism, antisemitism, homophobia,

---

96   "En la calle enfrente de las gradas de San Felipe, que hay unas pasaderas y va a salir a la del Arenal, se ha de poner la danza del negro valiente en Flandes que da el sesmo de Vallecas" ["In the street in front of the steps in front of the church of San Felipe, where there are some stepping stones and planks that lead to Arenal street, they should stage the Valiant Black Man in Flanders dance"] (AGVM, Secretaría, ASA 2-58-13, see Appendix D). For more on this dance, registered in the Archivo General de la Villa de Madrid, see the Performance History in this volume.

and physical violence. Juan's meticulous adherence to the valiant man's narrative, far from making him exceptional, places him at the center of a mainstream theatrical tradition occupied until then only by legendary white soldiers. Furthermore, Juan expands the limits of the genre of the valiant military man by including a critical examination of early modern society, and an overtly anti-racist denunciation that would have been obvious to the denizens who frequented the steps of San Felipe.

Abraham Teniers's portrait of the Black page rests today in the darkness of a storage room at the Museo del Prado.[97] Similarly, *El valiente negro en Flandes* was excluded from the literary canon. Despite its poetic merits and the extreme popularity it enjoyed in its time and beyond, the play has rarely been performed on modern stages, with the exception of clear instances of anti-colonialism and Black pride affirmation (see Performance History). The stories of Juan de Alba, Alonso de Venegas, and many others that are yet to be retold call us to re-examine the past in search of others who may have been forgotten, marginalized, or intentionally hidden.

---

97 According to the Museo del Prado's official website, the painting has only seen the light once at least since the early nineteenth century, at a temporary exhibition in Sevilla titled 'Los objetos hablan. Colecciones del Museo del Prado' (Oct 26, 2016–Jan 29, 2017).

CRITICAL ESSAY

Antón's Linguistic Blackface and Freedom

Baltasar Fra-Molinero
Bates College
Nelson López
Independent Researcher
Manuel Olmedo Gobante
Cornell University

The other Black character in the play is Antón. He is the second valiant Black man in Flanders. Our reading of Antón is not as a typical *gracioso*, the comic relief character who acts as foil to the main ones. Neither does Antón correspond to the type of the Black *gracioso* whose presence in some plays is exclusively to produce comedy through their use of *habla de negros* [Black speech] (Rodríguez López-Vázquez 1997, 9; Pérez Jiménez 2012, 6). Antón's *habla de negros* is a form of linguistic or oral racialization that can be traced back to literary texts in the second half of the fifteenth century. This practice has its origin in medieval plays that mixed Latin with vernacular languages to produce a comic effect (Weber de Kurlat 1967, 695). Not all Black comic characters of the Spanish *comedia* speak in *habla de negros*, yet *habla de negros* had become a staple ingredient in the creation of Black *graciosos* by the time Claramonte created Antón.[98]

The literary form of *habla de negros* originates during the early stages of modern slavery in Portugal, and it imitated the idiosyncratic form of speech of Africans on Portuguese soil (Lipski 2005, 71). Its popularity was a result of the printing revolution of the time. It was originally used in poetry, but it soon became a fixture in theater

---

98 For instance, Catalina, in Mira de Amescua`s *El negro del mejor amo*, is a Black woman who speaks in standard Spanish and her words amount to a serious critique of the clergy of the time (Panford 2003, 30–31).

whenever a secondary Black character had to speak. It became an aesthetic choice with ideological implications, a signifier of difference and perceived inferiority, a marker of Blackness.

Nicolas R. Jones theorizes on the relation of *habla de negros* as the linguistic element of the blackface that characterizes the *bozal*, the newly arrived enslaved Black who does not speak Spanish well. Both represent a figure of excess (2019, 79–82). While *habla de negros* mimicked to a certain extent the way newly arrived Africans spoke in the Iberian Peninsula and the West Indies, it was mainly a literary device to identify the character as a *bozal*, a Black person born in Africa who spoke Spanish in a different or deficient manner. The word *bozal* also has animalistic connotations, as it means the muzzle applied to dogs' mouths.[99] It was used as a racial marker to differentiate enslaved Black characters from whites or free Blacks, who generally spoke standard Spanish. Thus, *habla de negros* was a mark of slavery. Its use became standard in theater up to the twentieth century.[100]

Antón's *habla de negros* is a polygenic koiné, the combination of a theatrical praxis Andrés de Claramonte inherited and the additions and subtractions by the different hands that intervened in the text for the next two hundred years. In Antón's speech there are elements of the Portuguese language, phonological phenomena that point to West African languages, and the presence of colloquial forms of Spanish that the public would identify as non-standard and different.

There are different opinions about what *habla de negros* is and

---

99   *Bozal* meant a Black person who could not speak any language but their own: "Bozal. El negro que no sabe otra lengua que la suya" (Covarrubias 2020, 350). Its association with a dog's muzzle follows immediately in Covarrubias' definition: "También es bozal cierto género de frenillo que ponen a los perros y a los demás animales para que no puedan morder" ["*bozal* is also certain kind of muzzle that is put on dogs and other animals to prevent them from biting"] (2020, 350).

100   We can see its use in Tomás Gutiérrez Alea's *La Última Cena* [The Last Supper] (1976). Pascual is an old African who speaks like a *bozal*. So does Bengoché, who is an African king recently enslaved, and Sebastián, the rebel. In contrast, younger slaves express themselves in standard Spanish. The linguistic difference among Blacks is a marker of foreignness in this movie, unlike in the film *Maluala* (1979), by Afro-Cuban director Sergio Giral, another historical fiction of resistance to slavery. In this film Black maroons (*cimarrones*) speak in standard Spanish.

represents. It has been compared to the rustic *sayagués*, the slang of urban criminal types, called *germanía*, or even to the cultured poetry of Gongora and his followers – all literary languages of doubted authenticity. However, *habla de negros* is more than another case of Spanish *comedia*'s taste for special languages during the early modern period. At this time the Castilian dialect started being regulated through grammar books as the de facto official language of the Empire. As such, *habla de negros* underwent also its own standardization as it became an essential part of the theatrical repertoire.[101]

Most scholars agree that *habla de negros* is chiefly a hackneyed, artificial code, with little resemblance with the way Black people actually spoke in early modern Spain.[102] There are, however, compelling studies that suggest that literary *habla de negros* may reflect the linguistic reality of Black speakers, either in individual learning processes of Spanish as a second language (Santos Morillo 2020, 92–99) or in the wider context of the creolization of the Afro-Hispanic languages (Lipski 2005). Opinions differ on how to interpret *habla de negros*. Some scholars see it as a deformed, simplified, and mistake-ridden language – if not pure gibberish – that cannot but signify stupidity and childishness. These scholars do not always note that most of the linguistic characteristics of *habla de negros* – e.g., *seseo* and *yeísmo* – were and are still present in common everyday Spanish.[103] Jones (2019) de-automatized this line of

---

101 In his *Libro de todas las cosas y otras muchas más*, Francisco de Quevedo humorously teaches playwrights how to produce *habla de negros*, suggesting that this was an indispensable trick of the trade: "Si escribes comedias y eres poeta, sabrás guineo en volviendo las erres eles y al contrario, como Francisco, Flancisco; primo, plimo" ["If you write *comedias* and are a poet, you will become fluent in Black language by turning the r's into l's and the other way round, as in Francisco, Flancisco, primo [cousin], plimo"] ([1631] 2003, 464).

102 For the debate on the authenticity of *habla de negros*, see Weber de Kurlat (1962, 1970), Baranda Leturio (1989), Lipski (2005, 71–94), and Santos Morillo (2020, 56–61).

103 López Prudencio (1915) considered *habla de negros* a *jerga inextricable* [inextricable jargon] (quoted in Fra Molinero 1995, 23). Santos Morillo (2020) highlighted "su elementalidad expresiva, sus errores y deformaciones" ["its expressive simpleness, its mistakes and deformations"] (2020, 97). Similarly, Ndiaye (2017, 182, 205–10) also interprets *habla de negros*, or 'blackspeak', as a

interpretation by convincingly analyzing instances of *habla de negros* as genuine expressions of Black African agency. Fra-Molinero, who has studied the role played by *habla de negros* in the creation of a comical image of Black people, acknowledged that it could also be a legitimate vehicle for conveying a distinct point of view (1995, 23). This is the case of Antón in *The Valiant Black Man in Flanders*. Although he retains some traits of the *gracioso* type – in fact, Antón is one of the less comic *graciosos* we know – there is nothing especially childish or stupid in his characterization. Antón is never criticized or mocked for his use of *habla de negros*. In fact, he is perfectly understood by the rest of the characters. However, Antón's words were not always fully understood by either contemporary or subsequent copyists of the play, much less by present-day readers.

Antón's speech shows most of the traits that define *habla de negros*. Regarding his vocalic system, Antón manifests a variation of unstressed vowels that is typical in early modern Spanish but emphasized in his case (*plumeto, par dios, sior*). In final positions, this variation leads to an often-comical subversion of gender pronouns and suffixes (2219, 2247), a quirk that is overemphasized in the 1651 manuscript *M* (see Textual History). Paragogic vowels are also common in Antón's speech, although mainly in specific words such as *Dioso* and *seoro*. Stressed vowels rarely show variation, at least in the earliest versions of the play (see line 863 in the Critical Apparatus), with the exception of /o/, which often closes (*turo* for *todo*).

With respect to consonants, as in many other instances of Africanized Spanish, Antón's speech is formalized using an alternative, phonetic-oriented spelling. This writing system sometimes emphasizes traits that are common in most of the Hispanic world, such as the neutralization of sibilants /s/ and /θ/ (both *seseo* and *ceceo*), the fall of the /s/ sound in final position (*damo* for *damos*), the de-lateralization and palatalization of the voiced palatal lateral approximant /ʎ/, also known as *yeísmo* (e.g., *Antoniyo* for *Antonillo*), or the neutralization of liquid consonants /l/ and /r/ (both *plimo* for *primo* and *notabre* for *notable*, sometimes *pluquá* for *por qué* and *siolo* for *sioro*).

---

sign of infantilization (206).

While it shares linguistic traits that are present in other varieties of Spanish, both standard and dialectal, *habla de negros* maintains some elements that are exclusive to it. A frequent feature is the stop/flab realization of intervocalic /d/ (*turo* for *todo*, *cumira* for *comida*) that is still present today in some Afro-Spanish dialects (Lipski 2005, 222). Antón's speech shows the intrusive nasalization and prenasalization present in some West African languages (Lipski 2005, 233–39), which is spelled out in the text either by adding a syllable to the beginning of a word (*enbrancas* for *blancas*), or by adding it at the end (*notable en* for *notables* in line 1252). In some cases <n> or <m> are inserted before, after, or in the middle of a word (*parecen cosan* for *parece cosa*, *aquintura* for *aquí toda*, *alambarda* for *alabarda*). Despite the efforts made by copyists, Spanish spelling was at pains to reflect in a systematic manner these nasalizations that had an African linguistic origin. We conclude that what may seem like variants are in fact different spellings of the same thing: *espadan saco*, *espada ensaco* and *espada sanco* (see line 2120 in the Critical Apparatus), or *sun lacayo* and *su lancayo* (line 1340).

The greatest challenge in the interpretation of Antón's speech as a minimally accurate imitation of Afro-Spanish comes from its linguistic inconsistency and profound instability, even within each textual version of the play. In some versions, Antón distinguishes sibilant consonants /s/ and /θ/, and sometimes he neutralizes them. This would be considered normal if not for the fact that his speech sometimes favors the [θ] sound (*ceceo*) and sometimes the [s] sound (*seseo*), which is extremely rare, even when taking hypercorrection into account. The same goes for the neutralization of liquid consonants, both in favor of [l] and of [r] in the same text. It becomes even more complicated when we examine Antón's speech across the textual history of the play and consider the extraordinarily high rate of variants. Antón has virtually no line without at least one variant.

The morphosyntax of Antón's *habla de negros* has been described as simplified, although it could also be described as more economical or efficient. It tends to omit articles (*sa gente preto* for *son gente los prietos*), something that sometimes compensates for peculiar expressions (*gente brancas* for *los blancos* lines 2045 and 2115). His speech conjugates verbs and uses verbal tenses differently. He uses the present indicative tense all the time. The first-person plural is used regardless of the person and number of the referent (*damo* for *dad* in 1242, but also for *dará* in 1330, and *dais/daréis/dais* in 1959). The only exception to this rule is the use of the verb *sa* or *za*, which he uses as both *ser* and *estar* indistinctly, although occasionally *samo* or *zamo* are used instead. Another feature of Antón's grammar is his use of syntactic agglutination (*jur'an dioso* for *juro a Dios*), which is also common in colloquial Spanish. These linguistic forms are emphasized by the spelling in the texts (Santos Morillo 2020, 180). All of these traits, in sum, have been documented in Afro-Spanish both inside and outside the Iberian Peninsula (Lipski 2005).

Antón's lexicon shows the presence of Portuguese terms (*preto* for *prieto*, *branco* for *blanco*), which is a reminder of the Portuguese origins of *habla de negros* and Claramonte's awareness of the origin of many Black slaves in the Portuguese Atlantic. Antón's words sometimes are shortened by apheresis (*simulo* for *disimulo*, *belesados* for *embelesados*). He uses scatological alterations of common words (*cagayera* for *caballero*, *culobesate* for *calabazate*, dessert made of sweetened pieces of pumpkin) that do not necessarily obey any phonological rule. We will return to Antón's use of scatology.

Antón's original text – what came from Claramonte's hand – has been lost, obscured by a myriad of misunderstandings and interventions by other copyists and editors. The methodological fundamentals of stemmatics do not guarantee the restoration of Antón's lines in *X* (see Editorial Methods). On the one hand, the Critical Apparatus in this edition shows that printers and copyists did not always understand Antón's words. They most probably believed that some of his linguistic traits were typos. This produced several *easier readings* or simplifications that tended to standardize (de-racialize) the character's speech. On the other hand, as suggested by the Critical Apparatus, most printers and copyists had clear – although different – ideas of how a Black theatrical character should talk to 'sound Black'. They did not hesitate to further 'Africanize' or exoticize Antón's speech as the opportunity offered itself. These interventions by hands other than Claramonte's undermine the critical principle of *lectio difficilior potior* (the more difficult reading is the strongest). Antón's textual transmission also problematizes the idea of 'conjunctive error', that is, a mistake shared by two different texts that proves they both have been copied from a common original. *Habla de negros* being a widespread stereotype – it was present in literary manifestations on both sides of the Atlantic – some of the exoticizations present in Antón's textual history are indeed polygenetic, that is, the same innovations were produced independently, without copying one from another. In any case, it is almost impossible to determine which variant is an added Africanization and which is a simplified error.

Antón's *habla de negros* has the theatrical function of acting as the negative of Juan de Mérida/Juan de Alba's elevated standard Spanish. Juan, as archetypical choleric man (Olmedo Gobante 2018), is overly preoccupied with appearing well-spoken, and dignified:

JUAN DE ALBA	Más a espacio y más severo.	
ANTÓN	*Aspacio y severo andamo.*	
JUAN DE ALBA	Antonillo, ¿qué parezco?	
ANTÓN	*Rey Mago y yo sun lacayo.*	1340
JUAN DE ALBA	¡Antón!	
ANTÓN	*¿Sioro?*	
JUAN DE ALBA	Respeto, que soy sargento de Flandes.	
ANTÓN	*Turu lu mundo sabemo.*	
JUAN DE ALBA	Antón.	
ANTÓN	*¿Sioro?*	
JUAN DE ALBA	Camina.	
ANTÓN	*Parece cosa de neglos.*	

[JUAN DE ALBA	Slowly and give me more space.
ANTÓN	*Slowly and we walk with more space.*
JUAN DE ALBA	Little Antón, how do I look?
ANTÓN	*Like the Wise King, and I'm his lackey.*
JUAN DE ALBA	Antón?
ANTÓN	*Seh?*

JUAN DE ALBA	Show some respect;
	For I am a sergeant of Flanders now.
ANTÓN	*Everybody knows it by now.*
JUAN DE ALBA	Antón?
ANTÓN	*Seh?*
JUAN DE ALBA	March.
ANTÓN	*This must be a Black thing.*]

(lines 1337–1345)

Antón will make fun of Juan by proclaiming the two of them as two figures in a Nativity scene, the Black King and his lackey. Juan's fear is that his new military rank will not bring him respect from others. His proclamation of the obvious – he is a sergeant in Flanders – receives an answer from Antón – "Turu lu mundo sabemo" ["everybody knows it by now"] – that confirms the fact and puts the matter in question at the same time. All the world knows Juan is a sergeant in Flanders, so the insistence speaks of the nagging insecurity Juan feels. Antón's last words in the scene are addressed to the public: To you this is a Black thing, it is a Black mess, confusion. I know how you see us.

The play treats both Antón and Juan as *bozales*, African-born Black persons who speak Africanized Spanish or Portuguese.[104] Yet, even though Antón speaks *habla de negros*, he is never referred to as a *bozal*. In fact, there are no references in the text to a possible African place of origin for Antón. He has no stated place of origin, although he calls himself "Antonillo de Vera" (line 1027) and consequently he is not dubbed a foreigner. Yet he speaks foreign, since the *bozal* is a foreigner by definition (Pichardo 1875, quoted in Santos Morillo 2020, 89).

In spite of his use of standard Spanish, Juan de Mérida also uses a form of linguistic blackface. Juan's speech is a reversal of Antón's *habla de negros*. Juan and Antón, as Black theatrical personae, are articulated as reversals of one another and together as reversals of whiteness. Ironically, it is Juan who calls himself a *bozal*, in a comparison between Flanders and Guinea as opposites and the same. Born in Mérida – everybody knows that – and speaking standard

---

104   For a discussion of *habla de negros* as *bozal* speech, see Jones (2019, 79–82).

Spanish make him Spanish, but his skin color and slave genealogy make him a permanent foreigner. In his soliloquy after being promoted to sergeant, Juan reflects on the paradox of being Black in Flanders, a land of whites whom he is allowed to attack. He imitates the Dutch language as *habla de blancos*, parallel to the *habla de negros* that all Blacks are supposed to speak in Guinea:

> Lengua peor que la mía,
> donde negro bozal soy.
> Para mí, en Guinea estoy,
> que por yerro blancos cría.

> [This
> Tongue is worse than mine,
> Where I am a new Black slave.
> I am thinking I am in Africa
> Populated by whites.]
> (lines 1102–1105)

Flanders is a Guinea of whites, and Dutch is a *bozal* language of whites. But being in Flanders, his standard Spanish makes him a *bozal* there. The term *bozal* changes meaning in Juan's enunciation. A *bozal* is no longer just an African foreigner who speaks Africanized Spanish. Juan turns upside down this equation of speech, place, and phenotype through the power of his enunciation. For the Flemish, Spanish is a *bozal* language. He is reviving the diasporic essence of *habla de negros*. In Flanders Juan de Mérida is again a *bozal* like his ancestors were on arrival on Iberian soil. His inability to understand Dutch is turned into the inability of the Dutch to make themselves understood. By calling himself *negro bozal* in Flanders, he is calling every white Spaniard a *bozal* in Flanders, too. Juan becomes the possessor of the linguistic norm because he speaks the standard Spanish that the play's audience understands. But his use of court standard Spanish is a stage oddity for a Black character, and Juan is self-conscious about it. "Their speech is worse than mine, a Black man," he comes to say. His ultimate linguistic referent is *habla de negros*, the linguistic blackface that 'makes' a Black character on stage. A Black man now represents the linguistic norm, and the white soldiers who have rebelled against the King of Spain are the foreigners, the speakers of a *bozal* language who inhabit a foreign land. The whites of Flanders are *bozales*, foreigners. He, a Black man who speaks standard Spanish, is the foreigner of the foreigners.

Antón's use of *habla de negros* is the main contradiction of his character. Black characters since the middle of the sixteenth century were figurations of slavery. Blacks and slavery were seen as one and the same thing. Through the use of *habla de negros*, the Black character is supposed to represent someone comically uneducated (Wynter 1977, 16). With this premise in mind, *habla de negros* in Antón's mouth betrays a profound knowledge of social institutions and mores. His speech is urban, denoting a streetwise demeanor that does not correspond to the 'ignorant' *bozal* that *habla de negros* is supposed to connote. As already mentioned, nowhere in the play is it said that he was born in Africa, which would justify his *habla de negros*. In fact, his name is associated to the aristocratic Vera family of Mérida, and he is saluted by Juan de Mérida in Flanders as a fellow Mérida denizen. Why does Antón speak *habla de negros* when he seems like anything but a *bozal*? *Habla de negros* in Antón is artifice, a case of linguistic blackface that serves several purposes.

Antón uses *habla de negros* as a means to gain freedom. What makes Antón a different secondary Black character is his agency, represented by his independent agenda with respect to the two characters he serves, Doña Leonor and Juan de Mérida/Juan de Alba.[105] Antón's speech is not just a vehicle to launch barbs against other characters, but a textual referent of his growth as a character.

---

105   In his lecture-performance of 1938 in Havana, Rafael Marquina decided to exclude Antón from the selected scenes to be performed: "A este negro Antón, de escaso relieve en la obra dramatica de Claramonte, le dejaremos hoy en la sombra de su color, porque el tipo genérico a que se adscribe su peculiaridad hemos de hallarlo más acentuado y patente más adelante en otras obras teatrales. En ésta, apenas es figura de relleno sin espiritual caracterización digna de señalamiento" ["This Black Antón, given his scarce relevance in Claramonte's play, we will leave in the darkness of his color, because the generic type his peculiarity belongs to shall be found later more sharply defined in other plays. In this one he is barely a fill-in figure lacking any spiritual characterization worthy of note"] (Marquina 1938, 564).

Antón has to straddle two competing powers, both promising him freedom and yet at the same time representing physical danger. Freedom is the prize Doña Leonor offers him for accompanying her to Flanders. Antón is the only one who knows the secret of her male disguise, a powerful yet dangerous piece of information. The word freedom (*libertad*), pronounced by Doña Leonor, acquires its entire legal and ethical modern meaning in Antón's response:

DOÑA LEONOR   Yo libertad te daré
                  si me guardas el secreto
                     que te fío.
ANTÓN   *Preto samo*
                  hombre de bien, y cayamo,
                  que también sa gente preto.

[DOÑA LEONOR   I will grant you your freedom
                  If you keep the secret
                  I entrust to you.
ANTÓN   We Blacks
                  Are good people, we know how to keep quiet
                  Because Blacks are people too.]
                     (lines 859–863)

Antón uses the terms Juan de Mérida had applied to himself (*hombre de bien*) to establish his humanity (*sa gente preto*) through his agency, in this case the choice of silence to keep a secret. His prudence makes him a parallel to Juan de Mérida himself. Prudence is a companion to *virtù*, the manly virtue, the valor that a man has to display in actions and words.

Antón is different from other *graciosos* who avoid putting themselves in physical danger. He is Black and he is not a coward. Antón's quest for freedom is subtle but unequivocal. He conquers it not as an act of emancipation, but by his deft use of language and action. He seeks freedom by performing it in a manner similar to Juan de Mérida: through the use of violence against white men but also through the eloquence of his *habla de negros*. He is as violent as Juan de Mérida: Upon his first encounter with Don Agustín in Flanders, he proposes to Doña Leonor – who is in male dress – that she beat the false lover up (lines 885–856). For a Black slave to attack a white officer would be a death sentence (López 2006, 101).

Antón displays contradictory signs of identity. In line 1027 of the first act, Juan de Mérida calls him Antón de Vera. This last name makes him, as an enslaved person, related to the family of Juan de Mérida's future wife. However, his entrance on stage is as a slave of Doña Leonor de Vargas. The text does not make reference to Antón's age, yet his position as a page, to Leonor/Esteban in act one, and to Juan de Mérida/Juan de Alba in act three, might indicate that he is rather young. In the 1997 Alcalá production, the role was interpreted by actress Victoria Buika (Pérez Jiménez 2000, 7), who gave Antón an element of fierceness regarding Doña Leonor's revenge against Don Agustín. During the first scene of homoerotic banter, Victoria Buika turns the sexual economy of homophobia into a bisexual interracial triangle for the audience:

DOÑA LEONOR	Yo, no es posible que duerma sin compañía.
JUAN DE ALBA	Antón puede dormir con vos.
ANTÓN	*¡Guardan fuera!* *¿Yo con brancos? ¡Osten putas!*
DOÑA LEONOR	(Bien mi venganza se ordena. Disimula, Antón.)
ANTÓN	*(Simulo.)*

[DOÑA LEONOR	It is not possible for me to sleep Without company.
JUAN DE ALBA	Antón can Sleep with you.
ANTÓN	*Get out!* *Me with white folks? Forget that!*
DOÑA LEONOR	*[Aside]* I will get my revenge now; Play along, Antón.
ANTÓN	*[Aside]* *I'll play along*] (lines 1061–1066)

Antón rejects the idea of replacing Juan in bed with Leonor/Esteban with an expletive: "*¿Yo con brancos? ¡Osten putas!*" ["Me with white folks? Forget that!"] [(lines 1064–1065)]. In his case, Antón rejects the sleeping arrangement on racial terms: To sleep with whites is for him as terrible as a same-sex liaison. Antón knows that Esteban is in reality a woman, a white one. Instead of one woman dressed as a man, the 1997 production had a Black woman representing a Black man all throughout the play. Victoria Buika's identity as someone of Equatorial Guinean descent adds one more facet to the prism of the coloniality of the play. The irony of Antón's rejecting the possibility of sharing a bed with a white man who is really a white woman becomes evident at the end of the play, when the one who will share a bed with a white woman is Juan, in another performative reversal of the two Black characters of the play.[106]

Antón, beyond being a foil to Juan de Mérida as a typical *gracioso*, follows the same steps of the protagonist but with a more poignant goal. Antón puts his own life more at risk than even Juan de Mérida does. Antón follows Doña Leonor to Flanders and to a military environment: "*También venimos an guerras*" ["We came here to fight too"] (line 1029). Like so many Blacks in modernity, Antón is in the middle of a war but with a different agenda, one in which his skin color and slave condition could prove fatal (López 2006, 100). Antón shares a complicity with the section of the audience belonging to the lower strata, the *vulgo* Lope de Vega had in mind in his *Arte nuevo de hacer comedias*. Antón can say almost anything he pleases without fear of punishment. Censors will not take him seriously, because he is a Black *gracioso* who speaks in *habla de negros*. He is the nobody who expresses the *vox populi* disguised in his *habla de negros*. Those who choose to listen carefully understand his signifying, the communicative attitude he had started with his *cayamo*: We say nothing, but we know everything, and we will talk later. He is the

---

106 In María de Zayas's 'El prevenido engañado', in her *Novelas amorosas y ejemplares*, a white woman goes to see her Black slave in the stable at night, a scene that her jealous husband spies to his horror. It seems that this was not the first encounter, as the Black lover, deadly ill, rejects her presence.

slave who seeks freedom, and knowledge of a secret is the key to gain it. The information he holds can knock down the structures of power in society. Because he is a slave, this knowledge could turn against him at any time. He knows Doña Leonor is not a young man; he knows that Don Agustín lied to Doña Leonor and made her lose her honor; he knows that Don Agustín has recognized Doña Leonor dressed as a man in Flanders. He is the astute slave of the Roman comedy, wiser in many ways than Juan de Mérida. His words denote wisdom from experience in life.

While Juan de Mérida leaves his hometown in act one with a *carta de ahorro*, his freedom papers, Antón attains his freedom by a deft change of masters. His prudence in keeping the secret of Leonor/ Esteban's true identity allows him to string along Juan de Mérida's homophobic panic. Rather than revealing that the page is really Doña Leonor, he presents his position as one of necessity, speaking as an enslaved Black man to another Black man:

JUAN DE ALBA	Vil, si más	
	con este paje te veo	
	en estos países nunca,	
	en público o en secreto,	
	te he de quemar.	
ANTÓN	*¿Pues quién damo*	1330
	comira a Antón?	
JUAN DE ALBA	Yo.	
ANTÓN	*Comiendo*	
	Antón, al paje olvidamo	
	y a Juan por sior tendremo.	
	Vamo y llevamo alabarda.	
JUAN DE ALBA	¿Prometes lealtad?	
ANTÓN	*Plumeto.*	
[JUAN DE ALBA	Villain! If I ever	
	See you with this page	
	In these countries,	
	In public or in secret,	
	I'm going to burn you.	

ANTÓN	*Who will put food in*
	Antón's mouth?
JUAN DE ALBA	Me.
ANTÓN	*Well, if*
	Antón is fed the page he'll forget,
	And takes Juan as his Lord.
	Let's go and we'll carry the halberd.
JUAN DE ALBA	Do you promise loyalty?
ANTÓN	*I promise*]

(lines 1325–1335)

Antón's answer to Juan's threatening enforcement of heteronormative behavior is that he needs to eat. As an enslaved person, he lets Juan believe he will have to indulge his master's requests, including sexual ones. As an enslaved Black man in Flanders, he might flee or denounce his master as a sodomite, and he will starve to death. All this is summarized in the question of who will feed Antón. The change of masters is an act of self-emancipation on the part of Antón, who exploits Juan's homophobic panic in a private ceremony of fealty. Antón now will be a free page, one who carries the halberd, another Black man in possession of a weapon. His word *"plumeto"* ["I promise"] is the word that only a free person can pronounce meaningfully.

At the start of the third act, Antón shows his willingness to resort to violence in defense of dignity as a Black man. Although not stated, it is understood that Antón is now a *paje de jineta*, or captain's page, to Juan de Alba. As discussed by Olmedo Gobante in this volume, clothes and military insignia make the man. The military role as a captain's page has transformed Antón, even if his role as a page is to follow Captain Juan de Alba and carry his *jineta* spear or round shield. His clothes are a visual sign of his evolution as a character since he takes the initiative when some courtiers at the Royal Palace insult him and Juan for being Black. He chooses silence no more:

Estornudan
JUAN DE ALBA	¿Qué es esto?
ANTÓN	*Estornudar gente branca*
	haciendo burla de preto.

DON FRANCISCO	¡Uchúa!
DON PEDRO	¡Mandinga!
DON GÓMEZ	¡Aché!
JUAN DE ALBA	Calla, y no hagas caso de ellos.
ANTÓN	*¿No hagan caso? ¡Jur' an Dioso,*
	si espadan saco…!

[*They sneeze.*

JUAN DE ALBA	What's this?
ANTÓN	*White people sneezing*
	Making fun of us Blacks.
DON FRANCISCO	Achoo!
DON PEDRO	Mandinka.
DON GÓMEZ	Achoo!
JUAN DE ALBA	Shut up and ignore them.
ANTÓN	*Ignore them? I swear to God,*
	If I draw my sword!]
	(lines 2114–2120)

The supposed comedy of *habla de negros* is based on an effect of distortion that the Black character pronouncing it seems to be unaware of. Antón, however, is aware of the effect his (mis)pronunciation creates. This becomes clear in his use of scatological language. It was expected by the public, but Antón's scatological moments are also loaded with double meaning. In the eyes of whites, Black people were associated with scatology: In the same scene of act three the two courtiers insult Juan and Antón by farting in front of them, which was considered a customary insult against Blacks. The scatological insult racializes the two Black men equally, which is something Antón does not miss:[107]

---

107   The report that provoked the banning of the Black confraternities of Seville in 1604 cites farting as one of the forms of public insult by whites against Blacks especially during religious processions:"hacen burla de ellos, peyéndoles y diciéndoles palabras que unas vece los provocan a que se enojen y otras veces provocan risa" ["they make fun of them, farting in their presence and calling them things that some times provoke their anger and other times provoke laughter"] (Moreno 1997, 85).

JUAN DE ALBA	¿Peyeron?
ANTÓN	*Sí.*
JUAN DE ALBA	¿A quién de los dos peyeron?
ANTÓN	*A vosancé.*
JUAN DE ALBA	Negro, a ti.
ANTÓN	*¿A Antón?*
JUAN DE ALBA	Sí.

Vuelven a peer.

ANTÓN	*¿Y a quién peemo*	2130
	angora?	

[JUAN DE ALBA	Did they fart?
ANTÓN	*Yes.*
JUAN DE ALBA	Which one of us did they fart at?
ANTÓN	*At you, sir.*
JUAN DE ALBA	No, at you, *Negro!*
ANTÓN	*At Antón?*
JUAN DE ALBA	Yes.

They fart again.

ANTÓN	*And who of us did*
	They fart at now?]

(lines 2126–2131)

Antón's use of scatology becomes a form of Black signifying that demolishes the edifice of a seigneurial society that practiced slavery. His use of the word *cagayera* (line 869) for *caballero* (knight) becomes a pun with the word *cagar* (to shit) and acquires a destabilizing meaning. Antón is talking about Don Agustín's dishonorable behavior towards Doña Leonor, and he is also voicing sentiments that members of the public would not dare say in standard Spanish. While his *habla de negros* appears to be a debased form of 'good' Spanish, the vehicle is a mirror of what the audience cannot voice, a mirror of its fear and anger. It is to be noted that the other characters present do not respond in any way to his scatological debasement of the powerful. They do not correct him. Antón's *habla de negros* becomes a special form of aside between him and the public.

Speech is a site of freedom for Antón. Another word he uses is the Portuguese *merda* (shit) for Mérida, Juan's birthplace, which a Spanish-speaking public would understand perfectly. So, while the play seems to praise Mérida, as the place where action takes place, it also diminishes it. In front of the Duke of Alba he refers to Juan as "la flor de merda" (line 931), thus debasing the praise due to Juan, *la flor de Mérida* [the flower of Mérida], as *la flor de merda* [the flower of shit]. But Antón's language always points in two directions. It is not so much Juan who is debased, as the city Mérida-*Merda*, as a referent of Juan's terrible beginnings, and the place of Antón's own enslavement.

Scatology is also tied to food in Antón's *habla de negros.* Antón, in contrast to Juan de Mérida, mentions the pleasures of the body. This is part of a Black orality in which the mouth names food and claims the right to Black joy (Jones 2019, 72–77):

ANTÓN	*¿Habrá notables comiras*
	y culaciones diversos?
	¿Grangea, culobesate
	y cagalones?
[ANTÓN	*Will there some fancy meals*
	And some serious tasting?
	Crème booboole, fried fritters, and
	pahteh of fart grass?]

(lines 1252–1255)

Depending on the edition (see Critical Apparatus), Antón's *habla de negros* changes the word *colación* (snack) for *culación* (a made-up word related to ass, *culo*). The word *culobesate* [to kiss your ass] appears for *calabazate*, a dessert made with pieces of pumpkin boiled in syrup. *Cagalones* (turds) is another example of the relation Antón establishes between food and defecation, as well as a possible Andalusian joke. The *cagalones* were, and are, a form of fried dough in the region, a dish Andrés de Claramonte was possibly familiar with, that adds a lexical element to locating the writing of the play in Seville. The scatological naming of food in Antón's speech becomes a repertoire of dishes that denote his cosmopolitanism – foods associated with America or Andalusia – and the expenses incurred in preparing them. They are luxury items that he, as a slave and part of this capitalist exchange, transforms into excretal products through his pointed use of *habla de negros*.

Scatological language is an expression of freedom that Antón uses to criticize even the most sacred institutions. In his mouth, *habla de negros* acquires a degree of political irreverence that complements Juan de Mérida's discourse of racial honor. Unlike Juan, Antón is not fazed by the trappings of that discourse of honor. Antón calls out certain things for what they are. If Juan expresses awe at the prospect of meeting the King in the third act, Antón answers, "Isn't he a man?" (line 2205). When he sees the King in person, he echoes the typical expressions of veneration to his quasi-divine body, yet his *habla de negros* produces a contradictory rhetorical effect:

ANTÓN   *¿Esta sa el Rey? ¡Jur' an Dioso,*
                           que branco tornamo al preto
                           den temor y den respeto!
                           Cagayera sa espantosa.
                           Sioro, sioro, estamo
                           belesados.

ANTÓN   *Was that the king? I swear to God,*
                           That Black men turn White
                           Out of fear and respect.
                           He's the Knight of Knights.
                           My Seh, my Seh, we
                           Are dumberstruck.]
                                   (lines 2248–2253)

The vision of the King could turn Antón's skin from Black to white, as in Black saints' plays, in a comical comparison the public of the time would appreciate. However, by calling the King *cagayera*, a combination of *caballero* (knight) and *cagar* (shit), Antón is once again expressing the unspeakable through the oral mask of *habla de negros*. Furthermore, the scatological *cagayera* renders the hyperbolic words of admiration, fear, and trembling the King should inspire in a subject's body into their opposite. The King is associated with defecation, like food.

As other *graciosos* in the *comedia*, Antón is a character who subverts the social order by demolishing its rhetorical edifice. Thus, *habla de negros*, as used by Antón, goes beyond the linguistic signification of his blackness. The *habla de negros* he uses is a signifier of his quest for freedom. Antón's urban, streetwise retorts and asides define him as a character with agency and an individual goal. While Juan de Mérida/ Juan de Alba establishes the dignity of his Blackness through the exercise of arms, Antón uses his linguistic Blackness as the ultimate weapon to attain freedom. Nobody seems to be able to use a putdown against him. He is a master of timing and space, whether in Flanders, Madrid, or Mérida. Antón attains his de facto freedom by a strategic change of masters in Flanders. Doña Leonor/Esteban promises him freedom in exchange for keeping the secret of her gender identity, but this could be costly, as the homoerotic scene that ensues demonstrates. In the second act he decides to follow Juan de Alba as his new master. The choice of master is in itself an act of freedom. Once again, he exploits the homophobic scenes between Doña Leonor and Juan de Mérida/Juan de Alba to make an advantageous choice. From being a slave, Antón moves up to squire of a knight of the Order of Santiago. He leaves his legal slave condition forgotten in Flanders, coming back to his hometown of Mérida a new man, with new clothes, and a sword. A Black man bearing a sword is no longer a slave. He is a free man.

BIBLIOGRAPHY

Adiele, Pius Onyemechi. 2017. *The Popes, the Catholic Church and the Transatlantic Enslavement of Black Africans 1418–1839*. Hildesheim/Zurich/New York: Georg Olms Verlag.

Aguado, Simón. *Entremés de los negros*. Biblioteca Nacional de España, MSS/17434.

Aguado de los Reyes, Jesús. 2005. Lisboa, Sevilla, Amberes: eje comercial y financiero en el sistema atlántico (primera mitad del siglo XVII). In *El sistema atlántico español (siglos XVI–XIX)*, edited by Carlos Martínez Shaw and José María Oliva Melgar, 101–26. Madrid: Marcial Pons.

Alciato, Andrea. 1549. *Los emblemas de Alciato traducidos en rhimas Españolas. Añadidos de figuras y de nuevos emblemas en la tercera parte de la obra*, translated by Bernardino Daza. Lyon: Guilleimo Rovillio.

Allen, Paul. 2000. *Philip III and the Pax Hispanica, 1598–1621: The Failure of Grand Strategy*. New Haven: Yale University Press.

Ambrosi, Paola, Silvia Bigliazzi and Peter Kofler (eds). 2013. *Theatre Translation in Performance*. New York: Routledge.

Andioc, René and Mireille Coulon. 2008. *Cartelera teatral madrileña del siglo XVIII (1708–1808). Vol. 2, Índices y bibliografía*. Madrid: Fundación Universitaria Española.

Anonymous. 1982. *La vida de Lazarillo de Tormes y de sus fortunas y adversidades*, edited by Alberto Blecua. Madrid: Castalia.

Anonymous. 1908. *The Life of Lazarillo de Tormes, His Fortunes and Adversities*, translated by Clements Markham. London: Charles and Adam Black.

Ashcom, B. B. 1960. Concerning 'La mujer en hábito de hombre' in the Comedia. *Hispanic Review* 28(1): 43–62.

ASALE and RAE. 'Maricón'. *Diccionario de la lengua española*. https://dle.rae.es/

Austria, Alberto de. 1597. *Edicto y ordenanza sobre los desafíos, llamamientos y duelos. Decretada y mandada publicar por el serenísimo señor príncipe archiduque cardenal Alberto, gobernador lugarteniente y capitán general destos estados bajos y Borgoña*. Brussels: Roger Velpius.

Bainton, A. J. C. 1978. The 'comedias sueltas' of Antonio Sanz. *Transactions of the Cambridge Bibliographical Society* 7(2): 248–54.

Ball, David. 1983. *Backward and Forward*. Chicago: Southern Illinois University Press.

Ball, William. 1984. *A Sense of Direction: Observations on the Art of Directing*. New York: Drama Book Publishers.

Baranda Leturio, Consolación. 1989. Las hablas de negros. Orígenes de un personaje literario. *Revista de Filología Española* 69: 311–33.

Barceló Jiménez, Juan. 1980. *Historia del teatro en Murcia*. Segunda edición aumentada. Murcia: Academia Alfonso X el Sabio.

Barceló Jiménez, Juan 1978. Andrés de Claramonte, Juan de Mérida. Notas a la comedia *El valiente negro en Flandes*. In *Libro-Homenaje a Antonio Pérez Gómez*. Vol. 1, 55–63. Cieza: La fonte que mana y corre.

Barnard, Mary E. and Frederick A. de Armas (eds). 2013. *Objects of Culture in the Literature of Imperial Spain*. Toronto: Toronto University Press.

Barroso, Bernardino. 1628. *Teórica, práctica, y exemplos compuestos por el capitán Bernardino Barroso*. Milán: Carlo Antonio Malatesta.

Barsacq, Alain and Bernardo J. García García (eds). 2005. *Hazañas bélicas y leyenda negra: argumentos escénicos entre España y los Países Bajos: Coloquio Internacional, Béthune, 25–26 de marzo de 2004*. Madrid: Fundación Carlos de Amberes.

Basnett, Susan. 1991 Translating for the Theatre: The Case Against Performability. *Traduction, Terminology, Redaction* 1(4): 99–111.

Beckerman, Bernard. 1979. *Dynamic of Drama. Theory and Method of Analysis*. NewYork: Drama Book Specialist.

Benoist, Valerie. 2014. El 'blanqueamiento' de dos escogidas negras de Dios: Sor Esperanza la negra, de Puebla y Sor Teresa la negrita, de Salamanca. *Afro-Hispanic Review* 33(2): 23–40.

Berco, Cristian. 2007. *Sexual Hierarchies, Public Status: Men, Sodomy, and Society in Spain's Golden Age*. Toronto: University of Toronto Press.

Beusterien, John. 2006a. *An Eye on Race: Perspectives from Theater in Imperial Spain*. Lewisburg: Bucknell University Press.

Beusterien, John. 2006b. Teaching Race in *El valiente negro en Flandes* by Andrés de Claramonte. In *Approaches to Teaching Early Modern Spanish Drama*. Edited by Laura Bass and Margaret Greer, 174–81. New York: Modern Language Association.

Billiani, Francesca. 2007. Assessing Boundaries – Censorship and Translation: An Introduction. In *Modes of Censorship and Translation: National Contexts and Diverse Media*, 1–25. London: Routledge.

Blecua, Alberto, Guillermo Serés and Xavier Tubau. 2008. *La edición del teatro de Lope de Vega: las "Partes" de comedias. Criterios de edición.* Bellaterra (Barcelona): Grupo de Investigación Prolope, Universitat Autònoma de Barcelona.

Bravo-Villasante, Carmen. 1955. *La mujer vestida de hombre en el teatro español (siglos XVI–XVII)*. Madrid: Revista de Occidente.

Brendecke, Arndt and Peter Vogt. 2017. *The End of Fortuna and the Rise of Modernity: Contingency and Certainty in Early Modern History*. Berlin/ München/Boston: Walter de Gruyter GmbH.

Brodie, Geraldine. 2018. *The Translator on The Stage*. New York: Bloomsbury Academic.

Buchanan, Milton (ed.). 2016. *Spanish Poetry of the Golden Age*. Toronto: University of Toronto Press.

Calderón de la Barca, Pedro. 2009. *El árbol del mejor fruto*, edited by Ignacio Arellano. Kassel: Reichenberger.

Calderón de la Barca, Pedro. c. 1748–1775. *La sibila de Oriente y gran reina de Sabá*. Sevilla: Joseph Padrino.

Calvo, Thomas. 2019. *Espadas y plumas en la monarquía hispana. Alonso de Contreras y otras "vidas" de soldados: 1600–1650*. Madrid: Casa de Velázquez.

Camarena Castellanos, Ricardo, 1995. *El control inquisitorial del teatro en la Nueva España durante el siglo XVIII*. México, D.F.: Instituto Nacional de Bellas Artes.

Canfield, Curtis. 1963. *Verse drama*. In *The Craft of Play Directing*. New York: Holt, Rhinehart, and Winston.

Cano Aguilar, Rafael. 2009. Los contactos lingüísticos entre el español y las lenguas de Bélgica. In *El Hispanismo Omnipresente. Homenaje a Robert Verdonk. Amberes, Bélgica*, 89–103. Antwerp: University Press Antwerpen.

Canonica-de Rochemonteix, Elvezio. 1991. *El poliglotismo en el teatro de Lope de Vega*. Kassel: Reichenberger.

Caro y Mallén de Soto, Ana. 1993. *Valor, agravio y mujer.* Edited by Lola Luna. Madrid: Castalia.

Carreres, Ángeles, *et al.* 2018. *Mundos en palabras*. New York: Routledge.

Castro, Guillén de. 2019. *The Force of Habit/La fuerza de la costumbre*, edited by Melissa Reneé Machit, translated by Kathleen Jeffs. Liverpool: Liverpool University Press.

Castro Ibaseta, Javier. 2010. Mentidero de Madrid: la Corte como comedia. *Opinión pública y espacio urbano en la Edad Moderna*, coordinated by Antonio Castillo Gómez and James S. Amelang. Gijón: Ediciones Trea.

Cervantes Saavedra. Miguel de. 2015. *Comedias y tragedias*, edited by Luis María Gómez Canseco; Fausta Antonucci; Real Academia Española; *et al*. Madrid: Real Academia Española

Cervantes Saavedra, Miguel de. 2013. *The Complete Exemplary Novels/ Novelas Ejemplares*, edited by Barry W. Ife and Jonathan Thacker. Oxford, UK: Aris & Phillips.

Cervantes Saavedra. Miguel de. 2004. *Don Quijote de la Mancha*. Edición del IV Centenario. Madrid: Real Academia Española/Asociación de Academias de la Lengua Española.

Cervantes Saavedra. Miguel de. 1982. El amante liberal. In *Novelas Ejemplares*, Edición, introducción y notas de Juan Bautista Avalle-Arce. Vol. 1: 159–216. Madrid: Editorial Castalia.

Cervantes Saavedra. Miguel de. 1982. La gitanilla. In *Novelas Ejemplares*, Vol. 1. Edición, introducción y notas de Juan Bautista Avalle-Arce. Vol. 1: 71–158 Madrid: Editorial Castalia.

Chauchadis, Claude. 1997. *La loi du duel: le code du point d'honneur dans l'Espagne des XVIe–XVIIe siècles*. Toulouse: Presses universitaires du Mirail.

Che, Suh Joseph. 2005. The performability and Speakability Dimensions of Translated Drama Texts. *Translation Today* 2, no. 2 (October): 169–84.

Cires Ordóñez, Juan Manuel and Pedro E. García Ballesteros. El 'Tablero de Ajedrez' sevillano: Bautizos y matrimonios de esclavos. In *La antigua Hermandad de los Negros de Sevilla. Etnicidad, Poder y Sociedad en 600 años de Historia*, edited by Isidoro Moreno, 493–99. Seville: Universidad de Sevilla.

Cires Ordóñez, Juan Manuel *et al*. Negros antes que esclavos. *Archivo Hispalense* 72.219 (1989): 29–44.

Claramonte, Andrés de. 2022. *El burlador de Sevilla o El convidado de piedra*, edited by Alfredo Rodríguez López-Vázquez. Madrid: Cátedra.

Claramonte y Corroy, Andrés de. 2016. *El valiente negro en Flandes*, edited by Ana Ogallas Moreno. www.clasicoshispanicos.com

Claramonte, Andrés de. 2010. *La estrella de Sevilla/El gran rey de los desiertos*, edited by Alfredo Rodríguez López-Vázquez. Madrid: Cátedra.

Claramonte y Corroy, Andrés de. 2005. *El valiente negro en Flandes*, edited by Nelson López. Kassel: Edition Reichenberger.

Claramonte y Corroy, Andrés de. 1997. *El valiente negro en Flandes*. Introduction by Alfredo Rodríguez López-Vázquez. Alcalá de Henares, Spain: Aula de Artes Escénicas y Medios Audiovisuales de la Fundación General de la Universidad de Alcalá de Henares.

Claramonte y Corroy, Andrés de. 1857. *El valiente negro en Flandes*, edited by Ramón de Mesonero Romanos. Biblioteca de Autores Españoles. Vol. 43: Dramaturgos contemporáneos a Lope de Vega. Madrid: Rivadeneyra.

Claramonte y Corroy, Andrés de. 1613. *Letanía moral*. Sevilla: Matías Clavijo.

Contreras, Alonso de. 1998. *Discurso de mi vida*, edited by Henry Ettinghausen. Madrid: Espasa-Calpe.

Coromines, Joan. (1961) 2008. *Breve diccionario etimológico de la lengua castellana*. Madrid: Gredos.

Correas, Gonzalo. [1627] 2017. *Vocabulario de refranes y frases proverbiales y otras fórmulas comunes de la lengua castellana...: van añadidas las declaraciones y aplicación adonde pareció ser necesaria, al cabo se ponen las frases más llenas y copiosas / que juntó el Maestro Gonzalo Correas*. Alicante: Biblioteca Virtual Miguel de Cervantes.

Covarrubias Horozco, Sebastián de. (1611) 2020. *Tesoro de la lengua castellana o española*, edited by Ignacio Arellano and Rafael Zafra. Madrid/Frankfurt: Iberoamericana/Vervuert.

Crowe Morey, Tracy. 2010. *Between History and Fiction. The Early Modern Spanish Siege Play*. New York: Peter Lang.

Degroot, Dagomar. 2018. *The Frigid Golden Age: Climate Change, the Little Ice Age, and the Dutch Republic, 1560–1720*. Cambridge, United Kingdom: Cambridge University Press.

Diamante, Juan Bautista. 2017. *El negro más prodigioso*. Cádiz, en la Imprenta de Marina, por D. Manuel Bosch y Compañía. Alicante: Biblioteca Virtual Miguel de Cervantes.

Díaz Cassou, Pedro. 1895. *Serie de los obispos de Cartagena: sus hechos y su tiempo*. Madrid: Establecimiento Tipográfico de Fortanet.

Domínguez Ortiz, Antonio. (1952) 2003. La esclavitud en Castilla durante la Edad Moderna. In *La esclavitud en Castilla durante la Edad Moderna y otros estudios de marginados*, 1–64. Granada. Spain: Comares.

Elliott, J. H. 1989. *Spain and Its World, 1500–1700: Selected Essays*. New Haven: Yale University Press.

Erauso, Catalina de. 2021. *Vida y sucesos de la Monja Alférez*, edited by Miguel Martínez. Madrid: Castalia.

Enríquez Gómez, Antonio (Fernando de Zárate y Castronovo). (1655) 1988. *Las misas de San Vicente Ferrer*. In *Parte veintitrés de comedias nuevas, escritas por los mejores ingenios de España*, edited by José M. Regueiro Carrete. Madrid: Woodbridge Research Publications, Inc.

Enríquez Gómez, Antonio. *El negro más alevoso y pirata del honor*. Biblioteca Nacional de España, Madrid. MS. 16090.

Espino López, Antonio. 2001. *Guerra y cultura en la época moderna.* [Madrid]: Ministerio de Defensa, Secretaría General Técnica.

Fagel, Raymond. 2020. Orange's Spanish Mulatto and Other Side-changers: Narratives on Spanish Defection During the Revolt in the Low Countries. In *Early Modern War Narratives and the Revolt in the Low Countries*, edited by Raymond Fagel, Leonor Álvarez Francés and Beatriz Santiago Belmonte, 107–24. Manchester: Manchester University Press.

Fagel, Raymond. 2017. Describir la guerra. Narrativas de la primera década de las guerras de Flandes, 1567–1577. In *Estudios sobre guerra y sociedad en la Monarquía Hispánica. Guerra marítima, estrategia, organización y cultura militar*, coordinated by Enrique García Hernán y Davide Maffi, 507–18. Valencia: Albatros Ediciones.

Fagel, Raymond, Leonor Álvarez Francés, Beatriz Santiago Belmonte and William G. Naphy (eds). 2020. *Early Modern War Narratives and the Revolt in the Low Countries*. Manchester: Manchester University Press.

Faini, Marco and Severini (eds). 2016. *Books for Captains and Captains in Books. Shaping the Perfect Military Commander in Early Modern Europe*. Wiesbaden: Harrassowitz Verlag.

Fanon, Frantz. 1967. *Black Skin, White Masks*. New York: Grove Press.

Ferrer Valls, Teresa *et al. Base de datos de comedias mencionadas en la documentación teatral (1540–1700). CATCOM.* http://catcom.uv.es.

Ferrer Valls (director). 2008. *Diccionario biográfico de actores del teatro clásico español* (DICAT). Kassel: Reichenberger.

Fernández Martínez S. J., Luis. 1988. *Comediantes, esclavos y moriscos en Valladolid. Siglos XVI y XVII.* Valladolid: Secretariado de Publicaciones de la Universidad de Valladolid, 1988.

Figueroa, Melissa. 2019. *El valiente negro en Flandes* de Andrés de Claramonte. Review. *Comedia Performance* 16(1): 112–14.

Figueroa y Córdoba, Diego, and José Figueroa y Córdoba. (1746) 2014. *Mentir, y mudarse a un tiempo, el mentiroso en la Corte.* Alicante : Biblioteca Virtual Miguel de Cervantes.

Fra Molinero, Baltasar. 2014. Los negros como figura de negación y diferencia en el teatro barroco. *Hipogrifo* 2(2): 7–29.

Fra-Molinero, Baltasar. 2005. Juan Latino and His Racial Difference. In *Black Africans in Renaissance Europe*, edited by T. F. Earle and K. J. P. Lowe, 326–44. Cambridge, UK: Cambridge University Press.

Fra Molinero, Baltasar. 2000. Ser mulato en España y América: Discursos legales y otros discursos literarios. *Negros, mulatos, zambaigos: Derroteros africanos en los mundos ibéricos*, edited by Berta Ares Queija and Alessandro Stella, 123–42. Sevilla: Escuela de Estudios Hispano-Americanos.

Fra Molinero, Baltasar. 1995. *La imagen de los negros en el teatro del siglo de oro*. Madrid: Siglo Veintiuno editores, 1995.

Fracchia, Carmen. 2019. *Black But Human: Slavery and Visual Arts in Hapsburg Spain, 1480–1700*. Oxford, UK/New York, NY: Oxford University Press.

Fradejas Lebrero, José. 2008. Notas sobre la Relación de *El valiente negro en Flandes* de A. Claramonte. *Murgetana* 119: 95–114.

Frank, Jill. 2004. Citizens, Slaves, and Foreigners: Aristotle on Human Nature. *The American Political Science Review* 98(1): 91–104.

Franzosini, Lorenzo. 1638. *Vocabulario italiano e spagnuolo*. 2 volumes. Rome,

Fuchs, Barbara. 2003. *Passing for Spain: Cervantes and the Fictions of Identity*. Hispanisms. Urbana: University of Illinois Press.

Fuchs, Barbara. 2009. *Exotic Nation. Maurophilia and the Constrution of Early Modern Spain*. Philadelphia: University of Pennsylvania Press.

Ganelin, Charles V. 1987. Introduction to *La infelice Dorotea*, by Andrés de Claramonte. London: Tamesis Books.

García García, Bernardo José. 2006. Las guerras de Flandes en la prensa. Crónica, propaganda y literatura de consumo. In *La imagen de la guerra en el arte de los antiguos Países Bajos*, edited by Bernardo José García García, 247–98. Madrid: Fundación Carlos de Amberes and Editorial Complutense.

García Hernán, David. 2006. *La cultura de la guerra y el teatro del Siglo de Oro*. Madrid: Sílex.

García Norro, Juan José. 2002. ¿Es correcta la división aristotélica de los predicables? *Anuario filosófico* 35(72): 165–82.

García Reidy, Alejandro. 2019. La presencia escénica de Andrés de Claramonte en el Siglo de Oro a partir de las bases de datos Manos y CATCOM. *Bulletin of the Comediantes* 71(1–2): 135–54.

García Reidy, Alejandro. 2008. Una comedia inédita de Andrés de Claramonte: *San Carlos o las dos columnas de Carlos*. *Criticón* 102: 177–93.

Giral, Sergio (director). 1979. *Maluala*. New York: First Run Features.

Girón Pascual, Rafael M. 2016. 'Cruzando aceros'. El comercio de espadas entre España e Italia en los siglos xvi y xvii. *Gladius. Estudios sobre armas antiguas, arte militar y vida cultural en oriente y occidente* 36: 161–79.

Gómez-Centurión Jiménez, Carlos. 1999. El conflicto de los Países Bajos en tiempos de Felipe II en el teatro de Lope de Vega. In *Felipe II y su tiempo. V reunión científica de la Asociación Española de Historia Moderna*, Vol. II, edited by J. L. Pereira and J. M. González Beltrán, 31–42. Cádiz: Universidad de Cádiz/Asociación Española de Historia Moderna.

Góngora y Argote, Luis de. 1974. *Góngora y El 'Polifemo'*, edited by Dámaso Alonso. Madrid: Editorial Gredos.

González García, José María. 2006. *La diosa Fortuna. Metamorfosis de una metáfora política.* Madrid: Mínimo Tránsito, Antonio Machado Libros.

González García, José M. 2017. Fortuna in Seventeenth-Century Spain: Literature, Politics, and the Visual Arts. In *The End of Fortuna and the Rise of Modernity: Contingency and Certainty in Early Modern History*, edited by Arndt Brendecke and Peter Vogt, 108–24. Berlin: Walter de Gruyter GmbH.

González de León, Fernando. 2009. *The Road to Rocroi. Class, Culture and Command in the Spanish Army of Flanders, 1567–1659.* Leiden: Brill.

Grimm, R. 1992. Two African Saints in Medieval Germany. *Die Unterrichtspraxis/Teaching German 25(*2): 127–33.

Guerrero, [Manuel] Vicente. *El negro valiente en Flandes.* Edited, introduced and with notes by Moses E. Panford, Jr. Boulder, CO: Society of Spanish and Spanish-American Studies, 2003.

Gutiérrez Alea, Tomás (director). 1976. *La Última Cena.* 1976. New York Video.

Hale, John R. 1985. *War and Society in Renaissance Europe, 1450–1620.* London: Fontana.

Hall, Kim F. 2005. Othello and the Problem of Blackness. In *A Companion to Shakespeare's Works*, edited by Richard Dutton and Jean E. Howard, 357–74. Oxford, UK: Blackwell Publishing Ltd.

Harari, Yuval Noah. 2008. *The Ultimate Experience. Battlefield Revelations and the Making of Modern War Culture, 1450–2000.* Basingstoke and New York: Palgrave.

Harden, Faith S. 2020. *Arms and Letters: Military Life Writing in Early Modern Spain.* Toronto: University of Toronto Press.

Haywood, Louise M., Michael Thompson and Sándor Hervey. 2009. Genre: Text Type and Purpose. In *Thinking Spanish Translation. A Course in Translation Method: Spanish to English*, edited by Louise M. Haywood, Michael Thompson and Sándor Hervey. London and New York: Routledge.

Heliodorus of Emesa. 1961. *An Ethiopian Story*, translated by Sir Walter Lamb. London: J. M Dent.

Hicks, Dan and Mary C. Beaudry. 2010. Introduction: Material Culture Studies: A Reactionary View. In *The Oxford Handbook of Material Culture Studies*, edited by Dan Hicks and Mary C. Beaudry, i–xvi. Oxford, United Kingdom: Oxford University Press.

Hossain, Mohamed Shahadat. 2017. Translating Drama: Speaking the Unspeakable in Other Words. *Crossings* 8: 78–90.

Hugo, Victor. 2004. *Hernani*. In *Four Plays*. New York: Bloomsbury.

Hurston, Zora Neal. (1937) 2000. *Their Eyes Were Watching God*. New York: HarperCollins.

Ibsen, Henrik. 1992. *A Doll's House*. Translator unknown. New York: Dover Publications, 1992.

Irigoyen-García, Javier. 2005. Ascensión social y enfrentamiento entre negros en *El valiente negro en Flandes* de Andrés de Claramonte: Una aproximación postcolonial. *Afro-Hispanic Review* 24(2): 151–64.

Israel, Jonathan. 1995. *The Dutch Republic: Its Rise, Greatness and Fall, 1477–1806*. Oxford: Oxford University Press.

Jiménez de Enciso, Diego. 1951. *El encubierto y Juan Latino: comedias*, edited by Eduardo Juliá Martínez. Madrid: Aldus.

Johnson, Lemuel. 1971. *The Devil, the Gargoyle, and the Buffoon: The Negro as Metaphor in Western Literature*. Port Washington: Kenikat Press,.

Johnston, David. 2015.*Translating the Theatre of the Spanish Golden Age: A Story of Chance and Transformation*. London: Oberon Press.

Johnston, David. 2014. Valle Inclan: The Meaning of Form. In *Moving Target: Theatre Translation and Cultural Relocation*, edited by C.-A. Upton, 85–99. New York: Routledge, 2014.

Jones, Nicholas R. 2019. *Staging* Habla de Negros*: Radical Performances of the African Diaspora in Early Modern Spain*. University Park, Pennsylvania: The Pennsylvania State University Press.

Kaplan, Paul H. D. 1987. Black Africans in Hohenstaufen Iconography. *Gesta* 26(1): 29–36.

Kaplan, Paul H. D. 1985. *The Rise of the Black Magus in Western Art*. Ann Arbor: UMI Research Press.

Kirschner, Teresa J. 2002. El discurso bélico en *El asalto de Mastrique* y *El sitio de Bredá*. In *Calderón 2000: homenaje a Kurt Reichenberger en su 80 cumpleaño*s, edited by Ignacio Arellano, 269–82. Kassel: Reichenberger.

Lapesa, Rafael. 1981. *Historia de la lengua española.* Madrid: Editorial Gredos.

Latinus, Johannes (Juan Latino). 1573. Ad Catholicum et invictissimum regem Philippum elegia. In *Ad Catholicum, pariter et invictissimum Dei gratia Hispaniarum Regem, de felicissima Serenissimi Ferdinandi Principis nativitate...* Granada: Hugonis de Mena.

Leavitt, Sturgis E. 1931. *The 'Estrella de Sevilla' and Claramonte.* Cambridge: Harvard UP.

Lee, Christina Hyo Jung. 2016. *The Anxiety of Sameness in Early Modern Spain.* Manchester, United Kingdom: Manchester University Press.

Legnani, Nicole D. 2020. *The Business of Conquest: Empire, Love, and Law in the Atlantic World.* University of Notre Dame Press, Notre Dame, Indiana.

Le Roy Ladurie, Emmanuele. 1971. *Times of Feast, Times of Famine: A History of Climate Since the Year 1000.* Garden City, NY: Doubleday.

Lipsius, Justus. (1589) 2004. *Politica. Six Books of Politics or Political Instruction*, edited and translated by Jan Waszink. Assen: Uitgeverij Van Gorcum.

Lipski, John. 2005. *A History of Afro-Hispanic Language: Five Centuries, Five Continents.* Cambridge, United Kingdom: Cambridge University Press.

Loftis, John. 1987. *Renaissance Drama in England and Spain. Topical Allusion and History Plays.* Princeton: Princeton University Press, Princeton.

López, Nelson. 2007. Andrés de Claramonte y Corroy: El actor-autor-poeta. In *El valiente negro en Flandes*, edited by Nelson López, 5–8. Kassel: Edition Reichenberger.

López, Nelson. 2006. Antón, el servidor de dos amos en *El valiente negro en Flandes* de Andrés de Claramonte y Corroy. *Comedia Performance* 3(1): 91–120.

López Prudencio, José. 1915. *Diego Sánchez de Badajoz. Estudio crítico, biográfico y bibliográfico.* Madrid: Tipografía de la Revista de Archivos.

Londoño, Sancho de. 1593. *Discurso sobre la forma de reduzir la disciplina militar a mejor y antiguo estado, compuesto por don Sancho de Londoño maestro de campo.* Madrid: Luis Sánchez.

Lozano Bartolozzi, María del Mar. 1997. Los conventos de Mérida en la historia moderna. Fundaciones, supervivencia, transformación, ruina o reutilización. *Norba-Arte* 17: 121–48.

Lucena Salmoral, Manuel. 1995. La esclavitud americana y las Partidas de Alfonso X. *Indagación: revista de historia y arte* 1: 33–44.

Marquina, Rafael. 1938. El negro en el teatro español antes de Lope de Vega. *Ultra* 4: 555–68.

Martín, Adrienne. 2014. Antisemitismo canino en las Coplas del perro de Alba. *Creneida. Anuario de Literaturas Hispánicas*: 298–315.

Martin, Adrienne. 2008. Sodomitas, putos, doncellos y maricotes en algunos textos de Quevedo. *La Perinola* 12: 107–22).

Martin, Darnel (director). 2005. *Their Eyes Were Watching God*. United States: Touchstone Home Video.

Martín Casares, Aurelia. 2016. *Juan Latino. Talento y destino. Un afro-español en tiempos de Carlos V y Felipe II*. Granada: Editorial Universidad.

Martínez, María Elena. 2008. *Genealogical Fictions: Limpieza de Sangre, Religion, and Gender in Colonial Mexico*. Stanford, CA: Stanford University Press.

Martínez, Miguel. 2020a. Narrating Mutiny in the Army of Flanders. Cristóbal Rodríguez Alva's *La inquieta Flandes* (1594). In *Early Modern War Narratives and the Revolt in the Low Countries*, edited by Raymond Fagel, Leonor Álvarez Francés and Beatriz Santiago Belmonte, 89–107. Manchester: Manchester University Press.

Martínez, Miguel. 2020b. La vida diaria del soldado. In *Soldados de los tercios*, edited by Julio Albi et al., 24–39. Madrid: Desperta Ferro Ediciones.

Martínez, Miguel. 2016. *Front Lines: Soldiers' Writing in the Early Modern Hispanic World*. Philadelphia: University of Pennsylvania Press.

Martínez-López, Enrique. 1998. *Tablero de ajedrez: imágenes del negro heroico en la comedia española y en la literatura e iconografía sacra del Brasil esclavista*. Publications du Centre Culturel Calouste Gulbenkian. Paris: Centre Culturel Calouste Gulbenkian.

Matthews, Dakin. 2021. Workshop on Translating for Performance. *Resituating the Comedia, Conference 2: Made for the Stage: Translation and Performance*. Saturday, February 6, 2021. Unpublished Conference paper. UCLA Virtual Conference.

Mattos, Hebe. 2008. 'Black Troops' and Hierarchies of Color in the Portuguese Atlantic World: The Case of Henrique Dias and His Black Regiment. *Luso-Brazilian Review* 45(1): 6–29.

McKendrick, Melveena. 1974. *Woman and Society in the Spanish Drama of the Golden Age: A Study of the Mujer Varonil*. London: Cambridge University Press.

Méndez Rodríguez, Luis. 2001. Gremio y esclavitud en la pintura sevillana del Siglo de Oro. *Archivo Hispalense* 256–57: 243–55.

Merriam-Webster.com Dictionary, Merriam-Webster, 'Faggot'. https://www.merriam-webster.com/dictionary/faggot. Accessed 12 September, 2021.

Micón, Juan. 1691. *Arcadia de entremeses, escritos por los ingenios más clásicos de España. Primera parte*. En Pamplona, por Juan Micón, impresor del reyno.

Miller, Daniel. 2017. *Stuff*. Cambridge: Polity Press.

Miller, Daniel. 2005. Materiality: An Introduction. *Materiality*, edited by Daniel Miller, 1–50. Durham: Duke University Press.

Mira de Amescua, Antonio. *El negro del mejor amo*, edited by José Luis Suárez García y Antonio Muñoz Palomares. Alicante: Biblioteca Virtual Miguel de Cervantes.

Moll, Jaime. 1976. Un tomo facticio de pliegos sueltos y el origen de las 'Relaciones de comedias'. *Segismundo: revista hispánica de teatro* 12(23–24): 143–69.

Montes Pérez, Dámaris. 2019. *Los libros vernáculos en el Índice expurgatorio de Bernardo de Sandoval (1612–1628)*. Ph.D. dissertation. Universitat Autònoma de Barcelona.

Moreno, Isidoro. 1997. *La antigua Hermandad de los Negros de Sevilla. Etnicidad, Poder y Sociedad en 600 años de Historia*. Seville: Universidad de Sevilla.

Mout, Nicolette. 2017. Justus Lipsius (1547–1606): Fortune and War. In *The End of Fortuna and the Rise of Modernity: Contingency and Certainty in Early Modern History*, edited by Arndt Brendecke and Peter Vogt, 63–81. Berlin/München/Boston: Walter de Gruyter GmbH.

Muravyeva, Marianna. 2014. 'Do not rape and pillage without command': Sex Offences and Early Modern European Armies. *Clio. Women, Gender, History* 39: 55–81.

Murrin, Michael. 1994. *History and Warfare in Renaissance Epic*. Chicago: Chicago University Press.

N'Damba Kabongo, Albert. 1975. *Les esclaves à Cordoue au debut du XVIe siecle, 1600–1621: provenance et condition sociale*. Thesis. Université de Toulouse le Mirail. Microfiche. Paris: Micro Editions Hachette.

Ndiaye, Noémi. 2017. *Marking Blackness: Embodied Techniques of Racialization in Early Modern European Theatre*. Ph.D diss., Columbia University.

Neuschel, Kristen Brooke. 2021. *Living By the Sword: Weapons and Material Culture in France and Britain, 600–1600*. Ithaca: Cornell University Press.

Ogallas Moreno, Ana. 2010. La prosodia de *El valiente negro en Flandes* de Andrés de Claramonte. PhD diss., Universidad de Córdoba..

Olmedo Gobante, Manuel. 2022. In Search of the Black Fencer: Race and Martial Arts Discourse in Early Modern Iberia. In *Empire and its Aftermath: Transatlantic Dialogues on Diaspora*, edited by Jerome Branche. Vanderbilt University Press.

Olmedo Gobante, Manuel. 2019. Del frente a la palestra: esgrima y ejército en la carrera autorial de Jerónimo Sánchez de Carranza. In *Vidas en armas. Biografías militares en la España del Siglo de Oro*, edited by Abigaíl Castellano López and Adrián J. Sáez, 101–14. Huelva: Universidad de Huelva.

Olmedo Gobante, Manuel. 2018. 'El mucho número que hay dellos': *El valiente negro en Flandes* y los esgrimistas afrohispanos de *Grandezas de la espada*. *Bulletin of the Comediantes* 70(2): 67–91.

Olmedo Gobante, Manuel. 2016. Ni caballeros ni cortesanos: bizarría y autorretrato biográfico en la *Suma* de Diego García de Paredes. In *¡Muerto Soy!: Las expresiones de la violencia en la literatura hispánica desde sus orígenes hasta el siglo XIX*, coordinated by Cristóbal José Álvarez López et al., 105–14. Seville: Renacimiento, 2016.

Olmos, Angel Manuel (ed). 2020. Teatros de Madrid, vol. 5. In *Papeles Barbieri* 18. Madrid: Discantus more hispano.

Olsen, Margaret M. 2004. *Slavery and Salvation in Colonial Cartagena de Indias*. Gainesville: University Press of Florida.

Pacheco de Narváez, Luis. 1600. *Libro de las grandezas de la espada en que se declaran muchos secretos del que compuso el comendador Jerónimo de Carranza. En el cual cada uno se podrá licionar y deprender a solas, sin tener necesidad de maestro que le enseñe*. Madrid: Herederos de Juan Íñiguez de Lequerica.

Pan y Agua, Juan Carlos, 2018. *Black Bride of Christ: Chicaba, an African Nun in Eighteenth-century Spain*, edited and translated by Sue E. Houchins and Baltasar Fra Molinero. Nashville: Vanderbilt University Press.

Panford, Moses E. 2003. Introducción. [Manuel] Vicente Guerrero, *El negro valiente en Flandes*, edited by Moses E. Panford, 9–61. Boulder: Society of Spanish and Spanish-American Studies.

Panford, Moses. 1999. La 'Comedia famosa de Juan Latino': el discurso hegemónico como artefacto socio-político. *Afro-Hispanic Review* 18(2): 3–9.

Parker, Geoffrey. 2014. *Imprudent King. A New Life of Philip II*. New Haven, Conn.: Yale University Press.

Parker, Geoffrey. (1975) 2004. *The Army of Flanders and the Spanish Road*. Cambridge, United Kingdom: Cambridge University Press.

Parker, Geoffrey. 2000. Soldados del imperio. El ejército español y los Países Bajos en los inicios de la Edad Moderna. In *Encuentros en Flandes. Relaciones e intercambios hispano-flamencos a comienzos de la Edad Modern*a, edited by Werner Thomas and Robert A. Verdonk, 275–90. Leuven: Leuven University Press/Fundación Duques de Soria.

Parker, Geoffrey. 1977. *The Dutch Revolt*. Ithaca, NY: Cornell University Press.

Patton, Pamela Anne. 2016. *Envisioning Others: Race, Color, and the Visual in Iberia and Latin America*. Leiden: Brill.

Pavis, Patrice. 1992. *Theatre at the Crossroads of Culture*. London and New York: Routledge.

Peale, George. 2007. Conflagraciones teatrales: fichas para una poética de la guerra en la Comedia Nueva (Cajón LVG). In *Guerra y paz en la comedia española: [actas de las] XXIX Jornadas de Teatro Clásico de Almagro. 4, 5, 6 de julio de 2006*, coordinated by Felipe B. Pedraza Jiménez, Rafael González Cañal and Elena E. Marcello, 49–86. Almagro: Ediciones de la Universidad de Castilla-La Mancha.

Pedraza Jiménez, Felipe. 2012. Episodios de la historia contemporánea en Lope de Vega. *Anuario Lope de Vega. Texto, literatura, cultura* 18: 1–39.

Pérez Fernández, Desirée. 2007. La figura del soldado amotinado en el teatro del Siglo de Oro. In *Locos, figurones y quijotes en el teatro de los Siglos de Oro: actas selectas del XII Congreso de la Asociación Internacional de Teatro Español y Novohispano de los Siglos de Oro: Almagro, 15, 16 y 17 de julio de 2005*, coordinated by Germán Vega García-Luengos and Rafael González Cañal, 361–78. Universidad de Castilla-La Mancha.

Pérez Jiménez, Manuel. 2000. La figura del negrillo gracioso en el teatro español: estrategias para una didáctica teatral. *Lenguaje y textos* 15: 1–9.

Pérez Montalbán, Juan. 1998. *La monja alférez*, edited by Vern Williamsen. www.comedias.org.

Pérez Pastor, Cristóbal. 1913. Nuevos datos acerca del histrionismo español en los siglos XVI y XVII (segunda serie). *Bulletin hispanique* 15(3): 300–15.

Periáñez Gómez, Rocío. 2008a. *La esclavitud en Extremadura (siglos XVI–XVIII)*. Ph.D diss., Cáceres: Servicio de Publicaciones de la Universidad de Extremadura.

Periáñez Gómez, Rocío. 2008b. La investigación sobre la esclavitud en España en la Edad Moderna. *Norba: Revista de historia* 21: 275–82.

Pichardo, Esteban. 1875. *Diccionario provincial casi-razonado de voces cubanas*, fourth edition. La Habana: Imprenta El Trabajo.

Prickett-Barnes, David. 1999. 'The Filthiest Service in the World': Sodomy, Emasculation, Honor and Shame in the Early Modern Period. In *Wahrnehmung und Herstellung von Geschlecht*, edited by U. Pasero and F. Braun, 37–46. Opladen/Wiesbaden: Westdeutscher Verlag GmbH.

Quatrefages, Ren. (1983) 2015. *Los tercios*. Madrid: Ministerio de Defensa.

Quevedo, Francisco de. 2007. *Poesía burlesca. Tomo II: Jácaras y Bailes,* edited with glossary and notes by Ignacio Arellano. Alicante: Biblioteca Virtual Miguel de Cervantes, 2007.

Quevedo, Francisco de. 2006. *El sueño del infierno*. México: Siglo Veintiuno Editores.

Quevedo, Francisco de. (1631) 2003. *Libro de todas las cosas y otras muchas má*s. Reproducción digital a partir de *Obras de Francisco de Quevedo Villegas... [tomo primero]*, En Amberes, por Henrico y Cornelio Verdussen: 457–68. Alicante: Biblioteca Virtual Miguel de Cervantes.

Quevedo, Francisco de. 1971. Poema heroico de las necedades y locuras de Orlando el Enamorado. In *Obra poética*, edited by José Manuel Blecua, 409–52. Madrid: Editorial Castalia.

Quintero, Maria Cristina. 2013. The Things They Carried: Sovereign Objects in Calderón de la Barca's *La gran Cenobia*. In *Objects of Culture in the Literature of Imperial Spain*, edited by M. E. Barnard and F. A. de Armas, 80–98. Toronto: University of Toronto.

Quiñones de Benavente, Luis. 2001. *Entremeses completos I: Jocoserias*, edited by I. Arellano, J. M. Escudero, and A. Madroñal. Madrid: Iberoamericana.

Restall, Matthew. 2000. Black Conquistadors: Armed Africans in Early Spanish America. *The Americas* 57(2): 171–205.

Restori, Antonio. 1903. *Piezas de títulos de comedias. Saggi e documenti inediti o rari del teatro spagnuolo dei secoli XVII e XVIII*. Messina: Vincenzo Muglia Editore.

Rickford, John R. What is Ebonics (African American Vernacular). Linguistic Society of America. https://www.linguisticsociety.org/content/what-ebonics-african-american-english.

Rodríguez Cáceres, Milagros, Elena Elisabetta Marcello, and Felipe B. Pedraza Jiménez (eds). 2014. *La comedia española en sus manuscritos. Coloquio internacional, Parma, 17, 18 y 19 de octubre de 2013.* Corral de comedias. Cuenca: Universidad de Castilla-La Mancha.

Rodríguez Hernández, Antonio José and Aitor Díaz Paredes. 2020. Enrolarse en los tercios. *Soldados de los tercios*, edited by Julio Albi et al., 10–23. Madrid: Desperta Ferro Ediciones.

Rodríguez López-Vázquez, Alfredo. 2016. *El condenado por desconfiado* y su atribución: problemas críticos, metodológicos y procedimentales. *Lemir* 20: 439–76.

Rodríguez López-Vázquez, Alfredo. 2010a. Nuevos documentos en torno a Andrés de Claramonte. *Murgetana* 122: 67–70.

Rodríguez López-Vázquez, Alfredo. 2010b. Introducción. Andrés de Claramonte. *La estrella de Sevilla. El gran rey de los desiertos*, edited by Alfredo Rodríguez López-Vázquez. Madrid: Cátedra.

Rodríguez López-Vázquez, Alfredo. 1997. Prólogo. In Andrés de Claramonte. *El valiente negro en Flandes*, edited by Alfredo Rodríguez López-Vázquez, 5–20. Alcalá de Henares, Spain: Aula de Artes Escénicas y Medios Audiovisuales de la Fundación General de la Universidad de Alcalá de Henares.

Rodríguez López-Vázquez, Alfredo. 1987. *Andres de Claramonte y 'El burlador de Sevilla'.* Kassel: Ed. Reichenberger.

Rodríguez López-Vázquez, Alfredo. 1983a. "La estrella de Sevilla" y Claramonte. *Criticón* 21: 6–31.

Rodríguez López-Vázquez, Alfredo. 1983b. La autoría de "El burlador de Sevilla": Andrés de Claramonte. *Castilla: Estudios de literatura* 5: 87–108.

Rodríguez Pérez, Yolanda. 2009. El amotinado como español ejemplar. Rojas Zorilla y *Los amotinados de Flande*s de Vélez de Guevara. In *Alianzas entre historia y ficcion. Homenaje a Patrick Collard*, edited by Eugenia Houvenaghel and Ilse Logie, 237–48. Geneva: Droz.

Rodríguez Pérez, Yolanda. 2008. *The Dutch Revolt through Spanish Eyes: Self and Other in Historical and Literary Texts of Golden Age Spain (c. 1548–1673).* Oxford and Bern: Peter Lang.

Rodríguez Pérez, Yolanda. 2005. Alonso Vázquez en Johan Brouwer. Een zestiende-eeuwse spaanse militair en zijn twintigste-eeuwse vertaler. *Armada*, 38 (March): 10–17.

Rojas Villandrando, Agustín de. (1603) 1995. *El viaje entretenido*, edited by Jean Pierre Ressot. Madrid: Castalia.

Roncero López, Victoriano. 2014. La guerra hispano-holandesa en la pintura y teatro español del siglo XVII. *Arte Nuevo: Revista de Estudios Áureos* 1: 75–84.

Rowe, Erin Kathleen. 2016. After Death, Her Face Turned White: Blackness, Whiteness, and Sanctity in the Early Modern Hispanic World. *The American Historical Review* 121: 727–54.

Rowe, Erin Kathleen. 2019. *Black Saints in Early Modern Global Catholicism*. Cambridge, United Kingdom: Cambridge University Press.

Ruiz-Fornells, Enrique. 2011. *El español y su literatura en los Estados Unidos. Homenaje a la Real Academia Española*. Burgos, Spain: Fundación Instituto Castellano y Leonés de la Lengua.

Rupp, Stephen. 2014. *Heroic Forms: Cervantes and the Literature of War.* Toronto: Toronto University Press.

Rylance, Mark. Interviewed. Shakespeare's antisemitic lines must be censored at times, says Rylance. *The Guardian*. WEbMedia. Accessed, August 20, 2021.

Sánchez Arjona, J. 1898. *Noticias referentes a los anales del teatro en Sevilla desde Lope de Rueda hasta fines del siglo XVII*. Sevilla: Imprenta de E. Rasco.

Sánchez Cano, David. 2005. Dances for the Royal Festivities in Madrid in the Sixteenth and Seventeenth Centuries. *Dance Research: The Journal of the Society for Dance Research* 23(2): 123–52.

Sanchez Jiménez, Antonio. 2006. *El sansón de Extremadura: Diego García de Paredes en la literatura española del siglo XVI*. Newark: Juan de la Cuesta.

Sánchez López, Virginia. 2019. Aportaciones al estudio del melólogo en España e Hispanoamérica: *El negro sensible* entre dos orillas y varios contextos. *Revista Musical Chilena* 73(231): 9–38.

Sandoval, Alonso de. *Un tratado sobre la esclavitud [De instauranda aethiopum salute]*, Introducción y transcripción de Enriqueta Vila Vilar. Madrid: Alianza Universidad, 1987.

Sanz Camañes, Porfirio. 2004. Las relaciones entre el teatro y la política en la creación de imágenes sobre Flandes en la España del Barroco. In *VIIª reunión científica de la Fundación Española de Historia Moderna 2002*, edited by F. Aranda, Vol. 1, 957–89. Cuenca: Universidad de Castilla-La Mancha.

Samson, Alexander. 2016. ¿Rebeldes o luchadores por la libertad? *Los amotinados de Flandes*. In *La leyenda negra en el crisol de la comedia. El teatro del Siglo de Oro frente a los estereotipos antihispánicos*, edited by Yolanda Rodríguez Pérez and Antonio Sánchez Jiménez, 121–39. Frankfurt am Main: Vervuert Verlagsgesellschaft.

Santos Cabota, María del Rosario. 1997. El mercado de esclavos en la Sevilla de la primera mitad del siglo XVII. In Moreno, 501–09.

Santos Morillo, Antonio. 2020. *¿Quién te lo vezó a decir? El habla de negro en la literatura del XVI, imitación de una realidad lingüística.* Madrid: Iberoamericana.

Sentaurens, Jean. 1984. *Séville et le théâtre. De la fin du Moyen Âge à la fin du XVIIIe siècle*, Vol. 2. Bordeaux: Presses Universitaires de Bordeaux.

Shannon, Robert M. 1995. Historicity and Universal Truth: Lope de Vega's American and Flemish Plays. In *Texto y espectáculo*, Proceedings of the Thirteenth International Golden Age Spanish Theatre Symposium (March 17–20, 1993) at the University of Texas, El Paso, edited by José Luis Suárez García, 84–90. York, South Carolina: Spanish Literature Publications Company.

Shergold, N. D., and J. E. Varey. 1963. Some Palace Performances of Seventeenth-Century Plays. *Bulletin of Hispanic Studies* 40(4): 212–44.

Sorentino, Sara-María. 2019. Natural Slavery, Real Abstraction, and the Virtuality of Anti-Blackness. *Theory and Event* 22(8): 630–73.

Speidel, M. Alexander. 1992. Roman Army Pay Scales. *The Journal of Roman Studies* 82: 87–106.

Stanislavski, Constantin.1989. *An Actor Prepares*, translated by Elizabeth Reynolds Hapgood. New York: Routledge.

Stella, Alessandro. 1998. Herrado en el rostro con una S y un clavo: El hombre-animal en la España de los siglos XVI–XVIII. *Palabras de la Ceiba* 1: 22–31.

Stoll, Anita K. 2000. Cross-Dressing in Tirso's *El amor médico* [Love, the Doctor] and *El Aquiles* [Achilles]. In *Gender, Identity, and Representation in Spain's Golden Age*, edited by Anita K. Stoll and Dawn L. Smith, 86–108. Lewisburg: Bucknell University Press.

Stroud, Matthew D. 2007. *Plot Twists and Critical Turns: Queer Approaches to Early Modern Spanish Theater*. Lewisburg: Bucknell University Press.

Taylor, Scott K. 2008. *Honor and Violence in Golden Age Spain*. New Haven and London: Yale University Press.

Thacker, Jonathan. 2018. 'Seré lo que tú quisieres': Female Cross-Dressers in Three Comedies by Tirso de Molina. *The Modern Language Review* 113(2): 338–59.

Thompson, I. A. A. 2013. El soldado, la sociedad y el estado en la España de los siglos xvi y xvii. *Historia militar de España*, edited by Luis Antonio Ribot García, Vol. 3, Tome 2, 448–470. Madrid: Imprenta Ministerio de Defensa.

Tobar, María Luisa, y María Teresa Morabito. 2017. Escenificación de Juan Latino y Juan de Mérida, dos insignes negros en la España del siglo XVI. *Theatralia* 19: 87–117.

Torrico, Benjamín. 2008. De sitios y sitiados: El subgénero bélico como nueva tragedia. In *Hacia la tragedia áurea: Lecturas para un nuevo milenio*, edited by Frederick A. De Armas, Luciano García Lorenzo, and Enrique García Santo-Tomás, 277–85. Madrid/Frankfurt: Iberoamericana/Vervuert.

Treviño Trejo, Alex. 1977. *Edición crítica de El valiente negro en Flandes de Andrés de Claramonte*. Ph.D. Dissertation. Los Angeles: University of Southern California.

Todorov, Tzvetan. 1987. *La conquista de América: el problema del otro*. México: Siglo Veintiuno Editores.

Upton, Carole-Ann (ed.). 2014. *Moving Target: Theatre Translation and Cultural Relocation*. New York: Routledge.

Urzáiz Tortajada, Héctor et al. n.d. Censuras y licencias en manuscritos e impresos teatrales. CLEMIT. http://buscador.clemit.es.

Usandizaga, Guillem. 2014. *La representación de la historia contemporánea en el teatro de Lope de Vega*. Madrid: Iberoamericana, 2014.

Valencia, Felipe. 2021. *The Melancholy Void: Lyric and Masculinity in the Age of Góngora*. Lincoln: University of Nebraska Press.

Vázquez, Alonso. (c. 1577–1588) 1879. *Los sucesos de Flandes y Francia en tiempo de Alejandro Farnese, por el capitán Alonso Vázquez, sargento mayor de la milicia de Jaén y su distrito. Escrito en seis libros*. Madrid: Imprenta de Miguel Ginesta. [Based on BNE Mss/2767. olim I.132, vi].

Vázquez, Luis. 1987. Documentos toledanos y madrileños de Claramonte y reafirmación de Tirso como autor de 'El burlador de Sevilla y convidado de piedra'. *Estudios* 156–57: 9–50.

Vega García-Luengos, Germán. 2021. Juan Ruiz de Alarcón recupera *La monja alférez*. In *Sor Juana Inés de la Cruz y el teatro novohispano*, edited by Rafael González Cañal and Almudena García González, 89–149. Cuenca: Ediciones de la Universidad de Castilla-La Mancha.

Vega y Carpio, Lope de. 2006. *Arte nuevo de hacer comedias en este tiempo*, edited by Enrique García Santo-Tomás. Madrid: Editorial Cátedra.

Vega y Carpio, Lope de. 1985. *Cartas*, edited by Antonio Marín. Madrid: Editorial Castalia.

Vega y Carpio, Lope de. 1984. *El negro del mejor amo*, edited with introduction and notes by José Fradejas Lebrero. Madrid: Universidad Nacional de Educación a Distancia.

Vega y Carpio, Lope de. 2005. *El prodigio de Etiopia*, edited by John Beusterien. Pontevedra: Mirabel Editorial.

Vega y Carpio, Lope de. 1998. *El perro del hortelano*. Madrid: Editorial Cátedra.

Vega y Carpio, Lope de. 1930. *Comedia de Julián Romero*, edited by Emilio Cotarelo y Mori. http://artelope.uv.es.

Vega y Carpio, Lope de. 1894. *El santo negro Rosambuco de la ciudad de Palermo*. In *Obras de Lope de Vega publicadas por la Real Academia Española,* Vol. 4. Comedias de vidas de santos, 361–92. Madrid: Sucesores de Rivadeneyra.

Vega y Carpio, Lope de. 1890. *Obras de Lope de Vega, publicadas por la Real academia española. [Tomo I–VI]*. Madrid: Sucesores de Rivadeneyra.

Vega y Carpio, Lope. *El asalto de Mastrique*. http://artelope.uv.es.

Vega y Carpio, Lope de. *El Galán Castrucho*. http://artelope.uv.es.

Vega y Carpio, Lope de. *El vaquero de Moraña.* http://artelope.uv.es.

Vélez de Guevara, Luis. 2019. *The Mountain Girl of La Vera/La serrana de la vera*, translated by Harvey Erdman. Liverpool: Liverpool University Press.

Vélez de Guevara, Luis. 2010. *Virtudes vencen señales*, edited and annotated by William R. Manson and C. George Peale. Introduction by José María Ruano de la Haza. Newark, DE: Juan de la Cuesta.

Vélez de Guevara, Luis. 2012. *El negro del Serafín*, edited by C. G. Peale and Javier J. González Martínez. Newark: Juan de la Cuesta.

Vélez Sainz, Julio and Antonio Sánchez Jiménez (eds). 2016. *El teatro soldadesco y la cultura militar en la España imperial*. Madrid: Ediciones del Orto.

Verdonk, Robert A. 2017. La aportación de la lengua española de Flandes al léxico del español general a finales del siglo xvi y durante el siglo xvii. *Scriptum Digital* 6: 112–26

Verdonk, Robert A. 1986. La 'Vida y hechos de Estebanillo González', espejo de la lengua española en Flandes. *Revista de filología española* 66(1/2): 101–109.

Weber de Kurlat, Frida. 1962. El tipo cómico del negro en el teatro prelopesco. *Filología* 8: 139–68.

Weber de Kurlat, Frida. 1967. El tipo del negro en el teatro de Lope de Vega: tradición y creación. In *Actas del Segundo Congreso Internacional de*

Hispanistas, 695–704. Nijmegen: Instituto Español de la Universidad de Nijmegen.

Whicker, Jules. 2002. La caballería bajo fuego: la representación de la virtud militar española en *El asalto de Mastrique* de Lope y *El sitio de Breda* de Calderón. In *Calderón 2000: homenaje a Kurt Reichenberger en su 80 cumpleaños*, coordinated by Ignacio Arellano Ayuso, 411–24. Kassel: Reichenberger.

Woodhouse W. (2007). La quijada que cuentan los morenos. *Nueva Revista de Filología Hispánica* (NRFH) 31(2): 296–301.

Wright, Elizabeth R., Sarah Spence and Andrew Lemons. 2014. *The Battle of Lepanto*. Cambridge, Mass.: Harvard University Press.

Wynter, Sylvia. 1977. The Eye of the Other: Images of the Black in Spanish Liteerature. In *Blacks in Hispanic Literature: Critical Essays*, edited by Miriam DeCosta-Willis, 8–19. Port Washington, NY: Kennikat Press.

Wynter, Sylvia. 1972. Review of *One Love – Rhetoric or Reality? – Aspects of Afro-Jamaicanism*, by Audvil King, Althea Helps, Pam Wint and Frank Hasfal. *Caribbean Studies* 12(3): 64–97.

Young, Carol M. 1981. Lizardi's 'El negro sensible'. *CLA Journal* 24(3): 369–75.

Zayas y Sotomayor, María de. 2000. *Novelas amorosas y ejemplares*, edited by Julián Olivares. Madrid: Editorial Cátedra.

ILLUSTRATIONS

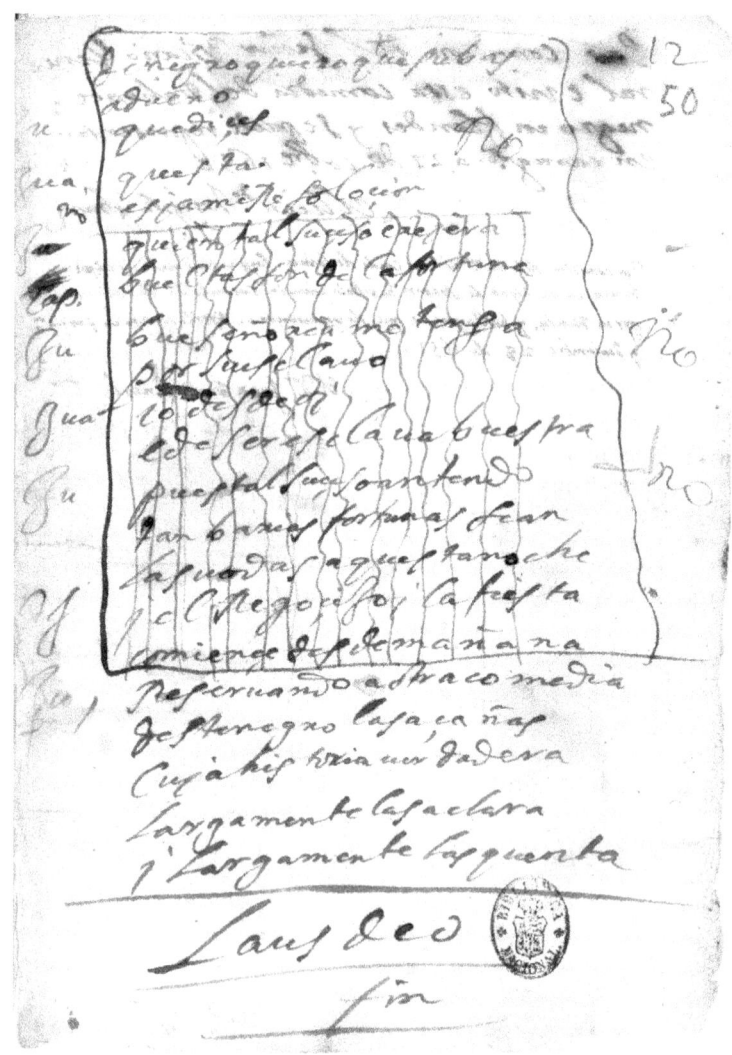

Figure 1. Censorship in M (folio 50r, see Textual History in this volume).
Courtesy of the National Library of Spain (Biblioteca Nacional de España)
in Madrid, Spain, MSS/15690.

EVO , Y CURIOSO ROMANCE,
que fe refieren las grandes hazañas del va-
nte Negro en Flandes , llamado Juan de
Alva , y lo mucho que el Rey nueftro
Señor premiò fus hechos.

lerofa Infantería	Señores de grande Salva,
de la efclarecida Efpaña,	fiendo hijo de una negra,
tre todas las Naciones	que fuè de Don Pedro efclava;
valor te feñalas:	mas por fus buenos fervicios,
e un valiente Negro	la libertad alcanzára.
za , y valor que alcanza,	Llevòme la inclinacion
e acompañan con èl	de fervir al Rey de Efpaña,
la Llave dorada,	y en efte dichofo tiempo
s , Condes , y Marquefes,	unas compañias marchan

Figure 2. Front page of The Ballad of the Valiant Black Man in Flanders.
Courtesy of the British Library, item T23, in volume T.1957.

Figure 3. Chafariz d'el Rey *(1560–80), Anonymous oil on board, probably Flemish. Courtesy of The Berardo Collection Museum (Museu Coleção Berardo) in Lisbon, Portugal.*

Figure 4. Chafariz d'el Rey *(1560–80, detail), An unidentified Black knight of the prestigious Order of Santiago. Courtesy of The Berardo Collection Museum (Museu Coleção Berardo) in Lisbon, Portugal.*

Figure 5. Un cuerpo de guardia (A Guard Post, 1650-1670), oil on copperplate by Abraham Teniers. Courtesy of the Prado Museum (Museo Nacional del Prado) in Madrid, Spain, P001784.

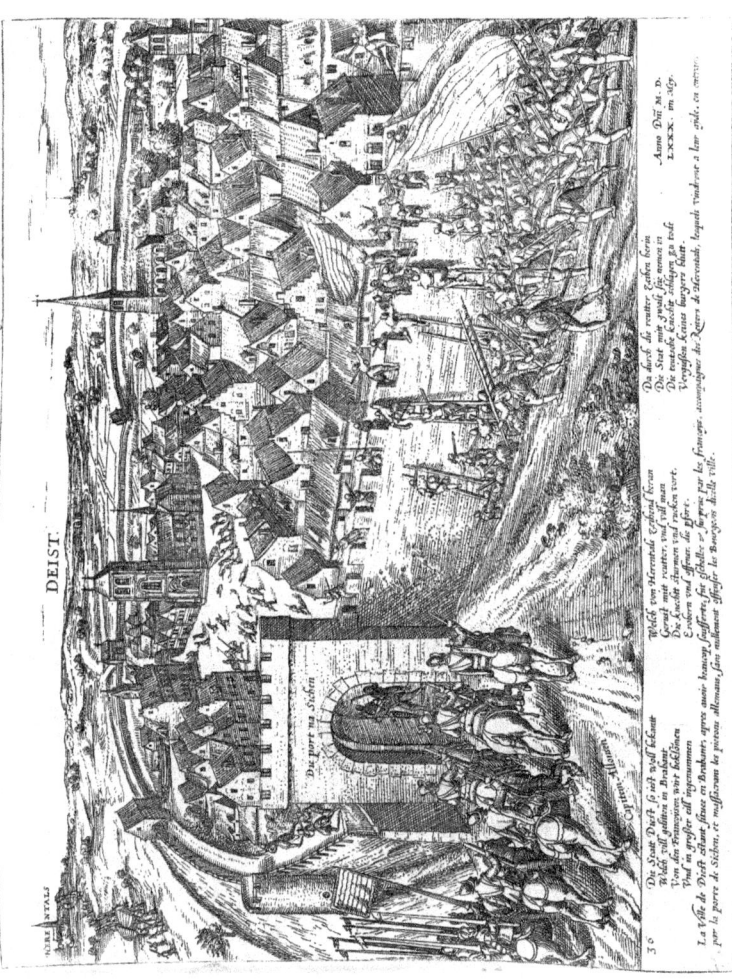

Figure 6. The Siege of Diest, 1580 (Verovering van Diest, 1580). Etching by Frans Hogenberg, 1580–1582. Courtesy of the Rijksmuseum in Amsterdam, Netherlands, Album 345, RP-P-OB-78.784.

Fuſſus in hoſtiles cuneos, noctuq̃ diẽq̃
Peruigil, indomito robore pronus agor.

Figure 7. Arquebusier (labeled as 'Helmeted Musketeer'), Officers and Soldiers series (plate 11). Engraving by Jacques de Gheyn II after Hendrick Goltzius, 1587. Courtesy of the National Gallery of Art in Washington DC, United States, 2004.8.11.

Ante ferox Signanus ago promptum agmen ad arma,
Haud̃ parum debent parta trophæa mihi.

Figure 8. 'Sergeant', Officers and Soldiers (plate 8). Engraving by Jacques de Gheyn II after Hendrick Goltzius, 1587. Courtesy of the National Gallery of Art in Washington DC, United States, 2004.8.8.

Figure 9. Officer, probably a captain (labeled as 'Colonel'), Officers and Soldiers (plate 11). Engraving by Jacques de Gheyn II after Hendrick Goltzius, 1587. Courtesy of the National Gallery of Art in Washington DC, United States, 2004.8.1.

CRITICAL APPARATUS

This section contains an index of variants, as well as a list of the most significative handwritten notes and marks in *M* and *S1* (see Textual History in this volume). Critical notes follow this order: Each entry is headed with the line number, followed by the selected or amended reading, which is delimited with the symbol] . This is continued by the variants, followed with the respective witnesses in italics. Readings of the same locus are separated by the symbol : . Different loci with variants or amendments are separated with the symbol | . Some verses have several entries, marked with the letter a, b, or c at the end of the line number to facilitate reading.

Variants are annotated negatively, which means that only deviations from the restored text are shown. I include only significant readings that change the meaning of a passage or clarify the textual transmission. Most of the obvious errata and other cases of textual garbage are omitted. I use the subarchetypes of the *stemma* shown in the Textual History section: *X*, *α*, *β*, *γ*, *δ*, *ε*, *ζ*, *η*, *θ*, and *ι*. For example, I write *δ* instead of *S3S4S5*, *ε* instead of *S1S8S9*, *ζ* instead of *S6S7*, etc. When there is a deviance within a subarchetype, it is marked in parentheses subsequently. The subarchetypes are arranged, roughly, in chronological order, with *α* being the earliest and most authoritative witnesses, and *S8S9* being the latest and furthest from *X*, which is the text I intend to restore. When an entry does not have the symbol] , it is because there is an addition in some version that does not correspond to any passage of the fixed text. Similarly, the phrase *Omitted in* is used to annotate absences. As explained in the Textual History section, *S2* is excluded from the index because it is virtually identical to *S1*.

Regarding manuscript texts and marks in *M* and *S1*, I annotate interventions following the Prolope Research Group system and using the following symbols:

    <-text>   Text deleted by strokes
    <+text>   Text added on top of another text
    <???>   Illegible text
    </text>   Text added to the line (either to the right or to the left)
    <\text>   Text added between lines (above or below)
    <\\text>   Text added to the margin (either to the right or to the left)

Headings LA GRAN / COMEDIA DEL / VALIENTE NEGRO / en Flandes *P* : De d[o]n Andrés de Claramonte / El valiente negro en / Flandes *M* : COMEDIA FAMOSA. / EL VALIENTE NEGRO / EN FLANDES / *DE DON ANDRÉS DE CLARAMONTE S1S3S5* : El valiente negro en Flandes / 3º ap[un]te / El amor y la razón / y el negro hablador *S1* [manuscript cover] : COMEDIA FAMOSA / EL VALIENTE NEGRO / EN FLANDES. / *DE DON PEDRO CALDERÓN DE LA BARCA S4* : COMEDIA FAMOSA, / EL VALIENTE NEGRO EN FLANDES. / *DE D. ANDRES DE CLARAMONTE S6* : COMEDIA FAMOSA, / EL VALIENTE / NEGRO EN FLANDES. / *DE DON ANDRES DE CLARAMONTE S7S8* : COMEDIA FAMOSA. / EL NEGRO / VALIENTE / EN FLANDES. / PRIMERA PARTE. / *DE DON ANDRES DE CLARAMONTE S9*.

Dramatis Personae. I fully amend the *dramatis personae* to include all the characters in the play, arranging them in order of appearance and adding information pertinent to the performance according to current conventions.

Hablan en ella las personas siguientes. El Capitán don Agustín. / Un Alferez. / Sargento Barrientos. / Juan de Mérida negro. / Un criado. / Dos capitanes. / Dos soldados flamencos. // Doña Leonor dama. / Doña Juana dama. / Elvira criada / Isabel criada. / Antón negro. / El Duque de Alba *P*.
+El Duque de Alba / +Don Agustín capitán / +El sargento+ / +El alférez- / mons de vivanble / Doña Le<-???/onor> + / +Doña Juana / +Elvira / +Inés / +Don Fr[francis]co 2 / +Don Gómez / +Mons de Vila / +Mons de lastrec, 2 / +Don Juan viejo / +Juan de Alva+ / +Soldados / +Antón negro+ / +El Príncipe de Orange / El Rey *M*.

Hablan en ella las personas siguientes. // El Duque de Alba. / Juan de alba, negro. / Don Agustín, capitán. / Un Sargento. / Un Alférez. / Don Juan, viejo. / <Don Pedro> / <D[o]n Fran[is]co- D[o]n Gómez> // El Rey. / El Príncipe de Orange. / Mons de Villa. / Mons de Lastrec. / Mons de Simbamblec. / Antonillo, negro gracioso. / <Dos flamencos> // Doña Juana, dama </2ª> / Doña Leonor, dama </1ª> / Elvira, criada </3ª> / Isabel, criada </4ª> / Soldados </y criados>. / Acompañamiento. / <\\Dos capitanes> *S1* (print).

El Duq[ue] de Alba / Ju[an] de Alba / D[o]n Agustín <\\menos estos todos> / D[oñ]a Juana / D[oñ]a Leonor / El sargento // <-Capitan 1º> / Alférez + / D[on] Juan viejo / D[o]n Pedro / D[o]n Fran[cis]co / D[o]n Gómez / Dos flamencos / Capitán 2º y 3º / Antonillo, negro / <-el Rey> / Elvira / Ysabel // El rey / El de Orange / Mons de Vila / Mons de Lastrec / Mons de

Simblanbleq / Soldados y criados / Un Mus[i]co *S1* (handwritten text on the back of the cover page).

Hablan en ella las personas siguientes. // El Duque de Alba. / Juan de Alba, negro. / Don Agustín, capitán./ Un sargento./ Un alférez// Antonillo, negro gracioso./ Mons de Biblamblec, tudesco. / El príncpie de Orange. / Mons de Vila./ Mons de Lastrac. // Dos soldados. / Don Juan de Vera. / Doña Leonor, dama./ Dos criados./ Don Juan, viejo *η*.

Hablan en ellas las personas siguientes// El duque de Alba / Juan de Alba, negro / Don Agustín, capitán / Un sargento / Un alférez // Antonillo, negro gracioso / Mons de Biblamblec, tudesco / El Príncipe de Orange / Mons de Villa / Mons de Lastrac // Dos Soldados / Doña Juana de Vera / Doña Leonor, dama / Dos criados/ Don Juan, viejo *S5*.

Personas que hablan en ella. // El duque de Alva. / Juan de Alva, que es negro. / Don Agustín, capitán. / Un sargento. / Un Alférez. // Antonillo negro, gracioso / Mons de Siblamblec, Tudesco. / El principe de Orange. / Mons de Vila. / Mons de Lastroce. // Dos solados. / D. Juana, dama / D. Leonor, dama. / Dos Criados. / D. Juan, viejo *ζ*.

Hablan en ella las personas siguientes // El Duque de Alba. / Juan de Alba, negro. / Don Agustín, Capitán. / Un sargento. / Un alférez. / Don Juan, viejo. // El rey. / El Príncipe de Orange. / Mons de Vila. / Mons de Lastrec. / Mons de Simbamblec. / Antonillo, negro gracioso // Doña Juana, dama. / Doña Leonor, dama. / Elvira, criada/ Isabel, criada. / Soldados. / Acompañamiento *S8*.

Hablan en ella las personas siguientes // El rey Felipe Segundo. / El duque de Alba. / Juan de Alba, negro. / Don Agustín, capitán. / Don Pedro Osorio. / Don Juan Estrada, viejo. // Doña Juana de Vera, dama. / Doña Leonor, dama. / Elvira, criada. / Isabel, criada. / Antonillo, negro, gracioso. / Un alférez. Un sargento // El Príncipe de Orange. / Mons de Bibamblec. / Mons de Lastrac. / Mons de Vila. / Unos pretendientes. / Soldados. Criados. *S9*.

Jornada I

1   CAPITÁN DON AGUSTÍN] CAP[ITÁN] *X* (AGUSTÍN *S9*) | <\\ Ojo lo ataga ???i no> *M*. See line 1085 and Textual History.
1b   JUAN DE MÉRIDA] JUAN *X* (<-AL +JU> *M*).
3   el color] la color *Pζ*.
5   ese] este *S1*.
6   turco] moro *P*.

8   qué vendrá] lo que vendrá *P*. | ¿qué? será] será *P*.
10   plana] planta *ζ*.
10–11   puesto en … profundo] *M* inverts the order of the lines.
16   con] en *M*.
20   y si exceden] y exceden *ζ*.
33   Oiga] Oigan *M*. | filosóficos] filosofito es *S7*.
37   abrasa] abraza *P*.
41   me] es el *P*.
48   este color] mi color *γ* : mi valor *δ*.
56   el mundo se] <-la tierra sc \el mundo> *M* : al mundo se *ζ* : el mundo
        le *S1S8*.
60   el alma de los] la que exalta o postra *ε*.
61   pórfido] pérfido *S4S6* : prófido *S5*.
62   medra] media *P*.
63   pentarbe] partible *γ* (pantarbe *S9*) ; pantarbe *δ*.
67   agora] ahora *γ*.
70   JUAN] SARGENTO *η*.
72   y soy] pero *ε*.
76   de aquellos] en aquellos *S1*.
80   y a él] S1 | le] lo *ε* (le *S9*).
83   pero] mas *P*.
87   su] la *S1*.
92   jamás] ya más *P*.
93   consintió] concentio *P* : recibió *M*.
94   si el rey no fuera] y cuando el rey fuera *P*.
96   *Acuchíllalos*] Omitted in *X* (*Acuchíllalos S9*). See line 100.
100   *Mete mano a la espada y acuchíllalos γ* (Omitted in *S9*) : *Mete mano
        a la espada y acuchíllalos Juan δ*.
104   ansí] así *β*.
106   Aquesta] aqueste *P*.
107   Prendedle, dadle un garrote] prendeldo y dalde *P* : prendelde, dalde
        Mδ : prendedlo, dadle *ζ* : prendedle, dadle *ι*.
109   dejarte] dejaros *M*.
110   puedas] podáis *M*.
111   ansí] así *β* | han] has *P* : ha *Mδ*.
112   matarlos] matarle *P* : matarla *β* (matarlos *MS8*).
113   casas] cosas S5.
115   *Sale* DOÑA LEONOR, *dama.*] *Sale* DOÑA LEONOR, *dama α* : *Entranse,*

y sale Leonor dama δζ: Entrase, y sale Leonor dama ε (*Entranse, y sale doña Leonor dama S9*).

116   mis casas] mi casa ε (mis casas *S9*) | *Sale el capitán S8* : *Sale d. Agustín S9*.

123   que en su] que su ζ.

122   alba] <-dia /alba > *M*.

125–128   <\\no no> *M*.

127   será] sería *S1S6*.

128   todo es nieve] toda es nieve ζ | nácar] <-alva /nacar> *M*.

134   declara] declaran *M* | omnipotencia] grande poder ε.

135   retirándose entró] retirando se entró δ*S9*.

136   alcanzan] pasan *P*.

137   plazas] plaza *S1* | de cielo] del cielo β.

140   alcanza] gana *M* : enlaza *S5*.

141   paz] pues *P*.

142   si] y ι.

148   consagro mil] consagrad mil δ : consagran mil ζ : consagro mis ι.

150   tal día, que aunque la fama] con estas : <-tal día que aunque la fama\ con estas???> *M* : cal día, que aunque la fama *S4*.

151–156   <\\no no no no> *M*.

154   azucenas] azucena *S1*.

156   Tan bien] también *X* (tan bien *M*).

158   claras] <-grandes/claras > *M*.

161   *Salen todos con* JUAN DE MÉRIDA *sin espada*] *Salen todos con el negro sin espada X* (*Salen el alférez, el sargento y soldados que traen prisionero a Juan de Alba S9*).

168   llevadle] llevalde *M* : llevadle β (llevadlo *P*ζ) | señora] señor *S1*.

169   hijo] negro *M* | julianillo δ.

171   de Vera] mi prima *P* : <-mi prima/de vera> *M*.

172   mi prima? JUAN DE MÉRIDA A mi madre llaman] JUAN Señora a mi madre llaman *P*.

178   aquí] ha que *P*.

181–182   Quedando… carta] Omitted in β.

183   eternamente] que eternamente δ : este moreno ε.

185   en perderla] el perdella *P* : en perderla β (en perdella *MS6*).

186   el ganarla] el ganalla *PS6* : ganalla M : el ganarla δ*S7* : ganarla ι.

189   herido] <-muerto/herido> *M*.

191   obedecer] respetar *M*.

193   Doña Leonor Yo el favor estimo. Sargento Barrientos ¡Oh,
        pese…!] soltar Doña Leonor Yo el favor estimo *P* : <-soltar \Leo.
        Yo el favor estimo. Sar. ¡Oh, pese…!> *M.*
198   espaldas] espadas *β.*
200   Sargento Barrientos] *Cap. S7.*
200b   ahora] agora *P* : pues *S7* | la que te rescata] la que te recate *δ* : quien
        te rescata *S7.*
202   la] tu *P.*
204   ladran] alagan *ε.*
205   al] el *P.*
207   Juan] pues *γ.*
209   pobre] hombre *ζ.*
210   si gratitudes] si en gratitudes *S1* : mis ingratitudes *ζ* : si ingratitudes *S8.*
211   esta] y esta *S1.*
212   dais] deis *δ.*
213   la ofreced] le ofrecéis *S6.*
217   a apaciguar] a paciguar *ζ.*
224   *Vanse y quedan el capitán* don Agustín *y* doña Leonor] : *Vase X*
        (*Vanse y queda el Capitán y Leonor M*).
227   <\\+Vega+> *M.*
233   deja] dejáis *M1.*
234   permitiendo] permitidme *ε.*
235   lo] o *γ.*
237   sol] el *P* | mundo] día *M.*
239–251   <\\no no -si+no no -si+no > *M.*
242   alas] aras *γ.*
243   desde] después *ı* | le dio] te vio *ζ* : me vio *ε.*
244   coronado] coronada *ζ.*
246   poca aurora] poco bozo *ε.*
247   la inclinación de] mi inclinación a *S1.*
250   las cajas] cajas *MS1.*
252   agora] ahora *γ* | el] en *S1.*
253   <-a España /a Flandes> *M.*
255–266   <\\si si +no si > *M.*
259   escurecido] obscurecido *ε.*
261   le] lo *ζ.*
264   blandas] blancas *S5.*
266   sangrientas batallas] reñida batalla *M.*

267–270 Vos sola podréis… fénix del alma] Omitted in all but *P*.

272   de Estrada] Leo. Repara *P*.

273   con quien pretendió casaros] mi memoria en vuestro nombre *P*.

274   El señor don Juan de Vargas] Con quien os tuvo casada *P*.

278   no di] negué *M*.

280   en vos] <-yo no \en vos> *M* : yo no *β*.

282   esta] esto *S9*.

283   agora] ahora *ζ1*.

283–286   <\\no no > *M*.

286   mi] su *β*.

287   desprecié] despreció *ε* (desprecié *S9*).

288   ya aguardan] y guardan *ε* (ya aguardan *S9*).

291–298   A todo rigor… paz descansa] Omitted in *M*.

295   la] el *P*.

296   agora] ahora *ε* (agora *S1*)

301   os ofrezco] es forzoso *S5*.

304   esos] sus *P* | la] a *S1*.

305   honrad] honró *S6* : honra *S7*.

307   flemas] flema *S2* : llamas *ı*.

308   priesas] prisas *Pε*.

310   rigor] valor *M*.

312   acción igual] ocasión tal *M*.

313   mi] el *S8* : Omitted and added by hand in *S1*.

314   me] de *S1*: le *ı*.

316   vista] vida *ε* (vista *S9*)

323   violento] Violante *S6*.

324   casto] callo *ζ*.

332   que hoy] de que *P* : como *S8*.

335   esta] esa *γ*.

338   haré aquí] haced que *γ* : haré que *δ* .

339   otorgaré] firmaré *M* | yo] hoy *ζ*.

340   pusiere] pudiera *P* : quisiere *ζ* : quistere *S8*.

341   invencible] invisible *P*.

342   *Don Agustín se arrodilla*] Omitted in *X*.

343   la] Omitted in *S1*.

347   os quedéis] quedéis *P*.

349   Amor, ya] qué presto *P* | vencida] vencido *δ*.

350   esta noche] siendo así *P*.

351   si en el papel concedéis] esta noche, donde haréis *P* | <\\López> *M*.

353   y tu] esa *M* : vuestra *ε*.

356   *Vanse. Salen Doña Juana y Juan de Mérida*] *Salen Doña Juana y Juan de Mérida P* : *Vanse. Salen Doña Juana y el negro M* : *Salen doña Juana y Juan de Alba S1* : *Vanse, y salen doña Juana y Juan de alba, negro δ* : *Vanse / Sale doña Juana y Juan de Alba negro ζ* : *Vanse y sale doña Juana y Juan de Alba ι*.

357   se pueden] se puede *M* : te puedo *ζ* : te no puedo *ε*.

358   pendencia] imprudencia *ι*.

364   así] ansí *M*.

368   y] que *γ* | ello] eso *M* : ellos *S1δS8* | les] le *ζ* | dan] den *ι*.

372   los] les *β* (los *αS1S8*).

375   todo el] cada *M*.

376   azacán? ¿yo, aguador?] a casa?, ¿yo agua? *ζ*.

378   valor es] valor no es *S8*.

379   pues] que *γ* | quiero] quiera *ζ*.

381–388   Eso ha de ser… de tu casa] Omitted in *M*.

381   Eso ha de ser] <-no repara> <-eno ha de ser /eso a de se> *S1*.

386   comido] Cercado *β*. Omitted in *M*.

387   brasa] brase *P*.

388   este] de este *ζ* | *Doña Juana le da un papel*] Omitted in *X*.

392   y con] ya con *ε* | acabo] acabe *M*.

393   ya mi] y mi *Pγ*.

394   he sido] soy *ε* (he sido *S9*)

397   le] la *δζ*.

402   las mercedes] la merced *P* : más mercedes *δS9* | hoy] hoy no *P*.

404   quiero] quiera *S1*.

405   pasar quiero] pasareme *ζS8*.

408   agora] ahora *γ* (agora *S1*) | espanto soy, si] espanto soy </y> si *S1*.

409   hoy me afrenta] me ofende *M*.

410   triunfante] constante *M*.

412   oro] humo *ζ* | o del] <-y la +o del> *S1*.

412b   *Vanse y salen Elvira, Isabel, y Pineda, criados*] *Vase. Salen Elvira y Isabel, criadas, y un criado P* : *Vase y salen Elvira y Isabel, criadas M* : *Vanse, y sale Elvira y Isabel, criadas S1* : *Vase y sale Elvira y Isabela, criada δ* : *Vanse, y sale Elvira y Isabel, criada ζ* : *Vanse, y sale Elvira e Isabel, criada S8* : *Vase, y salen Elvira e Isabel, criadas S9*.

413 PINEDA] CRIA. *X* (ISABEL *Mε*). I amend every name cue in this scene using context, since variants abound, and no witness offers a congruent version. In manuscript *M*, name cues have numerous marks of rewriting, showing that, most likely, all the witnesses descend from a text that did not clarify who said what in this scene. *M* and *ε* reallocate Pineda's lines between Elvira and Isabel, eliminating Pineda. The name of the servant is later stated in all versions, and it is made clear that he is the one who saw the departure of Don Agustín, legitimizing the stage direction in *P* (see 412b).

413b le] lo *PS8* : </le> *S1*.

415 tropa, cuando] tropa </y> cuando *S1*.

417 de la] del *PS1S8* | aurora] auro,</ra> *S1*.

418 ISABEL ... PINEDA] ISABEL ... CRIA. *Pδ*: ELVIRA ... CRIA. *ζ* : ELVIRA ... ISABEL *ε*.

419 le] la *η*.

420   Reniega] Renie<-a +o> *S1* : Reniego *ζ*.

421–424   Cuando ruega ... pecho rigor] Omitted in all but *P*.

425 *Vase* PINEDA] Omitted in *X*.

426 las nuevas] la nueva *M* | dará] dura *S4*.

427 es que en] en *P* | está] no está *P*. Line added in *M*.

431 amiga] Elvira *P*.

432 firmeza] fineza *γ* (firmeza *S9*).

433 <-mas\mas> re <-tirate que yo \-monos/tirate> *M*.

434 cierta] una *M*.

435 decirle] decille *P* : decirla *ε*.

435b *Vanse. Sale* DOÑA LEONOR] *Sale doña Leonor δζ* : *Vanse y sale Leonor ε* (*Retírase Elvira. Sale Leonor S9*).

439 despertar] desperta<-d +r> *S1* | sol] son *M*.

440 entre] en *P*.

444 alférez] alteza *ζ* | seré] hoy seré *S7*.

449–450   Las ternezas ... celebrando agora] Omitted in all but *P*.

451 que aquesta noche han pasado] que aquesta noche he gozado *P* : <-que aquella noche han pasado> *M*. Omitted in *ε* (<\\-que aquella noche han pasado> *S1*).

452 *Canta* ELVIRA *dentro*] *Cantan Pδ*: ELVIRA *canta dentro S1* : CRIADO *ζ* : ELVIRA *canta ι*.

453 un] una *S1*.

454 en] y en *M* | la caja] a la marcha *S8* : la marcha *S9*.

456   cantado] cantando *S1*.

459   el amor] un amor *ζ* | del] de un *δζ*.

460   un] una *δS9*.

461   un] una *PS9*.

462   así] ansí *P*.

463   de un] que un *P*.

464–467   Y aunque en amar … tocando la caja] Omitted in all but *P*.

468   agora] ahora *γ*.

472   mas] pero *P*.

473   propósito no viene] proponer no conviene *ζ*.

474   agora] ahora *γ*.

475   *Salen Elvira e Isabel*] *Sale Elvira ε*.

476   ELVIRA] ISABEL *M* | Es decirte] es decir *M* : decirte *S1S8*.

477   en la canción] la canción *Pζ* : en la ocasión *δS9* | te prevengo] que prevengo *Pε* (a que vengo *δS9*).

480–487   porque la canción … engaño conozca] Omitted in all but *P*.

488   ELVIRA] ISABEL *M*.

491   lienzos] brazos *ι* | de la] del *PS8*.

493   calladas] callando *γ*.

494   tropas] tropa *β* (tropas *S1S8*)

496   digáis] digas *ζ*.

499   *Vanse ELVIRA e ISABEL*] Omitted in *X*.

500–503   Loca estoy … mis congojas] Omitted in all but *P*.

505   soldado] soldados *S1* | deshonras] deshonra *S9*.

508–511   No te ha dado … sol le asombran] Omitted in *M*.

512   sea esta afrenta] esta infamia sea *M*.

515   se] los *ζ* : la *ε*.

516–519   Decirlo a su padre … a sus glorias] Omitted in *M*.

516   decirlo] decillo *P* : decirla *β* (decirle *ε*). Omitted in *M*.

520–535   <\\no no> *M*.

521   de esta] de la *P* : desta *β*.

522   *Saca el papel*] Omitted in *X* (*Saca un papel S1S8*).

526   más las] las más *ε*.

528   con todo] por todo *P*.

531   partes] parte *S9*.

532   venganza] palabra *M*.

534   mis] <-mis /tus> *M* | intentarlo] intentarla *β* (intentalla *PS6* : inten<-talle /tarlo> *M*).

536   seguirlo] seguillo *PS6* : seguirle *Mε*.

537   buscando] burlando *P* : <-buscando /surcando> *M* : surcando *ε* (sulcando *S1*). See Textual History for a justification of this amend.

538   abismos] abismo *ζS9*.

540–544   Corra tras ... desprecios la honra] Omitted in all but *P*.

544–547   <\\no> *M*.

548–552   Las joyas con que pensé ... en mis funerales pompas] Omitted in *M*.

548   pensé] creía *ε* (cria </creia> *S1*).

551   en] con *ζ*.

552   <\\Çifuentes> *M*.

556–559   Cielos, rayos ... hay en vosotras] Omitted in *M*.

560–567   <\\no> *M*.

562   que esté, pues di] que pues te di *P*.

563   poca] loca *M*.

565   bronces] bronce *ζ* | bronces, libros] libros, bronces *ι*.

566   mis] mal *P*.

567   que el] el *ε* | tiempos] cielos *M* | lloran] llora *ζ*.

568   el] que el *ε*.

569   un hora] una hora *P*.

570   en] que en *ι* | caja] marcha *S9*.

571   *Vase. Tocan cajas y salen los capitanes* DON PEDRO *y* DON JUAN] *Vase. Tocan cajas y salen dos capitanes P* : *Vase, y salen dos soldados β* (*Vanse, y salen los soldados S1S8*)

572–588   No se ha visto ... nos prometen] Omitted in *M*.

572b   CAPITÁN DON PEDRO] 1 *Pβ* (UNO *S1S8*). I restore the captains' name cues on the basis of lines 1951–1953 and other points of the play.

573   CAPITÁN DON JUAN] 2 *Pβ* (OTRO *S1S8*). See 572b.

573b   no han sido naos sino] no han sido sino *ζ* : en lo veloz fueron *S1*.

576   felice marinaje] feliz marineraje *β* (feiz marineraje *S3*). Omitted in *M*.

577   tocó de] tocó el de *S6* | metas] netas *β* (necta *S6*).

578   césar es] es Cesar *ε*.

579   a hallar] a haber *β* (aver *S1* : a ver *S4*). Omitted in *M*.

580   le ha recibido] le ha recebido *P* : lo ha recibido *ζι*.

582   unos] vos *ζ*.

583   Y es todo amable] es todo amable *β* (es amable *ζ*)

586   *Dentro cajas ε* | guarda al] guarda del *S8*.

587   la gloria] las glorias *ζι*.

587b   *Tocan cajas. Salen soldados y el sargento* BARRIENTOS *echando*
         a empujones a JUAN DE MÉRIDA] *Tocan cajas, salen soldaos,*
         y el sargento echando a empujones a Juan P : *Salen soldados y*
         el sargento echando a rempujones a Juan β (*Salen soldados y el*
         sargento echando a empujones a Juan ε).

588   <\\Bosque> *S1*.

590   esta] esta<-n> *S1*.

594   hileras] filas *ε* (<-filas +hileras> *S1*).

601   quebrarle] quebralle *M* : quebra<-nta>rle *S1*.

602   asta] estaca *ζ* | pasito] paso *ζ*.

603   seor] sor *Pδ*.

605   vuesarcé] voace *δ* : voarce *ζ*.

606   bajarla] bajalla *αS6*.

609   ella] él *β* (ella *ζ*)

610   agora] ahora *γ* (agora *S1*).

611   saltos] francos *M*.

612   el] los *M*.

614   CAPITÁN DON PEDRO] 1 *P δζ*: ALFÉREZ *M* : UNO *S1S8* : SOLDADO *S9*.

615   Está con vos] con vos está *S8*.

617   yo] ya *S1S8*.

622   CAPITÁN DON JUAN] 2 *Pβ* (UNO *S1S8*) : ALFÉREZ *M* | oigan] oiga *S7*.

623   CAPITÁN DON PEDRO] 1 *Pδζ* : OTRO *S1S8* : SARGENTO *S9* | sufrirlo]
         sufrillo *αS6S8*.

625   mal] más *P*.

626   CAPITÁN DON JUAN] 2 *Pδ* : 1 *ζ* : OTRO *S1S8* : SARGENTO *S9* | Suenan
         cajas] Omitted in *X* (*Cajas PS9*).

627   ya va] va ya *β* | *Vanse todos, y queda* JUAN DE MÉRIDA *solo*] *Vanse*
         αS9 : *Suenan cajas, y vanse, y queda Juan solo S1* : *cajas suenan δ*:
         suenan cajas ζS8.

628   que esto es] esto es *M*.

629   este] esta *γ* (este *S9*).

631   al cielo, al tiempo] al tiempo, al cielo *P* : al cielo, al mundo *M*.

632   ¡Oh, reniego] a pesar *M* : reniego *S9*.

634   almas] armas *ζ*.

636   servirle] serville *Pζ*: serviré *S1S8* | solo] mismo *M*.

640   pasa] viene *M*.

642   capitanes famosos] generales famoso *P*.

643   maeses] maestres *ε*.

645 que ser] que el ser *M* | afrente] afrenta *S1ζ*.

649 mis] mas *δ*.

653 *Sale el DUQUE DE ALBA, leyendo una carta. Salen el sargento BARRIENTOS, los capitanes DON AGUSTÍN, DON PEDRO y DON JUAN y soldados*] *Sale toda la compañía y el duque, armado, leyendo una carta P* : *Salen todos y el duque leyendo una carta M* : *Salen los soldados que puedan, y el duque de Alba va leyendo una carta S1S8* : *Sale toda la compañía y el duque de Alba leyendo una carta δζ* : *Salen el duque de Alba, leyendo una carta, don Ahustín, el sargento, soldados S9*. *M* and *S9* put this direction here, the rest put it below line 654.

654 ¡Óigame vuestra excelencia!] dígame vuestra excelencia *ζ* : Señor, oiga vueselencia *ε*.

655 apártate] apártese *Pγ*. I select the *tú* form because Don Agustín uses it in line 659.

656 *Se arrodilla JUAN DE MÉRIDA*] Omited in *X* (*Arrodíllase S9*).

659 CAPITÁN DON JUAN] 2 *Pδζ* : SARGENTO *MS9* : OTRO *S1* : UNO *S8* | ya] yo *S1S8*.

661 está, glorioso] estáis, glorioso *M* : estrellaroso *ζ*.

662 CAPITÁN DON PEDRO] 1 *Pδζ* : ALFÉREZ *M* : UNO *S1S8* : SARGENTO *S9*.

663 asiros tengo del brazo] solicito vuestro amparo *S7*. Omitted in *S6*.

665 dejadlo] dejaldo *α*.

670 miedo es de] miedo sino *γ* (miedo es de *S9*).

671 no es] que *M* : es *δ*.

673 alba] sol *M*.

681 me hacen mil] no me hacen *S8* | pedazos] podazos *S9*.

682 CAPITÁN DON JUAN … CAPITÁN DON PEDRO] 2 … 1 *Pδζ*: OTRO … UNO *S1S8* : SARGENTO … SOLDADO 1 *S9*.

683 CAPITÁN DON AGUSTÍN] CAPITÁN *Pβ* (SOLDADO 1 *S9*] : ALFÉREZ *M* | dejadlo] dejaldo *α*.

688 desechan] desprecian *M* | plaza] plazo *S6*.

690 suplicarle] suplicalle *αS6*.

694 que] le *ι*.

695 de cuerda] de guarda *P* : pólvora *M* | frascos] frasco *ζ*.

698 sin que] <-aun /sin \sin>que *S1* : aunque *S8* : y no que *S9* | lo] le *ζ*.

700 y sin] y con *β* | lisonjas] hazañas *S1S9*.

701 negregura] negrura *S1S4ζ*.

702 lo desmerezca] no lo merezca *M*.

704   negro] rey δ : rey negro *S6*.
706   lo] le ε.
707   y el valor, el cielo] el cielo el valor ı | honradlo] honraldo α.
713   nuestro] vuestro *S9*.
714   Capitán don Juan] 2 *Pδ*: Sargento *M* : 1 γ (Uno *S1S8*) | dadme]
         dame β (dadme *S9*).
715   aqueso] aquesto *P*.
716   Capitán don Juan] 1 *Pδ* : Alférez *M* : 2 ζ : Otro *S1S8* : Sargento
         S9.
717   fías] fiais δζ | casos] pasos δζ.
721   Pues de] que de *P*.
724   *Vase el capitán don Agustín*] Omitted in *X* (*Vase M*).
728   que entonces] entonces *S5*.
729   yo os] hoy os *S1* : os ı | ocaso] estado δ | *Vanse todos, y queda Juan
         de Mérida solo*] *Vanse PS7S9* : *Vanse todos M* : *Vanse y queda Juan
         solo S1S8* : *vase S6*.
733   ni el] y el *P* : el *M*.
734   <\\Al[ons?]o> *M*.
737   ¡vive el cielo!] voto a crispo *M* | matarlo] matallo *S1S6*.
740   puedo hallar] puede haber ζ.
742   de donde he] donde le he de *M*.
743   coces] <-coces +golpes> *S1*.
746   yo] ya *S7*.
748   y las] y en las *Mγ*.
751   *Vase. Sale el capitán don Agustín vestido de flamenco*] *Vase. Sale
         el Capitán vestido de tudesco P* : *Vase y sale el Capitán disfrazado
         M* : *Vase y sale el capitán con una banda en el rostro* β (*Vase. Sale
         el don Agustín disfrazado S9*).
752–763   <\\ no no no no> *M*. In *M,* this passage is bracketed and deleted
         with one oblique stroke.
755   bárbara] y bárbara *M*.
757   pecho] valor ı.
758   tenebrosa] es tenebrosa *M*.
760   hazaña es] acana *M* : la hacen ε : la hace ζ.
763   montes] <-montes /copos> *M* : copos β | ampos] campos ζ.
765   y voy] voy γ | <-es flamenco \he mudado> M
769   bebe] llueve *M*.
769b   *Sale Juan de Mérida con máscara*] *Sale Juan con máscara P* : *Sale*

el negro M : *Sale Juan con una mascarilla S1* : *Sale Juan con su máscara δ*: *Sale Juan con mascarilla ι*.

771 alcanzarle] alcanzalle *αS6* | suerte es mía] suerte mía *γ*.

775 amigos] amigo *ε*.

779 Dé el nombre] responda *β*.

781 San Mauricio] San Mamerto *γ* (Mauricio *S9*) : Mauricio *δ* | muera] miente *M*.

783 Orange] Orange y te aseguro *S8* | JUAN DE MÉRIDA También] valerte. JUAN DE MÉRIDA También *S8*.

784 cobarde afeminado] cobarde afemidado S4. Omitted in *ζ*.

788 tu persona] por tu persona *δS9*.

789 tienes] tiene *ζ*.

791 de que] del que *ε* | te abona] abono *ζ*.

792 *Riñen S9*.

793 soy demonio] más que hombre *M* : <-fu +so>i demonio *S1* : fui demonio *ζS8*.

795 *Riñen. Cae el capitán* DON AGUSTÍN] *Riñen β*. Omitted in *α*. It is uncertain when the fight begins, most likely from line 791. *S1*, *ζ* and *S8* put this direction in line 794. *S9* puts it in line 792. I add Don Agustín's fall on the basis of line 801.

799 soy] fui *M*.

803 era] fue *P*.

805 empresa] impresa *S1* | manca] franca *M*.

806 mas en] pero en *MS1S8* | plana] pluma *ζ*.

809 tan] mas *ζ*.

812–815 Darte puedo aquí la muerte … blanco mi suerte] Omitted in *γ* (not in *S9*).

815 salió] quedó *M*. Omitted in *γ* (not in *S9*) | <-negro \blanco> *M*.

816 te haré] haré *ζ*.

817 rinda] prenda *ε*.

819 llevaré] tomaré *M*.

821 *Toma la banda*] Omitted in *X* (Tómala *S9*).

828 esta] esa *Mβ* (esta *ζ* : eso *S8*).

831 otra] otro *δ*.

832 alma] honra *P* : alba *δ*.

835 *Vase el capitán* DON AGUSTÍN] *Vase X* (Omitted in *S1*, *S6* and *S8*).

839 ya la] esta *ε* | *Se quita la máscara*] Omitted in *X* (*Quítasela S9*).

844–847 Ya en púrpura … voy a emprender] Omitted in *M*.

845   el aurora] la aurora β. Omitted in *M*.

846   que] y β. Omitted in *M*.

849   agora] ahora γ.

855   *Vase. Sale* DOÑA LEONOR *vestida de paje y* ANTÓN] *Vase. Doña Leonor de regacho, y Antón negro P : Vase y sale Leonor, de hombre, y Antonillo, negro M : Vase y sale Leonor de page y Antonillo* β (Vase. Sale Leonor de paje y Antonillo S1 : Vase. Sale Leonor de paje y Antonillo negro S9).

856   turo] turu *M* : tuto δ. Almost every line said by Antón has significant variants.

857   me] le γ | Antón] a Antón *S1*.

858   neglo] negla *M* | sabemo] sabemos *S1*.

861   samo] zamo ε.

862   hombre] hombra *M* : homble *S1* | cayamo] callamo *M*ζ.

863   sa gente] za gente *S1* : zagante *ı* | preto] el preto γ.

865   <\\Çifuentes> *M*.

866   vengamo] tengamo δ | del] de *M*ε.

868   sa] zale *S1* : sal δ*S9* : sale *S8*.

869   aquí] que ζ.

870   *Disparan. Salen el* DUQUE DE ALBA *y los capitanes* DON PEDRO *y* DON JUAN] *Disparan. Sale el Duque. y capitanes P : Disparan y sale el Duque y capitanes* δ : *Disparan y sale el Duque y soldados* γ (*Sale el Duque de Alba y criados S9*).

871   CAPITÁN DON PEDRO] 1 *P*β (UNO *S1S8* : CRIADO 1 *S9*) : SARGENTO *M*. See variants in line 572.

872   CAPITÁN DON JUAN] 2 *P*β (OTRO *S1S8* : CRIADO 2 *S9*) : [SARGENTO] *M*.

873   ha] han *S1S8*.

875   proezas] promesas β.

876   que] a quien ε | tantos] todos ζ : tanto ε.

878   sa] za *S1S8* : es ζ | duque] duco *M*.

879   podemos] podemos *S1* | espantos] ispanto *M* : ezpanto *S1S8* : espanto ζ*S9*.

880   la espía] espía *MS1S8*.

881   escuadrón] escuadra *S9* | alborotó] ha alborotado ζ.

881b   *Sale el capitán* DON AGUSTÍN] *Sale el capitán* α : *Sale el capitán don Agustín* δζ : *Sale el capitán alborotado* ε (*Sale d. Agustín S9*).

885   cagayera] caganyera *S1*.

886   yeguemo] llegamo *M* : lleguemo *S8* | darle] dallo *P* : dalle *M*δ*S9* : daya *S1S8* | matraca] maltraca *S1*.

887   la acción] mi honor ε (el mentir *S9*) : el mentir δ : el honor ζ : | me cueste] cuesta ζ : le cueste *S1S8*.

889   los pies me dé] démelos ya *S8*.

893   con] fui δ | o] y *P*.

894   volver] <-volver +venir> *S1*.

896–901   pero, como a la fortuna … ardides y estratagemas] Omitted in all but *P*.

902–903   por mayor seguridad / fingí las galas tudescas] Omitted in *M*.

903   tudescas] flamencas ε.

904   camino] caminé *M*.

907   dibujados] divisados *S1S8*.

912   en] en en *S1* : de *S6* | casal] casar *M*.

916   gloriosamente] dichosamente ε.

917   cuesta] le cuesta *S1*.

921   se ilustra en la] le ilustra la *M* : me ilustra la δ.

923   está] esté δ | *Sale* JUAN DE MÉRIDA *con dos* SOLDADOS FLAMENCOS *y dos arcabuces*] *Sale Juan con dos soldados flamencos con sus arcabuces P* : *Sale Juan con dos soldados y dos arcabuces M* : *Sale Juan con dos soldados flamencos* β (*Sale Juan con dos soldados S1S8*).

924   SOLDADO FLAMENCO 1 … 2] FLA. 1 … 2 *P* : 1 … 2 *Mβ* (UNO … OTRO *S1S8*).

924b   Nite … Nite] | Mite … Mite *S1S8* : Mate … Mita ζ | Nitead] niteat *P* : nitear *M* : mitead γ (nitead *S9*).

926   DUQUE DE ALBA] 1 *Pβ* (Criado 1 ε) : DUQUE *M* | Viene aquí] vine aquí *P* : viene allí *M* | <\\criado> </1° +2°> *S1*.

928   siora] siolo *S1S8* : sioro ζ.

929   sa] ya ε (la *S9*) : la δ | soldado] soldada *P*.

931   za] sa *M*.

932   excelentísimo] invicto duque ε.

933   señor] de Alba ε.

934   soy] estoy *M*.

937   vergüenza] venganza δ.

939   a que] porque γ (a que *S9*).

940   yo, y dos] y traigo dos *MS1S8* : y hoy dos traigo $\delta\zeta S9$. Note that "yo y" and "y oy" have the same letters.

941   el uno] uno *S8*.

942   dos arcabuces] arcabuces *S6* : pues arcabuces *S7*.

944   sola] solo γ.
946   mi] me *S1S8*.
947   lo] la ζ.
948   otra vez] Omitted in *M*.
949   la jineta] las jinetas *M*.
950   las tiendas] la tienda ζ.
951   las] a las δ*S9*.
953   la] su γ (la *S9*).
955   castigando soberbias] castiga la soberbia γ : castigando soberbias (*S9*).
959   antes que con estos diera] todo envidia y todo lengua β. See line 971.
962   despojos] despojo *S1*.
964   a] en β.
965   *Dale la banda al* Duque de Alba] Omitted in *X* (*Dásela S9*).
966   al] el β (al *S9*).
968   que es justo] que quiero *P* | un] el ζ.
969   desecha] desprecia *M*.
971   hinchado con gran soberbia] todo envidia y todo lengua *P*. See in line 959.
973   afrentas] ofensas *M*.
975   esa] esta *P* | <-la va /esa banda > *M*.
976   hacéis] haces ζ.
977   mirad] mira ζ.
978   lo] *le MS1S9* : la *S8*.
979   esa] esta *S1*.
980   ansí] así β.
981   guardadla] guardalda *M* | pierda] os pierda γ.
982   soldados] soldado *MS1S8* | con] de *S1*.
983   respetan] respeta *M*γ (respetan *S9*).
984   Capitán don Pedro] 1 *P*β (criado *S1* : 2 *S8*) : Alférez *M*.
987   ansí] así β.
991   jamás] ya más *P*.
993   traigo] la traigo *S1*.
995   nacéis] tenéis *S7*.
998   vuestra] vuestro *P*.
999   Juan de Alba] Juan *X*.
1002   venerar] vencer γ (venerar *S7*) | el] al *M* : este ε.
1003   ya] hoy *M*.

1009 estas fieras] esta fiera *M*.

1010 he] ha *S8* | gentes] gente *M*.

1011 los ladre] la ladre *P*.

1012 de esas dos] destas dos *P* : de esos dos *S1* | espías] <-soldados / espías> *S1*.

1014 esos] estos *S1*.

1015 *Vase el capitán* DON AGUSTÍN] Omitted in *X* (*Vase don Agustín S9*). In *S9*, this direction is in line 1017.

1018 soy] sois *M*.

1019 ceñido] corrido *P*.

1023 dos plazas sean] sean dos plazas *S1*.

1023b *Vanse, y quedan solos* JUAN DE ALBA, DOÑA LEONOR *y* ANTÓN] *Vanse X*.

1025 doscientas] docientas *P* : ducientas *M* : doscientas *β* (ducientas *ζ*).

1026 primo] plimo *Mε* (primo *S9*) | <\\+Al[ons?]o> *M*.

1027 de Vera] dembera *P*.

1028 los brazos] uno abraso *S1* : un abrazo *S8*.

1029 también] tanbén *P* : també *S1S8* | an] a lan *S1* : a la *S8* : en *S9*.

1030 me abrazad] abrazadme *γ* (abrazarme *S8* : me abrazad *S9*).

1034 Esteban, el que servía] El que servía de paje *P*.

1035 don Juan] de san Juan *δS9*.

1045 *Toma a* JUAN DE ALBA *de las manos*] Omitted in *X*.

1049 las manos] la mano *γ* (las manos *S9*).

1051 diera] diese *M* | os hospedan] se hospeda *γ*.

1054 una] cierta *ζ*.

1055 regalarnos puedan] regalarnos pueden *P* : regalaros pueda *MS8*.

1063 guardan] guarda *γ* (guardan *S9*) | fuera] fueras *MδS9* | osten putas] osten putos *ε*.

1068 hostería] estaréis *ζ* | no sé] no señor *S7*.

1070 de la] de una *S7S9*.

1072 tiznarase] tiznarate *ζ* : tiznarete *S1S8*.

1073 taracea] ataracea *β* (taracea *S1S8*).

1076 brindis] brindes *S1*.

1081 amoroso] cariñoso M : amorosos *ε* (amoroso<-s> *S1* : amoroso *S9*).

1083 que me come] <-que me come /gastaremos> *S1*.

1085 trujo] trajo *γ* | <\Fin> *M*.

There is a list of plays in folio 20r of *M*, probably part of the repertoire of Toribio de la Vega's acting company: "*Amar a quien no se piensa*

/ *Pavia* / *El negro* / *Lorenço* / *S[an]ta Juana* / *Peor está que estaba* / *No hay dicha ni desdicha* / *Mentir y mudarse a un tiempo*".
In folio 21v of *M*, there is a warning note: Ojo / [Ojo] Gregorio lo [ātagado] ni lo <\no> has de sacar / Ojo". It may indicate that Gregorio has crossed out [*atajado*] the undesired lines.

Jornada II

1085b   <\2ª *X*[*ornada*]*da del Negro*> *M*.

1085c   *Sale* JUAN DE ALBA *solo*] Sale Juan de Alba solo α : Sale Juan de Alba β (Sale Juan ζ).

1086   aunque] y aunque *S1*ζ.

1087   lo] le *Mı* | <-su /mi > *M*.

1091   <\\+Lopez> *M*.

1096   en el] el δ.

1099   sus sargentos] su sargento *S1S8* | Grambot] Gran bot *P* : y tambor *S1S8* : gran boc ζ.

1100   moltuin] multruc *M* : multum γ (moltuin *S9*) | butir] bierret *M* : buturo *S1S8* : burir δ*S9* : barit ζ | estricot] estricón *S1S8* : estricor ζ.

1101   flinflán] frin *M* : fistan *S1* : ifillam *S6* : fillem *S7* : o fifan *S8*.

1105   yerro] yerros δ.

1108   *Se esconde. Salen el* SARGENTO BARRIENTOS *y los capitanes* DON AGUSTÍN, DON PEDRO Y DON JUAN] *Sale don Agustín, capitán, y el sargento y otros dos capitanes P* : *Retírase y salen el sargento y el capitán M* : *Escóndese. Salen el capitán, el sargento y otros* </dos:> *S1* : *Sale don Agustín y el sargento con él* δ : *Sale don Agustín y el sargento y otros* ζ : *Escóndese. Salen el capitán, sargento y otro S8* : *Retírase. Salen don Agustín, el sargento y soldados S9*.

1108b   CAPITÁN DON AGUSTÍN] Capitán *X* (SARGENTO *M* : AGUST. *S9*).

1109   SARGENTO BARRIENTOS] Sargento *X* (Capitán *M*).

1112   *Al paño S9*.

1113   del más] de mi δ | intento] ingenio *S9*.

1114   CAPITÁN DON PEDRO] 1 *P*β (UNO *S1S8* : SOLD. 1 *S9*) : <-JUAN -ALF -SAR> *M* .

1114b   honrarlo] honrallo *X* (honralle ε).

1115   porque es negro] por negro *P* |

1115b   CAPITÁN DON JUAN] 2 *P*β (OTRO *S1S8* : SOLD. 2 *S9*) : ALFÉREZ *M* :: | ha sido] ha salido *P* | <-valiente\dichoso> *M*.

1117   sufro] sufr<-o +a> *S1* : sufra ı | callo] call<-o +e!> *S1* : calle ı.

1118   Capitán don Pedro] 1 *Pβ* (Otro *S1S8* : Sold. 1 *S9*) : Alférez *M* | facciones] acciones *γ* (facciones *S9*).

1122   Capitán don Juan] 2 *P β* (Otro *S1S8* : Sold. 2 *S9*) : Alférez *M* | ya en el] ya el *δ* : y en *ζ*.

1123   temen] teme *δ*.

1126   habemos de hacer] haremos decir *β*.

1130   afrentarlos] afrentallos *α* : afrentarlos *β* (afrentallos *S1S8*).

1132   tengo] quiero *P* | con] por *β*.

1133   Capitán don Juan] 2 *Pδ* : Alférez *M* : <-Uno +Cap.n> *S1* : 1 *ζ* : Uno *S8* : Sold. 1 *S9* | amotinarlos] amotinallos *αS8* : amotinarnos *ζ*.

1134   jineta] alabarda *ε*.

1135   *Vanse los capitanes y quedan solos* Juan de Alba *y el* sargento Barrientos] *Vanse y quedan Sargento y Juan P* : *Vanse, queda el sargento y sale Juan ε* (*Vase S9*) : *Vanse y queda el Sargento ζ*. Omitted in *M* and *δ*.

1136   envidia] tierra *M*.

1137   la sujeta] <\no> acobarda *S1* : no acobarda *ι*.

1138   esto es todo] todo es *γ* (<-todo> es *S1*).

1143   salirle] salir *γ*

1143   *Sale S9*.

1145   escaparme] escusarme *β* (escaparme *ι*)

1148   las noches siempre] siempre las noches *P* : la noche siempre *β*.

1149   anochezco] anochesco *P*.

1151   prietos] negros *M*.

1152   así] ansí *P* | siempre andamos] andemos siempre *S8*.

1154   ha de holgarse] ha <\\de> holgarse *S1*.

1155   mis] sus *ζ*.

1156–1157   In *M*, these lines were written by a second hand, which intervenes again in lines 1839–1927. Either the first hand left a blank space for the second one to fill, or – less likely – the first hand briefly paused copying to allow a second one to intervene.

1158   ya] yo *η*.

1159   sus] las *ζ* | *aparte P*.

1161   dado] sido *S8*.

1163   la] el *P*.

1164   comprar] buscar *β* (<-buscar \comprar> *S1* : comprar *ζ*).

1166   soy] esto *M*.

1167   lo] la *M*.

1168   </-con la suya > *M*.

1170   negrura] ventura γ (negrura *S9*).

1172   servirle] servile *P*.

1179   yo] ya *S1*.

1180   ser su igual] ser igual *PS8*.

1182   Monicongo] monicongo *M*.

1184   *Toma* JUAN DE ALBA *la alabarda*] Omitted in *X* | le quito] quiero *S6* : me dé *S7*.

1185   y porque] porque ζ.

1188   más bien] mejor *M*.

1189   *La pone en el suelo*] Omitted in *X*.

1191   llegue y álcela del suelo] y será del uno el precio *S7*. Omitted in *S6*.

1195   *Saca* BARRIENTOS *la espada*] Omitted in *X*. See line 1207.

1201   todos] a todos β.

1202   las] sus γ.

1208   *Vase* BARRIENTOS] *Vase M*. Omitted in *S5*. *P* has this stage direction in line 1210. *S1*, η, ζ, and *S8* have it in 1211. *S9* has it in 1212.

1208b   Y ¡vive Dios!] y vive cristo *S9*.

1209   emperro] me emperro *MδS9*. Rule of majority cannot be applied.

1210   *Vase el sargento P*.

1210   que le haga] que haga ε.

1211   *Vanse el sargento, y toma Juan la alabarda S1S8* : *Vase ηζ*. See stage direction in line 1208.

1211b   <-able mas y que /obre me -nos /able menos> *M*.

1212   *Vase el sargento S9*.

1216   *Toma la alabarda*] Omitted in *X*.

1216b   Bien me está] bien está δ : que le siguen γ. Someone annotated on a copy of *S3*: </hecho lo que habemos hecho>. See 1217.

1217   la alabarda, ya parezco] muy bien hecho está lo hecho γ. Omitted in δ.

1218   otro hombre, ya] la alabarda β.

1226   *Salen* DOÑA LEONOR *vestida de paje y* ANTÓN] *Sale Leonor con una bengala y Antón P* : *Salen Leonor y Antón M* : *Sale leonor y Antonillo β* (*Salen Leonor y Antonillo δS9*).

1229   JUAN DE ALBA] JUAN *X* (JUANILLO η : ANTÓN *S5*).

1231   brasero] braseros β.

1232   algalia] argalia *M*.

1233   entre tus brazos] con nueva alegría ε.

1234   alegría] ventura ε | turu] turo β (tuto δS9) | samo] zamo ε : somos ζ.

1235   contentos con sus contentos] contentus con su contentus *M* : contenta
       con su contento *S1* : contenta de su contento *ι*.
1237   decimo] decimos *ζ*.
1241   seso] esto *δ* : suso *S6* | perdemo] perdemos *S1*.
1242   damo] demo *δ* : dame *ζ* : damos *S1S8*.
1244   cagayera] cangayera *S1*.
1248   así] aquí *P*.
1249   Quieran] quiera *S1* | Dioso] diozo *P* | pasemo] pasemos *S1*.
1250   mis] más *P*.
1252   habrá] habrás *δ* *ζ* | notables] notable en *P* : notabre *M* | comiras]
       comidas *Pβ* (comiras *ε*) : cumira *M*.
1253   y culaciones] y culacionos *P* : e curaciones *M* : y culaciones *β* |
       diversos] diversas *δ*.
1254   grangea] garajea *M* : glagea *ε* : gragea *S7* | culobesate] culo besalte
       P : curunbasate *M* : culobasate *S1S8* : culabazate *S9*.
1255   y cagalones] e cagallones *M*.
1256   enojo yo] tanto enojo *γ*.
1257   efecto] efeto *X* (estremo *M*).
1260   a afrentar] afrentar *P*.
1262   me] se *M*.
1265   sioro] seoro *S1S8* : sior *δS9*.
1268   tenerte] tenerme *PS7S8*. I add the question marks.
1270   abrazo] brazos *δS9*.
1273   partes] prendas *S9*.
1274   amo] sirvo *S8* | regalo] adoro *M*.
1275   y en mi mesa los asiento] dedicando mis afectos *S1S8*.
1276   la cama y la mesa] la mesa y la cama *Pζ* : a amarlos, que es el amor
       S1S8.
1279   argumentos] cumplimientos *M*.
1280   <-un amigo???\ a mi gusto> *M*.
1281   quien] que *M*.
1283   hermoso] <-hermoso \airoso> *M*.
1287   es el] él *M*.
1288   ese es] que es *S9*.
1290   y a vos] yo a vos *δS9* | lo] le *M*.
1291   Sí, amigo, a vos os lo debo] Sí, a vos, a vos os le debo *M*. Omitted in *δ*.
1292   vos, vos] vos que *γ* (pues vos *S9*) | le] lo *S8* | disteis] distes *P* : distis *M*.
1295   le] lo *P* : te *γ* | trajeron] trujeron *M*.

1297   arrojarlo] arrojarle M*γ*.
1300   tras del] tras el P*γ*.
1305   un pot de] alguna *γ* (un poco de *S9*).
1308–1309   *A reveder* ... lo divierto] Omitted in M*γ*.
1309   lo confundo y lo divierto] le confundo y le divierto *δ*.
1312   vamo angora] vamos ahora *ζ* | voy] vamos *M*.
1314   por su talle y su donaire] el rato que no le asisto *S1S8*.
1315   no es muy lindo, no es muy bello] tanto le estimo y le aprecio *S1S8*.
1316   y no tengo muy buen gusto?] yo no tengo muy buen gusto *β* (dime,
        no tengo razón *S1S8*).
1317   seoro] sioro M*ε* | *Vase* DOÑA LEONOR] Omitted in *X* (*Vase MS9*).
1317b   deshonesto] perverso *S1S8*.
1318   qué lascivo] afeminado *S1S8*.
1319   sello] resto *γ*.
1322   y tú] tú *γ* (y tú *S9*).
1323   sa] so *S1S8*.
1325   por qué] pluqué *S1* : pluqua *S8* | Juan] en Juan *P*.
1326   Antoniyo] Antonillo M*β* (Antoniyo *PS1S8*) | vil, si] si de hoy *γ*.
1328   en estos países nunca] jamás en estos países *S1S8*.
1329   o en] ni en *M*.
1332   al] el *P* | olvidamo] olvidado *S9*.
1333   y a Juan] y Juan *M* | sior] sioro *M* : siolo *ε* (seor *S9*) : señor *δζ* |
        tendremo] tenemo *M* : tendlemo *S1S8* : tendremos *S6*.
1334   vamo] damo *P* : vamos *S6* | llevamo] yevaremo *S1* | alabarda]
        alambarda M : la alabarda *ζ*.
1335   plumeto] prometo P*β* (plumeto *MS1S8*).
1337   a espacio] espacio P*ı* : aspacio *M*.
1338   aspacio] a espacio *β*.
1339   que] que te *ζ*.
1340   mago] magro *M* : mao *S1S8* | sun lacayo] su lancayo M : son lacayo
        S1S8 : sun lacayos *δS9* : son lacayos *ζ*.
1341   sioro] siolo *δS8*.
3141–1344   <\\Çifuentes> *M*.
1343   turu lu mundo] turo mundo *S1* : tuto lo mundo *δS9* : turo lo mundo
        ζS8 | sabemo] sabremo *P* : lo sabemo *γ* (sabemo *S9*).
1344   sioro] siolo *S1δS8*.
1345   Parece cosa] parecen cosan *P* : parese cosa *M* | neglos] negros P*β*
        (neglos M*ı*).

1345b *Vanse. Salen el* D<small>UQUE DE</small> A<small>LBA</small> *y los capitanes* D<small>ON</small> A<small>GUSTÍN</small>, D<small>ON</small>
P<small>EDRO</small> *y* D<small>ON</small> J<small>UAN</small>] *Sale el Duque de Alba y los capitanes P* : *Vanse*
y salen el Duque y los capitanes Mδ : *Sale el Duque de Alba y los*
capitanes ε (*Salen el duque, don Agustín y don Pedro S9*) : *Vanse y*
sale el duque y los capitanes ζ.

1346 a nuestro honor] Vuestro honor *ζ* : Para el honor *ι* (<-pará el \a
nuestro> *S1*) | a la opinión] la opinión *γ.*

1347 es afrentosa] afrentosa *δζ.*

1348 <-??? \campaña> *M.*

1348b C<small>APITÁN DON</small> P<small>EDRO</small>] 1 *Pζ* : <\\-Cap+??? > *M* : U<small>N</small> *S1* : 2 *δ* : : U<small>NO</small>
S8 : P<small>EDRO</small> *S9*. The captains' cue names vary greatly in this scene.
Likely, all the extant witnesses descend from a text that did not
specify them. I amend the cue names to mantain coherence.

1348–1353 <\\si> *M.*

1349 vivir] el vivir *M.*

1351 la injuria] la su furia *M* | en copiosa] copiosa *β.*

1352 se desata] desata *S6* : desatada *S7.*

1353 y todo es confusión] que todo es confusión *PS1* | es hielos] hielos *M.*

1354 C<small>APITÁN DON</small> A<small>GUSTÍN</small>] C<small>AP.</small> *X* (<-Cap./A<small>LFÉREZ</small>> *M* : A<small>GUST.</small> *S9*).

1355 lama] llama *P* : calma *ζ.*

1357 Fortuna] fagina *β* (fatiga *ε*) | entre los lodos] entre lodos *P* : entre los
lados *S9.*

1358 <- A<small>LFÉREZ</small>/Cap.> *M* : O<small>TR.</small> </2°> *S1* : 2 *δζ* : O<small>TRO</small> *S8* : P<small>EDRO</small> *S9*.
There is a change of speaker in all but *P*. See 1354.

1358b soldados] los soldados *δζ.*

1358–1359 <\\si> *M.*

1360 invierno] ivierno *M* | extraña] Omitted in *ζ.*

1365 nos hacen contra el tiempo] contra el tiempo nos hacen *S1S8* |
poderosos] rigorosos *S8.*

1366 Vistamos] vistámonos *S8* | temor] <-amor \temor> *S1* : amor *S8.*

1369 aquí y que aquí está] aquí <-y está aquí /donde está> *S1* : aquí que
aquí está *δS9* : aquí y aquí está *ζS8.*

1370–1377 Afrentosa es señor … España entre sus manos] Omitted in all
but *P.*

1370 <-los reveldes son hijos de la nieve> *M.*

1378–1390 Los rebeldes son hijos … cielo quiso darnos] Omitted in *M.*

1381 ni el hielo] ni el yelo *X* (el yelo *ζ*). Omitted in *M*. | conservados]
conformados *γ* (con </f>ormados *S1* : congelados *S9*).

1383   defendidos de] defendido de *S1* : defendiendo los *S8*.

1386   ansí es] así es *β* (así es una *S9*). Omitted in *M*.

1388   encerrarnos] enterrarnos *γ* (encerrarnos *S9*).

1390   *Disparan*] See line 1391.

1391   *Sale Juan* DE ALBA *con una bandera*] *Disparan y sale Juan con una
        bandera P* : *Sale Juan M* : *Disparan dentro y sale Juan con una
        bandera del enemigo ε* (*Disparan. Sale Juan con una bandera S9*) :
        Disparan y sale Juan con una bandera del enemigo δζ.

1393   agora] ahora *γ* (agora *S1*).

1394   esos] sus *δζ*.

1397   un negro tanta infamia] tanta envidia un negro *M*.

1398   y pongo espanto] y espanto *ζ*.

1399   conviene] convienen *M*.

1400   hacer y el decir] decir y el hacer *P*.

1401   de azúcar] sin azúcar *S9* | alcorzas] alcorza *S1ζ* : alcozar *S8*.

1406   confieso] prometo *M*.

1411   Buenos está, alférez] <-alférez /alva> *S1* : Álvarez, bueno está *S8* :
        Bueno está, Alba *S9* | gran señor] señor *S8*.

1412   muero] muerdo *S1*.

1412b   *Sale el sargento* BARRIENTOS] *Sale el sargento X* (*Sale Çifuentes M*).

1413–1416   <\\si no??? si > *M*. Text bracketed and deleted with oblique
        strokes in *M*.

1415   en el bocado] el bocado *ζ*.

1416   espuma] espumas *PδS9*.

1417   tudesco] <-tudesco \flamenco> *S1* : flamenco *S9*.

1418   puñetes] puñadas *Mε*.

1419   Señor, venga] a señor venga *P* : señor que venga *S8*.

1420   SARGENTO BARRIENTOS] SAR. *Pβ* (DUQUE *S8*) : CAP. *M*.

1423   le] me *S8*.

1424   traza] y traza *γ* (traza *S9*).

1424–1426   Text bracketed in *M*. There is no other indication.

1426   me he de escapar] me escaparé *S1S8* : he de escapar *δS9*.

1426b   *Sale* MONS. DE VIVANBLEC RAVALLAC, *tudesco*] *Sale Mons de
        Bivanblec, Raballac P* : *Sale Mons de Vivanbleque, tudesco M* : *Sale
        Mons de Bivanblec ε* : *Sale Mons de Biblambec y Raballac, tudesco
        δ* : *Sale Mons de Biblambec y Rebellac, tudesco ζ.*

1430   por los desastrados] <-deshonrados \desastrados> *S1* : que por los
        honrados *ζ* : por los deshonrados *S8*.

1431 Hornos y el de Agamón] Agamon, y el de Hornos *P* | Agamón]
Agamont *ε* (Agamonte *S8*).

1433 <-???/tu venida> *M.*

1435 causas] cosas *M.*

1436 flamenco] tudesco *M.*

1438 DUQUE DE ALBA] JUAN *ζ.*

1439 Vivanblec] Bimbablec *Pζı* : Bibambleque *M* : Bibamblec *S1* :
biblambec *δ.*

1440 Ravallac] Raballac *X* (Raballaque *M* : Raballec *S1*).

1444 envidien] impiden *P* : envidian *S6.*

1452 <-pedirse/decirse> *M.*

1456 y el lugar] y <\el> lugar *S1.*

1464 uno elige] pues elige *Pδ.*

1474 humille] incline *M.*

1475 poca hazaña] baja acción *M* : corta hazaña *ζ.*

1479 soberbio alemán] flamenco arrogante *ε.*

1482 Rin] vino *S1S8* : río *ζ.*

1482b *Coge JUAN DE ALBA a MONS. DE VIVANBLEC en brazos, y vase*] *Cógele
debajo el brazo P* : *Cógele en brazos y métele dentro β* (*Cógele en
brazos y base S9*). Omitted in *M.*

1484 dividirle] dividille *PS1S8.*

1486 *Sale JUAN DE ALBA*] *Sale Juan β.* Omitted in *α* and *S8.*

1487 Ya Vivanblec Ravallac] y Bibanblec Barrabás *P* : ya bibanblés
raballac *M.*

1491 justo] bien *M* | que haga] <-que \me> haga *S1* : que ha haga *η.*

1492 <-avo cespide/a voces pide > *M.* This re-writing is made by a second
hand. It had the purpose of making clear that the Duke's remark
completes the line started by Juan de Alba.

1493 tal hazaña tan gran] tan grande hazaña tal *S1.*

1494 tiñe] tiñen *P.*

1496 le] Omitted in *S1.*

1499 CAPITÁN DON PEDRO] 1 *Pδζ* : CAPITÁN *M* : UNO <\\1°> *S1* : UNO *S8*
: AGUST. *S9* | le dé vuestra excelencia] vuestra excelencia le dé *ε.*

1501 jinetas] bengalas *M.* See line 1568.

1504 prometo] os prometon *S1* | servirles] servirle *P.*

1505 CAPITÁN DON JUAN] 2 *Pδζ* : ALFÉREZ *M* : OTRO <\\2°> *S1* : OTRO *S8* :
PEDRO *S9.*

1506 le] lo *P.*

1507 CAPITÁN DON PEDRO] 1 *Pδζ* : Çifu[entes]. *M* : UNO *S1S8* : AGUST. *S9*.

1507–1509 <\\si si> *M*. Text bracketed in *M*.

1509 CAPITÁN DON JUAN] 2 *P Pδζ* : ALFÉREZ *M* : OTRO *S1S8* : PEDRO *S9*.

1524 a persuadirle] persuadirle *P*.

1529 vengarlo] vengallo *PδS6*.

1532 tus] sus *X* (tus *M*). I amend with the reading in *M* to avoid ambiguity. In other instances, Juan uses the *tú* pronoun as a form of courtesy to address the Duke and the King.

1535 CAPITÁN DON JUAN]] 2 *Pδζ* : ALFÉREZ *M* : OTRO *S1S8* : PEDRO *S9*.

1542 y es el invierno] el invierno es muy *S1*.

1545 maese] maestre *S1*.

1548 tristes] y tristes *S1*.

1560 lo mismo graznando dice] graznando lo mismo dice *M*.

1564 vuestro pie] vuestros pies *M*.

1567 todas] todos *Pδ*.

1568 *Entréganle la bengala y la jineta, y vase DON AGUSTÍN⁺*] *Vase X* (omitted in *M*). See line 1501 and the footnote to line 1568.

1569 <-señor /antes pienso> *M*.

1570 y que se ríe] y se ríen *S1*.

1571 verse] verla *S1* | <-???/alba > *M*. Added by a second hand in *M*.

1572 color] valor *β* (blasón *ε*).

1575 nazca] alumbre *S1*.

1576 Filipe] Felipe *γ* : Phelipe *δ* | *Vanse todos, y queda JUAN DE ALBA solo*] *Vanse todos M* : *Vase el duque ε*. Omitted in *Pδ*.

1577 postrer] postrero *δζ*.

1578 la] mi *S1*.

1580 alta] grande *β*.

1583 hazaña] acción *S1*.

1584 gloria] digna *S1*.

1585 el sol] sol *S1*.

1586–1587 <\\=> *M*.

1589 ay] ah *Pδ*.

1590 y a] a *M* : oh *ε*.

1592–1593 con mi brazo y con mi espada / dejaros acreditada] dejaros acreditada / con mi brazo y con mi espada *M*.

1597 *Salen por otro lado el capitán DON AGUSTÍN y DOÑA LEONOR*] *Salen el capitán y Leonor P* : *Retírase y sale d. Agustín y Leonor S1* : *Salen don Agustín y Leonor δ* : *Sale don Agustín y doña Leonor ζ* : *Retírase*

y sale don Agustín y Leon S8 : *Salen don Agustín y doña Leonor S9.*
Omitted in *M*.

1597–1620 Las horas que he estado … de tales oprobios] Omitted in *M*.

1603 estima] estimo *S1*.

1606 debe ser] es algún *ε*.

1613 Dios] el cielo *S1*.

1613–1614 No sé, vive dios / cómo me reporto] Omitted in *α*.

1619 escarmiento sean] pongan el remedio *ε*.

1620 de tales oprobios] eficaz y prompto *ε* (eficaz y pronto *S1*).

1621–1622 Otra vez se abrazan / cómo me reporto?] Omitted in all but *P*.

1622 *Vase JUAN DE ALBA*] *Vase X* (*Vas. y sal. Ped. S1*).

1623–1630 Gente viene … gustos todos] Omitted in *M*.

1630 *Vase DOÑA LEONOR, y sale el capitán DON PEDRO con una carta*]
Sale el capitán primero P: *Vase y salen el Alférez y el Capitán M* :
Sale don Pedro γ (*Sale don pedro con una carta S9*). Omitted in *δS1*.
See line 1622.

1631 CAPITÁN DON PEDRO] 1 *Pδ* : ALFÉREZ *M* : PEDRO *γ* (DON PEDRO
S1S8).

1633 <-???da /tencia> *M*.

1636 venía] tenia *ζ*.

1637 dio] envía *δ* | *Entrégale la carta*] Omitted in *X*.

1638 Este es] ese es *M* : y es *ε* (y *S8*) | mi padre] mis padres *ε*.

1643 <-??? \su casa> *M*.

1646 acreditados] acreditado *S1*.

1649 plazos] pasos *β* (plazos *S1S9*).

1656 mas] y *S1*.

1665 su honor] honor *S1* | la] le *P*.

1666–1671 <\\no no> *M*. Bracketed text in *M*. All instances of *no* are
underlined.

1671 el] al *S1*.

1673 así] ansí *M*.

1679 dilata] dilate *S1*.

1680 CAPITÁN DON PEDRO] 1 *P* : ALFÉREZ *M* : PEDRO *γ* : 2 *δ* | disteis la]
distele *P* : distis la *M*.

1684 irlo] irle *M*.

1690 fénix] finix *M*.

1691 *Vanse, y sale JUAN DE ALBA con una daga desnuda*] *Vase. Sale Juan
de Alba con dos pistolas y dagas y máscara P* : *Vanse. Y sale Juan*

con una espada desnuda M : Vanse. Y sale Juan con una espada desnuda ε (Vanse. Sale Juan con una espada desnuda S1) : Vanse. Sale Juan la daga desnuda ζ : Vanse. Sale Juan con una daga en la mano desnuda δ. The agreement between *M* and ε suggests restoring "espada" (sword), but Juan de Alba later refers to his "daga" (dagger) in line 1758. The nineteenth-century ballad 'Valerosa infantería' also mentions a dagger ("puñal"). See Appendix C.

1693   y] Omitted in *S1*.

1695   salido] venido *M*.

1695–1696   <\\=> *M*.

1698   mi] la *M*.

1699–1712   Esta es la noche … festejada sea] Omitted in *M*.

1711   canciones] Omitted in ζ.

1712   festejada sea] festejar desea β | *Dentro, grita como de fiesta*] Omitted in all but *M*.

1713–1714   <\\ya> *S1*.

1721   sin pensar, con máscara] <-sin pensar \máscara> con máscara *S1* : sin máscara, máscara δ*S9*.

1721b   *Escóndese* JUAN DE ALBA, *y salen el* PRÍNCIPE DE ORANGE, MONS. DE LANSTREC *y* MONS. DE VILA] *Salgan los que pudieren con una estatua del duque, con vigüelas y máscara, y pasen el de Orange, Lastrec, y Mons de Vila P : Escóndese y salen el Príncipe de Orange, y Mos. de Lastraz y Mons. de Vila M : Sale el Príncipe de Orange, Mons de Lastrec, y Mons de Vila S1 : Sale el príncipe de Orange, y Mons de Lastrac y Mons de Vila* δ*S9 : Sale el príncipe de Orange, y Mons de Latons y Mons de Vila* ζ *: Sale el príncipe de Orange, y Mons de Lastrec y Mons de Vila S8.*

1722   MONS. DE LANSTREC] MONS. *P* : LAS *M*ζ : LAST ε (LASTRAC *S9*) : LASTR δ. Confer line 1721b above.

1722b   vuecelencia] vuestra alteza ε.

1730   vuecelencia] vuestra alteza ε*S7*.

1731   los dos] <-los dos /con dios> *M*.

1741   MONS. DE LANSTREC] Mons *P* : Las. *M*ζ : LAST ε (LASTRAC *S9*) : LASTR δ | excelso] invicto ε.

1743   MONS. DE VILA] VILA *X* (<-VIL> *M* : LANS. *P*) | quitó] rompió *M*.

1745   MONS. DE LANSTREC] MONS. *P*δ : LAS. *M*γ | publicarlo] publicalle *P* : publicallo *MS6*.

1747   verle] verlo *P*.

1751   del] de *PS1S7*.
1752   <-???ranos \airados> *M*.
1754   llevarlo] llevallo *P* : llevarle *MS7*.
1756   traición] soldados traición *P*. | ¡*Mons*. de Vila!, ¡amigos!] Soldados, traición *S8*.
1756b *Coge al* PRÍNCIPE DE ORANGE *en brazos, llévaselo a la tienda del* DUQUE DE ALBA] *Coge al príncipe en brazos, y entrando por una puerta, y sale por otra S1* : *Coge al príncipe en brazos y llevasele a la tienda del duque* η : *Coge al príncipe en brazos y llévale a la tienda del duque S5*ζ : *Coge al príncipe en brazos y entra por una puerta y sale por otra S8* : *Coge al príncipe en brazos y entra y sale en la tienda del duque S9.* Omitted in α.
1757   Here *M* copies 1755–1757 for a second time, forming an enjambment between "Calle" and "soldados, traición".
1761   *Salen el* DUQUE DE ALBA *y el sargento* BARRIENTOS] *Salen el duque y el sargento PS9* : *Sale el duque y el sargento S1*δ. Omitted in *M* . See line 1762.
1762   Juan de Alba] Ju[an] Ju[an] de Alba *M*. | *Salen el duque y todos M*. See line 1761.
1764   <-yo soy> *M*.
1765   entrego] traigo *S1*.
1767   dice] decís *S1*.
1772   porque] pues que *M* | tan] tal *S1*.
1774   su mano] la mano *MS8* : sus manos δ*S9* | vuecelencia] vuestra alteza γ.
1777   aunque] <\aunque> *S1*. Omitted in *S1*.
1778   la] su *S1*.
1781   gloria eterna es vencer tal enemigo] Omitted in ζ.
1785   ofenda] asombre *M*.
1786   el rey premiarlo] ser premiado ζ.
1787   agora] ahora γ.
1790   es capitán] el capitán γ | decille] decillo *S1*.
1792   este valor] <-este \su> <co +ba>lor *M* : este <-valor \color> *S1*.
1793   color] valor *S1* | el mundo] al mundo *P*.
1797   quién] que γ (q̄ ζ : quien *S9*) | el negro] negro γ.
1797b *Salen el capitán don* AGUSTÍN, *don* PEDRO *y don* JUAN] *Salen todos los capitanes Pβ* (*Salen los capitanes S8* : *Salen don Agustín y don Pedro S9*). Omitted in *M*.
1797c <\\mesa a prev \\salen los capitanes 1 y 2> *S1*.

1798   Capitán don Agustín] Cap. *X* (<-cap/alf] *M* : Agust. *S9*).

1805   Lanstrec] Lastrec *Mβ* (Lastrac *δS9* : Lastroc *ζ*).

1810   a esos pies y a esa clemencia] a esos pies y a esa excelencia *β* (al poder de vuecelencia *ε*).

1813   *Vase don Pedro*] Omitted in *X* (*Vase d. Pedro S9*)

1814   Soldado(*dentro*)]*Dentro*1*Pδζ*:*DentroMS9*:<-Duque>*S1*:Duque*S8*.

1814b   Capitán don Juan] 2 *Pδζ* : Capitán *MS9* : <-Uno \Cap.> *S1* : Uno S8.

1816   maese] maestre *S1*.

1817   la] esta *S1* | Capitán don Juan] 2 *Pδζ* : Alférez *M* : Uno *ε* (Sargento *S9*)

1820   Capitán don Juan] 2 *Pδζ* : Alférez *M* : Uno *ε* (Sargento *S9*).

1821   han de hallar] hallarán *S1*.

1823   le están diciendo a Dios sus] Le están cantando a dios mil *M* : diciendo a Dios están sus *S1*.

1823b   *Sacan la mesa*] Omitted in *X* (<\\mesa> *S1* : *Sacan la mesa* S9). *S9* places this stage direction in line 1819.

1826   <-hacerme? \acerme> *M*. Interventions made by a second hand.

1828   paciencia] <-paciencia /Presteza> *S1*.

1829   pues] que *P* : pues que *S1S8* | *Siéntase a la mesa y sale Juan de Alba*] *Siéntase y sale Juan de Alba P*. Omitted in *M*.

1835   la mancha está] está la mancha *M*.

1836   *Se levanta el Príncipe de Orange*] Omitted in *X*.

1839–1927   Written by a second hand in *M* – the same hand that wrote lines 1156–1157. See the Textual History section in this volume.

1842   sus hombros] los suyos *P*.

1846   Siéntese vuestra excelencia] <-Ea>, siéntese vuestra alteza *S1* : Ea, siéntese su alteza *ι*.

1854   su mesa] sus mesas *P*.

1856   grandes] <-grandes \\Reyes> *S1*: reyes *δS9*.

1857   que] a que *P*.

1868   *Siéntase Juan de Alba*] Omitted in *X*.

1875   *Salen músicos, y los capitanes don Agustín y don Juan sirven a la mesa*] Omitted in *X*. Amendment made based on line 1894.

1879   El negro terror de Flandes] El valiente negro en Flandes *M*.

1881–1885   Text bracketed in *M*. No further indication.

1893–1900   Mil años el cielo… y para ese paje] Omitted in all but *P*.

1900   *Sale el capitán don Pedro*] *Sale el capitán α* : *Sale un capitán β* (<-Sale un capitán> *S1* : *Sale el sargento S9*).

1901 CAPITÁN DON PEDRO] 1 *αδ* : CAP *γ* (SARGENTO *S9*).

1902 Lanstrec] Lastrec *MS1S8* : Lastrac *δS9* : Lastroc *ζ*.

1903 porque del] <-porque del \a de dar el?> *S1*.

1904 *Quitan la mesa*] Omitted in *X* (*Quitan la mesa S9*) | *y salen los generales* MONS. DE LANSTREC *y* DE VILA] *Salen Lanstrec y Vila P* : *Salen dos generales M* : *Salen los dos generales γ* (*Salen mons de Lastrac y mons de Vila S9*) : *Entran los generales δ*.

1906 nos] me *M* | alcen] se alcen *MS1*.

1908 disparates] <-sucesos /disparates> *M*. Correction made by a third hand in *M* (see critical note to 1839–1927).

1914 serán] se harán *M*.

1917 a su fortuna debe] debe a la fortuna *S1* | su] la *PS8*.

1918 le debo a mis partes] les debo a mi <-s partes /sangre> *S1* : le debo a mi sangre *S9*.

1919 es] fue *S1*.

1920 señor, acción] una facción *S1S8* : hacer acción *ζ*.

1925 esté] está *S1*.

1939 esto] eso *S1*.

1941 mis tiendas] mi tienda *S1*.

1944 <-??? /lo que> *M*.

1946 agrade] agradare *M* | JUAN DE ALBA *reparte el tesoro*] Omitted in *X*.

1949 tuson] toyson *S1* | lo] la *S1*.

1952 trencellines] centellines *α* : trencillenes *S8*. I amend.

1962 el] Omitted in *S1*.

1971 perrera] perrilla *ε* (<-perrilla /perera> *S1*) : pedrera *δ* : perra *ζ*.

1972 nueve] cuatro *M*.

1976 vuestra excelencia] Hoy vuestra alteza *ε* : vuecelencia *S6* : vuestra alteza *S7*.

1980 *Vanse todos, y quedan* JUAN DE ALBA, *el* DUQUE DE ALBA, ANTÓN *y* DOÑA LEONOR] Omitted in *X* (*Vase el Príncipe y los capitanes M*). See line 1996.

1980b *MONS. DE* LANSTREC] Lans *Pδ* : <-PRI> *M*. Omitted in *γ*.

1980–1981 qué vuelta tan miserable … dio en un hora la fortuna] Omitted in *γ*.

1985 soy] ya *S1*.

1986 ya] soy *S1*.

1991 hará] dará *M*.

1996 pudo] supo *M* | *Vase el* DUQUE DE ALBA] *Vanse* M | *Vanse y quedan*

Juan, Leonor y Antón P : *Vanse Mβ* (*Vas. Quedan Leonor, y Juan y Antonillo S1*). See line 1980.

2001   por qué? JUAN DE ALBA ¿Por qué?] quieres, por qué? *S1*.

2003   a solas] sola *M*.

2006   cuando] como *P*.

2007   en que soy doña Leonor] y sepas... JUAN: ¿Qué he de saber? *S7*. *S7* adds an alternative scene here. See Appendix A in this volume.

2014   Mira en qué puedo pagarte] Viven los tersos celajes *S7*. See Appendix A in this volume.

2014–2040 Mira en qué puedo pagarte ... mi venganza más notable] Omitted in *S6*. Substituted in *S7* (see line 2014). These lines are added back in line 2052 in *ζ*.

2019   casa] case *S1*.

2020   esta carta] este papel *M*.

2021   saqué] quité *M*.

2024   que el duque se embarque] al duque que se embarque *S8*.

2027   sioro] siolo *β* (Omitted in *ζ*).

2028   de branco] de en branco *P* : del branco *S8*.

2029   siola] siora *P* : seola *δ* : seora *S9*.

2030   vengamo] vengarno *S1*.

2031   si sioro] <\si> siolo *S1* : si seolo *δ* : siolo *S8*.

2034   simulas] simula *P*: burlaye *S1S8*.

2039   césar] ángel *S8* | porque] y que *S1*.

Jornada III

2040   <\fin // 3ª jornada del Negro en Flandes> *M*.

2040b   *Salen JUAN DE ALBA muy galán, DOÑA LEONOR de lacayuelo, y ANTÓN de paje*] *Salen Juan, galán, Antón de paje y Leonor de lacayuelo P* : *Salen Juan de Alba y Leonor y Antón M* : *Sale Juan vestido ricamente, y Antón de lacayuelo, y Leonor de paje S1* : *Salen Juan muy galán, y Antón de page, Leonor de Lacayuelo δ* : *Sale Juan muy galán, y Antonillo de paje, Leonor de Lacayuelo ζ* : *Sale Juan vestido ricamente, y Antón de lacayo, y Leonor de paje S8* : *Salen Juan de gala con bengala, Leonor de paje y Antonillo de Lacayo S9*.

2044   cansando] causando *S1S9* : cansados *ζ*.

2045   aquí tura] aquintura *P* : aquí turas *δζ* : aquí tutas *S9* | gente brancas] gente enbrancas *P* : gente branca *S1* : gentes brancas *δS9* : gente brancas *S8*.

2046   sa fisgonera] la fisgonera *P* : za filgonanzo *S1* : za fisgonera *δS9* : za fisgonando *ζ* : za fisgonazo *S8* | y hacemo] y cerno *M*.

2047   den preto] den presto *P* : de preto *MS1S8* : del preto *ζ* | peor] peors *P* : peora *M*.

2048   estornudamo] estornudando *S1*.

2052   *ζ* inserts here lines 2014–2040, previously omitted (see above).

2054   midiendo] miendo *S1*.

2055   ¡vive Dios!] voto a Dios *P*.

2056   estar primero] estar más presto *M*.

2060–2061   del Duque; y vengo resuelto / a salirme de Madrid] Omitted in *P*.

2062   sin ver al rey] tantos días *P*.

2064   partirse] partirnos P.

2069   esa] esta *P* : la *M*.

2074   encerrarse] encerrarle *β* (encerrarte *ε*).

2075   Olalla] Clara *P*.

2078   saldrá] saldrás *ε* : saldré *δ*.

2079   suyo] tuyo *δε*.

2080   suya] tuya *δε*.

2081   ha] has *S1S8*.

2084   el casamiento] los conciertos *M*.

2086   los dos] una vez *M*.

2088   *Vase DOÑA LEONOR*] Omitted in X (Vase LEONOR *S9*). *S9* places this direction in line 2087.

2089   lleguemo a buscamo] llegamo, buscamo *M* : yeguemo a buscar *S1*: lleguemos a buscar *S6* : lleguemos buscar *S7* | Duque] Ruque *S1*.

2092   palestras] palestra *S1S8*.

2096   santiguamo] santiguemo *β* (santiguome *S1S8*) | entremo] entro *P* : entlemo *S1*.

2098   *Salen DON FRANCISCO y DON GÓMEZ por una parte, y DON MARTÍN y DON PEDRO por otra*] *Salen DON GÓMEZ y DON PEDRO por una parte, DON MARTÍN y DON FRANCISCO por otra P* : *Salen DON FRANCISCO y DON GÓMEZ M* : *Salen D. FRANCISCO y D. GÓMEZ, y otros S1δ* : *Sale D. FRANCISCO y D. GÓMEZ, y otros ζ1* (*Salen unos pretendientes con memoriales S9*).

2098–2247   *M* erases Don Martín and Don Pedro, attributing their lines to Don Gómez. *ζ* repeatedly reads 'Fed' instead of Don Pedro (obvious typo for *Francisco*). Cue names vary greatly in this scene.

2099   *a don Pedro*] I add these stage directions to facilitate the reading.

2100 aguardarle] esperarle *M* : aguardarlo ζ.

2101 pasa] vase *M*.

2103 Don Martín] D. Gómez *M* : Uno ε (<-Un \\Solo Go> *S1* : 3 *S9*).

2106 Don Pedro] D. Gómez *MS8* : Gom *S1* : Fed ζ: 1 *S9*. | ¿No reparáis en los] Reparáis en los dos β (Reparad en los dos *S1S8*).

2108 Don Francisco] Fran *X* (Juan *S8* : 2 *S9*).

2109 ansí] así *S1*.

2110 Don Martín] D. Gómez *M* : Uno ε (Uno <*2°> *S1* : 1 *S9*).

2112 midiendo] siguiendo *M*.

2113 Don Pedro] D. Gómez *MS8* : Fed ζ: 1 *S9* | tres mil reales] tres mil ducados *M* : seis mil reales *S8*. See lines 2113–2145.

2113–2145 Bien valdrán … ah, villanos] Text in *S1* covered with a glued-on piece of manuscript that abridges the passage. See Appendix A.

2114 el amo] amo *PS6S8*.

2114b *Estornudan*]. Omitted in *X* (*D*. Go[mez] Ache *P* : *Estornudan M*).

2115 branca] enblancas *P*.

2116 gaciendp] hacindo *M* : batiendo *S4* | de preto] den pretos *P*.

2117 Don Francisco … Don Pedro … Don Gómez] Fran … Pedro. Martin *P*δζ: Fran … [Fran] … <-Go[mez] uchuhu> *M* : Uno … [Uno] … Gómez *S8* : 1 … 2 … 3 *S9*.

2117b ¡Uchúa!] uchua *P* : vihua δ*S9* : uchoa ζ : hachi *S8* ¡Mandinga!] mandiuga δ : mandigui *S8* | ¡Aché!] <-Go[mez] uchuhu> *M* : achú ζ: hachi *S8*. See 2113–2145.

2119 dioso] diosa β.

2120 espadan saco] espada ensaco *P* : espada sanco δ : espada saco ζ*ı* | Don Pedro] D. Go[mez] *M* : Uno *S8* : 1 *S9*.

2122 Don Francisco] 3 *S9*.

2123 Don Martín] Go[mez] *M* : Uno *S8* : 2 *S9*.

2125 Don Gómez] Omitted in α | ¡pu, pu, puy!] pu, pu, pu β. Omitted in *P*.

2126 Don Pedro] Fran *M* : Uno *S8* : 1 *S9* | Ha vuelto] <-el perro \ha vuelto> *M*.

2128 quién] cuál *M*.

2130 *Vuelven a peer*] Omitted only in *P* | angora] angoras *P* : agora *S6* : ahora *S7*.

2135 así] ansí *P*.

2137 Acuchíllalos] Omitted in *X* (Pégales *S8* : Acuchíllalos *S9*) | Don francisco] Go, *M* : 3 *S9* | Don Pedro] Fran *M* : 2 *S9*.

2138   JUAN DE ALBA] JUA *X* (ANTÓN *M*) | ¡Peedme agora!] peemo angora *M* : Peeme agora *δ* : peen ahora *ζS8* : peedme ahora *S9*.

2138b *Salen SOLDADOS 1 y 2*] *Salen alabarderos P* : *Sale el duque y gente M* : *sale un criado β* (*Salen soldados*). Later, the Duke calls them "soldados" (soldiers) many times (see lines 2150 and 2154).

2138c SOLDADO 1] 1 *P* : DUQUE *M* : CRIADO *β* (SOLDADO 1 *S9*).

2141   SOLDADO 2] DON GÓMEZ *M* : UNO *S8* : 2 *S9* | ¡Oh, negro!] oh, perro *S8* : ah, negro *S9* | DON MARTÍN] DON FRANCISCO *M* : OTRO *S8* : 3 *S9* | ¡Oh, vil!] oh <-lo il /villano> *M* : Ah vil *S9*

2141b DON FRANCISCO] Duque *M* | ¿Tú, a nosotros?] ¡Hola! *M* : ¿A nosotros? *S8*.

2142–2149 Matadlo o llevadlo … colgar de una reja] Omitted in *M*.

2142   DON GÓMEZ] CRIADO 2 *S8* : 2 *S9* | matadlo … llevadlo] mataldo … llevaldo *P* : matadle … llevadle *ζS8*. Omitted in *M*.

2143   DON PEDRO] OTRO *S8* : 2 *S9* | asidlo] asildo *P* : asidle *β*. Omitted in *M*.

2145   DON FRANCISCO] 1 *S9* | villanos] villano *β* (villanos *PS9*).

2146   DON PEDRO] CRIA 1 *S8* : 2 *S9*.

2148   DON GÓMEZ] 1 *S9* | Soldado 1] 1 *Pδ* : CRIA</2°> *S1* : 2*ζ* : CRIA *S8* : SOLD 1 *S9* | ha] he *δ1*. Omitted in *M*.

2149   *Sale el Duque con bastón de mayordomo*] *Sale el duque con bastón de mayordomo X* (*Duque dentro … Sale el Duque con bastón de mayordomo S1* : *Sale el duque S9*). Omitted in *M*.

2152   bárbaro] villano *S8*. This line was written in *M* by a second hand.

2153   SOLDADO 2] 2 *X* (GO *M* : CRIA 1 *S1S8* : SOLD 1 *S9*).

2154   tened] teneos *S1*.

2158   ocasionados] ocasionado *PS8*.

2159   unos] estos *M*.

2162   en lazo] el lazo *S1* : enlace *S6* : en lance *S7*.

2163   la] de la *S1*.

2164   DON MARTÍN … DON FRANCISCO] DON MARTÍN … DON PEDRO *P* : DON GÓMEZ … DON FRANCISCO *MS8* : GÓM. … FER *S1* : 2 … 3 *S9*.

2165   DON GÓMEZ] D. FRANCISCO *P* : OTRO <1°> *S1* : D. PEDRO *ζ* : OTRO *S8* : 1 *S9* | este] que este *P*.

2166   DON FRANCISCO] UNO <1°> *S1* : UNO *S8* : 2 *S9*.

2168   <\\-vanse > *M*.

2169   mi color] mi <\color> *S1* | DON GÓMEZ] DON FRANCISCO *M* : 1 *S9* |él] el el duque *S1*.

2172   opuesto] <\o>puesto *S1*.

2175   Alba soy] <-soy> Alba </soy> *S1*.
2178   este] su *P*.
2179   so Antonillo] sa Antonillo *P* : soy Antoniyo *S1* : soy Antonillo *S8*.
2180   callamo] cayamo *S1* : habraremo] abraremo α.
2184   parezco] me ha hecho *M*.
2188   mi color] <-vueselencia /mi color> *M*.
2195   sus manos] la mano *MS8*.
2196   verlo] ver <-???+lo> *M*.
2197   agora] ahora γ.
2199   *Ruido dentro*] Omitted in *X* (*Ruido dentro M* : <\\ruido y2> *S1*)
2200   mas] que *M*.
2203   advertirle] advertirlo *S1S8* : advertille *M*ζ | *vase MS9* : yéndose *S8*.
2205   no] non *M* | <\\es> *S1*.
2206   dice] dicen *M*ι.
2207   cuidadoso el cielo en él] </tal> cuidado el cielo en él *S1* : puesto
       cuidadoso el cielo en él *S6* : el cielo en él horror *S7* : su cuidado el
       cielo en él *S8*.
2209   lo] le β.
2211   cuervo] cuerpo *P*ζ.
2212   feudos] feudo *M*ε (feudos *S9*).
2216   *Sale el DUQUE DE ALBA, y el REY, tomando memoriales*] *Sale el*
       *Duque y el Rey tomando memoriales P*δζ : *Salen el Duque y el Rey y*
       compañamiento MS8 : *Sale el Rey, el Duque y acompañamiento S1*
       : *Salen el Duque y el Rey tomando memoriales S9*.
2216   <*y> *S1*.
2217   aquel] aqu<-i +el> *S1*.
2218   sioro] siolo δ*S9*.
2219   es] es<-ta> *S1*.
2220   hacedle llegar] hacelde llegar α : hacedle que llegue *S6* : haced que
       llegue *S8*.
2227   <-negro> *M*.
2229   admirándole] admirándolo *P*.
2230   DUQUE] <-duq +Rey> S1 | sosegaos] sosega<-d +os> *S1*: sosegad
       ζ*S8* | miserable] admirable *M*.
2239   baña] honra *P*.
2240   sin] en su δζ.
2246   y] y hoy *S1* | da] dé *P* | a vos] Omitted in *S1*.
2246b *Vanse, y quedan solos JUAN DE ALBA y ANTÓN*] *Entrase P* : *Vanse M*
       : *Vas* γ (*Vase* δ*S9* : *V* ζ).

2247 ¡jur' an Dioso!] jurandioso *Pδ* : jurandiosa *MεS7*.
2248 branco] blanco *P* | al preto] pleto *M* : a preto *S1S8*.
2249 temor] temol *S1*.
2250 cagayera] cangayera *S1* | sa] la *P* : za *β* (esta *S7*). Omitted in *S6* | espantosa] espantoso *P*.
2251 sioro, sioro] siolo siolo *δS9*.
2252 belesados] belensados *P* : belesaro *S1S8* | sin mí estoy] estoy sin mí *P*.
2253 decir hoy] decir *P*.
2254 negro] neglo *Mε*.
2257 hablase y me honrase] honrase y hallase *S1* | a mí] aquí *M*.
2261 habramo] habraremo *S1* | a su] su *P* : a zu *S1S8*.
2262 a preto] apreto *P* : ya neglo *M* | za ya entonado] yaza entornado *P* : samo entonado *M*.
2267 honró] habló M : honra *β* | ya al] y al *S1*.
2267–2270 <\\no> *S1*. Text bracketed in *S1*.
2270 imaginé] imagina *P* | *Sale el DUQUE DE ALBA*] *Sale el Duque Pβ*.
2272 se … qué] vue que *S1*.
2275 sin duda, y se equivocó] sin duda se equivocó *P*. Omitted in *S1*.
2276 ¿Yo señoría? ¿Yo, yo?] voseñoría yo yo *P* : yo ser señoría yo *S1S8*.
2277 honores] horrores *S1ζ*.
2280–2291 De un hábito de Santiago … acredita su color] Omitted in *P*. This passage was censored in *P*, like other points of the play. This one is especially relevant because it is the reason why many modern editors questionably preferred *P* over *M*. See witness description in the Textual History section in this volume.
2288 valor] color *M*.
2291 color] esplendor *ε*.
2292–2295 La cruz su valor publica … en el que le califica] Omitted in *α*. See 2280–2291.
2292 valor] lustre *ε*. Omitted in *α*.
2293 la ultraje] le ultraje *ε* : se ultraje *ζ*. Omitted in *α*.
2296 agora] ahora *γ*.
2297 <-renta /renta> *M*. A second hand re-wrote the word.
2298 ansí le] así se *S1* | <\\la vida> *S1*.
2299 la virtud] la vida *γ* (<-la vida +la virtud> *S1*).
2301 DUQUE DE ALBA] ANTÓN *S1S8* | espanto] ezpanto *S1*.
2302 pensó] entendió *S1*.
2304 maese] maestre *S1* | en esta] <-??? + enes>ta *M*.

2307   gran señor, apuesta] <-competenci \gran señor>a puesta *S1* :
        competencia puesta *S8*.
2311   estremo] mudanza *M*.
2312   el hado loco] helado y loco *P*.
2313   agora] ahora *γ*.
2315   el mérito] alimento *P*.
2319   premio] sueño *M*.
2320   es ya] ya *P* | <\\2° Barba, capitán Agustín y D[oñ]a Juana> *S1*.
2323   la osadía] la cortesía *P* : la fortuna *M* : el mérito le *ε*. Hypermetrical
        line in *P*.
2325   señor] <-tener \señor> *M*.
2326   tiene] tuvo *M* : <-tiene \tuvo> *S1*.
2334   hijo] y yo *P*.
2335   de España] el alba *β* | estrella] la estrella *P*.
2336   el aurora] las auroras *P*.
2338   primo] plimo *Mε* (primo *S8*) | <-vase> *M*.
2339   ay neglo comendadora] ay negro grande señoras *P* : sa negla
        comendadora *M* : ay negro comenzadora *S6*.
2341   hábito] título hoy *P*.
2342   Antonillo] Antón *MS8* | sior] sor *P* : sioro *Mγ* (Sior *S9*).
2343   porque] que *P*.
2345–2347 a mérida. ANTÓN Vamos … a mojicones casar] Omitted in *P*.
2345   ANTÓN Vamos] ANTÓN Vamo *δS9*.
2347   mojicones] bofetadas *β* | *Vanse. Salen* MÚSICOS, *el capitán* DON
        AGUSTÍN *y* DOÑA JUANA] Omitted in *X* (*Salen músicos, el Capitán y
        doña Juana bizarra P* : *Vans. Sale don Juan Viejo, el Capitán don
        Agustín y doña Juana S1*). See line 2320.
2348–2383 Toquen alarma la gloria … no influyen ellas] Omitted in all but *P*.
2361   merecerlo] Omitted in *X* (merecello *P*).
2383   Cuando espira el amor] Omitted in *X* (Quando y espira *P*). Mesonero
        Romanos amended to "Cuando respira el amor"; a decision followed
        by López (2005). Ogallas Moreno (2010) amended to "Y cuando
        espira amor" (276). An interpretation of *y* as a locative adverb would
        be anachronical.
2383b   *Sale* DON JUAN, *padre*] *Sale don Juan viejo P* : *Vanse y salen don
        Juan, viejo, y don Agustín, que es el capitán, y doña Juana M* : *Vanse
        y salen don Juan viejo y el capitán don Agustín y doña Juana δζ* :
        Sale d. Juan viejo, el capitán d. Agustón y doña Juana S8 : *Salen don
        Juan de Estrada, viejo, don Agustín y doña Juana de Vera S9*.

2384   Don Juan] D. Iua *P* : D.J *M* : D. Ju<-. +an> *S1* : Juan δ : Jua *S6*
       : D. Jua *S7* : D. Juan *S8* : Estrada *S9*. From here until the end of
       the play, *iua* and *d. iua* were equally used for the name cues of three
       characters: Doña Juana, Don Juan, and Juan de Alba. I amend them
       on the basis of context.

2389   el] de ζ.

2391   la] te *M*.

2392   Don Juan] D. Juan *PS8* : Juana M : Ju<-a +n> *S1* : Juan δ : Jua *S6*
       : D. Jua *S7* : D. Juan *S8* : Estrada *S9*. See 2385.

2393(letter)   aquellos rebeldes países] los países bajos ε | resista] resista
       deje y asista γ | donde le sirvo] con el empleo *S1* | y así] y ansí *P* :
       y <\aunque quiere que le sirva> así *S1* | nombrar un maese] poner
       <-al \un> maestre *S1*| para mis ausencias] por mi ausencia *S1* | que
       conozca] por *S1* | obligándole] que obligándole *S1* | que vea que soy
       muy suyo y] a que lo haga y *P* : vea soy muy suyo *S1* | Madrid y
       mayo] Omitted in *S1*.

2395   le] la *PδS6S9*. The word *favor* could be feminine in the period. I
       amend it to avoid the ambiguity.

2396   que es infierno] que es infinito *S6* : pues según el *S7*.

2397   ojos] otros *P* | la esperanza] esperanza *S1*.

2403   disgusta] dis<-culpa /gusta> *M*.

2404–2409   y en el más breve instante ... las glorias mías] Omitted in *P*.

2405   hace] y hacer ζ.

2406   Don Juan] Juana *MS9* : D. Ju<-a +n> *S1* : Juan δ : Jua ζ : don
       Juan *S8*. Omitted in *P*. See 2385.

2407   si es de este] de aqueste *M*.

2408   Don Juan] Juana *MS9* : Juan δ : Jua ζ : don Juan *S8*. Omitted in
       P. See 2385.

2408–2421   <\\no no no> *S1*.

2409   a celebrar] a cantar *S6* : pues a cantar *S7*. Omitted in *P*. It is not
       clear who Captain Don Agustín is talking to in this line. He may be
       addressing the musicians, as the readings of ζ suggest. However,
       the musicians only appear in *P*. These lines, on the other hand, are
       absent from *P* but appear in all the other versions of the play.

2410   D. Juan *S7S8*.

2410–2421   <\\no> *M*. Bracketed passage and deleted with strokes in *M*.
       The *no* is also bracketed.

2414   casarse] casarme *P* | el asaltar] asaltar *S1*.

2415   muros] muero *S1* | trincheras] trinchera *S1*.

2416   ni fajinas] hacer fajina ε : fajinas *S7* | deseas] espera ε : desea *S6* : forzar ileras *S7*.

2417   tu] su *S1*.

2418   alista] asista *S1*.

2419   y en] ya en *S1*.

2420   maese] maestre *S1*.

2422   Doña Juana] Juan *PδS8* : Juana *MS9* : Juan</a> *S1* : Capitán ζ. See 2385.

2426   Don Juan] Juan *Pδ*: Don Juan *MS8* : </Juan> *S1*: Jua ζ : Estrada *S9*. Omitted in θ. See 2385.

2429–2433   <\\no> *M*. Bracketed text and deleted with many vertical and wavy strokes in *M*. Underlined *no*.

2430   impedirlo] impidillo *P* : conseguirlo *Mδ* : dilatarlo ε : conseguir ζ.

2433   *Salen dos* Caballeros] *salen dos caballeros, galanes de boda P* : *Sale <-un caballero> M* : *salen dos caballeros β* (<-Salen los dos caballeros \\Galan. Criados> *S1*) | Caballero 1] Ca 1 *PδS9* : Alférez *M* : Cab. *S1S8* : Cap ζ.

2433–2469   <\\ no no> *S1*.

2435   sin que ninguno lo crea] Omitted in *M*.

2439   Caballero 2] Ca 2 *P* : Alférez *M* : Cav 2 *β* (Cav ζ).

2442   le] que *S1*.

2443   la ciudad] las verdes *P*.

2444   cuyas] que en *P*.

2445   parecieron] parecían *P*.

2446   Caballero 1] Cap *P* : Alférez *M* : Un *S1S8* : Ca 1 *δS9* : Cap 1 ζ.

2446   los vieron] lo vieron *S1*.

2447   y yo los vi] y los dos *P* : y yo lo vi *S1*| si es así] pues si es así *P*.

2448   *Vase don Juan y el caballero M* : *Vase don Juan S9*.

2452–2463   Del tálamo de flores … grandeza se imagina] Omitted in α. Don Juan's monologue is in all *sueltas*. It could be an addition of *β*. See lines 2465–2470.

2452   Don Juan] Juan *δ* : Jua : Cab 1 *S9*. Omitted in α.

2453   dilatéis] dilatáis *β* (dilateis *ı*) | eternidades] a eternidades γ. Omitted in α.

2456   almas] en almas *S9*. Omitted in α.

2458   el] en γ. Omitted in α.

2463   gozo] goza *S1*.

2464–2469   Más ventura no quiero … ventura ha merecido?] Omitted in

P. Here *P* keeps omitting, but not *M*, nor the *sueltas*. Juana seems to be answering Don Juan, suggesting that lines 2452–2463 – or something in its place – also were in the original.

2468   dichosa] dichoso S1.

2468b   <\\que hazeis> *S1*. There is a handwritten arrow from line 2433 to 2469 in *S1*. See lines 2433–2469.

2469   *Sale un* CRIADO] *Sale un criado P* : *Sale M* : Omitted in *β* (*Salen Juan de Alba y criados S9*)

2470   CRIADO] CRIA[DO] *X* (ALF[érez] *M* : CRIA. 1 <1°> *S1* : CRIAD 1 *S8*).

2471   está aquí. DON JUAN ¿Qué dices? Llego] está aquí. JUAN ¿qué dices? Llega *S1S8* : está aquí. JUANA ¿qué decís? Llego *δ*: está aquí. JUA ¿qué decís? Llego *ζ*: está aquí. JUAN ¿qué decís? Llega *S9*. Omitted in *P*.

2472   Amor permita] A mi amor permite *P*.

2473   *Sale* JUAN DE ALBA *con el capitán* DON PEDRO *y toda la compañía*] *Sale toda la compañía, y Juan de Alba P* : *Salen toda la compañía con Juan de Alba M* : *Sale Juan de Alba y criados ε* : *Sale toda la compañía con Juan de Alba δζ*.

2474   JUAN DE ALBA] JUAN *X* (CRIADO *P*).

2480   DOÑA JUANA] DON JUAN *PS7S8* : JUANA *MδS9* : D. JU *S1*: JUA *S6*.

2485   así] ansí *P*.

2487   y así] así *S1*.

2489   con la venera] ya de manera *P*. See note to lines 2280–2291.

2490   de Santiago a quien añade] que estoy rico pues me da *P* : de Santiago a quien <-a honrado \añade> *M* | quien] que *S1*. See note to lines 2280–2291.

2492   maese] maestre *S1*.

2495   esto todo] todo esto *S1*.

2500   lo] le *X* (lo *Pζ*).

2501   lo] le *X* (lo *Pζ*).

2504   asentar mi] asentarme *S1*.

2509   ansí] así *X* (ansí P*η*).

2511–2510   pudiera, / como negro,] There are different interpretations depending on how punctuation is modernized. With only one comma, after *pudiera*, Juan would talk about *vengarse como negro* (to take revenge as a Black man) instead of querer honrarlo como negro (to honor him as a Black man). I put commas before and after to maintain the ambiguity.

2514   blanco en las] que es blanco en sus *S1*.

2517   seis] tres *P*.

2518   aunque] y aunque *P* | en] <-es +a> *S1*.

2519   poca correspondencia] es para correspondencias *P* : muy poca paga aquesta *M*.

2522   glorioso] dichoso *M*.

2525   los pies] <-las manos /los pies> *M*.

2528   negro] esclavo *M*.

2531   de lo que ha sido se afrenta] quien de lo que fue se afrenta *M*.

2539   aumenta] aumentan *Pδ*. I amend the agreement of *aumenta* because it makes more sense: Virtue increases merits, not otherwise. See Baltasar Fra Molinero's essay in this volume.

2543   polos] pasos *P*.

2544   ellos] ellas *S1*.

2546   nobles] blancos *M*.

2547   así] ansí *P*.

2553   la norabuena] tan buena nueva *P* : la enhorabuena *S1*.

2557   tanta renta] encomienda *M*.

2558   vistis] visteis *β*.

2559   Capitán don Pedro] Cap 1 *P* : 1 *Mδζ* : Cria. 1 </1°> *S1* : Criado 1 *S8* : Criado *S9* | <-aunque enferma \ma> *M*.

2560–2563   <\\-no> *M*. Bracketed text in *M*. *No* was deleted with a stroke.

2562   pues nada se ha sabido] después nada he sabido *S8*.

2563   alguna que] será ya *S1*.

2564   nuevas] noches *ζ*.

2565   no pensó bodas tan negras] <–no tendrá nuevas tan negras \\no entendió pascuas tan negras> *S1*: no querrá prendas tan negras *ζ* : no tendrá nuevas tan negras *S8*.

2567   tener] <-hoy /tener> *S1* : tener oy *S8* | sa a] está a *Pε* (sa a *S9*) : sa *δ*: a *ζ*.

2567b   *Sale Antón*] Sale Antón *P* : Sale Antonillo *β* (*Sale Ant S8*). Omitted in *M*.

2569   dile] dila *γ*.

2575   daré] doy *M*.

2577   *Antón saca a doña Leonor*] Saca a doña Leonor del paño *M* : Saca a Leonor *β* (*Sale Leonor S9*). Omitted in *P*.

2578   en la trampa hemos caído] en lan tampa hemos cahído *P* : en la tlampa hamo caíro *ε* (en la trampa hamo caído *S9*).

2579   par] por *Mδζ* : pal *S1S8* | ratonera] ratoneras *δζ*.

2580   Capitán don Agustín ¿Mi esposa?, ¿cómo ha de ser?] D. Juan: Ay de mí Cap Mi esposa, ¿como? *P* : Cap ¿Mi esposa?, ¿cómo ha de serlo? *β*.

2583   cásese] ca<-sar +se>se *S1*: casarse *ζS8*.

2586   Don Juan] Gob *P* : DJ *M* : D. Jua *S1S8* : Juan *δS9* : Jua *ζ* | maese] maestre *S1*.

2587   esto no] eso no *PS1γ* (esto *δS9*).

2588   le hace] ha sido *P*.

2590   esta diga] él la diga *P*.

2591   su obligación y su deuda] Omitted in *ζ* | *Dale un papel*] Omitted in *P*.

2592   es esto] esto es *S1* | así] ansí *M*.

2594   tú te] que te *β*.

2595   Juan de Alba] Omitted in *S1*.

2603   le] se *β* (le *αS9* : la *S1*).

2604–2609   Por ella me diste la vida … en nueva naturaleza] Omitted in *M*.

2604–2609b   <\\no> *S1*.

2606   por ti, por ella] por ti y por ella *ε*.

2610   ansí] así *β* | tú lo mandas] lo mandáis *S1*.

2611   ordenan] ordena *M*.

2612   amor] su amor *S1*.

2613   en este papel confiesas] esa cédula confiesa *M*.

2614–2644   In *M*, this passage was bracketed at several points, with many noes in the margin. Some of these noes were deleted with a stroke. The great number of handwritten interventions transmits anxiety and hesitancy.

2615   señor] señora *S8*.

2615–2616   <\\-no \\si> *M*. Bracketed text in *M*. *No* was deleted with a stroke.

2617–2629   <\\-no \\-no \\si si> *M*. Bracketed text in *M*. Instances of *no* were deleted with strokes.

2622   si aquí] ya que *S1*.

2625   fabricares] fabricaras *M* | que ese] ese *ε* (que ese *S9*).

2627   mis rentas] mi renta *M*.

2628   Doña Juana Pues, si ha de ser] D. Juan Yo te agradezco *P*.

2629   ya el casarme por tu cuenta] la noble correspondencia *P*.

2629–2639   ya el casarme … ser esclava vuestra] Omitted in *P*.

2630–2631   Bracketed text and deleted with heavy strokes in *M*. Almost illegible. No handwritten interventions in *S1*.

2630   y el cielo] el cielo *β* (y el cielo *MS9*). Omitted in *P*.

2631   que ha] y te ha *M*.

2632–2634   <\\no no> *M*. Bracketed text in *M*.

2634   resolución] resolocion *M*.

2635–2644   <\\no no> *M*. Bracketed text in *M*, deleted by multiple wavy lines.

2636   Cap(itán don Agustín) *M*.

2640   tenido] Omitted in *S1*.

2641   varias] buenas *P*.

2643   las fiestas] la fiesta *M*.

2644   comiencen] comience *M*.

2545   Juan de Alba] Juan *X* (Los dos *S8*)| Reservando a otra] Dando fin a la *S8*.

2646   las] y sus *S8*.

2647   cuya] por *S8*. *S8* ends at this line.

2648   largamente las aclara] prodigiosas las declara *S1S2*. Omitted in *S8*.

2649   y largamente las cuenta] y en tanto un vítor merezca *S1S2* : perdonad las faltas de esta *S9*. See 2646.

2649b   <\fin \Laus Deo> *M* | In *S1*, a hand added a different ending and a second one copied it below: "dando fin a la comedia / de *El negro valiente en Flandes* / y a su historia verdadera".

2649c   *M* includes two licenses to perform at the end of the manuscript:
Por comisión del señor vicario general, he vi[s]to esta comedia del Valiente negro en Flandes y se puede representar en caraga[oz]a a 27 de [l?] o[ctu]bre 1651. El licen[cia]do Joseph Iban[ez?] (By commission of the Vicar General, I have examined this play titled *El valiente negro en Flandes*. It may be performed. Zaragoza, October 27, 1651).
"Por comisión del Exc[elentísi]mo señor conde de Lemos, lugarteniente y capitán general en este reyno de Aragon, he visto la comedia *intitulada El valiente negro en Flandes*, y hallo que se puede representar. [Así lo siento?] en Çara[go]a y diciembre 28 de 1651. El D[oct]or Juan Fran[cis]co Andres [de Uztarroz]" ["By commission of his excellency the Lord Count of Lemos, lieutenant and captain general in this kingdom of Aragon, I have seen the play entitled *El valiente negro en Flandes*, and I find that it may be performed. [So this is my opinion] In Zaragoza, December 28, 1651. Doctor Juan Franco Andres [de Uztarroz]". The family name "de Uztarroz" was added in pencil by a modern hand. See Textual History in this volume.

APPENDIX A

Alternative Scenes
Doña Leonor Reveals Her True Identity (see lines 2007–2008).
Fragment inserted in *S7* (see Textual History).

DOÑA LEONOR   Yo sé que me aguardarás,
                 capitán, cuando repares
                 y sepas…

JUAN DE ALBA   ¿Qué he de saber?

DOÑA LEONOR   …que soy quien, en cierto lance,
                 te dio la vida.

JUAN DE ALBA   ¿Tú, a mí?

DOÑA LEONOR   Tú mismo lo contestaste.

JUAN DE ALBA   ¿Quién eres?

DOÑA LEONOR   Yo soy Leonor.

JUAN DE ALBA   ¿Tú, Leonor? ¿Qué dices?

DOÑA LEONOR   Hablen
                 mis ojos.

JUAN DE ALBA   ¡Cuerpo de Dios
                 ¿no lo hubieras dicho antes?

[DOÑA LEONOR   I know you'll take that back,
                 Capitan, when you realize
                 And know…

JUAN DE ALBA   What must I know?

DOÑA LEONOR   …that I am the one who, in a certain predicament,
                 gave you your life.

JUAN DE ALBA   You, saved me?

DOÑA LEONOR   You said it yourself.

JUAN DE ALBA   Who are you?
                 I am Leonor.

JUAN DE ALBA   You, Leonor? What are you saying?

DOÑA LEONOR   Let
                 My eyes speak for me.

JUAN DE ALBA   God lives!
                 Couldn't you have said this before?]

End of Act II (see lines 2014–2040)
Fragment inserted in *S7* (see Textual History)

JUAN DE ALBA	¿No lo hubieras dicho antes?
	Dame esa mano.
DOÑA LEONOR	La vida
	me debes, y a que me pagues
	desde Mérida he venido.
JUAN DE ALBA	¡Viven los tersos celajes!
	que por ti daré la mía.
DOÑA LEONOR	Pues como tú no me faltes,
	seré dichosa.
JUAN DE ALBA	Mi mano
	esta palabra afiance.
DOÑA LEONOR	Pues con ella me aseguro.
JUAN DE ALBA	Bien puedes asegurarte.
DOÑA LEONOR	Pues adiós, valiente negro.
JUAN DE ALBA	Bella Leonor, Él te guarde.
[JUAN DE ALBA	Couldn't you have said this before?
	Give me that hand.
DOÑA LEONOR	You owe me
	Your life, and I have come here
	From Mérida to collect the debt.
JUAN DE ALBA	As long as there are clear skies!
	I'll give my life for you.
DOÑA LEONOR	As long as you don't fail me,
	I'll be pleased.
JUAN DE ALBA	Let my hand
	Confirm my word.
DOÑA LEONOR	Then I feel assured by it.
JUAN DE ALBA	You can be sure of that.
DOÑA LEONOR	Then farewell, Valiant Black man.
JUAN DE ALBA	Beautiful Leonor, may God keep you.]

Quarrel with the Courtiers (see lines 2113–2152)
Fragment glued on *S1* at the beginning of act three.

1°	Bien valdrán tres mil reales.
2°	¡Achí!
3°	¡Achí!
JUAN DE ALBA	¿Qué es esto?
ANTÓN	*Estornudar gente branca*
	haciendo burla de prieto.
JUAN DE ALBA	Pues yo haré que aquestos blancos
	tengan más comedimiento:
	así desvergüenzas tales
	castigo.
1°	¡Válgame el cielo!
2°	¡Huyamos, que es un demonio!
3°	El duque sale.

Sale el DUQUE

DUQUE DE ALBA	¡Teneos!
	¿Este sagrado se ultraja?
	Soldados: ahorquen luego
	al villano que ha tenido
	tan bárbaro atrevimiento.

[1°	They'll be worth three thousand *reales*.
2°	Achoo!
3°	Achoo!
JUAN DE ALBA	What's this?
ANTÓN	*White folks sneezing*
	Making fun of us Blacks.
JUAN DE ALBA	Well, I'll make these white folks have more restraint:
	this is how I punish such shamelessness
	behavior.
1°	Oh my goodness gracious!
2°	Let's run away, he's a demon!
3°	Here comes the Duke.

Enter the DUKE

DUKE OF ALBA   Halt!
Who dares to violate this holy palace?
Soldiers: hang now
The villain who had
such a barbaric nerve.

APPENDIX B

An account written by Captain Alonso Vázquez on Alonso de Venegas, a defector from the Spanish army in Flanders

Fragmento de *Los sucesos de Flandes y Francia en tiempo de Alejandro Farnese, por el capitán Alonso Vázquez, sargento mayor de la milicia de Jaén y su distrito. Escrito en seis libros.* (Vázquez, [c. 1577–1588], 1879, 245–48).

Año de 1580. ...De allí a seis días [a Alejandro Farnesio] le vino aviso cómo la de Diste se había también perdido, y que la había ganado a escala vista Alonso de Venegas –mulato y español, natural de la ciudad de Andújar, del obispado de Jaén, que era capitán del Príncipe de Orange y muy su confidente– con ayuda de los calvinistas que estaban dentro, y la guarneció con un fuerte presidio de rebeldes. Y pues un solo español que les servía les había sido de tanta importancia, se deja considerar de la mucha que serían tantos como habían echado de Flandes, pues, por su ausencia, se iban perdiendo las villas sin haber quién las recuperase.

Este Alonso de Venegas, en tiempo del Duque de Alba, se fue de Flandes a Francia para buscar un enemigo que tenía. Sirvió en aquel reino a los franceses; y por su mucho valor, la Reina Madre le favorecía mucho y, deseando [él] volverse a los Países Bajos, le dio cartas para don Fadrique de Toledo, hijo del Duque de Alba, que en aquella ocasión gobernaba el ejército. Recibiole bien y agasajole mucho, encargando le hiciesen buena acogida entre los demás soldados españoles.

Servía con puntualidad y se preciaba de andar más bien armado que otros. Y como los que en la guerra lo están son preferidos, siempre le daban la primera hilera, y en los escuadrones ocupaba, por más bien armado, los mejores puestos. Envidiosos de esto, algunos oficiales reformados soldados particulares le cobraron odio, especialmente un ayudante de sargento mayor que después murió capitán –que excuso escribir su nombre por justos respetos y no haber tomado la satisfacción que le importaba de este Alonso Venegas, como adelante se dirá– deseaba atropellarlo, incitado de los que le querían mal; pero, como don Fadrique de Toledo le favorecía, nadie se le atrevió.

Un día de ocasión de pelear, quiso este ayudante –persuadido de lo que le aborrecían– quitarle de la primera hilera, habiendo dado ocasión a que otros le despreciasen como a negro y vituperasen –que poco han menester los soldados para semejantes cosas cuando se ven favorecidos y con alas de sus oficiales–. Quedó el mulato Venegas tan ofendido de esto que, desde luego, previno la venganza y, acabada la ocasión y deshecho el escuadrón, desafió al ayudante a reñir en campaña, no como a oficial sino como, a soldado, pues, en tal caso, podía ser su igual. Respondiole que no era hombre que había de reñir con un perro mulato, sino con otro de su calidad y color.

Hubo disputas en el ejército y pareceres que apoyaron esto. Otros, que, pues eran iguales en el hábito, lo habían de ser en las obras, demás de que era hombre de bien y buen soldado y podía reñir con él. Quedose así. No hubo amistades por parecerles había desigualdad, y que un soldado con un ayudante de sargento mayor no podía perder, ni le había para poder hacer caso de ello.

Pero Alonso Venegas quedó tan corrido del menosprecio que de él se hizo no respetando a su persona por el color, que, viendo le estorbaban la venganza sin considerar las obligaciones de cristiano y las que tenía a su nación; y, [viendo] que ya deshonrado no podía mostrar el valor que tenía, ni vivir entre los que le habían menospreciado y abatido; quiso que se conociese [su valor] entre los enemigos de la Iglesia, a los cuales se fue a servir;

Y procedió de manera entre ellos que le obligó al Príncipe de Orange a hacerle capitán y a casarlo con una mujer principal y de muy buenas partes. Y por los Estados rebeldes, se señaló valerosamente en las ocasiones que se le ofrecieron, y cobró tanta opinión que jamás se vio menospreciado, antes favorecido y estimado de todos los enemigos de Su Majestad.

Y pues en la infantería española son todos los soldados hijos de sus obras, no es justo despreciar a nadie, ni que ningún general ni superior lo permita, pues se ve claro que, por haber, en nuestros ejércitos, tenido en poco a algunos soldados, [ha de] sucedernos lo que con Alonso de Venegas. Y con Manzano, que tanto en Mastrique nos dio en qué entender por su mucho valor; que, por descuido de no haber hecho amigo con otro soldado que le había desmentido, no pudiendo o [por] no haber querido cobrar su honra, pareciéndole no estaba con su reputación en el ejército español, se fue con los rebeldes, donde también fue capitán del Príncipe de Orange…

…Y así, en ninguna manera se puede admitir disculpa de estos tales, ni creer de ellos cosa sino que, por mandar y vivir licenciosamente y fuera de la obediencia y disciplina militar de la nación española, dejan sus banderas y siguen las de los enemigos de la Iglesia. Pero todavía es bien quitarles la ocasión por el cuidado que estos tales han dado y puede dar. Alejandro le tuvo [el cuidado] muy grande con la pérdida de Diste, y le creció la confusión y el desengaño de poder resistir las fuerzas de los rebeldes.

[Excerpt of *The events of Flanders and France in the time of Alexander Farnese*, by Captain Alonso Vázquez, sergeant major in Jaén and its district. Written in six volumes.

Year of 1580. …Within six days Alexander Farnese received a report on how Diest had been also lost, when Alonso de Venegas climbed the walls in open combat. Venegas was a *mulato* and Spaniard, a native of the city of Andújar, in the bishopric of Jaén, who was captain of the Prince of Orange and very much his confidant. He took Diest with the help of the Calvinists who were within the walls, and he secured it with a strong garrison of rebels; And since a single Spaniard who served them had been of so much consequence, one can fathom the great importance the many others who had been driven out of Flanders would have, because by their absence, the towns were being lost without there being anyone to recover them.

This Alonso de Venegas, in the time of the Duke of Alba, went from Flanders to France to seek an enemy he had. He served the French in that kingdom, and, because of his great valor, the Queen Mother favored him greatly, and since Venegas wished to return to the Low

Countries, she gave him letters for Don Fadrique of Toledo, son of the Duke of Alba, who governed the army at the time. She received him well and gave him a great deal of hospitality, ordering that he be well received by the other Spanish soldiers.

He served punctually and prided himself on being better armed than others, and as those in war are, they always gave him the front line, and because he was better equipped in weapons, he occupied the best places in the squadrons. Envious of this, some of the reappointed and private soldiers hated him, especially an assistant to the sergeant-major who later died a captain – whom I have excused writing his name for the sake of respect and not having taken the satisfaction he cared for from this Alonso Venegas, as said – he wanted to abuse his power upon him, incited by those who wished him ill, but, as Don Fadrique of Toledo favored him, no one dared him.

One day on the occasion of fighting, this assistant officer – persuaded by those who loathed him – wanted to remove him from the front line, having given occasion for others to treat him unfairly as a Black man and to revile him. Soldiers need little goading for such things when they see themselves favored and under the wings of their officers. The *mulato* Venegas was so offended by this that he immediately set about revenge, and when the occasion was over and the squadron disbanded, he challenged the assistant officer to a fight in the field, not as an officer, but as a soldier, for in such a case he could be his equal. He replied he was not a man to quarrel with a *mulato* dog, but with another of his own status and color.

There were disputes in the army, and opinions that supported this. Others argued that since they were equal in profession, they should be equal in deeds; besides, he was an honest man and a good soldier and could fight with him. And that is how it ended. There was no peace between them because it seemed to them there was inequality, and that a soldier with a sergeant-major's assistant could not lose honor, nor was there an affront for him to take any notice of it.

But Alonso Venegas was so humiliated by the contempt made to him, not respecting his person because of his color, that seeing that it hindered him from revenge without considering his obligations as a

Christian and those which he had to his nation, and seeing that now disgraced, he could not show the valor he had, nor live among those who had despised and cast him down; he wished his valor to be known among the enemies of the Church, whom he went to serve.

And he so proceeded among them as to compel the Prince of Orange to make him a captain, and to marry him to a noblewoman and highborn. And for the rebellious Countries, he made himself valiantly known on such occasions as were offered to him; and he gained so high a reputation that all his Majesty's enemies did not despise him, but favored and esteemed him.

And, since in the Spanish infantry all the soldiers are self-made men, it is not fair to disdain anyone, nor that any general or superior should allow it; since it is clear that, because we have thought little of some soldiers in our armies, the same thing will happen to us as happened to Alonso de Venegas. And as with Manzano, who at Maastricht gave us so much to understand by his great valor, who through the carelessness of not having made friends with another soldier who had called him a liar, because he was not able or because he did not want to claim his honor, he thought he was without reputation in the Spanish army; he went with the rebels, where he also became a captain of the Prince of Orange...

...And so, one can neither accept this as an excuse for these events, nor believe from these dealings but that, by commanding and living licentiously and outside the obedience and military discipline of the Spanish nation, they leave their banners and follow those of the enemies of the Church, but it is still well to take occasion from them by the caution which these actions have given and may give. Alexander was hard hit with the loss of Diest and grew in confusion and the disappointment of being able to resist the forces of the rebels.]

APPENDIX C

Ballad of The Valiant Black Man in Flanders

The *Relación del valiente negro en Flandes* is an anonymous ballad that widely circulated in chapbooks (*pliegos sueltos*) during the eighteenth and nineteenth centuries (see Figure 2). Rodríguez López-Vázquez conjectured that this ballad preceded Claramonte's play (1997, 13), but this is unlikely. The earliest edition known is titled *Romance famoso en que se refieren las grandes hazañas del valiente negro en Flandes, llamado Juan de Alva*, and is listed in the catalogue of the Bancroft Library at University of California, Berkeley (PQ6429. R62 1680). We have not been able to examine this copy, but Panford allegedly did (2003). If the information in the Bancroft Library catalogue is correct, the printer, Francisco Sanz, would be the same that published *S1* (see Textual History). This dates the ballad to the last decades of the seventeenth century.

Relación del valiente negro en Flandes

Valerosa infantería
de la esclarecida España
que, entre todas las naciones,
por tu valor te señalas:
oye de un valiente negro
la fuerza y valor que alcanza,
pues se acompañan con él
los dos de la llave dorada,[1]
duques, condes y marqueses,
señores de grande fama:
Siendo hijo de una negra
que de don Pedro fue esclava
—mas por sus buenos servicios
su libertad alcanzara—,

---

1 *Llave dorada*: The golden key of the king's royal apartments. It was the insignia of the Gentilhombres Grandes de España, an institution founded by King Fernando VII in the early nineteenth century.

llevome la inclinación
de servir al Rey de España,
y en este dichoso tiempo
unas compañías marchan
a la ciudad de Lisboa;
con ellas va el Duque de Alba.
Fuime a ver al Duque un día
y, con briosa arrogancia,
le dije: "Gran Capitán,
sírvete de darme plaza,
que por el cielo que adoro,
y por esta humilde espada,
que he de seguir tus banderas
hasta morir en campaña".
El duque me pidió el nombre.
Dije que Juan me llamaba,
y respondió el duque invicto:
"Llámate desde hoy Juan de Alba,
que te he [de] dar mi apellido
porque tu valor me agrada".
Embarqueme, pasé a Flandes,
comenzando en sus campañas
a dar glorias a mi nombre
y nuevo asunto a la fama.
Un día me llamó el Duque
y dijo: "Amigo Juan de Alba,
aquesta noche conviene
a la corona de España
que traigas del enemigo
una posta maniatada".
Allí estaba un capitán
que don Juan de Rojas llamaban
que, ardiendo en airada envidia,
de esta suerte al Duque le habla:
"¿No es vergüenza de Españoles
lo que vuecelencia manda,
que vaya un negro a gozar
empresa tan noble y alta?,

¿no hay capitanes valientes,
sargentos, cabos de escuadra?
Y si no, yo iré, señor,
porque ese perro no vaya".
Mucho lo agradeció el Duque,
pero que fuese me encarga;
y yo, al mirar mi desprecio,
dije ardiendo en ira y saña:
¡Oh, capitán envidioso,
quién te cogiera en campaña!
Vieras la espada del negro,
y yo si obras como hablas".
Así que vino la noche.
Caminé hacia la estacada,
donde encontré al capitán,
que paseándose estaba.
Púseme una mascarilla
y al punto, saque mi espada.
Sacó el capitán la suya,
y a golpes y cuchilladas,
le abatí en el punto al suelo,
y luego sobre él me echara.
Él, despúes que se vio en tierra,
con una voz delicada,
me pide que no le mate.
Yo le dije que se vaya
y advirtiese, de camino,
que soy hombre de dos caras,
y si una aquí le perdona,
le matará otra mañana.
Quitele una banda roja
con rapacejos de plata,
que, por señal de mi triunfo,
hice que me la dejara.
A la tienda del gran Duque
fue diciendo en voces altas:
"Desgraciado fui, señor,
esta noche en la estacada.

Sintióme la centinela,
dio aviso, tocose al arma,
salió una manga furiosa,
reconoció la campaña:
Resistiéndome a su esfuerzo,
de entre todos me escapara".
Estando en estas mentiras,
yo, alegre y gozoso, entrara
con cuatro postas rendidas,
todas cuatro maniatadas.
Y el Duque, que me vido,
se ha levantado, me abraza.
Y volviendo al capitán,
con muy corteses palabras,
dije: "Señor capitán,
sírvase usted de esta banda
que le quité al enemigo
esta noche en la campaña".
El capitán, que lo advierte,
se ha turbado y no me habla,
mas el Duque mi señor
me honró, con su alabarda,
con título de sargento.
Con ella me paseaba;
ya murmuraban de mi
todos los tercios de España.
Y estando yo con el Duque
la víspera de Santa Ana,
llegó un soldado arrogante,
que Siblamei se llamaba,
desafiando al gran Duque
y a cuantos con él estaban.
Sin pedir licencia al Duque,
por el cuerpo le agarraba.
Apretele entre mis brazos
y la vida le quitara.
Echele en el mar y, luego,
volví a tomar mi alabarda.

Y apenas hube salido
seis pasos de la real casa,
cuando hallé algunos sargentos[2]
que, viendo que ellos me igualan,
en corrillos divididos,
de mí murmurando estaban,
Me silban y me estornudan,
me dicen: "perra bellaca,
¿quién la ha hecho soldadilla
no viniéndole de casta?"
Tanto de ver mi desprecio
me cegó la furia y rabia
que, ardiendo en ira y enojo,
metiendo mano a la espada,
acometí a todos juntos,
les quité cinco alabardas,
arrastrelas por el suelo
y les dije: "ruines mandrias,
pues que perdisteis la honra,
volved por el Rey de España,
que las insignias que os dio
hoy un negro las arrastra".
Mas viendo que no se atreven,
del suelo las levantara
y, con rendimiento humilde,
las besé, y dije al tomarlas:
"Perdonad, mi rey Filipo,
monarca invicto de España:
ellos la ocasión me dieron,
que yo no me la tomara,
pero su descortesía
dio a mi atrevimiento causa".
Vísperas de Navidad,
triste día para España.
El Duque de pena llora
de ver que sin gente se halla
porque, de la mitad que tenía,

---

2   The version examined reads "hallá". It could also be "allá" (there).

más de la mitad le falta;
pues, el feroz enemigo
unos prende y otros mata.
Más sin temor ni recelo,
a las trincheras contrarias
me acerqué buscando presa
que llevarle al Duque de Alba.
Vi que el Príncipe de Orange
en su tienda está sin guardia,
y al ver la ocasión tan buena,
determiné de lograrla.
Con un puñal a los pechos,
le dije: "Ríndete a España,
Príncipe, y date a prisión.
Si no, he de sacarte el alma".
Le desarmé y luego, al punto,
en los hombros me lo echara,
y hacia la tienda del Duque
corrí con él, que volaba.
El Duque, así como vio
que es el Príncipe de Holanda,
con gran gozo y regocijo,
le dice aquestas palabras:
"Estas visitas, señor,
me dan muy alegres Pascuas".
"Si tienes tales soldados
–respondió– que aquesto hagan,
¿qué mucho que tiemble el mundo
al valor de vuestra espada?"
Pónense a hacer colación
el príncipe y el Duque de Alba;
y el negro, a la cabecera,
entre los dos se sentara,
y en su aplauso, mientras cenan,
alegres coplas cantaba.
Ajustáronse las paces
como las quisiese España,

honrando el Príncipe y Duque
al negro por sus hazañas.
Vínose el Duque a Madrid,
quiso que le acompañara,
y de mí le contó al rey
muchas acciones bizarras.
El Rey, con gana de verme,
entrar al salón me manda.
Hinqué la rodilla en tierra
y el Rey me dijo: "Levanta,
noble maestre de campo,
lustre y honor de mis armas,
comendador de La Torre,
del orden de Calatrava:
seis mil ducados de renta
mando que os den en plata,
y capitán general
de la infantería de España".
De turbado, no acerté
a decir al rey palabra,
aunque, para engrandecer
lo que mi humildad ensalza
y lo bien que me ha premiado,
ruego a Dios que un rayo me haga
para postrar enemigos
de nuestro rey a las plantas.

[Ballad of The Valiant Black Man in Flanders

Valiant infantry
Of the illustrious Spain,
That, among all nations
For your valor, you stand out:
Listen from a valiant Black man
The valor and power he achieved,
For he is flanked
By the two of the Golden Key,
Dukes, Counts, and Marquises,
Lords of great fame:

Being the son of a Black woman
Who was Don Pedro's slave,
But for her exemplary services
her freedom did attain,
I felt inclined to
To serve the King of Spain,
And in this fortunate time,
Some regiments were marching
To the city of Lisbon:
With them goes the Duke of Alba.
One day I went to see the Duke
And, with spirited arrogance,
I told to him: "Great Captain,
Please give me a post,
That by the heavens that I adore,
And by this humble sword,
That I will follow your banners
Until I die in the battlefield.
The Duke asked me my name
I said I was called Juan,
And the undefeated Duke replied:
"From this day forth, call yourself Juan de Alba,
I will give you my surname
Because your valor pleases me."
I boarded the ship, I went to Flanders,
And began in his campaigns
To give glory to my name
And a new venture for fame.
One day, the Duke summoned me
And said: My friend Juan of Alba,
This evening it is in the interest
Of the Crown of Spain
That you bring me a sentry
In shackles from the enemy's camp.
A captain was there
Whose name was Don Juan de Rojas
Who, burning with envious anger,
Spoke to the Duke in this way:

Is it not shameful to Spaniards
What you command?
That a Black man should go to enjoy
Such a noble and lofty enterprise?
Don't we have here brave captains,
Sergeants, corporals of the squadron?
And if we do not, I will go, sir,
Because that dog should not go.
The Duke was very appreciative,
Yet he charged me to let him do it;
And I, seeing myself humiliated,
Said, burning with rancor and blinding fury:
O envious captain! If I would
Catch you on the battlefield!
You will see the Black man's sword,
And I shall see if you do as you said.
And so, the night came.
I walked towards the barracks,
Where I found the captain,
Who was walking about.
I put on a mask,
And at once I drew my sword.
The captain drew his,
And with blows and thrusts,
I struck him on the spot to the ground,
Then I threw myself on him.
And after he saw himself on the ground,
With a delicate voice,
He begged me not to kill him.
I told him to leave
And warned him on his way,
That I am man of two faces,
And if this one spares him here,
Another will kill him tomorrow.
I took off his red sash
That had woven silver fringes,
Which, as a sign of my victory,
I had him leave it to me.

To the great Duke's tent
He went crying out in a loud voice:
"I was unfortunate, Sir
Tonight at the stockade.
The sentry heard me,
Gave warning and sounded the alarm
A furious armed detachment emerged,
He discovered the ruse:
I escaped from all of them
Resisting their efforts."
While these lies were going on,
I entered elated and joyful
With four sentries all tied up,
And all four have yielded.
And the Duke, that saw me,
Stood up and embraced me.
And turning towards the Captain
With very courteous words,
I said: "Mr. Captain,
Help yourself to this sash
Which I took from the enemy
Tonight, in the countryside."
The captain, realizing it,
Is troubled and doesn't speak to me,
But the Duke, My Lord,
Honored me with his halberd,
With the rank of sergeant.
I would walk with it;
And all the Infantry of Spain
Were already talking behind my back
And while I was with the Duke
On the eve of St. Anne's Day
An arrogant soldier arrived,
Named Siblamei,
Challenging the great Duke
And all those who were with him.
Without asking the Duke's permission
I grabbed him by his upper body,

Clutching him in my arms,
And I took his life away.
I threw him into the sea, and then,
I picked up my halberd again,
And no sooner had I gone,
Six paces from the Royal house,
When I met some sergeants,
Who, seeing that they were my equal,
Were whispering about me,
In small circles here and there.
They hiss and sneeze at me,
And say to me: You insolent bitch,
Who has made him a soldier,
Given he lacks our caste?
Fury and rage blinded me
To see so much contempt towards me,
That, burning with rage and anger,
I reached for my sword,
And attacked them all at once,
Taking five halberds from them,
Dragged them across the ground
And said to them: "Worthless do-nothings,
Since you have lost your honor,
Go back to the King of Spain
Because the crests he gave you
A Black man today drags them down".
But seeing that no one would dare
To pick them up from the ground
And, with humble devotion,
I kissed them, and taking them said:
"Forgive me, My King Philip,
Undefeated Monarch of Spain:
They gave me motive,
One I should've not taken,
But their disrespect
Gave my boldness grounds for action".
Christmas Eve,
A sad day for Spain.

The Duke weeps with grief
To see that he is without people
Because of the half he had
More than half he lacks;
Because the fierce enemy
Seizes some and kills the others.
More without fear or suspicion
I approached the enemy's trenches
Looking for a target
To bring for the Duke of Alba.
I saw the Prince of Orange
Was in his tent, unguarded
And seeing the occasion so good,
I determined to follow through.
With a dagger to his chest,
I said: "Surrender to Spain,
Prince, and give yourself as a prisoner.
If you don't, I will take your soul."
I disarmed him, and then, in this moment,
I placed him over my shoulders
And I ran with him, as if I was flying
towards the Duke's tent.
The Duke, as he very well saw
That it was the Prince of Holland,
With great joy and delight,
Said these words to him:
"These visits, Your Grace,
give me a very joyful Christmas."
"If you have such soldiers,
– The Prince replied – that can do this,
How much should the world tremble
to the valor of your sword?"
The Prince and Duke began the talks
And the Black Man, at the head of the table
He sat between the two,
And in their applause, while dining
They sang joyful popular songs.
They made the peace accords

As Spain desired them,
With the Prince and Duke
Honoring the Black man for his deeds.
The Duke returned to Madrid,
He wanted me to come with him,
And he told the King of my
many valiant deeds.
The King, eager to meet me
Demands my presence in the hall.
I bowed my knee to the ground
And the King told me: "Rise
Noble Field Master,
Glory and honor of my weapons,
Commander of La Torre
Of the Order of Calatrava:
I order that they give you in silver
Six thousand ducats of income,
And Captain general
Of the Infantry in Spain."
I was overwhelmed and couldn't manage
To say a word to the King,
Although, in order to increase
What my humility exalts
And how well he has rewarded me,
I pray to God that he gives me a thunderbolt
To make me prostrate enemies
to the heels of our King.]

APPENDIX D

Memoria de gastos en 'La danza del valiente negro en Flandes' para las fiestas del recibimiento de la reina Mariana de Austria en el Archivo General de la Villa de Madrid (AGVM).

1. *Costes de la danza 'El valiente negro en Flandes', dados por Felipe Gómez, sesmo de Vallecas, para las fiestas del recibimiento de la reina* (AGVM, Secretaría, ASA 2-58-13, s/f)
1649, octubre 1, Ambroz
Memoria de lo que se gasta en la danza que se hace para el día de la entrada de la reina nuestra señora, de *El valiente negro en Flandes*, por el sesmo que llaman de Vallecas.

De librea para los danzantes: mil y cincuenta reales, 1.050.
A los danzantes, y músico y tamborilero; y del alquiler del aposento para vestirse: mil y trecientos y cincuenta reales, 1.350.

Que monta de dos mil y cuatrocientos reales, 2.400, los cuales se han de repartir por los lugares del dicho sesmo que son Fuencarral, Vicálvaro y Ambroz; Coslada, Fuente el Fresno, San Sebastián de los Reyes. Y por no saber firmar yo, Filipe Gómez, sesmero del dicho sesmo, lo signó a mi ruego un testigo, y juró a Dios y a una cruz es cierta y verdadera.
   Don Pedro Cornejo Gómez (firma)

2. *Extracto del mandamiento de Lorenzo R[...]es de Prado, caballero de Santiago, superintendente para las fiestas del recibimiento de la Reina, dado a Antonio Vidal para que requiera a los sesmeros de los sesmos de Villaverde, Vallecas, y Aravaca; y a las justicias de Vallecas para que tengan preparadas para el viernes 12 de septiembre danzas que tienen ofrecidas para la sobredicha fiesta* (AGVM, Secretaría, ASA 2-58-13, s/f)
Don Lorenzo R[...]es de Prado, caballero de la Orden de Santiago, del Consejo de su Majestad, y superintendente para las fiestas del

recibimiento de la reina nuestra señora, mando a vos, Antonio Vidal, que luego que este mandamiento se os entregue:

Requerir a Antonio Herrero, vecino del y sesmero del sesmo que llaman de Villaverde, que para el viernes doce de este presente mes tenga en esta manera las dos danzas que tiene ofrecidas el dicho sesmo, vestida y adornada en forma que la una es de muchachos zapateadores, y la otra de moros en forma de juego de cañas.

Asimismo, habéis requerir a las justicias del lugar de Vallecas que para el dicho día tengan en esta dicha villa la danza de espadas que es ofrecida, vestida y en forma.

Habéis de facer requerir a Felipe Gómez, vecino del lugar de Ambroz, sesmero del sesmo que llaman de Vallecas, que para el dicho día viernes doce deste mes tenga en esta dicha villa la danza de *El valiente negro en Flandes*, que tiene ofrecida, vestida y en forma.

Asimismo, haréis facer la misma diligencia con Diego de Vega, sesmero del sesmo que llama de Aravaca, y vecino del lugar de Alcorcón, que para el dicho día doce de este presente mes tenga en esta dicha villa la danza que ha ofrecido el dicho sesmo, que es un juego de cañas con alcancías.

Lo cual cumplan los unos y los otros, pena de cincuenta ducados, aplicados para los gastos de las dichas fiestas [...].

3. *Ubicación de la danza El valiente negro en Flandes, para las fiestas del recibimiento de la Reina que ofrece el sesmo de Vallecas. Extracto de la memoria de los lugares donde se situaban de danzas* (AGVM, Secretaría, ASA 2-58-13, s/f).

[...]Sesmo de Vallecas. Tablado Madrid. En la calle enfrente de las gradas de San Felipe, que hay unas pasaderas y va a salir a la del Arenal, se ha de poner la danza del negro valiente en Flandes que da el sesmo de Vallecas [...].

[Expense Reports Regarding the *Dance of the Valiant Black Man in Flanders* for the Festivities to Celebrate the Welcoming of Queen Mariana de Austria in 1649. General Archive of the city of Madrid (GACM).

1. *Expenses for the dance 'El valiente negro en Flandes;, given by Felipe Gómez, district of Vallecas, on the festivities to celebrate the welcoming of the Queen* (GACM, Secretariat, ASA 2-58-13, n.f.)
1649, October 1, Ambroz
An expense report on the dance that is held for the day of the entry of the Queen our Lady, for *The Valiant Black Man in Flanders*, in the district they call Vallecas.

- For the dancers' liveries: one thousand and fifty *reales*, 1,050.
- For the dancers, the musician, and the drummer; and for the rent of the room for dressing: one thousand and three hundred and fifty *reales*, 1,350.

That comes to the amount of two thousand and four hundred *reales*, 2,400, which are to be distributed throughout the villages of the referred districts, which are Fuencarral, Vicálvaro and Ambroz; Coslada, Fuente el Fresno, San Sebastián de los Reyes. And because I, Filipe Gómez, representative of the referred district, do not know how to write a signature, a witness signed at my request, and swore by God and by the Cross, to be true and accurate.
    Don Pedro Cornejo Gómez (signature)

2. *Extract from the order of Lorenzo R[...]es de Prado, knight of Santiago, superintendent of the festivities for the reception of the Queen, given to Antonio Vidal to require the representatives of the rural districts of Villaverde, Vallecas, and Aravaca; and the justices of Vallecas to have the dances they have offered for the aforementioned festivity ready for Friday 12 September.* (GACM, Secretariat, ASA 2-58-13, n.f.)
Don Lorenzo R[...]es de Prado, knight of the Order of Santiago, of His Majesty's Council, and superintendent for the festivities of the welcoming of the Queen our Lady, I command you, Antonio Vidal, that as soon as you receive this order, you:

– To require Antonio Herrero, neighbor of the district and representative of the said district that they call Villaverde, that by Friday the twelfth of this present month he mays fashion the two dances that the said district has offered, dressed and adorned attire in such a way that the one is that of the Spanish tap-dancing boys, and the others are Moors in the manner of a game of reeds.

– Likewise, the justices of the district of Vallecas are to be required to have the dance of swords that are offered, dressed and adorned, in this town for said day.

– Felipe Gómez, neighbor of the town of Ambroz, representative of the district they call Vallecas, is to be required to have the dance of *The Valiant Black Man in Flanders*, which he has offered, dressed and arranged for representation, in this town on the said day, Friday, the twelfth of this month.

– Likewise, you will do the same with Diego de Vega, representative of the district called Aravaca, and neighbor of the village of Alcorcón, who for the said twelfth day of this month will have in this said city the dance that the said district has offered, which is a game of reeds with balls of clay.

All of which the one and the other shall comply under penalty of fifty ducats, to be applied to the expenses of the aforementioned festivities [...].

3. *Location of the dance 'The Valiant Black Man in Flanders', for the festivities of the welcoming of the Queen offered by the rural district of Vallecas. Extract from the memorandum of the locations where the dances were performed,* GACM, Secretariat, ASA 2-58-13, n.f.)
[...] District of Vallecas. On a platform in Madrid. In the street in front of the steps of San Felipe church, where there are some walkways and goes out to the Arenal, the dance of *The Valiant Black Man in Flanders* is going to be performed by the district of Vallecas [...].